McNae's Essential Law for Journalists

McNae's
Essential Law for Journalists

Eighteenth Edition

Tom Welsh

Walter Greenwood

David Banks

OXFORD
UNIVERSITY PRESS

OXFORD

UNIVERSITY PRESS

Great Clarendon Street, Oxford OX2 6DP

Oxford University Press is a department of the University of Oxford.
It furthers the University's objective of excellence in research, scholarship,
and education by publishing worldwide in

Oxford New York

Auckland Cape Town Dar es Salaam Hong Kong Karachi
Kuala Lumpur Madrid Melbourne Mexico City Nairobi
New Delhi Shanghai Taipei Toronto

With offices in

Argentina Austria Brazil Chile Czech Republic France Greece
Guatemala Hungary Italy Japan Poland Portugal Singapore
South Korea Switzerland Thailand Turkey Ukraine Vietnam

Oxford is a registered trade mark of Oxford University Press
in the UK and in certain other countries

Published in the United States
by Oxford University Press Inc., New York

British Library Cataloguing in Publication Data
Data available

Library of Congress Cataloging in Publication Data
Data available

ISBN 0–19–928418–0   978–0–19–928418–4

3 5 7 9 10 8 6 4

Typeset by RefineCatch Limited, Bungay, Suffolk
Printed in Great Britain
on acid-free paper by
Ashford Colour Press Ltd, Gosport, Hampshire

Summary Contents

Contents

Preface

An 'avalanche' of legislation

Again, a new edition of *McNae* becomes necessary after two years because of many developments in media law. Lord Justice Rose in the Court of Appeal in January 2005 referred to 'a continuing avalanche of new complex legislation' (*R v Bradley*) and once again a number of statutes have added to the formidable array of restrictions on what may be published or broadcast.

- The Serious Organised Crime and Police Act (SOCP Act), which received Royal Assent on 7 April 2005, introduced a new range of offences that could be committed by newspaper publishers and broadcasters and their journalists (chapters 2, 24, and 25).

- The Courts Act 2003 saw new restrictions on covering some preliminary hearings of summary offences in magistrates courts (chapter 5).

- The Criminal Justice Act 2003 introduced new restrictions on reporting some appeals from crown court (chapter 7).

- The Sexual Offences Act 2003 brought changes during 2004 in reporting allegations concerning such offences (chapter 8).

- More changes to the reporting of sexual offences came with the implementation also in 2004 of parts of the Youth Justice and Criminal Evidence Act 1999 (chapter 8).

Under the SOCP Act it becomes an offence for the media or others to disclose new identities assumed by people under police protection, or the identities of witnesses, jurors or others involved in the legal system who are under protection because their personal safety may be at risk as a result of threats of violence or intimidation. It also becomes unlawful to disclose other arrangements made for their protection (chapter 2).

The Act also includes measures likely to widen police access to journalistic material when it is said to be needed to assist police investigations. The Police and Criminal Evidence Act 1984 allows the police to gain access to documents or search premises for evidence of 'serious arrestable offences'. But the SOCP Act virtually abolishes the category of serious arrestable offence which, in the criteria for PACE production order applications, is replaced by 'indictable offence' (chapter 24).

The Act also allows police to obtain a warrant to search all property occupied or controlled by the person in the warrant and not merely specific premises. This would appear to allow access to journalists' houses and other premises owned by a media organisation (chapter 24).

Another provision in the Act extends the powers to compel the production of documents and to demand information on specific issues. These powers already affect financial journalists when the Serious Fraud Office demands information and when the Department of Trade and Industry is investigating criminal misconduct in the City. The Act extends these powers to the police, the Serious Organised Crime Agency and Customs and Excise (chapter 24).

Journalists need to be aware that these provisions do not allow access to journalistic documents and records held in confidence, because the Act provides that no one can be compelled to disclose 'excluded material'. They will also need to note that a judge granting an all-premises warrant has to be satisfied the application meets additional criteria. Chapter 24 defines 'excluded material' and lists the additional criteria for all-premises warrants.

A proposal to make it an offence to publish matter said to incite religious hatred was dropped from the SOCP Act.

Other developments

Other developments since the publication of the 17th edition include:

- the declaration of the House of Lords in *Re S* limiting the power of courts to create new exceptions to the principle of open justice (chapters 1, 6, 12 and 30);

- clarification in the *Cream* case of the circumstances in which courts can impose interim injunctions in cases involving freedom of expression (chapters 1 and 30);

- new crimes relating to the grooming of children for sexual offences (chapter 2);

- restrictions on reports of a new form of preliminary hearing at magistrates court of offences to be tried summarily (chapter 5);

- proposals to remove the automatic anonymity of juveniles accused in the youth court of breaches of Asbos (anti-social behaviour orders) (chapter 6);

- a Queen's Bench Divisional Court ruling that restrictions on identifying juveniles apply only as long as the individual remains under 18 (chapter 6);

- a House of Lords decision, also in *Re S* (referred to above), that newspapers should not be restrained from publishing the identity of a defendant in a criminal trial in order to protect the privacy of the defendant's child not involved in that trial (chapter 6);

- the allowing of cameras for the first time into the courts, with an initial experiment in the Court of Appeal (chapter 7);

- the extension of automatic anonymity to complainants in a new range of sexual offences, including some where no physical contact is involved (chapter 8);

- new regulations under the Courts Act 2003 allowing a court to order that a third party such as the media pay costs which have been wasted in a trial through serious misconduct whether or not there has been contempt of court (chapters 12 and 17);

- proposed changes to the coroner system in the wake of the mass murders committed by general practitioner Harold Shipman (chapter 15);

- the introduction of conditional fee ('no win, no fee') agreements, believed to have a 'chilling effect' on investigative journalism (chapter 18);

- a cautionary judgment in the *Galloway* case on the limits of 'neutral reportage' by newspapers using the Reynolds defence (chapter 20);

- the outlawing of incitement to religious hatred was put on hold (chapter 25);

- the £1million-plus damages award against *Hello!* magazine in the *Douglas* case, marking a significant development in the use of the law of confidence to protect commercial interests based upon personality rights (chapter 23);

- full implementation of the Freedom of Information Act 2000 (chapter 27);

- a change in copyright law; the defence of fair dealing no longer extends to material that has not been in the public domain, for example, private letters (chapter 28);

- the establishment by the House of Lords in the *Naomi Campbell* case of 'unjustified disclosure of private information' as a new cause of action, arguably creating a law of privacy (chapter 32);

- The decision of the European Court of Human Rights in the *Princess Caroline* case that her rights were breached by photographs of scenes from her daily life (chapter 32).

Lords curb courts' power to gag

The Law Lords said that courts have no power to create new exceptions to the general principle of open justice and the right of the press to report criminal trials except in the most compelling circumstances. The declaration came at the end of a legal battle in which a child's guardian had sought to persuade the courts to uphold an injunction that would have banned the media from naming a woman charged with murdering her son. The injunction was aimed at protecting the woman's surviving child. Lord Steyn said there were already numerous statutory exceptions to the ordinary rule of open justice, put in place by Parliament in the interests of justice. He went on: 'Given the number of statutory exceptions, it needs to be said clearly and unambiguously that the court has no power to create by a process of analogy, except in the most compelling circumstances, further exceptions to the general principle of open justice' (*Re S (A Child)* [2004] UKHL 47) (chapters 1, 6, 12, and 30).

Prior restraint defence strengthened

The Court of Appeal in February 2003 shocked journalists by its interpretation of a provision that, it had been thought, gave them a strong defence against injunctions preventing publication of stories in the public interest. Judges refused to overturn an injunction preventing the *Liverpool Echo* from publishing a story about financial irregularities based on information it had received from the former accountant of Cream, the Liverpool night club and events organiser. Section 12(3) of the Human Rights Act 1998 says that no injunction affecting the exercise of article 10 of the European Convention (freedom of expression) is to be granted before trial 'unless the court is satisfied that the applicant is likely to establish [at trial] that publication should not be allowed' (see chapter 30, Human Rights Act 1998). The paper argued this meant that the party seeking the injunction had to show it was more likely than not to succeed when the matter came to trial, but the court held the words meant merely that there had to be a real prospect of success. Fortunately for the media, the paper (risking £600,000 costs if it lost) persevered with an appeal to the House of Lords which, in October 2004, overturned the injunction, allowing the paper to publish the story (*Cream Holdings Ltd v Banerjee* [2004] UKHL 44). See chapter 1, 'The rule against prior restraint' and, for the Lords' ruling, chapter 30, 'Protection against injunctions'.

New form of preliminary hearing at magistrates court

The Courts Act 2003 provides for magistrates to have preliminary hearings, where there has been a plea of not guilty and the case is to be tried summarily, to decide on admissibility of evidence and points of law. Restrictions on reporting these hearings were introduced simultaneously (chapter 4).

Anonymity not continued after 18

The Queen's Bench administrative court held that to continue to apply the ban, under the Children and Young Persons Act 1933, on identifying defendants in youth courts once they have reached the age of 18 would require a strained interpretation of the Act because the Act referred also to restrictions on identifying schools and applied to witnesses as well as defendants. The court rejected the submission that publication of the defendant's name even after his 18th birthday constituted an interference with his rights under article 8 of the European Convention on Human Rights (chapter 6).

Reporting of anti-social behaviour orders against juveniles

After complaints that reporting restrictions on anti-social behaviour orders against juveniles made it difficult for the press to make the local community aware of the orders, the SOCP Act provided that the usual anonymity should no longer apply where a juvenile was accused of a breach of an order. Nothing was contained in the Act, however, to deal with the anomaly that arises where a youth court convicts a juvenile of a criminal offence (automatic anonymity under section 49 of the Children and Young Persons Act 1933), and then immediately follows it with an Asbo (no automatic anonymity) (chapter 6).

Cameras in court, as an experiment

While photography in the precincts of the court remained banned during a trial, the Court of Appeal saw the beginning of an experiment to examine the issue of televising the courts. Cameras were fitted and hearings recorded, although at this stage filming was for consultation purposes and was not broadcast (chapter 7).

More offences where the complainant has anonymity

A wider range of offences where it is illegal to publish the identity of the alleged victim during his or her lifetime was introduced by further changes to the Sexual Offences (Amendment) Act 1992. Some of the offences, such as voyeurism, do not involve any physical contact between the defendant and the complainant. The amended 1992 Act now specifies that published matter which is likely to lead to the identification of the complainant is his or her name, address, school, or other educational establishment or place of work, or a moving or still picture of that person (chapter 8).

Orders to pay wasted costs in criminal cases

The Lord Chancellor, Lord Falconer, made regulations in 2004 allowing a magistrates court, a crown court, or the Court of Appeal, to order a third party to pay costs where there has been serious misconduct. The test of 'serious misconduct' falls short of the statutory test for strict liability for contempt of court—substantial risk of serious prejudice. The Department of Constitutional Affairs said the new measure was largely inspired by the abandonment, following a *Sunday Mirror* article, of the trial in the Leeds footballers case, wasting costs of about £1million. It seems likely that an order to pay wasted costs can be made if the 'serious misconduct' arises when a trial is aborted after a newspaper reports, before the end of the trial, matter heard in the absence of a jury, or before the jury is brought into court. This could arise even though the newspaper might have a defence under section 4(1) of the Contempt of Court Act against a charge of contempt if the court has failed to make an order postponing such reporting. The term 'serious misconduct' has been criticised as being too vague and it has been suggested that the risk of abuse of the power is strong enough to have a serious effect on freedom of expression (chapters 12 and 17).

Proposed changes to the coroner system

The murders committed by Harold Shipman gave rise to concern that the coroner system of England and Wales needed reform. A Home Office paper in 2004 proposed that all deaths should initially be reported to a medical team attached to the coroner's office. It also proposed a reduction in the number of coroners from 127 to between 40 and 60. A draft bill was due to be produced as *McNae* went to press (chapter 15).

Conditional fee agreements have 'chilling effect'

Stories about paupers used to carry little risk of attracting libel actions, but times have changed, leading media lawyer Andrew Caldecott QC warned journalists at a conference. He said the position of potential litigants without means to sue had been 'turned on it head' by the introduction of 'no win, no fee' conditional fee agreements. He said such litigants were now the most dangerous claimants because the solicitor of such a claimant could double his fee if his client won and, if the newspaper won, it had no real prospect of recovering its costs from the unsuccessful claimant. A judge said the development could have a 'chilling' effect on the media. (See chapter 18, 'The chilling effect'.)

Limits of 'neutral reportage' defence revealed

A 2004 case in which the *Daily Telegraph* was successfully sued by left-wing Labour MP George Galloway revealed the limits of the 'neutral reportage' defence which, in the *Al-Fagih* case in 2001, protected a newspaper that had objectively reported defamatory comments made in the course of a political dispute. In the *Galloway* case the judge said the reported allegations had been 'adopted' by the newspaper and its articles did not 'fairly and disinterestedly' report the context of the allegations. Mr Galloway was awarded £150,000 damages and the paper had to pay huge costs (*George Galloway MP v Telegraph Group Ltd* [2004] EWHC 2786, QB). (See chapter 20, 'Neutral reportage'.)

Government planned to outlaw religious hatred

The Government planned to extend the law outlawing incitement to racial hatred to cover incitement to religious hatred by amending the Public Order Act 1986 (chapter 25). The measure was contained in the Serious Organised Crime and Police Bill. Earlier, a coalition of comedians, writers and politicians had launched a campaign against the proposal because of fears it could damage freedom of speech. In the Commons David Blunkett, then Home Secretary, came under fire from MPs on both sides over the move. He told them:

> We are trying to stop groups of people who are prepared verbally, in writing and through the internet, to incite others to hate because of someone's faith not because of the argument about their faith. But the proposal was dropped shortly before Parliament was dissolved for the General Election.

Freedom of Information Act 2000 in force

In January 2005 the Act came fully into force and members of the public, journalists included, were able to request information from more than 100,000 organisations. The Act has been criticised for the number and nature of the exemptions which allow information to be withheld and in the early days of its working there were successes, and failures, in using it to obtain information (chapter 27).

More protection for personality rights

As recorded in the last edition of *McNae*, film stars Michael Douglas and Catherine Zeta-Jones, with *OK!* magazine, sued *Hello!* magazine for publishing snatched pictures of the couple's wedding. The couple claimed this was an infringement of their privacy. In the end, the judge in 2003 (to quote media lawyer Dan Tench) 'instead of basing his judgment on any new-fangled privacy law . . . considered that the images of the wedding were subject to an old-fashioned duty of confidence and were protectable by the couple in much the same way as a company can safeguard its trade secrets'. Old-fashioned or not, with the £1 million-plus damages awarded to *OK!*, the law of confidence appeared to take a substantial step in the direction of the protection of commercial interests based upon personality rights (chapters 23, 'Breach of confidence' and 32, 'Privacy'). *Hello!* appealed, and the decision of the Court of Appeal was awaited as this edition of *McNae* went to press.

Fair dealing protection restricted

The Copyright and Related Rights Regulations 2003 amended the law of copyright to restrict the fair dealing defence so that it applies only to work that has been made available to the public (chapter 28).

More steps towards privacy law

Two important cases in 2004 brought the development of a firm law of privacy closer for English courts. In the *Naomi Campbell* case in the House of Lords the judges unanimously held that English law provided a cause of action for the unjustified publication of private information. Lord Nicholls said the tort was now better named as 'misuse of private information'. Commenting in a lecture, Sir Charles Gray (Mr Justice Gray) referred to 'the new (or at least re-labelled) tort', and in a newspaper interview said that the Lords' judgment had, in effect created a law of privacy for the first time. Judges had taken the old-established law of confidence, which was founded on a prior relationship between two parties, and transformed it into a new law preventing misuse of information. In the *Princess Caroline* case the European Court of Human Rights held that respect for the private life of the princess was breached by photographs of scenes from her daily life, shopping or on holiday with her family, in public places (chapter 32).

Changes in McNae

McNae's Essential Law for Journalists is the recommended textbook of the National Council for the Training of Journalists (NCTJ), and its main object is to provide the young journalist with the knowledge of the law that he needs in his day-to-day work, in particular enabling him to challenge unjustified attempts to restrict his ability to report. For many years the book has also been an essential reference book in newsrooms. More recently, practitioners have begun to use *McNae* as a first point of reference when tackling an unfamiliar problem relating to the media, and they tell us they would welcome tables of cases and statutes. These tables are now, therefore, included for the first time.

For the first time also the book is supported by a website, which will enable the editors to update between editions. The website can be found at www.oup.com/uk/booksites/law/ The website will also include valuable supplemental material that fails to meet the 'day-to-day' test, such as the table giving step-by-step guidance to journalists on whether their proposed story will contravene the complex Official Secrets Act.

Also for the first time, the book contains a chapter on photographers and the law, a topic covered by the third edition of the book on the subject by the late Don Cassell, recommended by the NCTJ but now out of date.

As ever, the editors will be grateful to journalists and trainers who draw their attention to omissions.

Peter Carter-Ruck

Peter Carter-Ruck, the leading libel solicitor, who died on 19 December 2004 aged 89, made a valuable contribution to the training of journalists in legal matters, a cause in which he professed a keen interest. His publications, in addition to *Carter-Ruck on Libel and Slander*, his standard book for practitioners, included *Newspapers and the Law*, and valuable booklets for young journalists. His greatest contribution in the training field, however, was perhaps writing the chapters on defamation in the first edition of *McNae*, published in 1954. From 1979 onwards he read and, where necessary, corrected the chapters on libel for each edition and, when attending the launch of the 17th edition in London in July 2003, received warm applause from lecturers and newspaper trainers in recognition of his generous help. Carter-Ruck had a long-standing concern for the reform of the libel law. He was a member of Justice, the small and distinguished legal and human rights organisation that met under the chairmanship of Lord Shawcross (Sir Hartley Shawcross), and in 1965 produced the report 'The Law and the Press', calling for radical reform.

Acknowledgments

Our thanks are due to: District Judge Gordon Ashton, Preston; Paul Francis, political editor, *Kent Messenger*; Philip Jones, Assistant Information Commissioner; Sue Oake, solicitor, Newspaper Society; Santha Rasaiah, director of the political, editorial and regulatory affairs department (PERA) of the Newspaper Society; solicitor Dan Tench, Olswang; Antony White QC, Matrix Chambers; Bob Whitehouse, former justices' chief executive for County Durham. They have read new passages of the book and/or given valuable advice.

The NCTJ, and particularly its law examinations board, has given continued support. The editors have enjoyed working with staff of Oxford University Press, our new publishers, and we are grateful to have benefited from continued access to the online services of the former publishers, LexisNexis UK Direct.

Any errors or omissions are those of the editors, and we shall as ever be grateful to trainers and lecturers drawing our attention to them.

The law stated in the book is the law at 1 May 2005

Tom Welsh, media_lawyer@compuserve.com
Walter Greenwood, medialaw@fish.co.uk
David Banks, david.banks@ncjmedia.co.uk

Introduction

Journalists and the law

Britain has a tradition of a 'free press'. In many ways, as this book will show, the phrase is illusory, but even when journalists were less restricted in their work than they are today the words did not mean that they had rights distinct from those of the ordinary citizen—except in a few cases, all of which are explained in the pages that follow. The journalist has no legal right to go anywhere, do anything, say anything, or publish anything beyond what is the legal right of any private citizen in these matters.

The journalist's position in relation to the law was summed up by Sir John Donaldson (later Lord Donaldson) when he gave judgment in the *Spycatcher* case in the Court of Appeal in 1988. Sir John, then Master of the Rolls (head of the Court of Appeal), said:

> . . . a free press . . . is an essential element in maintaining parliamentary democracy and the British way of life as we know it. But it is important to remember why the press occupies this crucial position. It is not because of any special wisdom, interest, or status enjoyed by proprietors, editors, or journalists. It is because the media are the eyes and ears of the general public. They act on behalf of the general public. Their right to know and their right to publish is neither more nor less than that of the general public. Indeed it is that of the general public for whom they are trustees.

The importance of this role was emphasised in a case in 2000, when the House of Lords, the highest court in the land, ruled that a press conference was a 'public meeting' as regards the law of defamation, and therefore a fair and accurate report of what was said there enjoyed qualified privilege, a protection against libel actions. The purpose of the press conference was to raise support for a convicted prisoner. The senior law lord, Lord

Bingham, said the press representatives could either be regarded as members of the public themselves, or as 'the eyes and ears of the public, to whom they report'. A press conference was 'an important vehicle for promoting the discussion and furtherance of matters of public concern'.

The journalist may find he enjoys a number of privileges and facilities which private citizens do not enjoy, extended to him by people or organisations to make it easier for him to do his job. If these are withdrawn, he can and should protest, but these privileges are not rights and unless their withdrawal infringes the law he has no legal redress.

For example, reporting the courts is accepted as an important part of a journalist's work, and a press bench is generally provided for his use, but the journalist is in court, in nearly every case, merely as a member of the public. Normally he has no right to enter, or to remain, when the public has been legally excluded.

The other side of the coin is that the journalist, like any other citizen, may legally go anywhere and report anything provided that in so doing he does not transgress the laws of the land, such laws as those concerning theft, trespass, breach of confidence, and defamation.

Freedom of speech

The Human Rights Act 1998, which came into force on 2 October 2000, in effect incorporating the European Convention on Human Rights into English law, for the first time gave citizens specific legal rights, including the right to 'freedom of expression' (see below and chapter 30). Previously the rights of citizens were not guaranteed by statements of general principle as they are in some countries that have written constitutions. In Britain the rights were said to be 'residual'—that is, a citizen was allowed to do anything that was not specifically forbidden by law.

As a result, rights and freedoms could be and were whittled away by legislation. Let us consider that statement in relation to freedom of speech, the important right that journalists share with other citizens, and which includes not only the right to comment but the right to communicate information.

Without this freedom, democratic life as it is known in Britain would be impossible, because there would be no public discussion of the issues affecting citizens, and they could have no access to the facts upon which to base their opinions and decisions.

As Lord Bingham said in the House of Lords in 2000, in the case referred to above:

In a modern, developed society it is only a small minority of citizens who can participate directly in the discussions and decisions which shape the public life of that society. The majority can participate only indirectly, by exercising their rights as citizens to vote, express their opinions, make representations to the authorities, form pressure groups and so on.

But the majority cannot participate in the public life of their society in these ways if they are not alerted to and informed about matters which call or may call for consideration and action. It is very largely through the media, including of course the press, that they will be so alerted and informed. The proper functioning of a modern participatory democracy requires that the media be free, active, professional and inquiring.

Like other freedoms, however, freedom of speech may be restricted by law, and this book is largely concerned with these restrictions.

Most citizens, including journalists, believe it is reasonable that certain restrictions on their freedom of speech exist. For example, the law must strike a balance between the public interest in exposing wrongdoing and the individual's right to have his reputation defended from malicious and baseless attacks. The law of libel and slander tries to strike that balance.

Freedom of speech has been so highly valued in the United Kingdom, and the tradition of freedom has been so strong, that for many years legal restrictions were kept to a minimum. But in the 51 years since the first edition of this book was published, Parliament has made very many inroads into that freedom, passing a number of Acts that restrict the journalist's ability to report, particularly in the area of the courts of law.

For example, before the Contempt of Court Act 1981, it was extremely rare for a judge to use his power, derived from the common law, to order journalists to postpone the reporting of a criminal trial. Once that power had been expressed in the Act, and given for the first time to magistrates, it became a commonplace. The constitutional principle of open justice was thus eroded.

Many people believe such legislation restricts freedom of speech too severely. Journalists, even more than other citizens, should be alive to the danger that freedoms that have long been enjoyed may be lost if they are not defended with sufficient vigour.

It was assumed that they would receive help from section 19 of the Human Rights Act, which requires that a minister introducing a bill into Parliament must declare that its provisions are compatible with the European Convention, including a commitment to 'freedom of expression'.

But journalists were disappointed to find, after the section was brought into effect in 1998, that the declaration was attached to a number of bills which bore little evidence of having been examined with freedom of expression in mind. In particular, the declaration was attached to the Youth Justice and Criminal Evidence Bill, which was introduced into Parliament in December 1998, providing for wide ranging reporting restrictions. The bill, as drafted, contained a number of draconian provisions, not all of which were removed during its passage through Parliament.

For individual journalists a practical problem is that too often they are prevented from reporting matters of public interest by courts that make decisions while paying little regard to the judicial principle that justice must not only be done but must be seen to be done.

Some of the actions resulting from these decisions are invalid, and journalists should be alert to challenge such actions when they can. Chapter 12 of this book, 'Challenging the courts', should help them in doing so.

In the absence of a written constitution, freedom of speech in Britain has depended traditionally on two constitutional bulwarks, jury trial and the rule against prior restraint.

Jury trial

The history of the development of freedom of speech in Britain has several instances of journalists and others being brought before the courts and charged with publishing material which provoked the anger of the government of the day, and then being found not guilty by independently minded juries, sometimes in flagrant disregard of the strict legal position. An example of such a jury decision was seen in the trial of Clive Ponting (see chapter 27, Central government).

The jurist Albert Dicey said: 'Freedom of discussion is, then, in England little else than the right to write or say anything which a jury, consisting of 12 shopkeepers, think it expedient should be said or written.'

The rule against prior restraint

But if jury trial is to defend the journalist, there must first be a published story upon which the jury can adjudicate. That cannot happen when there is censorship, because a censor prevents the story going into the paper. Official censorship died out in England in 1695, and in the next century the jurist Sir William Blackstone said: 'The liberty of the press . . . consists in laying no previous restraints on publication, and not in freedom from censure for criminal matter when published.'

This 'rule against prior restraint', as it is known, has an important place in the English legal system, but it appeared to be losing its validity in cases affecting the media in the

1980s and 1990s. For example, in the network of cases relating to the book *Spycatcher* the then Government used the law of breach of confidence to prevent publication of stories it disapproved of by means of injunctions granted by judges sitting without juries, and the injunctions were enforced by the use of the law of contempt of court, again dispensed by judges sitting without juries (see chapter 23).

In 1987 the Court of Appeal declared that an injunction against one newspaper restraining it from publishing confidential information about *Spycatcher* caught all the media, even though they had not been named in the injunction and it had not been served upon them. The ruling was confirmed by the House of Lords in 1991. The development gave the Government a very effective means of silencing the entire press.

In 1991 the European Court of Human Rights at Strasbourg considered the use of injunctions in the *Spycatcher* saga and said that although the European Convention did not prohibit the imposition of prior restraints on publication the dangers inherent were such that they called for the most careful scrutiny on the part of the court.

That was especially so with regard to the press, for news was a perishable commodity and to delay its publication even for a short period might well deprive it of all its value and interest.

In the Human Rights Act 1998, the Government acknowledged media concern about the use of pre-trial injunctions by including a provision giving special protection in cases involving freedom of speech issues.

Section 12(3) requires that before issuing an injunction that will affect the right to freedom of expression the court must be 'satisfied that the applicant is likely to establish that publication should not be allowed'.

But this provision did not prevent a judge imposing an injunction preventing the *Liverpool Echo* from publishing confidential information it obtained from the former financial controller of events organiser Cream Holdings, making allegations about financial irregularities. The judge's decision was upheld by the Court of Appeal.

The *Liverpool Echo* appealed to the House of Lords, which in 2004 overturned the injunction, allowing the paper to publish the story (*Cream Holdings Ltd v Banerjee* [2004] UKHL 44). The Lords' ruling, which is reported in chapter 30 ('Protection against injunctions') was seen as a victory for the media.

Sources of law

The law is the set of rules by which the sovereign authority in a society regulates the conduct of citizens in relation to other citizens and the state.

In the United Kingdom there is no single written set of rules. We say the law in this country is not 'codified'. Whether an action is recognised as being in conformity with the law is determined by a consideration of various authorities. These authorities may be, for example, reports of decided cases ('precedents'), Acts of Parliament and statutory instruments, regulations of the European Community, articles of the European Convention, or byelaws of a local authority. If none of these fits the circumstances, the judge makes his decision by analogy with past decisions made in somewhat similar circumstances.

The main sources of the law have traditionally been custom, precedent, and statute. Now the European Convention on Human Rights and the precedents of the European Court on Human Rights are becoming an increasingly important source.

Custom

When the English legal system began to take shape in the Middle Ages, royal judges were appointed to administer the 'law and custom of the realm'. This part of the law was called 'common'—that is, common to the whole kingdom—in contrast to that which was particular or special, such as ecclesiastical law or local law.

Precedent

As judges applied the common law to the cases before them, their decisions were recorded by lawyers. Reports of leading cases give the facts found by the court, sometimes the arguments put forward, and the reasons given by the judge for coming to his decision. The principles on which these decisions are based are binding on all lower courts. The decisions are known as 'precedents', and the system as 'case law'.

A judgment of the House of Lords is binding on all other United Kingdom courts apart from Scottish criminal courts. The Lords can refuse to follow their earlier decisions in later cases, if circumstances make this desirable. However, if their interpretation of a point of law is contrary to the intentions, policies, or wishes of the government, it can be reversed only by new legislation.

Below the Lords, decisions of the Court of Appeal bind the High Court and the lower courts. Decisions of High Court judges, though binding on all lesser courts, can be disregarded by other High Court judges—although they do so reluctantly because the tradition of unanimity is strong.

Equity

The common law is supplemented by the rules of equity. In common speech, equity means fairness and impartiality. In the law, the word refers to a system of doctrines and procedures that developed through the centuries side by side with the common law; historically, the rules of equity were based on considerations of conscience.

Certain 'maxims of equity' are sometimes quoted in courtrooms and express important principles behind equitable doctrines, They include: 'Equitable remedies are discretionary', 'He who comes into equity must do so with clean hands', 'Equity acts on the conscience', and 'Equity regards the balance of convenience'.

Statutes and statutory instruments

Common law, supplemented by equity, remains the basic law of the land, but increasingly it is being modified or changed by statute, that is, by Acts of Parliament. Their interpretation by the courts gives rise to a great number of new precedents.

Governments are also making increasing use of delegated legislation known as 'statutory instruments'. Parliament frequently legislates on principles, leaving the detailed application of the new measure to be ordained by the Government or the departmental minister concerned, in detailed regulations made under powers given in the main statute. Statutory instruments are also used to bring legislation into force on dates different from those on which It becomes law, for administrative reasons. This process often causes uncertainty as to the current law.

As this edition of *McNae* went to press in 2005, sections of the Youth Justice and Criminal Evidence Act 1999, which were due significantly to affect the work of journalists, had still not been brought into effect.

European Community regulations

Under the European Communities Act 1972, Community treaties and legislation are part of United Kingdom law. In 1981, for example, the British Government banned importation of a German magazine carrying accounts of what the magazine claimed were tapes of telephone conversations between Prince Charles and Lady Diana Spencer (later the Princess of Wales), under article 36 of the Treaty of Rome, which allows prohibition of goods 'justified on grounds of public morality, public policy, or public security'.

European Convention on Human Rights

As stated above, Britain has no legally binding written constitution guaranteeing rights but by the Human Rights Act 1998, which came into force on 2 October 2000, the European Convention on Human Rights was in effect incorporated into British law, providing a guarantee of specific rights.

For journalists, the most important part of the Convention is article 10, which says in part: 'Everyone has the right to freedom of expression. This right shall include freedom to hold opinions and to receive and impart information and ideas without interference by public authority . . .'.

Restrictions on this right have to be justified. They must be 'necessary in a democratic society, in the interests of national security, territorial integrity or public safety, for the prevention of disorder or crime, for the protection of health or morals, for the protection of the reputation or rights of others . . .'

They must also be 'prescribed by law'.

Other important rights guaranteed by the Convention are fair trial (article 6) and privacy (article 8). (The full wording of articles 8 and 10, and an extract from article 6, are given in chapter 30.)

Even before incorporation, Britain was a party to the Convention, and UK courts were increasingly taking its principles into account in their decision-making. The 1998 Act says that a court determining a question in connection with a Convention right *must* take account of decisions of the European Court of Human Rights, which adjudicates on matters affecting the Convention—although UK courts will not necessarily be bound by those decisions. As stated above, new legislation must be compatible with the Convention rights.

Under the 1998 Act courts must, as far as possible, interpret existing legislation in a way that is compatible with the Convention. Lawyers defending people accused of criminal offences frequently cited the Act, particularly article 8, when arguing for identification bans, and such bans were sometimes imposed. In 2004, however, the House of Lords, considering such an application, declared that courts had no power to create new exceptions to the general principle of open justice and the right of the press to report criminal trials except in the most compelling circumstances (*Re S (A Child) (Identification:*

Restrictions on Publication) [2004] 3 WLR 1129). See also chapter 6, 'Juveniles in the news', and 30, 'Human Rights Act 1998'.

Divisions of the law

There are two main divisions of the law: criminal law and civil law.

Criminal law deals with offences that are deemed to harm the whole community and thus to be an offence against the sovereign.

A lawyer writing about a crown court case in which John Smith is accused of an offence will name it *R v Smith*. 'R' stands for Regina (the Queen) or Rex (the King), depending on who is reigning at the time.

When speaking about this case, however, he will generally refer to it as 'The Queen (or the King) *against* Smith'.

Civil law concerns the maintenance of private claims and the redress of private wrongs.

A case in which John Smith is sued by Mary Brown will be known in writing as *Brown v Smith*. Lawyers will speak of the case as 'Brown *and* Smith' (our italics).

In practice, the two divisions overlap to some degree. Many acts or omissions are not only 'wrongs' for which the injured party may recover compensation, but also 'offences' for which the offender may be prosecuted and punished. A road accident may lead to a claim for damages and also to a prosecution for dangerous driving. Similarly, defamation and breach of copyright, usually dealt with in the civil courts, may in certain circumstances be regarded as criminal matters, and dealt with in the criminal courts.

In spite of this overlap, the issues will generally be considered in different courts, depending upon whether the action is a criminal or a civil one. Young reporters must be careful to remember the basic differences in the nature of the actions.

It would be wrong, for example, to say that a defendant in a county court action is being 'prosecuted'. That is the language of the criminal courts.

In civil courts the person taking legal action, normally known formerly as the *plaintiff* and after 1999 as the *claimant*, is said to sue the other. The person sued is known as the *defendant*—the same term as in the criminal courts—but if he loses the case it is wrong to say that he has been 'found guilty': he is 'held liable'.

You should not describe the civil court's order in terms of punishment, as is generally the case with the *sentence* in a criminal court.

The legal profession

Lawyers adopt one of two branches of the profession: they become either solicitors or barristers.

By tradition and practice, solicitors are the lawyers who deal directly with lay clients. They advise the client. They prepare the client's case, taking advice, when necessary, from a barrister specialising in a particular branch of the law—although solicitors themselves increasingly specialise.

Solicitors may represent their clients in court, but in the past have generally been allowed to do so only in the lower courts—that is, the magistrates courts and the county courts. From 1993, solicitors with a record of experience as advocates and who have gained a higher courts qualification have been allowed to appear in the higher courts, where they compete with barristers in representing clients.

Even before 1993, solicitors could represent an accused person in the crown court in an appeal from a magistrates court or in a committal for sentence when they had represented the person in the lower court. They can also appear in the High Court in formal or unopposed proceedings, and in proceedings when judgment is delivered in open court following a hearing in chambers (in the judge's private room) at which they conducted the case for their client. In court, a solicitor wears a gown but no wig.

In other cases, the solicitor 'briefs' (instructs) a barrister to conduct the case. The title 'solicitor' derives from this procedure: on behalf of their clients, solicitors 'solicit' the services of a barrister.

Solicitors are officers of the Supreme Court and for misconduct may be struck off the roll or suspended for a period. In that case, they are unable to practise.

Barristers are so called because they practise at the 'bar' of the court. Originally, the bar was a partition or barrier separating the judges from laymen attending court. Nowadays, there is no physical barrier in most courts.

Barristers are known, singly or collectively, as 'counsel'. In court reporting, it is a common error to apply the word to solicitors, but this is incorrect.

Except for certain conveyancing matters counsel have hitherto not been allowed to accept instructions directly from lay clients. They had to be instructed by solicitors. Now, however, there is limited direct access for other professions such as surveyors, account-ants, and town planners seeking advice on the legal aspects of the disciplines.

Barristers wear a wig and gown in the higher courts, the crown courts and in the county courts, but not in the magistrates courts.

Successful barristers who have been practising for at least 10 years may apply to the Lord Chancellor for appointment as a Queen's Counsel. If this application is successful, they are said to 'take silk' because henceforth they will wear a gown of silk instead of cotton. They use the letter QC after their names.

The terms Queen's Counsel and King's Counsel are interchangeable: which is used depends on whether the reigning monarch is a queen or king.

For unprofessional conduct, barristers may be censured, suspended, or disbarred—that is, deprived of their standing as a barrister and therefore unable to practise.

Eminent lawyers—normally those who have pursued a political career—have in the past been able to aspire to the offices of Lord Chancellor, Attorney-General, or Solicitor-General, but as this edition of *McNae* went to press the position of the Lord Chancellor was under review. The person holding that post is head of the judiciary. He is a member of the Cabinet, Speaker of the House of Lords, and the senior judge in the House of Lords sitting as the Supreme Court of Appeal. That is, he is the only person who rises above the 'separation of powers' that normally prevails in the United Kingdom, having positions in the executive, legislative, and judicial branches of government, a situation regarded as undesirable in a democracy.

The main duty of the Attorney-General and the Solicitor-General, the two law officers, is to advise the government of the day on legal matters. Some holders of the post are ministers of cabinet rank. The Attorney-General or, in his absence, the Solicitor-General, conducts the prosecution in certain important types of cases. The Lord Chancellor and the law officers change with a change of government.

Starting proceedings: reporting the courts

Every journalist reporting or sub-editing court stories should be familiar with both criminal and civil procedure.

Many unlawful acts can result in both criminal and civil cases, as we have seen.

Types of offences

Magistrates courts deal with three types of criminal offences:

(1) those triable only on indictment at crown court, eg murder, rape, robbery;

(2) those triable either way—at crown court or at magistrates court—eg theft, indecent assault;

(3) those usually triable only at a magistrates court (summary offences), eg minor motoring offences, drunkenness.

An indictable offence is defined as one that *may* be tried by a jury.

Trials at crown court are listed as issues between the Queen and the accused (see chapter 1, 'Divisions of the law').

Most prosecutions, both at magistrates court and crown court, are the responsibility of the Crown Prosecution Service in each of the 43 police areas in England and Wales. It is the task of this state service to decide on prosecutions and to conduct prosecutions in court, except where the police prosecute in the most minor offences. Prosecutions can, however, be brought by private individuals, local authorities, and government departments.

Private prosecutions rarely go beyond the magistrates court. No one can be tried for certain serious offences without the Director of Public Prosecutions being informed, and the law allows the Crown Prosecution Service to take over the prosecution. The Attorney-General has the power to stop such a case.

Normally a criminal prosecution starts in one of two ways—either by the defendant being arrested without the need for a warrant in the case of an arrestable offence, or by the police laying an information (normally a document sent to the court electronically) giving particulars of the alleged offence) before magistrates or their clerk. Magistrates may not try a summary offence unless the information is laid within six months of its being committed.

Magistrates can, if satisfied that there are reasonable grounds, issue a warrant for arrest, or a summons to attend court at a stated time and date. Sometimes when a warrant is issued, it is 'backed for bail', thus allowing the defendant his freedom for the time being, once he has been to the police station to complete certain formalities. A magistrates clerk can issue a summons and may issue a warrant for arrest for failure to surrender to bail where defence do not object.

Applications for warrants or summonses can be heard either privately or in open court.

Arrestable offences

An arrestable offence is one for which the penalty on first conviction can be at least five years' imprisonment, or for which the penalty is fixed by statute (eg life imprisonment for murder). In addition, some offences, eg taking a car without authority or driving with excess alcohol, have been declared arrestable by Parliament, even though the maximum penalty is less than five years in jail.

A police officer may arrest a person without a warrant where he suspects that person of an arrestable offence.

Alternatively a police officer may seek a warrant from a magistrate for the arrest of any person suspected of having committed any indictable offence, whether arrestable or not.

A police officer may also arrest for any offence when a summons would be impractical or inappropriate, eg drunkenness, failing to stop after an accident.

'Helping the police with their inquiries'

This phrase, and 'detained for questioning', are often used to describe interrogation of suspects, but the latter is a legal fiction.

Under the Police and Criminal Evidence Act 1984, the police have no right to keep a person at a police station to help them with their inquiries unless he has been arrested. They are however entitled to question anyone. A person who attends a police station voluntarily is under no obligation to stay unless arrested.

The Act lays down that a person arrested must be told the grounds for the arrest. The information need not be given if it is not practicable to do so because of the person's escape from arrest before it can be given.

Under the code of practice adopted through the Police and Criminal Evidence Act, once a person has been charged, police questioning must stop.

Defendants are often detained for many hours without a charge being laid while they and witnesses are questioned and evidence is sifted. No person can be detained for more than 12 hours without being charged. If not charged within that time, further detention can be authorised only by a police superintendent up to a total of 36 hours. That can be extended by a magistrates court to a total of 96 hours, after which the detained person must be either charged or released. The Police and Criminal Evidence Act stipulates that the magistrates must not sit in open court when hearing applications for extended detention. A person can be detained for longer under the Terrorism Act 2000 and the Anti-terrorism, Crime and Security Act 2001.

If a person is subsequently released without being charged, his claim for damages for false arrest or wrongful imprisonment or both will depend on whether he was actually deprived of his liberty and, if so, whether the grounds were reasonable. If he is subsequently charged and convicted, such an action will fail.

While a person is in custody, his friends or solicitor can apply to the High Court for a writ of habeas corpus to secure his release, if no charge is brought against him within a reasonable time.

The phrase 'a man is helping the police with their inquiries' is a convenient one for a newspaper even though it has no legal force. But even at this stage proceedings may have become active and liability for contempt of court may have started under the Contempt of Court Act 1981 (see chapter 17).

Apart from this, if you name the man and he is later released without being charged, he may sue for libel, claiming the phrase imputes guilt. But the Defamation Act 1996 (see chapter 20) gives qualified privilege to a copy of, or extract from, a notice issued by or on behalf of the police, as these statements often are.

The Queen's Bench Divisional Court ruled in 1991 that the press has no automatic right to be told by the police the name of a person being investigated or who has been charged with a criminal offence.

Once charged, a man must either be granted bail by the police or be brought before a magistrates court no later than the next day, unless that day is Sunday, Christmas Day, or Good Friday.

Under the Bail Act 1976, the court is required to remand the accused on bail unless it is satisfied there are substantial grounds for believing he will abscond, commit other offences, or obstruct the course of justice; or he should be kept in custody for his own protection; or he is already serving a prison sentence; or there is not yet sufficient information available to make a decision. Before granting bail in respect of an offence which appears to have been committed while the defendant was on bail for an earlier offence, magistrates are required to take these circumstances into account when assessing the risk of the defendant committing other offences. Bail cannot be granted to a defendant charged with homicide or rape if he has been previously convicted of such an offence unless there are exceptional circumstances. It need not be granted if he is charged with an offence committed on bail.

The court must give reasons for refusing bail and must state the reasons for granting bail if bail is opposed by the prosecution.

If bail is refused by magistrates the defendant may apply to a judge in chambers. The prosecution can similarly appeal if its objection to bail is overruled.

A surety is a person who guarantees the accused will surrender to his bail. He agrees to forfeit a sum of money fixed by the court if the accused jumps bail. A surety cannot be compelled to deposit the money in advance, but he can be jailed if subsequently he cannot find the money.

(See also chapter 5, 'Committal for trial'.)

Witnesses in private

Under section 25 (implemented in 2001) of the Youth Justice and Criminal Evidence Act 1999, courts are given power to exclude the public when hearing a vulnerable or intimidated witness while evidence is being given in a sexual offence or where a person other than the accused might intimidate a witness. Under the Act, the court must allow at least one press representative to remain. Any other press representative, excluded from the hearing, has the same reporting rights as those not excluded. This is taken to mean that the proceedings will be deemed to have been held in public to meet the requirement for privilege to apply to reports (see later this chapter, 'Privilege', and chapter 11, 'Evidence in private in criminal courts').

Section 47 of the Act makes it an offence to report, before the end of the trial, any 'special measures' order made to protect a vulnerable or intimidated witness or to any prohibition on the accused cross-examining a witness. 'Special measures' may include taking evidence given by a witness by a live television link or behind a screen allowing him to be seen only by the judge, jury and lawyers in the case. The Queen's Bench Divisional Court held in May 2004 that the Act gives no powers to make a special measures direction for a defendant even if the defendant is giving evidence. The reporting restriction in this section does not extend to evidence or to any witness's identity. Prosecution for publication before the end of the trial of any 'special measures' order may be brought only by or with the consent of the Attorney-General.

Identification of witnesses

A Home Office statement on standards of witness care, issued in 1998, said that unless it was necessary for evidential purposes, defence and prosecution witnesses should not be required to disclose their addresses in open court. In exceptional cases, it would be appropriate for defence and prosecution to make application for the non-disclosure in open court of the names of witnesses. Courts sometimes allow a witness to write down his name or address to avoid unnecessary pain or distress.

Under section 46 of the Youth Justice and Criminal Evidence Act, operative from October 2003, a court is given power to ban the identification of a vulnerable witness over 18 during his lifetime. The Act states that matter likely to lead to identification includes the name and address of the witness, any educational establishment attended by him, his workplace or any still or moving picture.

Power to give anonymity to people under 18 concerned in criminal proceedings in an adult court already existed. However, guidelines on court reporting issued to crown court judges by the Judicial Studies Board in 2000 say: 'Strangely, it does not seem possible to give a reporting restriction order in respect of a witness under 18 that will last beyond his 18th birthday even in a case where the court would make a lifetime direction in relation to an adult' (see chapter 6).

The Act provides that a court may make an order banning the identification of a witness if it is satisfied that the quality of the witness's evidence or the level of his co-operation will be diminished by fear or distress and that his evidence and co-operation will be improved by an order being made. Home Office explanatory notes published in 1999 said that the words 'fear' and 'distress' were not intended to cover a disinclination to give evidence on account of the prospect of embarrassing publicity, and not every witness eligible for other protection (such as the provision of screens or a video link) because of fear or distress would also be eligible for a ban on identification.

The court is required by the Act to take into account the circumstances of the case, the age of the witness, his social and cultural background and ethnic origins, his domestic and employment circumstances and his religious beliefs and political opinions. Other circumstances include the behaviour towards the witness of the accused or of the accused's family and associates, or of anyone likely to be an accused or a witness. The court must also consider any views expressed by the witness.

A witness over 16 may give a written waiver dispensing with any order, provided no person interfered with his peace or comfort to obtain consent. Except where a sexual offence is involved, a parent or guardian of a witness under 16 may give the written waiver provided the parent or guardian had previously been given written notice drawing his attention to the need to consider the welfare of the person under 16.

The court is required to consider whether an order would be in the interests of justice, including, in particular, the desirability of avoiding a substantial and unreasonable restriction on the reporting of the proceedings. This requirement might provide grounds for the media to object to an order. A court or appeal court may revoke the order or relax it in the interests of justice, or because it imposes a substantial and unreasonable restriction on reporting and it would be in the public interest to relax it.

One of the first orders under section 46 was made by a recorder at Northampton crown court in November 2004 to prevent the identification of a vicar alleged to have been the victim of harassment by a GP and his girl friend who were also accused of conspiracy to pervert the course of justice

Witnesses such as blackmail victims can also be protected from identification by the court making an order under section 11 of the Contempt of Court Act 1981 (see later this chapter, 'Contempt of Court', and also chapters 12 and 17). The Court of Appeal held in 2004 that a police officer who was a potential witness at an inquest was entitled to anonymity for himself and his family if he had reasonable grounds for fearing for his life (*A v Inner South London Coroner* (2004) Times, 11 November). The Divisional Court had reached a similar conclusion in 1993 when it held that reasonable steps can be taken to protect and reassure witnesses, and witnesses who had already suffered violent attacks could be allowed to retain their anonymity.

In care proceedings, a court may afford anonymity to a professional social worker witness only in an exceptional case (*Re W (Care Proceedings): Witness Anonymity)* [2002] EWCA Civ 1626, [2003] 1 FLR 329).

Under the Serious Organised Crime and Police Act it becomes an offence to disclose new identities of witnesses under police protection because of violence or intimidation or to disclose other arrangements for their protection.

Intimidation of witnesses

If a person has been acquitted and the procedure has been tainted by intimidation of a witness (or a juror at crown court), the High Court can, under the Criminal Procedure and Investigations Act 1996, quash the acquittal, allowing the person to be tried again, thus departing from the general principle of British law that a person cannot be tried twice for the same offence. Before the High Court can exercise this power a person must have been convicted of interference with, or intimidation of, a witness or a juror and the court convicting him must have certified there is a real possibility that but for the interference or intimidation the person would not have been acquitted. If the court believes there is a possibility of a new trial of the person who was acquitted, it can, under section 4 of the Contempt of Court Act 1981, order the postponement of reporting of the proceedings, or part of the proceedings, against the person accused of the interference with, or intimidation of a witness, until after the new trial of the acquitted person.

Liability for contempt of court under the strict liability rule of the 1981 Act starts in relation to the new trial once the certificate is granted as a first step towards allowing the High Court to quash the original acquittal, thus restricting publicity generally about the acquitted defendant's role in the crime (see also chapter 7, 'Procedure at trials' and chapter 17, 'Tainted acquittals').

Reporting derogatory assertions in pleas of mitigation

Under the Criminal Procedure and Investigations Act 1996, a court has power to restrict reporting of an assertion made in a speech of mitigation where there are substantial grounds for believing that the assertion is derogatory to a person's character (such as where it is suggested that his conduct has been criminal, immoral, or improper) and that the assertion is false or the facts asserted are irrelevant to the sentence. The Act allows the court to order that the assertion made in mitigation shall not be reported for 12 months. The Act says that an order cannot be made if the assertion was made earlier in the trial which led to the conviction of the defendant on whose behalf the plea of mitigation was made (where there may have been an opportunity to rebut the allegation). Otherwise, the order can be made at any time before sentence is decided or as soon as reasonably practicable afterwards and may be revoked at any time.

The Act makes it an offence to publish the assertion during the 12 months even if the person whose character is attacked is not named, if the report contains enough information to make it likely that the public will identify him.

The order may also be made where a magistrates court has been hearing a plea of mitigation before considering sending the defendant to crown court for sentence.

Privilege

This book lists (see chapter 8) some of the many restrictions imposed by law on court reports in newspapers and broadcasting.

The court reporter should be aware of the restrictions which apply to the particular case or court which he is attending.

He also needs to be aware of the conditions which must be met if his report is to be protected against an action for libel.

The law recognises that the proceedings of the courts should be reported in the press and it has given such reports a special protection.

This protection, known as absolute privilege, requires the report to be a fair and accurate report of court proceedings held in public, published contemporaneously (see chapter 20).

To be fair and accurate a report need not be verbatim. It can be a paragraph. But it must be balanced, giving proper weight to both sides, stating for example that the accused denied the charge, and giving an outline of his defence if the report sets out the prosecution's case.

The reporter must be careful not to single out allegations made in court and present them as facts. He must attribute such remarks to the person who made them in court. A reporter can never be absolutely sure that opening statements made by barristers, solicitors, or police officers, when they outline the case they hope to prove, will actually be borne out by the evidence. Such statements should never be reported as fact without attribution to the speaker.

Care is also needed when the reporter, in writing his story, sets out to abbreviate and paraphrase complex charges. The danger is that in simplifying the legal jargon he commits inaccuracies or makes the charge seem more serious than it is. It is usually safer in the introduction to use a phrase like 'charges connected with' certain happenings, but the young reporter in doubt should consult his news editor.

An inaccurate statement in a court report does not have the protection of privilege, should the inaccuracy be defamatory.

Headlines and introductions to court stories are privileged only if they are fairly and accurately based on statements made in court.

As a working rule, a contemporaneous report means one that is published in the first available issue. All protection is not lost if a report is not contemporaneous, but the privilege is only qualified and is therefore subject to the proviso that publication is made without malice. (See chapter 20, 'Part I of the Schedule to Defamation Act 1996'.)

Privilege does not protect anything added to a court report that has not actually been said in court—for example, information given to a reporter after the hearing by a lawyer or a police officer. Nothing which is not part of the proceedings is protected.

Outbursts made in court by people who are not directly involved in the case need care in reporting, because they may be held not to be part of the proceedings. Many interruptions made by people in the public gallery are not defamatory and may be freely reported. Other remarks, however, may represent an attack on someone's character or truthfulness. In this case, it is wiser to report merely that the interruption was made, without using the actual words.

Written reports handed to the bench but not read out could also be ruled to be outside privilege.

They are not strictly evidence, but they become privileged if read out in the course of the case.

Contempt of court

Besides many statutory restrictions on court reports, the journalist also needs to recognise the limitations sometimes imposed by the law of contempt, as already indicated, although the Contempt of Court Act 1981 provides a limited defence for court reports published in good faith, as explained below and in chapter 17.

The courts have power under section 4 of the Act to order the postponement of publication of a report of any part of court proceedings to avoid the substantial risk of prejudice to the administration of justice in those proceedings or any other proceedings pending or imminent.

But this section also says that provided no such order has been made there is no strict liability for contempt for fair and accurate reports of proceedings held in public when published contemporaneously and in good faith. It remains possible that liability for contempt could arise if the report of the proceedings failed to meet the requirements of being fair and accurate and it created a substantial risk of serious prejudice under the strict liability rule. There is a danger that a newspaper publishing a report which causes a trial to be abandoned or delayed could be ordered under the Courts Act 2003 to pay the cost to public funds of the wasted time even though strict liability for contempt does not arise because no postponement order has been made. An example of this would be if a newspaper disclosed, before the end of the case, proceedings at crown court which had taken place in the absence of the jury and a fresh trial had to be ordered. (See chapter 17, 'Media could be ordered to pay costs'.)

Newspapers should in any case be careful to exclude references made in magistrates court to previous convictions and any extraneous material that could be prejudicial where a case is to be tried by a jury (see also chapter 5, 'Reporting restrictions at committal for trial and sending for trial').

The courts also have power under section 11 of the Contempt of Court Act to protect the identity of a witness or accused, but sympathy with a witness or accused is not a reason for making such an order. Section 11 orders are dealt with in greater detail in chapters 12 and 17.

03 Crimes

Misdeeds triable in the criminal courts are numerous and varied. Their names, together with the legal jargon associated with them, sometimes present problems to young journalists and their newspapers. For example, the crime of theft is sometimes referred to in introductions and headlines as 'robbery'; this not only makes the paper look foolish to those many readers who know the difference, but also puts the paper at risk of a solicitor's letter, because robbery is a much more serious offence.

There are two elements in most crimes, a criminal act and a guilty mind. Lawyers refer to these two elements as the *actus reus* (which they pronounce, in lawyers' Latin, actus reeus) and *mens rea* (menz reeah). Without a guilty intent, no crime is committed.

But for some crimes, no guilty intent is necessary. These crimes are said to be subject to *strict liability* and called 'absolute offences'.

The crime for which a journalist is most likely to appear, as a journalist, before a court is contempt of court. Under the common law, contempt is a crime of strict liability—the prosecution does not have to prove that the journalist intended to impede the course of justice. But the Contempt of Court Act 1981 limited the circumstances in which journalists could be guilty of contempt of court in the absence of intent (see chapter 17).

This chapter mentions some of the main crimes and indicates pitfalls in referring to them. Simple explanations are given that in many cases would not satisfy a lawyer. The journalist seeking further information is advised to consult *Stone's Justices' Manual*, a three-volume reference book for magistrates that some newspapers and public libraries have.

Crimes against people

Murder The unlawful killing of another human being 'with malice aforethought'—that is, with the intention to kill or cause grievous bodily harm to that person. A person found guilty of murder must be sentenced to imprisonment for life.

Manslaughter The unlawful killing of another person, but in the absence of malice aforethought.

Aiding suicide The killing of oneself is not a crime—though it was until 1961 and at one time resulted in the forfeiture of the dead person's property—but it is a crime to help another person to commit suicide or to attempt suicide.

Infanticide The killing of an infant under 12 months old by its mother, whose mind is disturbed as a result of the birth.

Assault and battery In these offences legal language differs from ordinary speech. Assault is technically a hostile act that causes another person to fear an attack. Battery is the actual application of force. It is normal newspaper practice to use the word 'assault' in court stories to indicate a physical attack.

ABH An assault (in the usual sense of the word) that causes actual bodily harm. The offence is frequently referred to as ABH, but in court lawyers sometimes refer to 'a section 47 offence', a reference to section 47 of the Offences Against the Person Act 1861.

Malicious wounding or GBH An assault (in the usual sense of the word) that causes a wound or grievous bodily harm. The offences are variously referred to as malicious wounding or GBH, or as 'a section 20 offence' (from the 1861 Act).

Wounding with intent or GBH with intent An assault (in the usual sense of the word) which causes a wound or grievous bodily harm, with the intention to do grievous bodily harm; the offences carry a maximum penalty of life imprisonment. They are often referred to in court as 'a section 18 offence' (from the 1861 Act).

Rape Having unlawful sexual intercourse with a person without his or her consent. The Sexual Offences Act 2003 extended the definition of rape to penetration, by the penis, of the vagina, mouth, or anus, and the law covers male victims as well as female. The Act classifies as rape any sexual intercourse with a child under 13, because a child under that age is deemed not capable of giving consent to any form of sexual activity.

Unlawful sex Having unlawful sexual intercourse with a girl under 16.

Sexual assault Known before the 2003 Act as indecent assault. A series of offences including assault by penetration other than by the penis.

Child sex offences A series of offences including those designed to deal with the increase in 'child grooming' as a result of developments in communications technology such as the internet. Offences introduced in the Sexual Offences Act 2003 include 'arranging intended child sex offences' and 'meeting a child following sexual grooming'.

Crimes against property

Theft The dishonest appropriation of property belonging to another with the intention of permanently depriving the other of it (Theft Act 1968). The act of theft is stealing. Do not refer to the offence as robbery.

Offering a reward for the return of stolen goods may be an offence (see chapter 8: Theft Act 1968).

Robbery Theft by force, or by threat of force.

Burglary Entering a building as a trespasser and stealing or attempting to steal; or inflicting or attempting to inflict grievous bodily harm. It is also burglary to enter a building as a trespasser *with intent* to steal, inflict grievous bodily harm, commit rape, or do unlawful damage. Before the Theft Act 1968, burglary was an offence which could be committed only at night.

Aggravated burglary The act of burglary while armed.

Obtaining property by deception The name defines the offence. It can safely be referred to as 'fraud'.

Obtaining services, or evasion of liability, by deception (Theft Act 1978). Again, the name defines the offence. An example is staying at a hotel, or filling a car tank with petrol, and leaving without paying.

Blackmail Making an unwarranted demand with menaces with a view to gain.

Handling Dishonestly receiving goods, knowing or believing them to be stolen; or dishonestly helping in their retention, removal, disposal, or sale by or for someone else.

Taking a vehicle without authority This offence does not imply an intention to deprive the owner permanently and must not be confused, either in text or headline, with theft. You can say the defendant took a car, but not that he stole the car. The offence is sometimes referred to on court lists as TWOC (taking without owner's consent).

Aggravated vehicle taking The offence was introduced in 1992 in response to increasing public disquiet over joy-riding. It occurs when a vehicle has been taken (as above) and, before it is recovered, injury or damage is caused.

Motoring crimes

Dangerous driving A person drives a motor vehicle dangerously if the way he drives falls far below what would be expected of a competent and careful driver.

Causing death by dangerous driving This and the previous offence were substituted for reckless driving and causing death by reckless driving by the Road Traffic Act 1991. The offences require only that bad driving be demonstrated through its consequences rather than by establishing a driver's intentions.

Careless or inconsiderate driving Driving a motor vehicle on a road without due care and attention or without reasonable consideration for others. The level of bad driving that must be proved is considerably less than that required in cases of dangerous driving.

Driving while unfit Driving a motor vehicle on a road while unfit to drive, through drink or drugs. The case will normally include evidence of the accused person's driving before he was stopped.

Driving with excess alcohol Driving a motor vehicle on a road at a time when the proportion of alcohol in the driver's body exceeds the prescribed limit; that is, 80 milligrammes of alcohol in 100 millilitres of blood, 35 microgrammes of alcohol in 100 millilitres of breath, or 107 milligrammes of alcohol in 100 millilitres of urine.

Causing death by careless driving when under the influence of drink or drugs The driver must be unfit to drive through drink or drugs; or must have consumed excess alcohol (as above); or must have failed to provide a specimen.

Magistrates courts: summary proceedings

All criminal cases in England and Wales start in the magistrates courts, except when, very rarely, a voluntary bill of indictment is granted, and 97 per cent of the cases are dealt with in their entirety by magistrates. The most serious (indictable-only) offences must be sent for trial at crown court while other (either-way) offences can be tried either summarily or on indictment at crown court. The procedure in both indictable-only and either-way offences and the reporting restrictions involved are described in chapter 5. Minor offences must usually be tried by the magistrates (summary proceedings).

Magistrates

Magistrates (or justices of the peace) are appointed to serve until the age of 70. They must sit between 26 and 35 half days a year and the occasional full day.

Over 30,000 men and women serve as non-salaried magistrates. They may draw expenses and an allowance for financial loss. They are appointed by the Crown on the recommendation of the Lord Chancellor, who acts on the suggestion of a local advisory committee.

At least two magistrates must sit for most summary trials; one is sufficient when the case against the defendant is going to crown court for trial (see chapter 5).

Magistrates also carry out some other duties in civil and administrative law (see chapter 9: Magistrates courts: civil functions).

In some courts, a district judge (magistrates courts), may sit. District judges, formerly known as stipendiary magistrates or, in London, metropolitan magistrates, are barristers or solicitors, and may sit alone and decide both on the law and on the facts of the case. These district judges are usually asked to take the lengthy and complex cases at magistrates courts in the area. The Lord Chancellor has power to appoint deputy district judges (magistrates courts), who also must be legally qualified.

The Queen's Bench Divisional Court ruled in 1986 that a magistrates' bench and their clerk who had withheld names of magistrates hearing cases from press and public were acting contrary to law. Lord Justice Watkins said there was no such person known to law as the anonymous JP (see chapter 11, 'Powers to prevent or restrict reporting', and 'magistrates court information').

The magistrates of each division appoint a chairman for the year. Because he cannot be present in every court, another magistrate, from a list of chairmen who have been trained for the work, presides in his absence.

Sitting in front of the magistrates in court is the legal adviser, formerly known as the court clerk. In charge of one or more magistrates courts is a clerk to the justices, a solicitor or barrister who advises the magistrates on the law and is also empowered to conduct an early administrative review in open court dealing with legal aid and bail where a person appears for the first time on a summary or either-way offence.

When the magistrates are in session he or one of the legal advisers sit in court to record the proceedings and advise the magistrates on law. In many large towns and cities where a number of courts are sitting simultaneously, some members of the staff act practically full-time as legal advisers.

Under the Courts Act 2003, all courts were unified into a single administrative system from April 2005. All court staff are civil servants under the direction of the Lord Chancellor. There is a new central administrative agency. A courts board, including two magistrates and one judge, exists in each area. Magistrates courts committees and justices chief executives have been abolished.

Pre-trial hearing

Magistrates may, under the 2003 Act, hold a pre-trial hearing to rule on the admissibility of evidence and on points of law where a not guilty plea has been entered on an either-way offence and it has been decided to try the case summarily. Reporting restrictions apply (see chapter 5: Either way offences: indication of not guilty plea). The Act prohibits reporting of any such ruling until the end of the trial. The prohibition may be lifted or relaxed by magistrates but if an accused objects, lifting or relaxation can be ordered only if it is in the interests of justice to do so.

Prosecutions

The Crown Prosecution Service rather than the police decides in most cases whether to charge a person and the appropriate charge or charges. The case is presented in court by a solicitor or barrister employed by the service. Some prosecutions are also brought by public bodies such as local authorities. Minor offences, mainly road traffic cases, are still prosecuted by the police.

It is possible for an individual to bring a private prosecution. He may either engage a solicitor or present the case himself but the prosecution may be taken over by the Crown Prosecution Service and even discontinued by them if, for example, they consider the prosecution frivolous.

The person prosecuting outlines the case to the magistrates, whether or not the defendant has pleaded guilty. If the defendant has pleaded not guilty, witnesses for the prosecution are called. The defendant, whether represented by a solicitor or conducting his own case, may himself testify and call witnesses. He cannot be compelled to give evidence.

If he goes into the witness-box himself, like any witness he is liable to be cross-examined by the other side. Adverse comment is allowed where a defendant over 14 who has pleaded not guilty chooses without good cause not to give evidence, or, when giving evidence, not to answer a question. Failure to give evidence or to account for incriminating circumstances cannot itself lead to a conviction however.

A witness can be compelled to give evidence if a court issues a witness summons or warrant. Magistrates have power to commit to custody for up to a month or fine any person who refuses to be sworn or to give evidence. But a person cannot be compelled to give evidence against his or her spouse or co-habitee, except where the spouse or co-habitee is charged with an offence against him or her or their children, and in a few other cases.

If a witness appears to be refusing to testify or to go back on the statement he made to the investigators, he may be treated as a hostile witness. The effect of this is that he may be challenged and asked leading questions by the side who called him, suggesting to him what answer is expected. Questions put by the side which calls the witness are called examination or evidence-in-chief. Questions put by the opposing side are known as cross-examination. (See also chapter 2, 'Intimidation of witnesses'.)

When the court has heard all the witnesses, the defence may address the court, arguing how the facts and the law should be interpreted. (Either side may, with permission, address the court twice.) If the magistrates find the defendant guilty, the court will be told of any relevant previous convictions. Often sentence is postponed to await a pre-sentence report about the offender. Usually the defendant's own bad character cannot be introduced by the prosecution until this stage. However under the Criminal Justice Act 2003 evidence of previous misconduct can be brought if it is relevant to an important issue between the defence and prosecution, including whether the defendant has a propensity to commit offences of the kind with which he is charged, to correct a false impression given by the defendant, or where the defendant has made an attack on another person's character. The older previous convictions are, the less likely they are to be admitted.

Sometimes the defendant may ask for other offences to be 'taken into consideration'. This should not be confused with previous convictions. It means that the defendant is also admitting other offences which are not on the charge sheet, so that he can be sentenced for these at the same time. Where magistrates find a person guilty, or he has pleaded guilty, the defence will be given an opportunity to make a plea in mitigation of punishment, citing extenuating circumstances. (See also chapter 2, 'Reporting derogatory assertions'.)

Sentences

Generally, sentences run from the moment they are announced. For summary offences, magistrates have wide powers in the way they deal with the defendant. They may not, however, impose a jail sentence of more than 12 months for one offence and 15 months for two or more offences. Prison sentences can be imposed for the first time only when the defendant is legally represented, or has been given the chance to apply for legal aid. Under the 2003 Act, custody plus sentences (a jail term of up to three months followed by a longer term of supervision in the community) replace short prison sentences of under 12 months. Intermittent custody orders, allowing the defendant out of jail for work, education or family ties are also introduced.

Consecutive sentences—that is, sentences running one after the other—may be imposed where the defendant is guilty of more than one offence.

Sentences may, however, be ordered to run concurrently. This means that the defendant remains in prison effectively only for the length of the longest sentence imposed.

Some prison sentences are suspended, with the effect that the defendant does not have to go to jail unless he commits a further offence, for which a jail sentence could be imposed, during the period the sentence is suspended. It should always be made clear in a court story that the sentence is suspended, and it is incorrect to refer to the defendant as being jailed. Community minus sentences are suspended sentences combined with supervision in the community.

Magistrates must consider the defendant's financial circumstances before deciding on the amount of any fine. Maximum fines are fixed by statute within a scale according to the offence. The normal maximum is £5,000 but higher penalties may be imposed for such offences as customs duty and tax evasion.

The court can, if it does not wish to impose a penalty, grant the defendant an absolute discharge. This means that he is discharged without any conditions. Alternatively, he may be conditionally discharged for a given period. Again, no penalty is imposed, but if the defendant commits another offence within the period laid down he is liable to be dealt with for the first offence as well as subsequent offences.

A defendant over 16 can be placed under a community order by which he can be told to carry out one or more of a number of requirements, including unpaid work in the community under the direction of a probation officer or a youth offending team set up by a local authority, or adherence to a curfew or drug or alcohol treatment. Offenders under 25 can be ordered to put in a stated number of hours at an attendance centre.

Magistrates have power to bind over to be of good behaviour any person such as a defendant, witness, or complainant, in cases of violence or the threat of violence. Sometimes the prosecution will drop such a charge if the defendant agrees to be bound over in this way. No conviction has been recorded if this happens because such an order is regarded as a civil matter. In common assault cases, often the complainant as well as the defendant is bound over instead of the case being tried to a conclusion.

Sometimes when a man has admitted, or has been convicted of, an offence the magistrates may feel the sentence they can pass is insufficient.

In this case they can commit him to crown court for sentence. It is important not to confuse this with his being committed for trial (see chapter 5).

Magistrates have powers to order a defendant to make restitution, and can order a motor vehicle used in the furtherance of theft, even shoplifting, to be confiscated. They can order an offender to pay compensation for personal injury, or for loss or damage to goods.

A magistrates court can vary or rescind a sentence within 28 days and, where it would be in the interests of justice, can re-open a case, to be heard by a different bench of magistrates, if a person has pleaded not guilty or has been tried in his absence.

Court lists

There is no provision in law for defendants' names to be made available to the press in advance of court proceedings (see chapter 2, 'Helping the police with their inquiries').

In 1989 the Home Office wrote to justices' clerks commending the practice of making available to the press court lists and, where they are prepared, provisional lists on the day of the hearings. The court may charge the economic rate for providing court papers and newspapers and news agencies may co-operate to share any such cost (Circular 80/1989).

The Home Office circular said that, as a minimum, the list should contain each defendant's name, age, address, and, where known, his occupation, and the charge he faced. The circular also approved the practice of some courts of supplying copies of the court register of the day's proceedings.

In 1967 and 1969, the Home Office recommended that addresses of defendants should be stated orally in magistrates courts. The 1967 Circular (No 78/1967) stated: 'A person's address is as much part of his description as his name. There is, therefore, a strong public interest in facilitating press reports that correctly describe persons involved.'

Lord Justice Watkins said in the Queen's Bench Divisional Court in 1988 that while no statutory provision laid down that a defendant's address had publicly to be given in court it was well established practice that, save for a justifiable reason, it must be (*R v Evesham Justices, ex p McDonagh* [1988] QB 553, 562).

The guide to reporting restrictions in the magistrates court, issued by the Judicial Studies Board in 2001, says: 'Announcement in open court of names and addresses enables the precise identification vital to distinguish a defendant from someone in the locality who bears the same name and avoids inadvertent defamation.'

The Department of Constitutional Affairs announced in 2004 that a register of fines in the magistrates courts, with name, date of birth and address would become available during 2005. A 'keeper and developer' of the register would be appointed, on similar lines to that provided for county court judgments.

(See also chapter 11, 'Addresses of defendants' and chapter 12, 'European Convention on Human Rights'.)

Under section 15 of the Defamation Act 1996 qualified privilege (subject to explanation or contradiction) is given to publication of a fair and accurate copy of, or extract from, a document made available by a court or by a judge or officer of a court. The Act does not state to whom the document must be made available for it to be privileged.

Court information and data protection

This subject is dealt with in chapter 33, 'Data Protection Act'.

Appeals

If a person pleads guilty, he or she cannot usually appeal against conviction, but may appeal to crown court against sentence. A person who pleads not guilty can appeal to crown court against conviction and/or sentence (see chapter 7).

Either defence or prosecution may appeal to the Queen's Bench Divisional Court on a point of law. The procedure is described in chapter 7.

See also chapter 9, 'Magistrates courts: civil proceedings'.

Magistrates courts: preliminary hearings

Many serious offences are not tried by magistrates but are sent by them for trial at crown court. Magistrates sitting at these hearings leading to trial by jury at crown court are said to be acting as examining justices.

Reporting of proceedings before examining justices is restricted by section 8 of the Magistrates' Courts Act 1980, the aim of which was to avoid a potential juror at crown court being prejudiced by earlier reports of the case when it was at magistrates court stage.

These restrictions, set out later in this chapter, apply to reports of earlier hearings before magistrates, prior to the case being formally moved to crown court for trial by either of the two main methods:

- *Committal for trial* (where the accused has indicated that he will plead not guilty to an either-way offence or the accused is a juvenile facing a serious charge); and

- *Sending for trial* on indictable-only offences such as murder, rape, and robbery, a fast track procedure for offences that *must* be tried by jury, as described later in this chapter.

Changes to the procedure will take place when more parts of the Criminal Justice Act 2003 become operative.

Either-way offences

(See also chapter 2, 'Types of offences'.)

When a person is brought before magistrates and charged with an 'either way' offence, the accused must be asked to indicate whether he will plead guilty or not guilty. This is known as plea-before-venue procedure.

Indication of guilty plea

If he intimates that he will plead guilty, the magistrates must proceed as for a summary trial and cannot commit him for *trial* at crown court. They must hear the prosecution case, after an adjournment if that is necessary. If there is a dispute as to the facts concerning the gravity of the offence (these have become known as Newton cases), magistrates must accept the defence version unless the prosecution proves another version. They must then sentence after hearing what is said in mitigation, adjourn the case for reports, or commit the accused for *sentence* at crown court if they believe their powers are insufficient. The purpose of this procedure in either-way cases is to ensure that an accused is given the opportunity to enter a plea of guilty as soon as possible and to ensure that cases which can properly be dealt with at magistrates court remain there.

Reporting restrictions under the 1980 Act do not apply to either-way offences as soon as the accused says he will plead guilty because the magistrates then cease to act as examining justices.

Indication of not guilty plea

Unless reporting restrictions are lifted, as explained later, the Act does not permit the reporting of the accused's indication to plead *not* guilty at this stage, but a report which mentions such an intention is unlikely to lead to a prosecution.

If the accused intimates that he will plead not guilty to an either-way offence or fails to indicate a plea the mode of trial will be decided by the magistrates. When the Criminal Justice Act 2003 becomes fully operative, the prosecution will be able to inform the court of any previous convictions and both prosecution and defence may make submissions as to whether the case should be tried summarily or at crown court. Magistrates must then decide on the mode of trial. Even if they believe the case should be tried summarily, the accused may still exercise his right to be tried by a jury at crown court. If he wishes, or the magistrates decide, for trial by jury at crown court the hearing will usually be adjourned for formal committal for trial proceedings, described below.

If he accepts summary trial of an either-way offence, to which he has decided to plead not guilty and magistrates agree, there are no general reporting restrictions under the 1980 Act.

However if magistrates then hold a hearing under the Courts Act 2003 in advance of summary trial to rule on the admissibility of evidence and on points of law where the not guilty plea, another type of reporting restriction applies under that Act. The Act prohibits reporting of any such ruling until the end of the trial—an unusual recognition of the possibility of magistrates being prejudiced by reports of an earlier hearing in the same case. The prohibition may be lifted or relaxed by magistrates but if an accused objects, lifting or relaxation can be ordered only if it is in the interests of justice to do so.

Committal for trial

Committal for trial at crown court may take place on either-way offences, as described above, or where a person under 18 is accused of an indictable offence.

Magistrates may commit the defendant for trial on the basis of written statements, sometimes known as depositions, without consideration of the contents of these documents, unless there is a defence submission that there is insufficient evidence to put the accused on trial, or one of the accused is not legally represented. Witnesses, whether for prosecution or defence, are not called to give oral evidence and any submission of insufficient evidence must be decided merely on contentions put forward by prosecution and defence. If magistrates decide there is insufficient evidence, they must discharge the accused.

Even if the accused has elected for the reporting restrictions to be lifted, there is no provision for the written statements or depositions to be made available to the press. If the magistrates accept a submission of insufficient evidence to go before a jury and none of the accused is committed for trial, reporting restrictions on the whole hearing are lifted. Additionally, the Magistrates' Courts Act 1980, as amended, provides that when the accused is not committed for trial, as much of the written statements or depositions as has been accepted as evidence shall be read aloud unless the court otherwise directs. Where a direction is given against reading the evidence aloud, an account must be given of such evidence.

If the accused is not committed for trial because of insufficient evidence, this should not be described as an acquittal because there has been no trial. It is possible, though rare, for the accused to be brought to court again if further evidence comes to light, since this would not infringe the general principle that a person cannot be tried twice for the same offence.

If the accused is sent for trial and is refused bail pending appearance at crown court, he can apply to a judge in chambers sitting in private to allow him bail.

The prosecution may object to bail, eg on grounds that the accused might abscond, interfere with witnesses or commit another offence.

Section 8 of the Magistrates' Courts Act restricts what may be reported of bail applications to 'arrangements as to bail on committal or adjournment'. This has been widely interpreted as meaning that any conditions as to bail may be reported, eg the amount of the surety, that the accused reports regularly to the police, that he surrenders his passport, or that he does not interfere with witnesses. But arguments as to whether bail should be granted are ruled out. So are the reasons for refusing bail, which magistrates must give under the Bail Act 1976.

The law obliges the clerk of the court to display at the court house a notice giving the accused's name, age, address, the charge(s), and whether he is committed (and to which court) or discharged. Exceptions are made in cases involving juveniles. A newspaper report of such a notice is protected by qualified privilege.

Bill of indictment

If magistrates rule there is insufficient evidence to go before a jury, the prosecution can turn to the rare procedure of applying to a High Court judge for a voluntary bill of indictment. The effect of this is that although magistrates have discharged the accused, he will still be brought to trial at crown court. The application for a bill of indictment will be heard by a judge in private. Under the Administration of Justice Act 1960, it would not be a contempt of court to report the judge's decision (see chapter 17, 'Report of hearings in private').

Under the Criminal Justice Act 2003 rules may be made for the committal for trial procedure and the notice of transfer procedure for serious fraud and offences against children, outlined later in this chapter, to be replaced by 'sending for trial' as described below.

Sending for trial

Under procedure for indictable-only charges against an adult, or a juvenile co-accused with an adult, magistrates, must after hearing any application for bail, *send for trial* at crown court, without considering the evidence. In many indictable-only offences, the accused will appear before magistrates only on this one occasion. There is no opportunity for the accused to submit there is no case to answer. In a few cases there may be an adjournment for a few days before *sending for trial*, for example to confirm that the indictable-only offence is the right one. If the accused is in custody he will appear at crown court for a first hearing (to learn whether he intends to plead guilty or not etc) within eight days. However, he may remain in prison for the first crown court hearing if he can be seen and heard by video link. There is no right of appeal against a *sending for trial* of a person accused of an indictable-only offence, but a sending that is invalid in law can be challenged in the Queen's Bench Divisional Court. However, within 14 days of the copies of documents containing the evidence being served on the defence and on the crown court, the accused may apply either orally or in writing to crown court for any charge to be dismissed on the grounds of insufficient evidence. A practice direction has been issued that the crown court should normally hear the application in public but reporting is restricted under the Crime and Disorder Act 1998, as is outlined later.

Reporting restrictions at committal for trial and sending for trial

Restrictions on newspaper or broadcast reports of committals for trial or sending for trial by the magistrates, introduced to avoid a potential juror being influenced, have been in place in various forms since 1968. The restrictions apply equally to early hearings such as the first appearances in magistrates courts leading up to committal or sending for trial (see *The Citizen* case later this chapter).

There are occasions when it seems difficult to present a report of preliminary proceedings that is fair to the accused if all the restrictions are strictly observed—such as where in an 'either way' charge the accused has himself chosen jury trial and is being formally committed for trial for this reason only, and not because of the seriousness of the offence or of his record. The same is true where an accused or his solicitor protests his innocence or complains of police treatment during questioning. Yet some reports which infringe the restrictions cannot be said to be in the interests of the accused. Almost daily, newspapers and broadcasters add to a court story background material either about the defendant or the alleged crime, even though reporting restrictions have not been lifted. It is arguable that such background material is not itself a report of the court proceedings and is not therefore a contravention of the Act (even though the general law of contempt still applies).

In 1975, however, the editor of a weekly newspaper was fined for a story which combined an account of a fire with a report of a man's first appearance before a magistrates court on an arson charge. The prosecuting solicitor contended that reports must be restricted to matters permitted by the Act. He said it did not matter where other information came from, whether it was said in court or was known to the reporter—it was a breach of the Act. This conclusion has not been contested in the High Court.

One legal view is that in this situation the newspaper ought to run separate stories, each with its own headline—a story on the incident, conforming to the law of contempt (see chapter 17) and a court story conforming to section 8 of the 1980 Act.

Apart from the exceptions, which follow, reports of preliminary hearings on offences triable by jury are limited by the 1980 Act to 10 points:

(1) the name of the court, and the names of the magistrates;

(2) names, addresses, and occupations of the parties and witnesses, ages of the accused and witnesses;

(3) the offence(s), or a summary of them, with which the accused is or are charged;

(4) names of counsel and solicitors in the proceedings;

(5) any decision of the court to commit the accused, or any of the accused for trial, and any decision on the disposal of the case of any accused not committed;

(6) where the court commits the accused for trial, the charge or charges, or a summary of them, on which he is committed and the court to which he is committed;

(7) where proceedings are adjourned, the date and place to which they are adjourned;

(8) any arrangements as to bail (which is taken to include any conditions as to bail, but not any reason for opposing or refusing it);

(9) whether legal aid was granted;

(10) any decision of the court to lift or not to lift these reporting restrictions.

These restrictions are not in force when:

(1) the accused applies to have them lifted. Under the 1980 Act magistrates are then required formally to make an order lifting restrictions. If there is more than one accused all of them must be given the opportunity to make representations before a decision on lifting the restrictions is taken. If any of the accused objects, restrictions may be lifted only on the grounds that it is in the interests of justice to do so. Even if reporting restrictions are lifted, newspapers should not refer to previous convictions or report other information that carries a substantial risk of serious prejudice to a fair trial at crown court.

(2) the court decides to send none of the accused for trial;

(3) the court decides to try one or more of the accused summarily. In this case, a report of the summary trial may be published even if it impinges on the case of other defendants not tried summarily. If the accused is committed for *sentence* to crown court, there are no restrictions on the report because he has been tried summarily;

(4) all the defendants have eventually been tried at crown court. This means that submissions made at the committal weeks or months earlier can now be reported, if thought newsworthy, without waiting for any appeal. This belated report of the committal proceedings, provided it is fair and accurate, will be treated as a contemporaneous report, and will be privileged under the Defamation Act 1996.

Some important interpretations of the Magistrates' Courts Act 1980 have been given by the High Court.

In one case it was ruled that where there is a multiplicity of charges which have properly been made the subject of one committal for trial proceeding, any lifting of the restrictions must apply to the whole of the committal.

In 1972, it was held in the Queen's Bench Divisional Court that once lifted, the restrictions cannot be reimposed (*R v Blackpool Justices, ex p Beaverbrook Newspapers Ltd* [1972] 1 All ER 388, [1972] 1 WLR 95). It is however possible to impose a postponement order under section 4 of the Contempt of Court Act 1981 (see chapter 17) but guidelines on reporting restrictions in the magistrates court prepared by the Judicial Studies Board in 2001 say the court should be slow to impose additional, discretionary reporting restrictions such as postponement orders.

There have been a number of prosecutions for reports that were in breach of the Magistrates Court Act even though it later transpired that the reports could not have influenced the subsequent crown court trial.

In 1996, the former editor of *The Citizen*, Gloucester, and the paper's owners were each fined £4,500 under the Act for a report of the first appearance in the magistrates court of Fred West, who was accused of several murders. The report was an accurate report of what was said in court but included a statement that West had admitted killing his daughter.

Every court reporter should understand the basis of the Act but not allow it to inhibit him more than necessary. For instance, point three of the ten permitted points allows the reporter to give detail *of the charge*. The reporter's difficulty is that the charge as set out on the information available to the reporter is often only a summary. If the case merits it on its news value, he should approach the clerk of the court or the prosecution to obtain particulars of the charge, such as where and when the offence is alleged to have been committed and against whom, information which the 1980 Act allows him to publish. In publishing the charge however, a newspaper must beware of disclosing the name of any complainant in a sexual offence (see chapter 8: Sexual offences and other statutory restrictions).

Notice of transfer

In an either-way offence involving violence or cruelty against a child, or involving serious fraud, the Crown Prosecution Service may serve a notice of transfer on magistrates and the case is then transferred to crown court. The only function of the magistrates is to make orders requiring witnesses to attend crown court or for bail or legal aid.

In both cases, of offences against children and of serious fraud, the accused can apply to crown court for the charge to be dismissed on grounds of insufficient evidence.

Reporting restrictions on preliminary hearings, under section 8 of the Magistrates' Courts Act 1980, described above, apply to hearings before magistrates where notice of transfer is served by the prosecution, although usually there will be little to report other than basic details. (See also chapters 6 and 7.)

Section 70 committal

On the application of the prosecution, magistrates may make an order under section 70 of the Proceeds of Crime Act 2002 committing the case of a convicted defendant to crown court for a hearing there to decide whether there should be a confiscation order to seize property obtained as a result of criminal conduct. Such a committal can take place alongside a committal for sentence. The prosecution may also make application for an order at crown court under the 2002 Act. Because magistrates are not acting as examining justices in section 70 committals, there are no reporting restrictions under the Magistrates' Courts Act 1980.

Restrictions on reports of applications for dismissal made at crown court

Applications at crown court for dismissal of indictable-only charges sent for trial by magistrates are subject to reporting restrictions under the 1998 Crime and Disorder Act unless all the applications for dismissal made at the proceedings are successful. Reports must be confined to:

(1) the name of the judge and of the court;

(2) names, ages, home addresses, and occupations of the accused and witnesses;

(3) the offence or offences with which the accused is charged;

(4) names of counsel and solicitors;

(5) where proceedings are adjourned, the date and place to which they are adjourned;

(6) arrangements as to bail;

(7) whether legal aid is granted.

The judge dealing with the application for dismissal may lift the reporting restrictions but where there are two or more accused and one of them objects to the lifting, the judge may lift the restrictions only if it is in the interest of justice to do so. The restrictions do not apply to any decision to lift or not to lift them and cease to apply at the end of the trial of all the accused.

The application must normally be heard in public (see chapter 11, 'Crown court').

Juveniles in the news

As long ago as 1993, a review carried out for the Lord Chancellor's Department pointed out the need for consistency in the law on access to and reporting of cases involving juveniles.

Since then the law has become even more anomalous. This chapter sets out to cover restrictions on reporting cases involving children involved in either criminal or civil proceedings.

Juveniles and the European Convention on Human Rights

After the Human Rights Act 1998 came into effect in 2000, courts were required to take account of rights guaranteed by the European Convention on Human Rights, including the right to freedom of expression and to impart information (article 10) and the right to respect for private and family life (article 8).

Lord Bingham, then Lord Chief Justice, explained the implications of this requirement in cases involving children when the Queen's Bench Divisional Court was considering whether a youth court had been correct in allowing the naming of a convicted juvenile offender.

He said there was tension between the two articles. It was a hallowed principle that justice was administered in public, open to full and fair reporting of the proceedings in court. But the principle came into collision with another important principle, that the privacy of a child or young person involved in legal proceedings must be carefully protected, and very great weight must be given to the welfare of such a child or young person.

The divisional court held however that the youth court had been correct to waive the restriction (*McKerry v Teesdale and Wear Valley Justices* (2000) 164 JP 355, [2000] Crim LR 594). (See later this chapter, 'When youth court anonymity may be lifted'.)

Another judge applied the Convention principles when she lifted an injunction which had prevented the *Mail on Sunday* from reporting that a council had removed a black girl from her loving white foster parents in accordance with the council's fostering policy. Mrs Justice Bracewell said this was not the kind of case under the Children Act 1989 which demanded the child's welfare should be the court's paramount consideration. She referred to section 12 of the Human Rights Act, which says that where a court is consider- ing whether to grant an injunction which would affect freedom of expression it must have particular regard to that right and where the proceedings relate to journalistic material, to the extent it would be in the public interest for the material to be published. A judge's job, she said, was not to carry out a balancing exercise between freedom of expression and other interests. On the contrary, she said, the scales were weighted at the beginning so that article 10 applied when given a narrow interpretation (*Richmond upon Thames London Borough Council v Holmes* (2000) Times, 20 October). (See also chapter 30, 'Human Rights Act 1998'.)

Similarly, in 2003 Mr Justice Munby applied the principles when deciding that a 17- year-old girl who became pregnant when she was 12 with a baby which was later adopted should have the right to tell her story through a newspaper. Article 8, he said, embraced both the right to maintain one's privacy but also the right to waive that privacy and to share what would otherwise be private with the world at large. The right to tell her story was protected not only by article 10, but also by article 8. The right of a child who had sufficient understanding to make his or her own choice had to be defended. Torbay Borough Council had opposed relaxation of an injunction which had hitherto prevented identification of the girl, her baby or the baby's father. The judge said that the council had sought to argue that in order to properly safeguard the child's interest it was necessary to prevent the media from publishing the mother's story. He rejected this contention. He said he emphatically agreed with the newspaper's assertion that it was in the public interest that the girl should be able to tell her story. Views of the children caught up in the family courts system and the wider social issues were matters which could and should be dis- cussed publicly and required open and public debate in the media. The injunction was varied to allow the girl to be identified but to prohibit publication of anything which might identify her child or the child's father. (*Re Roddy (A Child); Torbay Borough Council v News Group Newspapers* [2003] EWHC 2927 (Fam).

Youth courts

Juvenile courts, established in England and Wales under the Children and Young Persons Act 1933, were renamed youth courts in 1992, and deal with young people who were under 18 at the time they committed an offence. In law a child is defined as being under 14 years and a young person as being over 14 but under 18. A child under 10 cannot be charged with a criminal offence. However, magistrates sitting in family proceedings (see chapter 9) may make a child safety order under the Crime and Disorder Act 1998 to place a child below 10 under supervision of the local authority to prevent any repetition of behaviour which would be a criminal offence if he was over 10. Instead of a juvenile offender being brought before the youth court, the police may under the 1998 Act issue a reprimand or warning and if a further offence is committed a court may take this into account in the same way as a previous conviction. Once an offender has been given a final warning, any further offence must lead to prosecution. In many cases young offenders pleading guilty at youth court to a first offence are automatically referred to a youth offender panel comprising expert youth workers—the referral order. (See also anti-social behaviour orders against juveniles, later this chapter.)

The general public are barred from youth court although the court may make exceptions for people such as victims. Reporters are entitled to attend under the 1933 Act (see chapter 11, 'Admission to the courts').

When the youth court deals with a juvenile accused of a grave crime, it may commit him for trial at crown court. Reports of such a committal for trial are restricted by the Magistrates' Courts Act 1980 (see previous chapter) in addition to the restrictions on reports of youth court proceedings which now follow.

District judges (magistrates court), formerly known as stipendiary magistrates, may sit alone in the youth court, unaccompanied by other magistrates (see chapter 4).

Restrictions on reports

Under section 49 of the 1933 Act, reports of proceedings at a youth court must not contain:

(1) the name, address, or school, or any particulars likely to lead to the identification of any child or young person involved in the proceedings as a defendant or witness.

(2) any photograph of, or including, any such juvenile.

In a 1998 case in New Zealand the Court of Appeal decided that 'likely to lead to identification' meant an appreciable, as opposed to a fanciful, risk that the matter would lead to identification.

A district judge at Plymouth magistrates court fined the *Evening Herald* £2,500 in 2003 for the use of a photograph of a 15-year-old boy who had been convicted at youth court of stabbing a fellow pupil. The district judge said evidence by friends and family that they had recognised the boy, even though the face was partly blacked out, meant that the paper was guilty of breaching section 49. An appeal by the paper was rejected.

Reporters need to be careful not to include in a youth court story anything that could identify a juvenile. To say 'a 14-year-old Bristol boy' would not identify him but to use the name of a small village might, as would a statement that the boy was the 12-year-old twin son of a village policeman. The test must always be whether any member of the public could put a name to the child as a result of information given in the report.

There is nothing to stop the naming of adults concerned in youth court proceedings, provided this does not identify a juvenile. It should be noted that there is a complete ban on naming the juvenile's school, however large.

These restrictions also apply to reports of appeals from the youth court to a crown court or on a point of law to the Queen's Bench Divisional Court. They also apply to any proceedings in any court (for example, a crown court) for varying or revoking a supervision order against a juvenile, provided the restriction is announced in open court. The restrictions do *not* apply to reports of proceedings at crown court where a juvenile has been committed for trial or for sentence, unless an order is made under section 39 of the Children and Young Persons Act, or section 45 of the Youth Justice and Criminal Evidence Act (if implemented).

(If part of the Youth Justice and Criminal Evidence Act is implemented, this anonymity would apply from the start of a criminal investigation, to a person under 18 alleged to have committed the offence. That Act would also ban the identification of any place of work of anyone under 18 involved in the proceedings. See later this chapter, 'Anonymity before criminal proceedings start'.)

When youth court anonymity may be lifted

The normal anonymity for anyone under 18 involved in youth court proceedings does not apply when:

(1) the court lifts it to avoid injustice to that juvenile;

(2) the restrictions are waived in the public interest under the Crime (Sentences) Act 1997; or

(3) it is relaxed to trace a juvenile wanted for a serious offence.

Injustice to the juvenile

A youth court or the Home Secretary has the power to lift the restrictions on identifying any juvenile concerned in the proceedings to avoid injustice to him.

Public interest

Under the Crime (Sentences) Act 1997, section 49 of the 1933 Act was amended to give a youth court power to waive the restrictions on identifying a juvenile when he is convicted if magistrates believe it would be in the public interest. Before it can waive the restrictions, the court must allow parties to the proceedings to make representations. Under the Youth Justice and Criminal Evidence Act, mentioned earlier, a single magistrate would be able to waive the youth court restrictions in the public interest.

In a number of cases reporters attending youth court have successfully applied for the restriction to be lifted. A circular put out jointly by the Home Office and the Lord Chancellor's Department in 1998 said that the lifting of the restriction would be particularly appropriate where either the offending was persistent or serious or had had an impact on a number of people, or alerting others to the offender's behaviour would help prevent further offending. Factors where it would not be in the best interests of justice to lift the restriction would include where publicity might put the offender or his family at risk of harassment or harm, where the offender was particularly young or vulnerable, where the offender was contrite and ready to accept responsibility for his actions, and where naming the offender would reveal the identity of a vulnerable victim and lead to unwelcome publicity for that victim.

In the Queen's Bench Divisional Court in 2000, Lord Bingham, then Lord Chief Justice, said this power to dispense with anonymity had to be exercised with great care. It would be wholly wrong to dispense with a juvenile's right to anonymity as an additional punishment. It was extremely difficult to see any place for naming and shaming (a view contrary to that expressed by Home Office ministers previously).

Lord Bingham said the youth court had to be satisfied that it was in the public interest to lift the reporting restriction. That would rarely be the case and magistrates had to be clear in their minds why it was in the public interest.

The divisional court however upheld the decision of Teesdale and Wear Valley magistrates who, on the application of the editor of the *Northern Echo*, Darlington, had lifted the anonymity of a 15-year-old offender, giving as their reasons that he constituted a serious danger to the public and had shown a complete disregard for the law (*McKerry v Teesdale and Wear Valley Justices* (2000) 164 JP 355, [2000] Crim LR 594).

A report published by the Home Office in December 2000 said the lifting of reporting restrictions at youth court was felt to be useful on occasion but this should be used cautiously to avoid enhancing offenders' status among their peers. Naming of offenders, when necessary, should be done to alert the community to persistent offenders rather than being used as a punishment. (See also chapter 12, 'Challenging the courts'.)

Juvenile wanted for serious offence

Under the Criminal Justice and Public Order Act 1994, a youth court, on the application of the Director of Public Prosecutions, may dispense with the restrictions in order to trace a juvenile concerned in its proceedings who is charged with, or has been convicted of, a violent or sexual offence or an offence where an adult could be jailed for 14 years or more. The Act provides that the court may specify to what extent the restrictions are being lifted, which appears to allow it to stipulate how long the dispensation lasts.

Offenders who attain their 18th birthday

Any uncertainty as to whether a juvenile involved in youth court proceedings can be named after attaining his 18th birthday would be ended if part of Schedule 2 of the Youth Justice and Criminal Evidence Act is implemented. The Act would specifically ban publication of the juvenile's name 'while he is under 18'. Similarly under the 1999 Act, section 45 orders in the adult court, replacing section 39 orders, would be in force only while the juvenile is under 18.

Even without the implementation of this part of the 1999 Act, the anonymity for young people in the youth courts appears to end on their attaining the age of 18. This is because the Criminal Justice Act 1991 repealed the restriction on naming these 'over age' defendants and witnesses in the former juvenile courts without substituting any similar provision in the then new youth courts.

The Queen's Bench Division Administrative Court held in 2003 that the purpose of the legislation was not to protect the interests of young persons after they had ceased to be young persons and accordingly reporting restrictions applied only as long as the individual concerned remained a young person. The court dismissed an appeal against the decision of South Shields youth court, Tyne and Wear, that a defendant who was 17 when proceedings against him started in the youth court no longer had anonymity when the case resumed after his 18th birthday. The administrative court held that to continue to apply restrictions to persons reaching the age of 18 would require a strained interpretation of the 1933 Act since the Act referred also to restrictions on identifying schools and applied to witnesses as well as defendants The court rejected the submission that publication of the defendant's name constituted an interference with his rights under article 8 (Privacy) in the European Convention on Human Rights (*Todd v Director of Public Prosecutions* [2003] All ER (D) 92 (Oct).

Juveniles in adult courts

(See also chapter 11, 'Young defendants at crown court' and chapter 12, 'Juveniles in adult courts'.)

When a juvenile appears as defendant or witness in any court other than a youth court or other than in an appeal from a youth court, there is no automatic ban on identifying him in a report of the proceedings, but the court may impose such a ban.

Section 39 of the 1933 Act gives the court the power to direct that:

(1) no report of the proceedings shall reveal the name, address, or school, or include any particulars likely to lead to the identification of any child or young person concerned in the proceedings as being the person by or against or in respect of whom the proceedings are taken, or as being a witness;

(2) no picture shall be published of any child or young person so concerned.

Under section 45 of the Youth Justice and Criminal Evidence Act 1999, if implemented, an adult court would be able to direct that:

... there shall be no publication while he is under 18 of the name, address, school or other educational establishment or workplace of a minor involved in the proceedings as a person against or in respect of whom the proceedings are taken or who is a witness, nor shall any picture of or including the person be published if publication is likely to lead to his identification.

Section 39 orders would still be made in civil proceedings.

Guidelines for crown court judges issued by the Judicial Studies Board in 2000 say on section 39 orders: 'The power should not be exercised as a matter of routine but the court should balance the general requirement for open justice with the need to protect young people involved in the proceedings.'

(This matter is dealt with at greater length in chapter 12, 'Section 39 orders'.)

Courts have sometimes purported to make orders attempting to ban the identification of dead children—even though the name of the dead child has usually been published already in a report of the death or of an inquest. Several High Court judges have said the courts do not have this power and such an order appears to be a nullity (see chapter 12, 'Section 39 orders'). The guidelines issued to crown court judges in 2000 say that under section 39 it has been held that there is no power to make an order to prevent identification of a deceased child. The guidelines say this would appear to apply equally under the Youth Justice and Criminal Evidence Act.

Courts have also attempted to make orders in cases involving child battery or sexual abuse within families that the name of the adult defendant should not be published.

In 1991, however, the Court of Appeal held that the courts could not use section 39 to order that the names of defendants should not be published, unless such defendants were themselves young persons (see chapter 12).

Newspapers have frequently persuaded courts not to impose or renew orders to prevent identification of young babies who have been victims of violence. It is difficult to see that a child of such tender years would suffer any ill-effects from being named. For examples of successful challenges on these grounds, see chapter 12.

Court reports to which an order applies

Lord Justice Lloyd giving judgment in *R v Lee* [1993] 2 All ER 170, [1993] 1 WLR 103, CA said of section 39 orders: 'The section enables any court to make an order in relation to any proceedings. But any proceedings does not mean any proceedings anywhere: it must mean any proceedings in the court making the order.' From this, it would appear that if an order is made by magistrates in respect of a juvenile whose case they send for trial to crown court, that order is no longer in force when the juvenile reaches crown court. Consequently, for him to remain anonymous, a fresh order must be made by the crown court judge.

Jigsaw identification

Although the Court of Appeal decision means that while an order cannot stipulate that newspapers suppress the name of an adult defendant in order to prevent the identification of a child, there remains the danger of jigsaw identification of a child or young person who is the subject of a section 39 order—through one newspaper giving the name of the defendant and suppressing details of the relationship, and another paper, or radio or television programme, withholding the name but giving the full story.

The code of practice, adopted by the Press Complaints Commission in 2004, for newspapers to follow to avoid jigsaw identification, says:

In any press report of a case involving a sexual offence against a child:

(1) the child must not be identified;

(2) the adult may be identified;

(3) the word 'incest' must not be used where a child victim might be identified;

(4) care must be taken that nothing in the report implies the relationship between the accused and the child.

The code of practice also says that even where the law does not prohibit it, the press should not identify children under the age of 16 who are involved in cases of sexual offences, whether as victims or witnesses or defendants.

Although most newspapers have agreed to follow the recommendation of naming the defendant and suppressing matter that might suggest a connection with the child, some editors have felt it impossible to adhere to the practice where they considered the details of the story were more important than the name.

When a defendant accused of a sexual offence against a child first appears before a court and newspapers decide to give details of the relationship while omitting names, it will be difficult to have a change of mind and name the defendant.

Guidelines on reporting restrictions prepared for crown court judges by the Judicial Studies Board in 2000 commend the code of practice recommendations to avoid jigsaw identification and say: 'Since reports may already have appeared before the case reaches the crown court, the court should be very slow to interfere with this agreed practice since it may result in the sort of identification that the agreement is designed to prevent.' The draft code of practice prepared by OfCom (Office of Communications) lays emphasis on rules to safeguard the young, defined as under-15s. (See chapter 31, 'The Codes'.)

Anonymity before criminal proceedings start

Section 44 of the Youth Justice and Criminal Evidence Act would, if implemented, make it an offence once the police have started a criminal investigation to publish anything likely to lead to the identification of anyone still under 18 alleged to have committed the offence. It lists as matters likely to lead to such identification: his name, address, school, or other educational establishment or workplace, or any still or moving picture of him. Home Office notes on the Act published in 1999 state that reporting of any material (including the listed items) is not restricted if it would not lead to identification. Any appropriate criminal court may lift the ban in the interests of justice but must first consider the welfare of the suspect. A single magistrate may exercise this power.

The section contains no public interest defence and there is no provision for the suspect to waive his anonymity. The restriction would last until the individual reached the age of 18, or the offence became the subject of court proceedings, when other reporting restrictions might take effect, as explained earlier.

The former Independent Television Commission in its programme code issued in January 2001 stipulated that there should be no identification of those under 18 who were suspects, victims or witnesses in a criminal offence 'to reflect the requirements of the Youth Justice and Criminal Evidence Act 1999'. No part of the Act containing restrictions was in force at that time. The ITC later modified this stance and the code was amended so that broadcasters were required only to pay 'particular regard' in any pre-trial investigation to the potentially vulnerable position of witnesses and victims under 18 before identifying them and that 'particular justification' was required for identifying juveniles involved as defendants or potential defendants.

Anonymity for witnesses and victims under 18

The government also held back from implementing an additional restriction under the 1999 Act, a pre-trial ban on identifying witnesses or victims of crime aged under 18. Under the Act this additional restriction can come into operation only by a vote of both Houses of Parliament. The Press Complaints Commission code of conduct says: 'particular regard should be paid to the potentially vulnerable position of children who witness, or are victims of, crime. This should not restrict the right to report legal proceedings.'

Anti-social behaviour orders against juveniles

Magistrates (or a county court) may make an anti-social behaviour order (Asbo) prohibiting repetition of objectionable conduct, against a defendant aged over 10 years. The standard of proof of behaviour justifying the order is the same as for a crime (beyond all reasonable doubt) because a breach of an order is a criminal offence. The order may follow a breach of an acceptable behaviour contract (ABC) entered into by the defendant.

There are two types of Asbo application:

(1) *Applications brought by local authorities, registered social landlords or the police before magistrates in civil proceedings.* There is no automatic ban on identifying the juvenile but courts may impose anonymity under section 39 of the Children and Young Persons Act 1933.

(2) *Applications brought before a youth court after the court has convicted the juvenile of a criminal offence, which have become known as a 'bolt-on' Asbo.* The usual ban on identifying the juvenile in the report of the criminal proceedings will apply under section 49 of the 1933 Act. Oddly, there is no automatic ban on naming the juvenile in a report of the second proceedings (the Asbo application) although an order banning identification may be made under section 39 of the 1933 Act. The youth court has the power under section 49 to lift anonymity for a report of the criminal proceedings in the public interest once the juvenile has been convicted, thus making it possible for newspapers to report both hearings fully. (See, 'Public interest', earlier this chapter) Failing the removal in this way of the anonymity for a report of the youth court proceedings, the newspaper has the choice of reporting the Asbo without giving details of the criminal conduct outlined in the preceding youth court proceedings, or reporting both sets of proceedings without any names. The Justices Clerks Society suggested that during the Asbo proceedings, the court should be reminded of the criminal conduct.

If the juvenile breaches the anti-social behaviour order, he will normally be dealt with at youth court. Under the Serious Organised Crime and Police Act 2005, the usual youth court anonymity does not apply to juveniles accused of a breach of an Asbo, although the youth court has power to impose it by making an order under section 39 of the Children and Young Persons Act. If the court does make a section 39 order it is required under the Act to state its reasons.

See also chapter 9, 'Magistrates in civil proceedings' and chapter 12, 'Anti-social behaviour orders'.

Children in civil proceedings

The Children Act 1989 was introduced to rationalise the law on caring for, bringing up, and protecting children. The Act gives a court power to make care, supervision, contact, education supervision, and family assistance orders and provides anonymity for children involved.

Cases under the Act are heard in the magistrates court, the county court, or the Family Division of the High Court and may be transferred within these three tiers.

Reporting of family proceedings in the magistrates court is controlled by complex restrictions. It is governed by two overlapping acts—the Children Act 1989 and that part of the Magistrates' Courts Act 1980 originally dealing with the old domestic courts, but now relating to family proceedings courts, which besides handling children's cases also hear domestic issues between husband and wife.

The basic rule is that the press may attend. Section 69 of the Magistrates' Courts Act 1980, as amended by the Children Act, denies admission to the general public but says that representatives of newspapers or news agencies may attend these family proceedings, other than adoption proceedings. Nevertheless, magistrates in family proceedings do have power under magistrates courts rules to sit in private when exercising powers under the Children Act in relation to a child under 18.

See chapter 9, 'Family proceedings'.

If the press are admitted

Even where reporters are allowed to remain when children are involved, there are two sets of restrictions on what may be published if the proceedings are under the Children Act, as most of them are. The combined effect of the two Acts is that few details can be published and the child cannot be identified in any way, making it difficult for a meaningful story to be compiled.

Although section 71 of the Magistrates' Courts Act permits names to be published, if the case is under the Children Act this permission is removed in respect of children by section 97 of that Act, which makes it an offence to publish any material which is intended or likely to identify any child under 18 as being involved in proceedings in a court in which any power is being exercised under the Act, or to publish an address or school as being that of a child involved in any such proceedings. Under the Access to Justice Act 1999, the Children Act was extended to give anonymity to those under 18 involved in Children Act cases before the high court or the county court.

Section 71 of the Magistrates' Courts Act says no report of family proceedings in a magistrates court shall be published containing matter other than the following:

(1) the names, addresses, and occupations of parties and witnesses;

(2) the grounds of the application and a concise statement of the charges, defences, and counter-charges in support of which evidence has been given;

(3) submissions on any point of law arising in the proceedings and the decision of the court on the submissions;

(4) the decision of the court, and any observations made by the court in giving it.

If the court does not exclude reporters, the effect of the Magistrates' Courts Act restrictions is to prevent the reporting of evidence and the newsline in the case, unless the chairman of the magistrates refers to it in announcing the decision of the court (see item (4) above). Under the Children Act, magistrates are bound to give reasons for their decision.

By the use of the words 'as being involved in proceedings', this ban on identification appears to extend not merely to reports of the proceedings themselves but to any story, such as an interview with parents in dispute with social workers, which identifies the children as having been involved in such proceedings. The ban may be lifted or relaxed by the court or by the Home Secretary, if satisfied that the welfare of the child requires it. It is a defence for a publisher to prove that he did not know, and had no reason to suspect, that the material was likely to identify the child. In 2002, a woman wrongly accused of harming her twin babies, who were then placed in foster care, successfully applied, with the support of the *Daily Express*, to Mr Justice Coleridge, in the High Court Family Division for the restriction under section 97 of the Children Act to be lifted so that her name could be cleared after the children were returned to her (*Daily Express*, 17 December 2002).

Family proceedings concerning a child held in private

If family proceedings concerning a child are held in private in any court, the restrictions are even more drastic. It may be held to be a contempt of court to publish a report of the proceedings other than the decision of the court. Mr Justice Munby said in 2004 that the prohibition on publication without the court's permission of documents such as witness statements, reports, transcripts or notes of the judgment applied equally to documents that had been anonymised. Disclosure of material amounted a criminal offence under section 97 of the Children Act and a contempt of court under section 12 of the Administration of Justice Act 1960 (*Re B (A Child*) [2004] EWHC 411 (Fam),

See chapter 17, 'Reports of hearings in private'. For further details on family proceedings see chapter 9.

Adoption of children

Adoption cases are deemed to be family proceedings under the Children Act and under section 97 there can be no identification of the child, nor can any photograph of the child be published, in whatever court the proceedings take place. Under the Adoption Act 1976, adoption proceedings in the High Court may be heard in chambers. When the hearing takes place before magistrates, section 69 of the Magistrates Courts Act 1980 provides that the proceedings must be in private. Any report of the proceedings, such as one obtained afterwards is liable to be regarded as a contempt of court under section 12 of the Administration of Justice Act 1960 (see above, 'Children in civil proceedings' and chapter 17, 'Reports of hearings in private').

The Adoption Act 1976 (due to be replaced by the Adoption and Children Act 2002 when it comes into force) makes it an offence to publish an advertisement or information indicating that a child is available for adoption, the parent or guardian of a child wants the child to be adopted, a person wants to adopt a child, is willing to receive a child handed over to him with a view to adoption, or is willing to remove a child from Britain for adoption elsewhere.

Wards of court

Wardship applications are heard, usually in chambers, by a judge at county court or a judge in the Family Division of the High Court.

It is a contempt of court to publish any account of family proceedings concerning a child before a judge in chambers, eg medical or social reports, and the ward of court has anonymity under the Children Act.

Section 12 of the Administration of Justice Act 1960 deals with reporting such cases. While under this provision it is not normally a contempt to publish a report of *proceedings* in private, it is contempt to publish information about proceedings in private relating to children. For many years, it was considered that there was no automatic ban on identifying wards of court even though an account of the proceedings in chambers could not be published but Mr Justice Munby in *Kelly v BBC* [2001] Fam 59, [2001] 1 All ER 323 said this no longer applied.

Mr Justice Munby held that section 97(2) of the Children Act gave anonymity to wards of court. He said the position had changed since the Access to Justice Act 1999 extended the anonymity for children in proceedings under the Children Act to the High Court and the county court, in addition to the magistrates court. He said the combined effect of sections 8 and 10 of the Access to Justice Act was that the prohibition on identifying a person under 18 in family proceedings in section 97(2) of the Children Act applied to wardship proceedings. He added that section 97(4) still empowered a court to dispense with this restriction.

The position was summed up in *Media Lawyer* newsletter (Sept-Oct, 2002 issue):

(1) In the absence of an injunction there is nothing to prevent the media interviewing and writing about a child who is a ward of court, including the fact that he is a ward of court, provided they do not (a) identify him or (b) publish a report of the proceedings held in private. (Mr Justice Wilson in *X v Dempster* had fined the *Daily Mail* £10,000 and the columnist Nigel Dempster £1,000 for reporting that a woman had been portrayed as a bad mother in child proceedings before a judge in chambers. The judge said this trespassed into matters the court was considering in private proceedings).

(2) In the absence of an injunction there is nothing to prevent the media interviewing and writing whatever they like about a named child who is in fact a ward of court provided they do not (a) say he is a ward of court or (b) link him with proceedings of the type referred to in section 97.

(3) The media can accordingly write of a named child that he is a ward of court or otherwise involved in proceedings under section 97 only with the permission of a judge.

(4) It follows by implication from *Kelly* that once a ward of court has been named with the leave of the judge, the cat is out of the bag once and for all so that, in the absence of an injunction, the only restrictions are those arising under the Administration of Justice Act 1960 (see chapter 17, 'Reports of proceedings in private').

It was established in the Court of Appeal in 1977 that for there to be a contempt in reporting child cases in chambers, it has to be shown (1) that the publication was of information relating to proceedings before a court sitting in private; the words 'information relating to proceedings' cover confidential reports submitted to the court by, for example, the Official Solicitor or social workers, once wardship proceedings have been commenced and are not limited to information given to the judge at the actual hearing; and (2) that the publisher knew that he was publishing information relating to private wardship proceedings, or published the information recklessly not caring whether or not publication was prohibited. It followed, the court held, that it was a defence to a charge of contempt under section 12 that the publisher did not have guilty knowledge or intent in publishing the information (*Re F (A Minor) (Publication of Information)* [1977] Fam 58, [1976] 3 All ER 274).

Lord Justice Lane (later Lord Chief Justice) said in this case: 'Proceedings include such matters as statements of evidence, reports, accounts of interviews, and so on prepared for use in court once the wardship proceedings have been properly set on foot.'

In 1994, the *Sun* newspaper was fined £5,000 and its editor £1,000 for contempt of court arising from the publication of extracts from a doctor's report which had been presented at proceedings before a judge in chambers about a child.

There remains a danger for newspapers in publishing what is seen as a story of a parent's struggle to retain control of a child, should the story contain matters from the proceedings in chambers.

See also chapter 12, 'Wards of court' and chapter 17, 'Proceedings in private'.

Other civil proceedings involving a child or young person

The law governing publication of matter about wardship proceedings can also apply to other proceedings in chambers concerning children. In 1992, Lord Justice Balcombe said in the Court of Appeal: 'The court's inherent jurisdiction can be exercised whether or not the child is a ward.'

In 1998, the Court of Appeal, Civil Division, ruled that a restriction on the identification of a child was included in all Court of Appeal orders relating to children, whether or not a specific direction was given. However, the court said it was open to any party or the media to argue that the restriction should not apply in a particular case (*Re R (Minor) (Court of Appeal: Order Against Identification*) (1998) Times, 9 December).

Exercising the inherent jurisdiction, the High Court can issue an injunction forbidding identification or other information even if the child is not a ward of court. After two schoolboys, Jon Venables and Robert Thompson, had been found guilty at Preston Crown Court in 1993 of the murder of a young boy, James Bulger, Mr Justice Morland issued an injunction forbidding the seeking or publishing of information about their addresses, schools or their care or treatment, or the taking of further photographs or film of them.

Under section 12 of the Human Rights Act 1998, a court must not grant an injunction restraining publication without allowing representation by those against whom the injunction is directed unless there are compelling reasons why they should not be notified. The court must also have regard to the extent to which the material has been or is about to be made public, the public interest, and any relevant privacy code, such as press or broadcasting codes. (See chapter 30, 'Human Rights Act 1998'.)

Injunctions continuing after 18

In 1984, a judge imposed an injunction preventing the publication of any matter which could reveal the new identity of Mary Bell, a child murderer in Newcastle-upon-Tyne in the 1960s, and the identity of her child. The order was continued after Mary Bell became an adult in order to protect Mary's child, not Mary Bell herself.

The Family Division of the High Court in 2001 issued injunctions to continue to protect Venables and Thompson from publicity indefinitely even after they reached adulthood. The President of the Family Division, Dame Elizabeth Butler-Sloss, said there was a future risk of revenge attacks on the two. Applying the right to life enshrined in article 2 of the European Convention on Human Rights, their lives and well-being required protection, she said. The provisions of the Convention and the law of confidence could in exceptional cases be extended to protect individuals who were seriously at risk of death or injury if their identity or whereabouts became public knowledge. She granted injunctions restraining the media from disclosing information about the new identity of Venables and Thompson, their appearance or addresses when they were released from detention. To protect their identity and future whereabouts, no information could be solicited from secure units that might lead to identification for nine months. It was not necessary to protect information about their time in secure units as that information was already covered by the law of confidentiality or was not information that it was necessary to keep out of the public domain. (See also chapter 23, 'Breach of confidence'.)

Guidance on injunctions

In addition to the reporting restrictions on family proceedings in the magistrates courts and on children's cases before judges in chambers, it is possible for a local authority or individual to seek an injunction from a judge banning all reporting of the matter, even if the report does not identify the children.

In the past, local authorities, faced with allegations of widespread child abuse, have frequently sought injunctions in the interests of the children, or, possibly, to prevent the actions of their social workers from being open to public criticism.

Some wide-ranging injunctions have restrained identification of children. The courts have had to resolve the conflict between the interests of the child and freedom of speech. The Children Act 1989 provides for the interests of the child to be paramount but in several cases the Court of Appeal has ruled in favour of publicity for topics of genuine public interest.

The Court of Appeal in 1991 gave guidance to judges on how far these injunctions should go in banning publicity for children. Lord Justice Neill said a distinction could be drawn between cases of mere curiosity and cases where the press was giving information or commenting about matters of genuine public interest.

In almost every case, he said, the public interest in favour of publication could be satisfied without any identification of the child to persons other than those who already knew the facts. The injunction had to be in clear terms and had to be no wider than was necessary to achieve the purpose for which it was imposed.

In a case in 1989, the Master of the Rolls, Lord Donaldson, said if a temporary injunction had been granted in the absence of the other side (the newspaper), a judge should be ready and willing at short notice to consider any application by those affected to withdraw or modify it.

The House of Lords held in 2004 that the freedom of the press to report a criminal trial required that newspapers should not be restrained from publishing the identity of a defendant in a criminal trial in order to protect the privacy of the defendant's child who was not involved in the criminal proceedings (*Re S (A Child) (Identification: Restrictions on Publication*) [2004] UKHL 47). The law lords upheld the refusal of an injunction, which would have prevented the identification of a mother, or of the child she was accused of murdering, in order to protect a younger child. Counsel for the surviving child had maintained that under article 8 of the European Convention on Human Rights the child had a right to protection from publicity which could damage his health and well being and risk emotional and psychiatric harm. Lord Steyn said the impact on the child was essentially indirect and was not of the same order as cases of juveniles who were directly involved in criminal trials. If an injunction was granted in his case, it was easy to visualise circumstances in which attempts would be made to enjoin publicity of, for example the gruesome circumstances of a crime. The process of piling exception upon exception to the principle of open justice would be encouraged and would gain momentum.

Lord Steyn said a newspaper could always contest an injunction but even for national newspapers that was a costly matter. It was easy to consider the position from the point of view of national newspapers only. Local newspapers played a huge role, A sensational or serious criminal trial would be of great interest in the community where it took place. For local newspapers who did not have the financial resources of national newspapers, the spectre of being involved in costly legal proceedings was bound to have a chilling effect.

The impact of such a development on the regional and local press strongly militated against adoption of the injunction. If permitted it would seriously impoverish public discussion of criminal justice.

See also chapter 12, 'Wards of court'.

The crown court and the appeal courts

Crown courts try both criminal and civil cases, but the criminal business is greater.

Crown courts were set up in England and Wales in 1972 to replace the old assizes and quarter sessions. All serious crime is eventually tried there. Even the Central Criminal Court (the Old Bailey) in London is, in effect, a crown court.

When dealing with civil business, the crown court acts as a provincial branch of the High Court.

Crown courts have three main functions in criminal cases:

(1) to try indictable offences sent for trial by magistrates courts (some serious offences, for example murder and rape, must be tried at crown court);

(2) to deal with cases sent for sentence from magistrates courts; and

(3) to hear appeals from magistrates courts.

There are six crown court areas (known as circuits): South Eastern, Midland, North Eastern, Northern, Wales & Chester, and Western. Each has a circuit administrator, a senior civil servant who, with the assistance of courts administrators, runs all the crown courts in the circuit. There are in each circuit, however, two High Court judges, known as presiding judges, who guide circuit administrators on legal matters, on the allocation of cases, and on other administrative matters.

Three types of judges sit in crown courts—High Court judges, circuit judges and recorders. Up to four magistrates may sit with judges at trials, but this is not obligatory and here the magistrates' real contribution is in discussing sentence with the judge.

Any of the three types of judges has power to deal with civil cases.

High Court judges, for instance, while on circuit frequently hear Queen's Bench Division or Family Division cases, which would otherwise be tried in London.

Similarly, circuit judges and recorders may try civil cases in the county court (see chapter 10). Some circuit judges sit exclusively in the county court.

See also chapter 11, 'Crown court' and chapter 12, 'Obstructive courts'.

High Court judges

They are referred to in reports as Mr Justice Smith, or Mrs Justice Smith, *never* Judge Smith. There are 107 high court judges, they sit only in the more important centres and only they can try the most serious offences, like murder. Other serious offences such as unlawful killing and rape are also tried by them, unless referred to a circuit judge.

Circuit judges

Circuit judges are referred to in reports as Judge John Smith or Judge Mary Smith. They must be barristers of at least 10 years' standing or be solicitors who have been recorders. There are 643 circuit judges.

Recorders

They are part-time judges. They must be barristers, or solicitors who have held right of audience at crown court. Recorders are usually referred to as the recorder, Mr John Smith or Mrs Mary Smith.

Exceptions to the status of recorder are the Recorder of London, the historic title for one of the senior full-time judges who sit at the Central Criminal Court, and the Recorders of Liverpool, Manchester and Belfast, who are the senior circuit judges in the city crown courts. Additionally, some cities have themselves bestowed the honorary title of 'Recorder of——' on the senior circuit judge at the city crown court, who also carries out some ceremonial duties.

Rights of audience

Prosecutions at criminal trials are conducted by barristers, and barristers usually appear for the defence. Experienced solicitors with a record of experience as advocates and who have gained a higher courts qualification may also appear however.

Additionally, a solicitor may appear for the defence at appeals or committals for sentence at crown court if he or his firm has represented the accused at the lower court (see chapter 1, 'The legal profession').

Juries

A jury consists of 12 people aged between 18 and 70 taken from the electoral list. There are disqualifications for those who are on bail awaiting criminal proceedings or have been jailed in the previous 10 years, or have received a suspended sentence, a community service order or a probation order in the last five years. Those suffering from mental health problems which require them to be resident in a hospital, or receive regular treatment from a medical practitioner are not eligible for jury service.

The Criminal Justice Act 2003 ended a number of exemptions for certain professions and positions and judges, lawyers, politicians, doctors and peers all became eligible for jury service from April 2004.

This change resulted in at least two judges—Mr Justice Wood and Lord Justice Dyson—being called for jury service. The Recorder of London, Judge Michael Hyam, also rejected an application from an unnamed QC to be excused from the remainder of his jury service after he was rejected for three Old Bailey juries because he knew lawyers or judges involved in the cases.

This position was reiterated in guidance to judges by the Lord Chief Justice, Lord Woolf, who said only extreme circumstances would justify a judge being excused. He added that any judge sitting on a jury had to follow the directions of the trial judge and should not correct guidance he believed to be inaccurate.

Those over 65 are not compelled to serve. A judge may sit in chambers to hear a challenge against any person being on a jury.

Majority verdicts of 11–1 or 10–2 are allowed, but only if the jury has been out at least two hours and ten minutes and has failed to reach a verdict.

If a jury is reduced for any reason, a majority of 10–1 or 9–1 is possible.

A newspaper may report that a defendant has been convicted by a majority of the jury. It is regarded as undesirable, however, to report that a defendant is acquitted by a majority, as this suggests that some members of the jury did think him guilty and leaves a stain on his character even though he has been cleared.

Under section 8 of the Contempt of Court Act 1981, it is contempt of court to seek or disclose information about statements made, opinions expressed, arguments advanced, or votes cast by members of a jury in the course of its deliberations. The Royal Commission on Criminal Justice pointed out in 1993 that even it was barred by section 8 from conducting research into juries' reasons for their verdicts.

The House of Lords held in 1994 that the prohibition applies not just to the jurors themselves but to anyone who publishes the information they reveal. The law lords dismissed an appeal brought by the *Mail on Sunday* against being found guilty of contempt of court after it published interviews with jurors disclosing details of the discussion in the jury retirement room. Lord Lowry said at the Lords hearing that section 8 was aimed at keeping the secrets of the jury room inviolate in the interests of justice. The paper, the editor, and a journalist had been fined a total of £60,000.

Prosecutions under section 8 must be by a crown court or higher court, or be with the consent of the Attorney-General.

It is permissible to publish a juror's views at the end of the case provided they do not refer to statements made, opinions expressed, arguments advanced, or votes cast in the course of the jury's deliberations. This would seem to allow for publication of a juror's account of his general impressions of the case or his ability to follow the evidence. On the other hand some lawyers believe that the naming in a newspaper or broadcast of a juror who has had a part in reaching a verdict could be treated as a contempt of court at common law as this could expose the juror to intimidation or attack. Photographing a juror may also be regarded as a contempt. The danger in identifying jurors would not appear to apply where a juror is discharged in the middle of a case, for example.

If the jury returns a not guilty verdict it is usually final as far as the accused is concerned (see the exceptions below to the Criminal Justice Act 2003) although the Court of Appeal can be asked by the Attorney-General to give its opinion on a point of law. Additionally, a retrial may be ordered if there has been intimidation of a juror, or witness or new and compelling evidence emerges later, or a judge has stopped a trial and the prosecution has successfully appealed against his decision.

Juries are used in civil actions mainly for defamation, false imprisonment, or malicious prosecution. A judge has power, rarely exercised, to allow a jury in other civil actions. Fewer than 12 people may sit on the jury with the consent of the parties in the civil action.

Pre-trial hearings and preparatory hearings

Before a criminal trial, a judge may hold a preliminary hearing to decide on points of law and the admissibility of evidence and/or to clarify issues to go before the jury. This hearing can take place while the accused remains in prison if a video link allows him to see and hear the court and to be seen and heard by it. A pre-trial hearing, which may include a plea and directions hearing, usually takes place within a short time after the case has been remitted by the magistrates court, and is held before any preparatory hearing. The two forms of hearing are subject to different reporting restrictions.

Pre-trial hearings

The pre-trial hearing may include the taking of a plea of guilty or not guilty and the plea is not affected by the reporting restrictions. It is however an offence under the Criminal Procedure and Investigations Act 1996 to publish a report before the end of the subsequent trial of an application for a ruling, or its variation or discharge, at a pre-trial hearing such as a plea and directions hearing, unless the judge lifts the restriction. If any of the accused objects, the judge may lift the restriction only if he is satisfied it is in the interests of justice to do so.

Preparatory hearings

A preparatory hearing may be held for the longer and more complex trials. The hearing marks the start of the trial. When it takes place reports must, under the 1996 Act, be restricted to seven points:

(1) name of the court and the judge;

(2) names, ages, home addresses, and occupations of accused and witnesses;

(3) charges or a summary of them;

(4) names of lawyers;

(5) date and place to which proceedings are adjourned;

(6) arrangements as to bail;

(7) whether legal aid was granted.

Again, a judge may lift the restrictions but if any accused objects may do so only if he is satisfied that it is in the interests of justice.

In both pre-trial hearings and preparatory hearings, the restrictions cease when all the accused have been tried.

Procedure at trials

A man charged at crown court is said to be arraigned. The counts (charges) on the indictment are read out to him by the clerk of the court and his plea recorded.

The charges may differ slightly from those on which he was committed by magistrates for trial at crown court, and the reporter should not rely on cuttings of the earlier report. For instance, the dates between which an offence is alleged to have been committed may be different.

Counsel (a barrister) will appear for the prosecution, and a barrister or a solicitor will conduct the defence.

If the defendant pleads guilty, the prosecution will outline the evidence and his criminal record, and social inquiry reports will be given. The defendant or his lawyer may also be allowed to address the court in mitigation of sentence before it is passed. The court may restrict the reporting of derogatory assertions made during pleas of mitigation (see chapter 2).

The jury take no part, because the guilty plea has dispensed with their function.

If the defendant pleads not guilty, a jury of 12 will be sworn in and the substance of the indictment will be read to them.

Counsel for the prosecution will normally 'open the case', outline the evidence, and state the relevant law.

The defence knows beforehand what evidence the prosecution intends to call because it is set out in the documents containing the evidence which were served on the defence at the time the case was committed for trial, or in documents containing any additional evidence. The defence is also required to disclose information about its case before the trial, to narrow the issues in dispute.

Prosecuting counsel then calls his witnesses, who will be examined by him and cross-examined by the defence.

The defence then begins. Provided the defence lawyer intends calling witnesses on fact (as distinct from character) he has the right to address the jury before his witnesses are called. But if the only witness as to the facts is the accused, the defence may not 'open the defence' before the accused testifies.

After the case for the defence, prosecuting counsel makes his final speech and the defence addresses the jury last.

The judge then sums up the case to the jury. He directs the jury as to the law, but questions of fact are the province of the jury. The judge should, however, if he feels that the evidence is not sufficient to support the charge in law, direct the jury to bring in a verdict of not guilty.

If the jury returned a not guilty verdict, that was usually final as far as the accused was concerned. However, the Criminal Justice Act 2003 ended the so-called 'double jeopardy rule' which prevented someone being tried for the same offence twice.

If compelling new evidence comes to light, then with the authority of the Director of Public Prosecutions (DPP) the prosecution can apply to the Court of Appeal to have the acquittal quashed and a retrial ordered. The DPP has to be satisfied that the new evidence is reliable, substantial and highly probative and that it is in the interests of justice having regard to the likelihood of a fair trial and the length of time since the offence was committed.

The 2003 Act also gave judges the power to discharge a jury if jury tampering appeared to have taken place and the judge can order that the trial continues without a jury, but only if that would be fair to the defendant. If the judge believes it to be in the interests of justice then the trial must be terminated.

Proposals to limit jury trial in complex fraud cases and to allow defendants to waive their right to jury trial were dropped following opposition in the House of Lords.

Prosecution appeals – reporting restrictions

If a judge stops a trial on the grounds of insufficient evidence or for some other reason, the prosecution may under the Criminal Justice Act 2003 appeal to the Court of Appeal against the termination of the trial. The Act restricts reporting of the application (but not of the trial itself so far) to seven points, similar to those for preparatory hearings described earlier in this chapter.

Under the Criminal Procedure and Investigations Act 1996, where a court convicts a person of interference with or intimidation of a juror, witness, or potential witness in a trial at which the accused has been acquitted, application may be made to the High Court for an order quashing the acquittal, thus allowing a retrial. The court may order postponement of any report of the case until after the new trial of the acquitted person. (See chapter 2, 'Intimidation of witnesses'.)

Under the 2003 Act a prosecutor can apply to the Court of Appeal for an order quashing a person's acquittal and for him to be retried where there is new and compelling evidence. Once notice to apply is given it becomes an offence to report the application or anything in connection with it until the end of the retrial or the matter is dropped. The restriction may be lifted or relaxed by the Court of Appeal but if the acquitted person objects, lifting or relaxation can take place only if it is in the interests of justice to do so. The restriction ceases to apply after the trial is restarted or the matter is dropped.

The Attorney-General can, under the Criminal Justice Act 1972, ask the Court of Appeal after an acquittal to give its opinion on a disputed point of law, but under that Act the accused cannot be brought back to court. The Court of Appeal has power in giving its opinion to ban or restrict disclosure of the identity of the acquitted defendant.

Defendants' addresses

In 1989 the Lord Chancellor said it was reasonable for a crown court to supply a defendant's address to the press if it was available in the court record. Detailed instructions were sent to crown courts as to how this should be done (see chapter 11, 'Addresses of defendants').

Murder charges

The death penalty was abolished in 1965 for murder. Now the only sentence provided by law is one of life imprisonment. In cases where the accused is insane, an order for detention is not technically a sentence.

The judge may recommend a minimum term of the life sentence which the defendant should actually serve. Sometimes he may recommend that it should actually be for life. In practice, each case may be reviewed by the Parole Board, and it is the Home Secretary who has the ultimate power to order release. The Home Secretary must, however, consult the trial judge, if available, and the Lord Chief Justice before releasing a convicted murderer.

Sentences of life imprisonment may still be imposed for other offences (eg arson, robbery, rape, buggery with a boy under 16) where there is no statutory penalty limit, and the judge considers life proper.

Offences against children

The Criminal Justice Act 1991 provides for these cases to be transferred to crown court from the magistrates court, by-passing the normal procedure. Where a person's case is transferred to crown court in this way, he may apply at crown court for the case to be struck out on the grounds of insufficient evidence. Reports of such applications at crown court are restricted under the 1991 Act. The restrictions are similar to those for other applications at crown court for the case to be struck out (see later this chapter, 'Appeals').

Serious fraud charges

Similarly, where a serious complex fraud case has been transferred from magistrates court to crown court without the usual normal procedure, the defendant may apply to crown court for the case to be struck out on the grounds of insufficient evidence.

Where a serious fraud trial does go ahead at crown court, a judge may, as soon as a plea of not guilty is entered, order a preparatory hearing before the jury is sworn in to clarify the issues to go before them.

There are reporting restrictions on both applications for the case to be struck out and on the preparatory hearings. The crown court may order that these reporting restrictions do not apply if one or more of the accused requests. But if any accused objects to the request by his co-accused, the judge can grant the request only if he feels it is in the interests of justice.

The Criminal Justice Act 1987 says reports of such applications or of preparatory hearings before a judge must be confined to:

(1) the identity of the court and the name of the judge;

(2) the names, ages, home addresses, and occupations of the accused and witnesses;

(3) any relevant business information;

(4) the offence or offences, or a summary of them, with which the accused is or are charged;

(5) the names of counsel and solicitors engaged in the proceedings;

(6) where the proceedings are adjourned, the date and place to which they are adjourned;

(7) any arrangements as to bail;

(8) whether legal aid was granted to the accused or any of the accused;

(9) whether reporting restrictions are lifted.

'Any relevant business information' includes names and addresses of businesses concerned.

All the restrictions cease to apply if all applications for a case to be struck out are granted, or at the end of a trial of all the accused.

These restrictions, like those applying to applications under the Criminal Justice Act 1991 (see chapter 6, 'Offences against children'), do not allow the journalist to report a crown court judge's decision not to allow a case to be struck out.

Appeals

To the crown court

Where a magistrates court has sent a person over 18 for trial at crown court on an indictable-only charge, under the Crime and Disorder Act 1998 the accused may apply either orally or in writing to the crown court for any charge to be dismissed on the grounds of insufficient evidence. Reporting of such applications is restricted unless all the applications for dismissal made at the proceedings are successful. The restrictions are explained in chapter 5, 'Sending for trial'.

An appeal against conviction by magistrates will take the form of a complete rehearing but there will be no jury. It is for the prosecution to prove afresh the defendant's guilt. The court may confirm, reverse, or vary the magistrates' decision or send the case back to them for a re-trial.

In an appeal against sentence, the crown court may confirm the sentence or substitute a lesser penalty. The crown court may increase the sentence, but not to more than that which the magistrates could have imposed.

A person sent to crown court for sentence who receives more than six months' imprisonment may appeal to the Court of Appeal against the sentence.

To Queen's Bench Division

A man who has been dealt with by the magistrates or who has appealed unsuccessfully to the crown court may also appeal on a point of law to the Queen's Bench Divisional Court on the grounds that the decision was wrong in law.

This procedure, which is also open to the prosecution, is known as appeal by way of case stated. The magistrates or the crown court will be asked by the appellant to state their findings on fact and the questions of law which arose.

The divisional court can make an order of certiorari (quashing the lower court's decision), of mandamus (directing the lower court, eg to convict or acquit), or of prohibition, forbidding them to hear a charge not known to the law. A statutory instrument abolishing the use of Latin phrases changed these orders to quashing order, mandatory order and prohibiting order, respectively.

A further appeal is possible to the House of Lords. For this to take place, the divisional court must certify that there is a point of law of public importance. In addition, either the divisional court or the House of Lords must grant leave for the appeal as one that ought to be heard by the House.

To Court of Appeal

Appeals from crown court are heard by the judges of the Queen's Bench Division (although other High Court judges may also sit at the request of the Lord Chief Justice), who share the work of the Court of Appeal with the Lords Justices of Appeal. The Lord Chancellor may also appoint a circuit judge to sit with a High Court judge for a criminal appeal.

A significant change to the way courts are covered began in 2004 with the first experiments in televising the courts in England and Wales.

Four remote-control cameras were fitted in Court 4 of the Royal Courts of Justice, focused on the barristers and judges involved in the case. The first filmed hearing took place on 16 November 2004, although no footage had been taken for broadcast when this edition of *McNae* went to press. The pilot scheme was still in the consultation stage before a decision was made on whether to allow proceedings to be broadcast on TV news bulletins.

The accused's right of appeal on a point of law from a crown court trial is automatic.

Other appeals by the accused from a crown court trial require leave of the trial judge or of the Court of Appeal.

The Court of Appeal may, if it allows the appeal, quash a conviction. It may order a new trial at crown court, and this has resulted in at least one case of a man charged with murder being tried twice, and acquitted at the second trial.

The court also has power to substitute a conviction for a different offence. It does not have power to increase the sentence imposed by the crown court, but can order that the time spent in custody awaiting the hearing should not count towards the sentence.

Under the Criminal Justice Act 1988, the Attorney-General may ask the Court of Appeal to review an unduly lenient crown court sentence in a range of serious offences. The Criminal Justice Act 2003 also extends the powers of the Attorney-General in this respect and sentences for racially aggravated offences can be challenged. The Court of Appeal may change the sentence to any other sentence that was within the crown court's power.

See also chapter 17, 'Power to issue injunction to prevent contempt'.

08

Sexual offences and other statutory restrictions

The law gives anonymity during their lifetime to victims of most sexual offences. The range of offences where there is anonymity for both male and female complainants was greatly extended in 2004. The complainant cannot now be identified in a number of allegations where no physical contact is involved, like indecent exposure and voyeurism, such as where a man watches the private acts of a woman without her consent to obtain sexual gratification.

This anonymity is enforced through the Sexual Offences (Amendment) Act 1992 as amended by the Sexual Offences Act 2003 and by a part of the Youth Justice and Criminal Evidence Act 1999 which was brought into operation in 2004.

Failure to remember that complainants in sexual offences other than rape must also not be identified, either by name or by other particulars, has led to a number of newspapers being prosecuted.

Offences

Subject to a number of exceptions which follow, restrictions on identifying the complainant apply if the allegation is rape, which now includes assault by penetration, causing a person to engage in sexual activity without consent, assault of a child under 13 by penetration, causing or inciting a child under 13 to engage in sexual activity where penetration was caused, sexual activity with a person with a mental disorder impeding choice involving penetration, or attempting, conspiring or inciting the commission of any of these offences.

Other offences where there is anonymity for the complainant are : indecent assault, trespass with intent to commit a sexual offence, sexual intercourse with mentally handicapped person by hospital staff, indecent conduct towards young child, incitement by man of his grand-daughter, daughter or sister under the age of 16 to commit incest with him, procurement of a woman by threats or false pretences, administering drugs to obtain intercourse with a woman, intercourse with a girl under the age 16, intercourse with a mentally handicapped person, procurement of a mentally handicapped person, incest by a man or woman, buggery, assault with intent to commit buggery; and abduction of a woman by force.

Additionally, anonymity for the complainant is given where the offence is: sexual activity with a child or causing a child to engage in sexual activity, engaging in sexual activity in the presence of a child, causing a child to watch a sexual act, sex offences committed by a juvenile, arranging or facilitating commission of such an offence, meeting a child following sexual grooming, abusing a position of trust in any of these offences involving a child, sexual activity with a child family member, sexual offences involving careworkers, indecent photographs of children, abuse of children through prostitution or pornography, trafficking for sexual exploitation, administering a substance with intent to commit a sexual offence, indecent exposure and voyeurism.

Once an allegation has been made that a person has been the victim of one of these offences, no matter must be published during that person's lifetime if it is likely to lead members of the public to identify the person as a person against whom the offence is alleged to have been committed.

The amended 1992 Act specifies matter likely to lead to identification of the complainant as: name, address, school or other educational establishment, place of work or still or moving picture of the person.

The anonymity for the complainant remains in force during his or her lifetime even if the allegation is later withdrawn or the accused is eventually tried for a lesser offence. It also applies to victims of male rape—an offence created by the Criminal Justice and Public Order Act 1994. When a person is charged with rape and murder there is no restriction on naming the victim.

The prohibition on identifying a rape complainant does not apply to all reports of criminal cases. It does apply where the charge is one of those listed above. But section 1 of the amended 1992 Act says that it does not restrict publication of matter consisting *only of a report of criminal proceedings* where a person is charged with offences not listed in the Act. This overrides the normal anonymity. It was apparently intended to provide for the situation where the complainant makes a false accusation of a sexual offence and is later tried for wasting police time or perjury, but this exception to the normal anonymity applies whenever the charge is not one of those listed above.

The anonymity for life does apply to any report of *civil* proceedings, for example a claim for damages for rape, or to allegations made at an employment tribunal (see also the 'Trade Union Reform and Employment Rights Act 1993' later in this chapter).

A judge at a trial may remove the anonymity if he is satisfied that it imposes a substantial and unreasonable restriction on the reporting of the trial and it is in the public interest to lift it, but must not do so by reason only of the outcome of the trial, for example the acquittal of the accused. The judge may also remove the anonymity, on the application of the defence, to bring witnesses forward, where he is satisfied the defence would otherwise be substantially prejudiced or the accused would suffer substantial injustice. These powers to remove anonymity can also be exercised by magistrates at a summary trial or where the mode of trial of an either-way offence has yet to be decided.

In a number of cases, editors have written to the trial judge applying successfully for the judge to use his power to lift the restriction on naming a complainant because of the difficulty in reporting the case. The approach might be made informally in a note from the reporter to the judge, via the clerk.

Sometimes a newspaper gives certain particulars of a victim but withholds others, and in this way intends to protect the victim's anonymity, but another paper gives other particulars and the two stories read together make the victim's identity obvious. The former Press Council urged newspaper editors and broadcasting organisations to co-operate in following the same policy in the reporting of individual rape cases to avoid this patchwork identification.

The Solicitor-General said in 1983 that a report of rape proceedings could be an offence if no names or specific addresses were published but the particulars given were sufficient to identify the complainant in the minds of some people even though not in the minds of the community generally.

The Press Complaints Commission code of practice says that newspapers should not publish material likely to contribute to identification of victims of sexual assault, unless there is adequate justification and by law they are free to do so. In cases affecting children the code says that the adult should be identified and that care should be taken that nothing in the report implies the relationship between the accused and the child (see chapter 6: jigsaw identification).

Since the passing of the Criminal Justice Act 1988 there has been no legal anonymity for rape defendants—but publication of the identity of the defendant, combined with other particulars, could lead to the identification of the complainant, as where a husband is accused of raping his wife. The Sexual Offences Act contains no provision to allow a court to make orders imposing additional restrictions beyond those which apply auto-matically to protect the complainant's identity. Sometimes courts wrongly assume they have power to order that the accused should not be named (see chapter 12, 'Sexual offences').

The amended 1992 Act contains a provision for the complainant to give consent in writing to being identified, provided that no person interfered unreasonably with his or her peace or comfort to obtain that consent. A complainant under 16 cannot consent to being identified however.

It is a defence where a person is accused of a breach of these reporting restrictions to prove that the publisher was not aware, did not suspect and had no reason to suspect the publication was in breach of the Act.

A complainant is defined as a person against whom the offence is alleged to have been committed and thus the anonymity covers consenting parties, unless they are prosecuted.

An application to the court to introduce evidence or questions about a complainant's sexual history must be heard in public but in the absence of the jury, if there is one.

Other statutory restrictions

Other principal statutory reporting restrictions are as follows:

1 **Criminal Justice Act 1925**, section 41, prohibits the taking of any photograph in the court or in its precincts (or making any portrait or sketch, in court or in its precincts with a view to publication) of any juror, witness, party, or judge of the court. It makes it an offence to publish any such photograph, portrait, or sketch. The same section says that this shall apply also to any photograph, etc, taken of such a person entering or leaving the court or its precincts (see chapter 35, 'Photography').

2 **Judicial Proceedings (Regulation of Reports) Act 1926**, section 1(a), prohibits publication in any court report of any indecent medical, surgical, or physiological details which would be calculated to injure public morals and section 1(b) restricts reports of divorce, nullity, and judicial separation actions to four points (see chapter 13).

Publication of details of actual indecencies or perversions could also result in a prose-cution, although the mere reporting of a charge is not likely to have this effect.

The test of what would injure public morals in today's climate has yet to be applied.

See also chapter 21, 'Obscenity'.

3 Children and Young Persons Act 1933, section 49, says no report of youth court proceedings shall reveal the name, address, school, or any other particulars identifying any person under 18 involved in any way, and says that no photograph of *or including* any such juvenile shall be published.

Section 39 of the Act empowers a court to prohibit publication of any picture or other matter leading to the identification of juveniles under 18 involved in any way in proceedings before it (see chapters 6 and 12). In the criminal courts only, these orders are due to be replaced by orders under section 45 of the Youth Justice and Criminal Evidence Act 1999, if implemented (see below).

The restriction on identifying juveniles involved in any way in youth court proceedings may be lifted by the court or by the Home Secretary for the purpose of avoiding injustice to that juvenile. A youth court, on application on behalf of the Director of Public Prosecutions, may also lift the restriction to any specified extent where a juvenile is at large after committing a sexual offence or offence of violence.

The Crime (Sentences) Act 1997 also amends the 1933 Act to permit magistrates to make an order lifting the restriction on naming a convicted juvenile where they believe it is in the public interest to do so. Before making such an order they must allow representations from parties to the proceedings.

Under the Serious Organised Crime and Police Act 2005 there is no automatic anonymity in reports of youth court proceedings where a juvenile is accused of infringing an Asbo (anti-social behaviour order).

4 Wireless Telegraphy Act 1949 prohibits the use without authority of wireless apparatus with intent to obtain information about the contents of any message, and prohibits the disclosure of any such information (for example, police radio messages) (see also chapter 31).

5 Administration of Justice Act 1960, section 12, provides that publication of information relating to proceedings before a court sitting in private shall not of itself be a contempt of court, except in cases involving the Children Act, wardship, other proceedings relating to the maintenance or upbringing of a child, mental health, national security, or a secret process, or where a court which has the power to do so expressly prohibits publication. It also provides that the publication of the text or a summary of the whole or part of a court order shall not be contempt, in the absence of express prohibition (see chapter 6, 'Wards of court' and chapter 17, 'Reports of hearings in private').

6 Betting, Gaming and Lotteries Act 1963 and Gaming Act 1968 contain restrictions on advertising gambling. It is considered unlikely that a news story could contravene these restrictions but journalists wishing to ensure that story is safe should contact the Gaming Board (0207 306 6200).

7 Theft Act 1968, section 23, makes it an offence to offer a reward for the return of stolen goods, using any words to the effect that no questions will be asked. A newspaper has been fined for printing a news item referring to such an offer.

8 Domestic and Appellate Proceedings Act 1968 gives courts hearing appeals power to sit in private if the lower court had that power. It also restricts reports of applications for declarations of legitimacy and the like to the four points permitted in divorce hearings (see chapter 13).

9 Rehabilitation of Offenders Act 1974, section 8, says any newspaper, etc, when defending a libel action will not be able to rely on the defence of justification if publication of a spent conviction is shown to have been made with malice.

It also says that a newspaper will not be able to rely on privilege to defend a reference in court reports to a spent conviction where the conviction has been ruled to be inadmissible (see chapter 22).

10 Magistrates' Courts Act 1980, section 8, restricts reports of preliminary hearings of indictable offences at magistrates courts, except where a decision has been taken to try the case summarily (see chapter 5). Section 71 limits newspaper reports of family proceedings to four brief points (see chapter 9).

It says that only officers of the court and parties involved may attend adoption hearings (see later this chapter, 'Adoption Act 2002', and chapter 6, 'Adoption of children').

11 Contempt of Court Act 1981 modifies some of the common law on contempt, dealing in particular with the starting point for liability and the circumstances in which strict liability for contempt applies to publications (see chapter 17).

12 Public Order Act 1986 makes it an offence for a person to publish threatening, abusive, or insulting material if he intends to stir up hatred against any group in Great Britain defined by reference to colour, race, nationality, citizenship, or ethnic or national origins, or if it is likely to stir up hatred having regard to all the circumstances (see chapter 25).

13 Criminal Justice Act 1987 imposes restrictions on reports of serious fraud cases at crown court pre-trial hearings where (a) the defendant is applying for the case to be struck out or (b) the court is sitting to clarify the issues to go before the jury (see chapter 7).

14 Official Secrets Act 1989 makes it an offence to make an unauthorised disclosure which is, or is likely to be, damaging, of information on security, intelligence, defence, or international relations, or of information entrusted in confidence by Britain to another country or to an international organisation. It makes it an absolute offence to disclose telephone tapping etc which has been authorised by a warrant.

It makes it an offence to disclose without authority information obtained from a crown servant (including police and prison officers) or government contractor where such disclosure would, or would be likely to, result in: an offence being committed; escape from custody being facilitated; or the prevention, detection, or prosecution of crime being impeded

15 Children Act 1989 makes it an offence to publish any material intended or likely to identify a child (under 18) as being involved in family proceedings in a magistrates court, or his address or school, where the court is exercising powers under the Act. It also allows the court to sit in private when exercising such powers (see chapter 6). The anonymity for those under 18 was extended in 2000 to Children Act proceedings in the High Court or the county court.

16 Criminal Justice Act 1991 imposes restrictions on reports of pre-trial proceedings at crown court where the accused is charged with a sexual offence or an offence involving violence or cruelty against a child and is applying for the case to be struck out (see chapter 7, 'Offences against children').

17 Trade Union Reform and Employment Rights Act 1993 allows an employment tribunal to make a restricted reporting order preventing the immediate publication of the identity of a person complaining of sexual misconduct or of a person affected by such a complaint. The identity of a person complaining at an employment tribunal of a sexual offence against him or her is also protected by the Sexual Offences (Amendment) Act 1992 mentioned earlier (see also chapter 16, 'Employment tribunals').

18 Disability Discrimination Act 1995 empowers an employment tribunal to make an order banning immediate identification of any person complaining to the tribunal under the Act, where evidence of a medical or intimate nature which might cause significant embarrassment is likely to be heard (see chapter 16, 'Employment tribunals').

19 Criminal Procedure and Investigations Act 1996 allows a court to restrict reporting of derogatory assertions made in pleas of mitigation. The Act also makes it an offence to publish a report of a ruling made at crown court at a pre-trial hearing or to publish more than seven permitted points in a report of a preparatory hearing unless the judge permits it (see chapters 2 and 7).

20 Crime and Disorder Act 1998 creates a new procedure for sending indictable-only cases for trial and sets out restrictions on the reporting of applications made at crown court for dismissal of the case on grounds of insufficient evidence (see chapter 5).

21 Youth Justice and Criminal Evidence Act 1999, if fully implemented, would make it an offence to identify a juvenile suspected of an offence from the time the offence is being investigated until court proceedings start. It would substitute a new power to suppress the identity of a juvenile in an adult criminal court in place of section 39 of the Children and Young Persons Act (see chapter 6). Power given to criminal courts under the 1999 Act to ban publication of the identity of adult witnesses was implemented in 2004 (see chapter 2).

22 Regulation of Investigatory Powers Act 2000 prohibits intentional and unlawful interception of communications by post or phone or other telecommunications system. It supersedes the Interception of Communications Act 1985 but, unlike the 1985 Act, it applies to private systems as well as public systems (see also chapter 32).

23 Adoption Act 2002 when fully implemented will prohibits publication of an advertisement or information indicating that a parent or guardian of a child wants the child to be adopted, or that a person wants to adopt a child, was willing to receive a child with a view to adoption or was willing to remove the child from the United Kingdom for adoption elsewhere (see chapter 6).

24 Criminal Justice Act 2003 makes it an offence to report, following an acquittal, a prosecution application for a retrial on grounds of new and compelling evidence. It also imposes restrictions on reporting a prosecution appeal against a judge's decision to stop a trial (see chapter 7).

25 Courts Act 2003 introduced regulations for criminal courts to order a third party to pay the costs of a wasted or aborted trial incurred by serious misconduct, whether or not a contempt of court is alleged (see chapter 17, 'Wasted costs').

The Act also prohibits the reporting of any ruling given at a magistrates court pre-trial hearing on admissibility of evidence and points of law where a not guilty plea to an either-way offence has been entered and the case is to be tried summarily (see chapter 4).

26 Serious Organised Crime and Police Act 2005 removes anonymity for reports of youth court proceedings where a juvenile is accused of breach of an Asbo. The Act makes it an offence to disclose information about a person assuming a new identity or about protection arrangements.

Effect of contravening restrictions

The Rehabilitation of Offenders Act contains no sanctions under the criminal law for offending reports.

Newspapers contravening any of the other Acts above, other than the Contempt Act itself, are usually prosecuted in summary proceedings in the magistrates court under the terms and penalties laid down in the Act concerned, rather than for contempt of court. (Magistrates have no power to deal with contempt by publication.)

In 1998, the Queen's Bench Divisional Court held that the managing director of a publishing company, who was effectively the sole person in control, could be guilty of an offence under the Sexual Offences Act when his newspaper published a story which identified a complainant in a rape case. The managing director of the company owning *Sunday Business* had appealed against his conviction on the grounds that his principal role was of financial backer and that he had not read the story and did not know or suspect that it was going to be published.

A judge who has made an order under an Act of Parliament restricting reporting may use his inherent powers to treat defiance of the order as a contempt although this has been discouraged by the Court of Appeal. In January 1997 a judge at Newcastle Crown Court fined Tyne-Tees Television £10,000 for contempt after a news broadcast had quoted prosecuting counsel's statement that a man accused of indecently assaulting a boy was a neighbour. Tyne-Tees had not disclosed the street in which the accused lived, but newspapers had published his address. At the start of the trial the judge had made an order under section 39 of the Children and Young Persons Act 1933 prohibiting publication of anything leading to identification of the boy. (The order was unnecessary because the boy's anonymity was automatically protected under the Sexual Offences Act) If the matter had been dealt with as a breach of the 1933 Act, the maximum fine would have been £5,000. The Court of Appeal later quashed the conviction. Lord Justice Beldam said that as long ago as 1759 in the case of *Robinson* it was held that when Parliament had provided a statutory remedy for an offence, it was not open to a court to pursue a remedy by way of contempt proceedings. It was undesirable for a trial judge to deal with the matter in his own court or to deal with it as a contempt of court. The proper course would have been for the matter to be reported for summary proceedings against the television company to be considered under the Children and Young Persons Act (*R v Tyne Tees Television* (1997) Times, 20 October, CA).

However in 2001 the BBC was fined £25,000 and one of its reporters £500 for contempt of court in identifying, in a report of a trial at Exeter Crown Court, a man who complained of a sexual attack he had been subject to while a child. It was said his identification interfered with the administration of justice in that the man was distressed by the report, threatened to withdraw his evidence and initially refused to attend court next day.

A person who believes he has been injured by a contravention of one of these Acts restricting reporting may be able to sue in the civil courts. In 1994 a rape victim won £10,000 damages from a free newspaper that gave sufficient details about her to enable her to be identified. In doing so, the paper was liable for the tort of breach of statutory duty. The paper had not been prosecuted under the Sexual Offences (Amendment) Act (see also chapter 32, 'Privacy').

Magistrates courts: civil functions

Family proceedings

Family proceedings before magistrates courts were constituted in 1991 under the Children Act 1989. Nearly all family proceedings involving children are brought under the 1989 Act and a court has power to make care, supervision, contact, family assistance, and education supervision orders and affiliation orders (for the maintenance of a child).

Family proceedings, replacing the old domestic courts, also deal with husband and wife disputes and hear applications for maintenance orders, separation orders and adoption orders (see chapter 6, 'Adoption of children'). They also deal with the custody and upbringing of children (care cases), which formerly came before the juvenile court.

Under section 71 of the Magistrates' Courts Act 1980 reports must be confined to four brief points as described in chapter 6, 'Children in civil proceedings'.

Additionally, under section 97 of the Children Act, no particulars may be published that would lead to the identification of a child under 18 as being involved in proceedings *under that Act*, or his school (see chapter 6). The restriction can be lifted by the court or by the Home Secretary. In 2002, a woman wrongly accused of harming her twin babies, who were then placed in foster care, successfully applied, with the support of the *Daily Express*, to Mr Justice Coleridge, in the High Court Family Division for the restriction under section 97 to be lifted so that her name could be cleared after the children were returned to her (*Daily Express*, 17 December 2002).

Family proceedings are not open to the public. Representatives of newspapers and news agencies may attend under section 69 of the 1980 Act but the court *may* exclude them, under magistrates court rules, when exercising powers under the Children Act in relation to a child). A consultation paper reviewing access to and reporting of family proceedings, prepared for the Lord Chancellor's Department, said in 1993 that it seemed as if magistrates must make a specific decision as to the interests of the particular child and not simply rely on a general policy of excluding the press. Magistrates also have power under section 69 of the Magistrates' Courts Act 1980 to exclude the press during the taking of indecent evidence. Magistrates must exclude the press when dealing with adoption cases (see chapters 6 and 11). When proceedings concerning a person under 18 are heard by magistrates sitting in private, reporting of the hearing is subject (in the same way as children's cases before judges in chambers) to section 12 of the Administration of Justice Act 1960, which by implication assumes it is a contempt to publish a report of the actual proceedings other than the bare decision (see chapter 6, 'Children in civil proceedings').

Often during family proceedings, magistrates will take cases of arrears of payment of maintenance by a husband or will deal with the method of payment.

On their own, these cases can be reported without restriction, since a man may be sent to prison for his failure to pay.

But sometimes these cases are heard together with cross-summonses to revoke the original order on the grounds, for example, that the wife is living with another man. If this happens the whole hearing is subject to the reporting restrictions.

Applications for the variation, discharge, or temporary suspension of a maintenance order are also subject to the reporting restrictions, and where the application could be heard in private, any appeal may also be heard in private.

A maintenance order is an order to make payments to a wife and/or family. Such an order can also be made against a wife who, in certain circumstances, can be ordered to make payments to her husband if he is incapable of work, or cannot find work.

A separation order, which may or may not be made at the same time, is merely an order that the people are no longer bound to cohabit.

Consent to marry applications (by young people aged 16 or 17), now rarely heard, are treated as family proceedings and are subject to the same restrictions. They may be taken in private, and usually are. Permission to marry may also be sought from a High Court judge or a county court district judge, both in chambers.

Neglect to maintain

The restrictions which apply to reports of divorce proceedings (see chapter 13) were extended by the Domestic and Appellate Proceedings (Restriction of Publicity) Act 1968 to reports of proceedings for neglect to maintain or for a declaration of legitimacy, except that in the four permitted points 'particulars of the declaration sought' was substituted for 'a concise statement of the charges, counter charges and defences in support of which evidence has been given.'

Child safety, anti-social behaviour and sex offender orders

Another of the civil functions of magistrates is to hear an application under the Crime and Disorder Act 1998 for a child safety order to place a child under 10 under supervision to prevent repetition of criminal behaviour, an application for an anti-social behaviour order (Asbo) prohibiting a person who has caused harassment, alarm, or distress from committing further acts, and an application by the police for a sex offender order, compelling a convicted sex offender to obey directions laid down by the court, such as to comply with a curfew. There is no statutory provision for any of these orders to be heard other than in open court. These proceedings are not deemed to be family proceedings and therefore reports are not restricted by section 71 of the Magistrates' Courts Act (see earlier this chapter). Asbo applications may also be heard by a criminal court where that court has convicted the defendant of a criminal offence.

(See also chapter 6, 'Anti-social behaviour orders against juveniles'.)

The civil courts

As we have seen, criminal law is concerned with offences that are deemed to harm the whole community, while civil law deals with the resolution of private disputes and the redress of private wrongs. Nevertheless, civil proceedings can be brought against the state and public bodies.

The mass of civil litigation is concerned with:

(1) breaches of contract, including the recovery of debts;

(2) torts—that is, civil wrongs for which monetary damages are recoverable, such as negligence, trespass and defamation;

(3) possession proceedings against mortgagors and tenants, usually for failure to pay mortgage instalments or rent but also for other breaches of obligations;

(4) 'Chancery' matters, such as disputes relating to properties, business partnerships, trusts and the administration of estates;

(5) insolvency, including bankruptcy and the winding up of companies; and

(6) family proceedings, such as separation and divorce and associated disputes over matrimonial assets and over the residence of and contact with the children of divorced or separated parents (and also placing children in the care of the local authority).

Most civil litigation is dealt with in the High Court of Justice and the county courts. Magistrates courts have some civil jurisdiction and in family proceedings they can grant domestic violence injunctions and deal with applications that relate to children, whether between parents or involving local authorities (see chapter 9: Magistrates courts: civil functions).

Earlier editions of this book have drawn a sharp distinction between the work of the county courts (the lower tier of the civil justice system) and the High Court but, as a result of the Civil Procedure Rules 1998 (often referred to as the 'CPR'), which came into effect in April 1999 ('the Woolf reforms'), the procedure for both became virtually identical. The distinction is now not primarily between courts but between the 'tracks' selected for handling cases. Courts must now actively manage cases and apply the 'overriding objective' by ensuring that parties are on an equal footing, saving expense, and dealing with cases in ways that are proportionate, fair and expeditious while allotting no more than an appropriate share of resources.

Civil claims

Starting proceedings

Proceedings in both the High Court and the county courts are begun by the issue of a claim form. This document is prepared by the claimant (the person who begins the claim) and briefly sets out the nature of the claim and the remedies sought from the court. The remedy may be an injunction, a declaration (say about ownership of property), or an order to make payment. In the case of a money claim this will be a specified amount or damages to be decided by the court.

In all but the simplest cases full particulars of the claim must be set out and served on the defendant. The Court Service has produced a series of plain English guides that describe to litigants in person how to use the court. The guides are available from every county court and from the Court Service website (www.courtservice/gsi/gov/uk).

The vast majority of money claims do not proceed to a trial because the defendant does not file any defence and the claimant simply writes to the court asking for judgment to be entered 'in default'. Even in such cases, however, there may need to be a hearing to assess the amount of damages. As soon as judgment is entered, the claimant may enforce it by using the court's enforcement procedures. Claims for possession of land and return of goods under a hire purchase agreement are given a hearing date when the claim is issued and are generally decided at this hearing.

If the defendant disputes the claim he must file either a defence or an acknowledgment of service within 14 days of service of the claim form and in any case must file his defence within 28 days of that date.

The trial is confined to issues that the parties set out in their 'statements of case' (previously known as 'pleadings') these being the particulars of claim, defence and, if the defendant brings a counterclaim, claimant's defence to the counterclaim. The court can permit the parties to amend their statements of case, exceptionally even during the trial.

Case management

If a defence is filed the papers will be considered by a district judge or, in the Royal Courts of Justice, a master. In a money claim where the defendant is an individual and does not live in the area in which the claim form was issued the claim will be transferred to the court for the district in which he lives. In other cases the master or district judge may decide to transfer the case if another court will be more convenient to the parties. More importantly, he has to allocate the case to the appropriate 'track' based upon various factors including the financial value, complexity, the amount of oral evidence, the nature of the remedies sought and the circumstances of the parties.

There are three tracks:

(1) the small claims track;

(2) the fast track;

(3) the multi-track.

While the money value of the claim is not necessarily the most important factor, the basic approach is that all cases where the claim exceeds £5,000 (or £1,000 for personal injuries) but not £15,000 will be allocated to the fast track. Those below these levels are allocated to the small claims track but possession claims are excluded from this track.

Cases allocated to the fast track are intended to be heard within 30 weeks and concluded within a hearing lasting no more than one day. The court will give routine written directions in the form of a case preparation timetable and fix the period during which the trial is to take place.

The multi-track covers a very wide range of claims. Many are little more complicated than those on the fast track and written directions will be given. Others will require more care and the district judge or master will normally fix a case-management conference (sometimes by telephone) at which the issues in the claim will be clarified, efforts made to encourage a negotiated (or mediated) settlement, and appropriate directions given to ensure that the trial takes place as soon as is realistically possible.

The emphasis is now upon all evidence being disclosed up-front and parties are not to be taken by surprise at the trial. Expert evidence may be admitted only with the permission of the court to which any expert owes a duty of impartiality, and unless the expert evidence is likely to be strongly contested the court will appoint a single expert who will be jointly instructed by the parties.

Small claims hearings

On the small claims track cases are decided by the district judge and are intended to be heard within three months. The procedure is designed to allow litigants to present their own case without the need for a lawyer, but they have the right to be represented in their presence by a friend (known as a 'lay representative'). Proceedings are informal and strict rules of evidence do not apply. An inquisitorial approach is generally adopted by the judge rather than the usual adversarial procedure, but the judge must give reasons for the decision. These cases are now heard in public, though this will often be the district judge's 'chambers' (ie private room) with access allowed, but the judge has power to hold the hearing, or part of it, in private and even elsewhere (eg a private house or nursing home).

Trials

In fast track and multi-track claims there is a formal trial by a judge with no jury, unless the claim is for fraud, defamation, false imprisonment or malicious prosecution, when either party has a right to apply for trial by jury. Most parties instruct a solicitor to prepare their case. In consultation with the client the solicitor will either brief counsel or represent the client himself if the trial is in the county court. A brief consists of a 'file' comprising the solicitor's narrative of the case, the statements of case, the statements of the parties and their witnesses and copies of all relevant disclosed documents. Some solicitors now have right of audience in the High Court (see chapter 1, 'The legal profession').

A party may always appear in person and may generally be assisted by some other person (often called a 'McKenzie friend') although the judge may refuse to allow this. The judge's express permission is required if a litigant wishes this person to act as advocate and will be given only in exceptional circumstances.

Unless there is a jury, civil trials are now largely paper based. In contrast with earlier practice, the judge will probably not ask the claimant's advocate to 'open', that is, to give an account of the facts and of the documents relied on, with an overview of the relevant law. Instead, the claimant files an agreed bundle of papers with the court for the judge to read before the trial. The bundle will include witness statements, relevant documents and the parties' respective skeleton submissions on the law. With a few exceptions each party must serve his opponent with copies of all his proposed witness statements before the trial. The claimant's advocate will call his witnesses who may be asked in examination to do no more than confirm that the content of their statements are true, although usually the judge will allow some supplementary questions. There will then be cross-examination by the defendant's advocate and the judge may ask further questions. If the defendant calls witnesses there will be the same process of (brief) examination and cross-examination. Then the respective advocates make their submissions on the evidence and law.

Finally, the judge delivers judgment, giving his decision and the grounds on which it is based. In more difficult cases he may reserve judgment so that he can ponder on his notes and consult the law books. He will then write out his judgment, referred to as a 'reserved judgment' and may, at his discretion, read it out in court at a later date or have the judgment typed and 'handed down' at a similarly convened court hearing. The latter course has been increasingly adopted—mainly in the Court of Appeal, Civil Division, at the behest of the Master of the Rolls—to speed up justice and help to clear a backlog of cases. Accredited court reporters as well as lawyers are usually provided with a copy of the judgment.

If there is a jury, the judge will sum up after the advocates have made their submissions. In some cases he may ask them for a general verdict, but in the more complicated cases he will put a series of questions to them.

After the judgment there will usually be argument about costs and the judge must make an appropriate order although more discretion is now allowed and it is not simply a question of the loser paying the winner's costs.

Family proceedings

There is, as yet, no separate family court in England and Wales, but certain types of case are designated 'family proceedings' and the Family Proceedings Rules 1991 then apply to the exclusion of the CPR. The party bringing the proceedings will be the 'petitioner' or 'applicant' and the other party is known as a 'respondent'. Most family proceedings are dealt with by district judges but some circuit judges are nominated to deal with the more serious cases

Such proceedings are held in private and no documents on the court file other than a decree or order made in open court is open to inspection, nor can copies be taken. Proceedings under the Children Act 1989 (and adoptions) are treated as confidential and no documents, other than a record of an order, must be disclosed other than to the parties and their lawyers without the leave of a judge. This rule is to be modified so as to enable unrepresented litigants to disclose certain documents to support services.

In recent years there has been a welcome tendency towards greater openness. Some judges, even in the highly sensitive Family Division of the High Court, having heard matters in private will release their judgments to be reported if they consider the cases are of sufficient public interest or raise matters of legal importance. However, such judgments normally refer to the parties only by initials, and it is up to journalists not to disclose any information that might lead to identification of the parties.

County courts

County courts were originally intended to provide an inexpensive court for the trial of the small, everyday kind of civil disputes in which the ordinary person is likely to get involved. Nowadays they have virtually unlimited common law jurisdiction and can be regarded as the normal civil court, the High Court being used increasingly for more specialised cases.

Many county court cases are landlord and tenant matters or concern debt. But these courts also deal with complaints of disability discrimination, dissolution of partnerships, actions for work done, cases of negligence, recovery of land and questions of title, bankruptcies and winding up of companies, and divorce, children and adoption proceedings.

County courts have nothing specifically to do with counties. There are some 217 of them situated so as to be convenient to the centres of population they are intended to serve. The courts are organised into groups consisting of one or more courts, depending on the amount of work to be done, and some are civil trial centres or family hearing centres where the longer trials take place.

Circuit judges

In some courts where sessions are virtually continuous there may be two or more senior judges known as circuit judges; in other groups the circuit judges may travel between several towns. Circuit judges may also sit in the Crown Court to deal with criminal cases. They are referred to the first time in copy as Judge John Smith or Judge Mary Smith, and later as Judge Smith or the judge. Recorders are barristers and solicitors who sit part time with the jurisdiction of a circuit judge, whereas retired circuit judges who continue to sit part time are known as deputies.

Circuit judges hear some fast track and most multi-track trials, actions for divorce that have not been previously disposed of by the district judge (see chapter 13) and more serious children disputes, both those between parents and those involving local authorities. They may also hear appeals from district judges. Appeals from a circuit judge lie direct to the Court of Appeal.

District judges

Each court has one or more district judges, who are appointed from among practising solicitors and barristers. They deal in open court with many of the fast track and small claims track claims and also deal privately in their own chambers with claims for possession of land and many family disputes, insolvency matters and procedural matters. They may be referred to in reports as District Judge John Smith, but are increasingly being referred to in newspapers as Judge John Smith. Deputy district judges are part-time appointments.

The district judge also acts as the 'costs judge' on the detailed assessment of costs where these are not assessed by the judge conducting the trial. The assessment of costs is the manner of deciding how much the paying party must pay the receiving party when a costs order is made.

See also chapter 11, 'Admission to the courts and access to court information'.

The High Court of Justice

The administrative centre of the High Court is at the Royal Courts of Justice in The Strand, London, but district registries are located in the larger county courts. Cases are heard both in London and 'on Circuit' when High Court judges travel to the larger cities, although a circuit judge may be authorised to try a case (referred to as a 'section 9 judge').

The High Court is made up of three divisions:

(1) *the Queen's Bench Division* (QBD), within which there are also specialist courts, the Admiralty Court, the Commercial Court and the Technology and Construction Court (formerly the Official Referee's Court). Some provincial district registries have sittings of the TCC and of the Commercial Court;

(2) *the Chancery Division* which deals primarily with company work, trusts, estates, insolvency and intellectual property. There are provincial district registries at

Manchester, Leeds and certain other places although the county court has a limited jurisdiction in this area;

(3) *the Family Division.*

The QBD has an appellate jurisdiction. The Divisional Court of the Queen's Bench Division hears appeals on points of criminal law from magistrates courts and from the appellate jurisdiction of the crown courts (see chapter 7). High Court judges normally sit singly to try cases, but a *divisional* court consists of two or, occasionally, three judges.

When the divisional court sits in a civil capacity it is called the Administrative Court. It reviews civil and family decisions of the magistrates courts on points of law and reviews administrative actions and the decisions of tribunals. It hears contempt of court cases brought against newspapers by the Attorney-General.

Court of Appeal

The Court of Appeal, presided over by the Master of the Rolls, is for most cases the court of final appeal. It hears appeals from the county courts, the High Court, the Employment Appeal Tribunal and the Lands Tribunal. Appeals are heard by three judges, though two will suffice in most circumstances.

Each member may give a judgment but the decision is that of the majority. A newspaper can make itself look foolish if it gives great prominence to the outspoken opinion of one judge without pointing out that this was overruled by a majority of his colleagues.

House of Lords

The House of Lords is the highest court in the hierarchy.

It hears no more than 40 to 50 cases a year of which about half are revenue appeals. It gives permission to appeal only in claims of public significance.

The court is not a sitting of the full House of Lords. Appeals are normally heard by five law lords (Lords of Appeal), paid professional judges holding life peerages in the House of Lords Appellate Committee. In cases of exceptional importance the number of judges sitting may be increased. In a case in 2004, nine law Lords presided over appeals against detention without trial by foreign terrorism suspects.

Peers who have held judicial office (including former Lord Chancellors) are entitled to sit in this court but the Lord Chancellor no longer does so. Majority decisions of four to one or even three to two are binding.

European Court of Justice

The European Court of Justice is part of the European Community. It adjudicates upon the law of the Community, and its rulings are binding on British courts. It sits in Luxembourg. (See chapter 1, 'Sources of law'.)

European Court of Human Rights

The European Court of Human Rights is part of the Council of Europe. It adjudicates upon breaches of the European Convention on Human Rights. English and Welsh courts determining a question in connection with a Convention right must take account of decisions of the European Court. It sits in Strasbourg. See chapter 1, 'Sources of law', and chapter 30, 'Human Rights Act 1998'.

For information on admission to the courts and access to evidence see chapter 11.

Admission to the courts and access to court information

Some courts seek improperly to exclude public and press when in fact the law does not permit them to do so.

As long ago as 1913, the House of Lords in *Scott v Scott* affirmed the general principle that courts must administer justice in public. Only if the administration of justice would be made impracticable by the presence of the public was their exclusion justified, it was ruled.

It was held by the Lords that considerations of public decency or private embarrassment are not sufficient to justify the exclusion of the public.

This principle that justice must as a general rule be done in public was upheld by the House of Lords in 1979 in a judgment often quoted by judges. Lord Diplock said:

> This principle can be departed from only where the nature and circumstances of the particular proceedings are such that the application of the general rule in its entirety would frustrate or render impracticable the administration of justice.
>
> The application of this principle of open justice has two aspects: as respects proceedings in the court itself it requires that they should be held in open court to which the press and public are admitted and that, in criminal cases at any rate, all evidence communicated to the court is communicated publicly. As respects the publication to a wider public of fair and accurate aspects of proceedings that have taken place in court, the principle requires that nothing should be done to discourage this. (*A-G v Leveller Magazine Ltd* [1979] AC 440 at 449,450)

Sir Christopher Staughton said in *Ex p P* (1998) Times, 31 March: 'When both sides agree that information should be kept from the public that is when the court has to be most vigilant.'

The European Court emphasised the principle of open justice in 1999 in declaring, 'by rendering the administration of justice transparent, publicity contributes to the achievement of a fair trial' (*Gautrin v France* Application 21257/93, (1998) 28 EHRR 196, para 42).

Article 6 of the European Convention on Human Rights ensures free access to the courts and to open justice by providing that everyone is entitled to a fair and *public* hearing within a reasonable time by an independent and impartial tribunal established by law.

The article qualifies this however by adding: 'Judgment shall be pronounced publicly but the press and public may be excluded from all or part of the trial in the interest of morals, public order or national security in a democratic society, where the interests of juveniles or the protection of the private life of the parties so require, or to the extent strictly necessary in the opinion of the court in special circumstances where publicity would prejudice the interests of justice.' Courts who wish to take this qualifying phrase into account will have to balance it against article 10 of the Convention (freedom of expression and to impart information). (See chapter 30, 'Human Rights Act'.)

Parliament has chosen to widen the range of statutory court reporting restrictions (mainly in the criminal courts) that are either mandatory or at the discretion of the court. It is therefore more important than ever that when attempts which are dubious in law are made to negate the open justice principle either by excluding the press or imposing restrictions on reporting they should be challenged in the public interest (see next chapter).

Powers to prevent or restrict reporting

Magistrates were told in 2001 in guidelines on reporting restrictions issued by the Judicial Studies Board that (1) proceedings must be held in public (2) evidence must be communicated publicly (3) fair, accurate and contemporaneous media reporting of proceedings must not be prevented by any action of the court unless strictly necessary.

The guidelines add: therefore unless there are exceptional circumstances laid down by statute law or common law, the court must not (1) order or allow the exclusion of the press or public for any part of the proceedings (2) permit the withholding of information from the open court proceedings (3) impose permanent or temporary bans on reporting of the proceedings or any part of them that prevents the proper identification, by name and address, of those appearing or mentioned in the course of the proceedings.

The reporter who finds himself excluded from court should find out under what powers the exclusion is taking place. He should tell his editor if he thinks he is being excluded illegally.

The powers that the courts have to sit in private in certain circumstances are limited. They can arise in three ways—at common law, by Act of Parliament or by rules of court (delegated legislation).

The common law principle of open justice has been reiterated by the courts many times.

In 1983 magistrates in Surrey were persuaded to exclude press and public to hear pleas in mitigation made on behalf of a defendant who had given assistance to the police.

Subsequently, the magistrates were strongly criticised in the Queen's Bench Divisional Court. Lord Justice Ackner said hearing a matter in private was a course of last resort to be adopted only if the proceedings in open court would frustrate the process of justice (*R v Reigate Justices, ex p Argus Newspapers* (1983) 5 Cr App Rep (S) 181).

In another case, in 1987 Malvern magistrates excluded press and public during pleas in mitigation on behalf of a woman who admitted driving with excess alcohol. The divisional court later held that although magistrates were entitled to use their discretion to sit *in camera*, it was undesirable that magistrates should do so unless there were rare compelling reasons (*R v Malvern Justices, ex p Evans* [1988] QB 540, [1988] 1 All ER 371, QBD).

It is generally held that exclusion of the press and public at common law extends only to:

(1) where their presence would defeat the ends of justice, for example, where a woman or child cannot be persuaded to give evidence of intimate sexual matters in the presence of many strangers;

(2) where a secret process is the subject of evidence and publicity would defeat the purpose of the litigation;

(3) matters affecting children, for example, wardship and guardianship cases;

(4) where the security of the state demands it;

(5) lunacy cases.

In certain cases there is specific provision in an Act of Parliament to sit in private.

If the public are lawfully excluded, does it follow that the press must go too? The question was considered in the Court of Appeal in November 1989 in a case brought by journalist Tim Crook (see next chapter).

Crook's counsel said that even if the public were excluded while a judge received information on a procedural matter the press could have been allowed to remain and publication of reports postponed by an order under section 4 of the Contempt of Court Act 1981 (see chapter 17).

Lord Lane, Lord Chief Justice, said it would not be right generally to distinguish between excluding the press and the public. There might be cases however during which the press should not be excluded with the other members of the public, such as a prosecution for importing an indecent film, where the film was shown to the jury and some members of the public might gasp or giggle and make the jury's task more difficult (*R v Crook (Tim)* (1989) 93 Cr App Rep 17, 24).

Witnesses in private

Under section 25 of the Youth Justice and Criminal Evidence Act 1999 courts have power to exclude the public when hearing a vulnerable or intimidated witness while evidence is being given in a sexual offence or where a person other than the accused might intimidate a witness. A court hearing evidence in private in this way must allow at least one representative of the press to remain (See later this chapter, 'Evidence in private in criminal courts'.) The Act makes it an offence to report, before the end of the trial, any 'special measures' order made to protect a vulnerable or intimidated witness or any prohibition on the accused cross-examining a witness. The restriction in this section does not extend to evidence or to any witness's identity however and does not apply where the judge informs the jury of the 'special measures' direction or prohibition on the accused cross-examining the witness. Prosecution for publication before the end of the trial of any 'special measures' order may be brought only by or with the consent of the Attorney-General.

Identification of witnesses

A Home Office statement on standards of witness care, issued in 1998, said that unless it was necessary for evidential purposes, defence and prosecution witnesses should not be required to disclose their addresses in open court. In exceptional cases, it would be appropriate for defence and prosecution to make application for the non-disclosure in open court of the names of witnesses. Courts sometimes allow a witness to write down his name or address to avoid unnecessary pain or distress (see also chapter 2, 'Identification of witnesses').

Under section 46 of the Youth Justice and Criminal Evidence Act, courts have power to ban the identification of a vulnerable witness over 18 during his lifetime. Power to give anonymity to people under 18 concerned in criminal proceedings in an adult court already existed under the Children and Young Persons Act 1933 (see chapter 6, 'Juveniles in adult courts'). However, guidelines on court reporting issued to crown court judges by the Judicial Studies Board in 2000 say: 'Strangely it does not seem possible to give a reporting restriction order in respect of a witness under 18 that will last beyond his 18th birthday even in a case where the court would make a lifetime direction in relation to an adult.'

The 1999 Act provides that a court may make an order banning the identification of a witness if it was satisfied that the quality of the witness's evidence or the level of his co-operation would be diminished by fear or distress and that his evidence and co-operation would be improved by an order being made. Home Office explanatory notes published in 1999 said that the words 'fear' and 'distress' were not intended to cover a disinclination to give evidence on account of the prospect of embarrassing publicity, and not every witness eligible for other protection (such as the provision of screens or a video link) because of fear or distress would also be eligible for a ban on identification.

The court is required by the Act to take into account the circumstances of the case, the age of the witness, his social and cultural background and ethnic origins, his domestic and employment circumstances and his religious beliefs and political opinions. Other circumstances include the behaviour towards the witness of the accused or of the accused's family and associates, or of anyone likely to be an accused or a witness. The court must also consider any views expressed by the witness.

A witness over 16 may give a written waiver dispensing with any order, provided no person interfered with his peace or comfort to obtain consent. Except where a sexual offence is involved, a parent or guardian of a witness under 16 may give the written waiver provided the parent or guardian had previously been given written notice drawing his attention to the need to consider the welfare of the person under 16.

The court is required to consider whether an order would be in the interests of justice, including, in particular, the desirability of avoiding a substantial and unreasonable restriction on the reporting of the proceedings. This requirement might provide grounds for the media to object to an order. A court or appeal court may revoke the order or relax it in the interests of justice, or because it imposes a substantial and unreasonable restriction on reporting and it would be in the public interest to relax it.

Witnesses such as blackmail victims can also be protected from identification by the court making an order under section 11 of the Contempt of Court Act 1981 (see chapter 2, 'Contempt of Court', and also chapters 12 and 17).

Hearings in private or in chambers

A court may sit *in private* for a trial or for other proceedings in closed court with press and public excluded—for example an Official Secrets Acts trial, or in other circumstances in *Scott v Scott*, outlined earlier, or mentioned in the civil procedure rules below.

A hearing is often held *in chambers*—that is in the judge's room—for applications to be heard, rather than a case to be tried, such as an application for bail made to a judge, or for administrative reasons. The Master of the Rolls, Lord Woolf (later Lord Chief Justice), said in the Court of Appeal in February 1998 that the public had no right to attend hearings in chambers but, if requested, permission should be granted to attend when and to what extent it was practicable. What happened in chambers was not confidential or secret, with the exception of cases involving national security, children, wardship of court, mental health or secret processes. A judgment in chambers was normally a public document even though there was no right to inspect it without leave. However, the judgment or order of the court could and should be made available when requested. If those who sought to attend could not be accommodated, the judge should consider adjourning the whole of the part of the proceedings into open court or allowing one or more representatives of the press to attend the hearing in chambers (*Hodgson v Imperial Tobacco*, [1998] 2 All ER 673, [1998] 1 WLR 1056).

Publication of reports of hearings in private is permissible except in cases involving children and a few other instances. (See chapter 17, 'Report of hearing in private'.)

Civil Procedure Rules (CPR)

Rule 39.2 of the Civil Procedure Rules for the High Court and the county court says that the general rule is that a hearing is to be in public but a hearing, or part of it, may be in private if:

(1) publicity would defeat the object of the hearing;

(2) it involves matters relating to national security;

(3) it involves confidential information (including information relating to personal financial matters) and publicity would damage that confidentiality;

(4) a private hearing is necessary to protect the interest of any child or patient;

(5) it is an application without notice and it would be unjust to any respondent for there to be a public hearing;

(6) it involves uncontentious matters arising in the administration of trusts or of a deceased's estate; or

(7) the court considers it to be necessary in the interests of justice.

The rules also state: 'The court may order that the identity of any party or witness must not be disclosed if it considers non-disclosure necessary in order to protect the interests of that party or witness'.

Professor CJ Miller in *Contempt of Court* (2000) says that the problem with this rule is that the focal point is the interests of parties and witnesses, without addressing the competing requirements of freedom of expression under article 10 of the European Convention on Human Rights. 'In any event section 3 of the Human Rights Act will require all such delegated legislation to be construed so far as is possible in a way compatible with the convention rights. . .'. The courts must interpret the rule with this requirement in mind.

The Lord Chancellor's Department told the editors of *McNae* however that Lord Woolf, then Master of the Rolls, had made it clear that a party or witness might be granted anonymity, as an exception to the general principle that proceedings should be in public, where that was shown to be necessary in the proper administration of justice (*R v Legal Aid Board, ex p Kaim Todner* [1999] QB 966, [1998] 3 All ER 541). The interests of the party or witness was relevant in determining what was in the interests of the proper administration of justice. The CPR rule reflected that position, and orders would be made under it only where a sufficient case was made out.

In 1999 Mr Justice Buckley said that once a proposed settlement of a claim by a child or a patient was approved, a judge could normally give approval in open court and he (Mr Justice Buckley) would. If the judge had sufficient material to satisfy himself in advance of the hearing that approval should be given, then the hearing could be in public. (*Beatham v Carlisle Hospitals NHS Trust* (1999) Times, 20 May.) A civil procedure rule that such hearings should take place in private unless the court directed otherwise has now been deleted.

High Court

All divisions of the court are entitled to hear some matters in private.

However the general rule is that a hearing is to be open to the public. The Human Rights Act 1998 abolished the former difference between 'open court' and 'chambers' hearings.

Now a judge may sit in his 'chambers' for a public hearing, or in a courtroom unrobed for a private hearing. If you are in any doubt about whether reporters are admitted to a hearing you should ask for a message to be sent to the judge.

The CPR provide that a hearing may be in private if publicity would defeat the object of the hearing, national security is involved or the hearing involves confidential information, including information relating to personal financial matters. The most important examples in this category include domestic violence injunctions, and mortgagees' and landlords' applications for possession of residential property. The judge is given discretion to hear certain other matters in private.

Even if the reporter is aware of details of proceedings in private, through contact with interested parties, it is unwise to publish without considering whether this could constitute contempt of court (see chapter 17, 'Reports of hearings in private').

Family proceedings

Under the Family Proceedings Rules 1991, child cases involving residence, or contact orders in the High Court or county court must be heard in private unless the court otherwise directs. Either side can apply for an open hearing or for judgment to be given in public. Wardship and other orders under the Children Act in the High Court must be made in private. Lady Justice Butler-Sloss said in the Court of Appeal in 1996 that the effect of this was that the courts were bound to hear child cases generally in private. If issues of public interest arose however it seemed entirely appropriate to give judgment in open court provided, where desirable in the interest of the child, directions were given to avoid identification (*Re P-B (a minor)* [1997] 1 All ER 58). In 2004 Mr Justice Hedley decided to sit in public for a case involving a dispute between parents and a hospital about baby's right to life, but said this was unique and afforded no precedent as to the future hearing of family cases in public.

It may be contempt of court to publish information from such family proceedings other than an order made by the court, although this too may be banned. In 2004 the Department of Constitutional Affairs proposed that the law on disclosure of information arising from family proceedings should be relaxed to assist public and voluntary organisations working with children and their families but stressed that the proposals would not allow publication to the media without the permission of the court. (see chapter 6, 'Juveniles and the European Convention on Human Rights', and 'Children in civil proceedings', chapter 10, 'The civil courts' and chapter 17, 'Reports of hearings in private').

In 2002 however the Court of Appeal held that family proceedings in private not concerning children were not automatically covered by secrecy. The court upheld the finding of Mr Justice Munby that in such cases there was no automatic bar on parties disclosing details of cases or court papers to the media.

Applications for legitimacy declarations must be heard in private unless the court directs otherwise and any report which is obtained afterwards must conform to the restrictions of the Judicial Proceedings (Regulation of Reports) Act 1926 (see chapter 13, 'The reporting restrictions').

Access to court information

Under rule 5.4(2) of the Civil Procedure Rules (as amended in 2004), any person who pays the prescribed fee can at the central office, or at a district registry of the High Court, search for, inspect and take a copy of a claim form once an acknowledgment of service or a defence has been filed; any judgment or order given or made in public, and any other document if the court gives permission (see also chapter 10). A party named in a claim form may apply to the court for availability to the form to be restricted, and/or for the form to be edited before non-parties are allowed to see it.

Statements of case are made available to the media in some cases—but not as a matter of course—for the purpose of ascertaining names, ages, addresses, etc. But they are not covered by privilege. Any other information taken from them must be treated with extreme care, especially when the case is settled and no details are announced in court. Settlement of a case—for instance the award of agreed damages in a personal injury claim—does not imply acceptance of liability by the defendant nor that any of the facts set out in the statement of case are admitted.

Because a reporter will not have read the trial bundle, the trial itself may have very little meaning. The onlooker may learn little from the cross-examination because this will be by reference to the trial bundle to which there is no access.

As stated, there is a general presumption in the CPR that the business of the court is to be done in public unless this is likely to lead to injustice. Rule 32.13 now provides that 'A witness statement which stands as evidence is open to inspection unless the court otherwise directs.' This enables public access during the course of the trial to written evidence relied on in court but not read out. However, the court may direct that the written statements should not be made available because of the interests of justice, the public interest, or the nature of any medical evidence.

A High Court case in 2004 resolved the question whether a journalist could obtain access to documents relating to a case that had concluded.

The *Guardian*, reporting an arms bribe case, applied to the court to receive witness statements disclosing huge payments by a leading British arms company to the daughter of the then President of Indonesia. The documents were disclosed in a hearing but the case unexpectedly settled before it could be reported.

Mr Justice Park, having equated the press with the public, continued: 'The public should not, by reason of modern practice, lose the ability to know the contents of witness statement evidence in chief which they would have had under the earlier practice when evidence in chief was given orally.' It had been argued that the statements sought by the paper should not be made available, among other things, because the case had ended. However, in the judge's view an application for documents could be made after a case had ended, and relevant documents included the pleadings (that is, the statement of case) and witness statements.

The judge also ruled: 'The fact that *The Guardian* did not have a reporter permanently in court does not in my view make any difference. Observations in some cases about how members of the public sitting in court should be able to know what is happening have to be read with realistic qualifications for the particular circumstances of the press.'

Re Guardian Newspapers Ltd (Court record: Disclosure) (8 December 2004, unreported).

There is no right of access to other statements of case or affidavits, or judgments and orders given or made in private. However the Department of Constitutional Affairs announced in 2004 that a register of High Court judgments, and fines in the magistrates courts, with name, date of birth and address would become available during 2005. A 'keeper and developer' of the register would be appointed, on similar lines to that provided for county court judgments (see 'County court', later this chapter)

Mr Justice Jacob said in the Chancery Division in January 1998 that, with very rare exceptions, and even when a hearing had been in private, no judgment could be regarded as a secret document. The best way to avoid ill-informed comments in the media in a case of high public interest was for the court to be as open as possible (*Forbes v Smith* [1998] 1 All ER 973).

New arrangements for judgments were announced by the Lord Chief Justice in April 1998 in a practice statement, which he said was to be regarded as experimental. He said that when the court handed down its written judgment, it would pronounce judgment in open court and copies of the judgment would then be available to accredited representatives of the media. In cases of particular media interest, it would be helpful if requests for copies could be made in advance to the judge's clerk. Anyone supplied with a copy would be bound by any order under section 39 of the Children and Young Persons Act 1933 or any other restriction.

The court may direct that the written statements should not be made available because of the interests of justice, the public interest, the nature of any medical evidence or confidential information or the need to protect the interests of a child or patient.

Lord Justice Judge, deputy chief justice, said in the Court of Appeal in 2003 that barristers should give journalists copies of the skeleton arguments they prepare for court hearings if they were asked to do so. He said it would be a waste of time for the skeletons to be repeated in court. The court had concluded that the principle of open justice led inexorably to the conclusion that written skeleton arguments, or those parts of skeleton arguments adopted by counsel and treated by the court as forming part of an oral submission should be disclosed of and when a request to do so was received.

Injunctions

Applications for injunctions are heard in private (with press and public excluded) in the Queen's Bench Division but are usually heard in open court in the Chancery Division (see also chapter 10).

In addition, masters and district judges of the High Court deal with many applications and summonses in the course of proceedings in chambers, as in the county court.

In the Family Division private hearings are the rule and open court hearings the exception. Most divorce matters are heard privately. In the Queen's Bench Division, interlocutory matters tend to be heard in chambers, but in the Chancery Division they are heard in public.

The Court of Appeal rarely sits in private. When it does so, it is in accordance with *Scott v Scott*, mentioned earlier.

County court

The Civil Procedure Rules provide that the general rule is that a hearing is to be in public but seven exceptions are listed (see 'Civil Procedure Rules', earlier this chapter). Practice direction 39, supplementing rule 39 of the Civil Procedure Rules, says that a judge should have regard to article 6 of the European Convention on Human Rights requiring that in general hearings should be held in public. The exceptions include cases involving children or a patient, or confidential information about personal financial matters. The practice direction says where there is no sign on the door of the court or of the judge's room (if a case is heard there), indicating that proceedings are in private, members of the public will be admitted where practicable. A judge may adjourn the proceedings to a larger room or court if he thinks it appropriate.

Any claim by a landlord for possession of a house, based on non-payment of rent must be listed as a hearing in private, as must any claim by a mortgagee for possession of a house. A judge has discretion to hear the case in open court and must hear any representations on whether the hearing is to be in public or in private.

The judge may hear some other matters in private. A judge may decide to have a small claims hearing in private. Applications for injunctions (other than a domestic violence injunction) heard where the person against whom the injunction is sought is represented, must be heard in open court. Applications which are made without notice (in the absence of the person against whom the application is sought) are heard in private.

District judges (formerly known as county court registrars) deal in open court with many of the smaller cases and often with actions for possession of land. They also deal in private with arbitration, many family disputes, and routine matters. When dealing with arbitration, they can give leave for other people to attend, although this is exceptional.

Other matters dealt with in private are pre-trial reviews and interlocutory applications.

Rule 5.4 of the Civil Procedure Rules stipulates that any person who pays the prescribed fee may during office hours search for, inspect and take a copy of a claim form where acknowledgment of service or a defence has been filed, any judgment or order given in public or, with the permission of the court, any other document. There is no right of access to other statements of case or affidavits, or judgments and orders given or made in private. Family Proceedings Rules stipulate that in children cases no document shall be disclosed other than to a limited range of people. In some cases a practice direction may supersede rule 5.4. A non-party may not search for, inspect or take a copy of a claim form which has been issued but has not been served. A claim form must normally be served within four months of issue.

It is intended that eventually a computer search of county court records will be possible.

Court lists are available for inspection but these do little more than name the parties although they may indicate the nature of the action.

Each court keeps records of proceedings, including the name and address of the defendant, the nature and amount of the claim, and concise minutes of the proceedings, including a note of any judgment, order, or decree.

Under section 73 of the County Courts Act 1984, judgments can be inspected by members of the public at a privatised central registry. A public register, under the control of the Lord Chancellor's Department, of names, occupations, and addresses of defendants, and amounts in all outstanding county court judgments (except for orders made in family proceedings, and some judgments in contested cases awaiting enforcement action) can be inspected by personal visit or by post on payment of £4.50 each judgment (one name and one address) at the time of going to press, at Registry Trust Ltd, 173/175 Cleveland Street, London, W1P 5PE (telephone 0207 380 0133). Judgments which are settled within a month of being registered can be cancelled. Those settled after a month stay on the register for six years.

Bankruptcy

In general, Civil Procedure Rules apply to bankruptcy actions. Rule 7.28 of the Insolvency Proceedings Rules 1986 allows for public inspection of the court's record of bankruptcy proceedings, including bankruptcy orders, but if the district judge is not satisfied with the propriety of a request to inspect the record, he may disallow the request. Postal searches for court orders still in force for bankruptcy or for voluntary arrangement may be made free of charge through the Insolvency Service, 5th Floor, West Wing, 45–46 Stephenson Street, Birmingham B2 4UP (telephone 0121 698 4000) (see chapter 14, 'Bankruptcy and company liquidation').

Evidence in private in criminal courts

Under part of the Youth Justice and Criminal Evidence Act 1999 implemented in 2002, a crown court may make 'special measures' directions to facilitate the giving of evidence by vulnerable or intimidated witnesses, such as a direction to exclude the public and the press while evidence is being given in a sexual offence case or where a person other than the accused might intimidate a witness. Under section 25 of the Act, a court hearing evidence in private in this way must allow at least one representative of the press to remain. Any other press representative, excluded from the hearing, has the same reporting rights as those not excluded. This is taken to mean that the proceedings will be deemed to have been held in public to meet the requirement for privilege to apply to reports.

Lord Williams of Mostyn QC, then Minister of State at the Home Office and later Leader of the House of Lords, said: 'We believe the court will rarely want to exclude the press. The power is much more likely to be used to exclude certain individuals who may be sitting in the public gallery. But there may be occasions where the court thinks that clearing the court, including the press, is necessary to ensure the surroundings in which the witness gives his evidence are as quiet and private as possible. The court will use their powers only where they believe (a) it would be in the interests of justice to do so and (b) it will maximise the quality of the evidence the witness will be able to give.

He did not think the power could be used simply to avoid embarrassing publicity. It would not be practicably possible for anyone other than the party calling the witness to make a successful application for special measures for that witness. Without the relevant information with which to mount such an application, access to the witness or knowledge of his views, he did not see how it could succeed. 'Special measures' directions were binding only on the proceedings to which they were related (and not for example to any subsequent appeal), lasted until the end of those proceedings and could be varied or discharged by the court (letter to the Guild of Editors, 27 January 1999).

Lord Williams said when evidence-in-chief and cross-examination were videoed it would be in private. However, once the videos had been admitted as evidence, press and public would be able to see and hear them when they were played to the court and to the jury, where there was one.

Sexual offences

When a court is hearing an application to introduce evidence or questions about a complainant's sexual history, the court must sit in private under section 43 of the Youth Justice and Criminal Evidence Act 1999. The court must give its decision and the reasons for it in open court but in the absence of the jury (if there is one).

Crown court

Guidelines issued to crown court judges by the Judicial Studies Board in 2000 begin: 'The general rule is that the administration of justice must be done in public. The media is in court to report the proceedings to the public, the majority of whom will be unable to be there in person but who have the right to be informed as to what has occurred. Accordingly, unless there is good reason, nothing should be done to prevent the publication to the wider public of fair and accurate reports of the proceedings by the media.'

Crown court rules allow a judge to order that the whole or part of the proceedings be held in private in certain cases, including bail applications and the issue of a summons or warrant. A party who intends to apply for all or part of a trial to be heard in private in the interests of national security or to protect the identity of a witness must give written notice to the court at least seven days before the trial (rule 24A). In 1998, Lord Justice Brooke giving judgment in the Court of Appeal said that if the defence applied for such an order on the grounds of national security, it was incumbent on the judge to ensure he received relevant evidence from those who were the guardians of national security so that he could balance any potential risk to national security against the risk to justice. A judge should not be left to infer, in the absence of relevant evidential material from the crown, whether national security would be at risk. Lord Justice Brooke said as open justice promoted the rule of law, citizens of all ranks in a democracy had to be subject to transparent legal restraint, especially those holding judicial or executive offices. Publicity, whether in the courts, the press, or both, was a powerful deterrent to abuse of power and improper behaviour (*Ex p Guardian Newspapers* [1999] 1 All ER 65, [1999] 1 WLR 2130).

Lord Lane, Lord Chief Justice, said in the Court of Appeal in 1991 that a judge should not adjourn into private as a matter of course, but only if he believed that something might be said which made determination in private appropriate. If he did sit in private, a judge should be alive to the importance of adjourning into open court as soon as exclusion of the public was not plainly necessary (*Re Crook (Tim)* (1991) 93 Cr App Rep 17, CA). In 2004 the Court of Appeal ordered that an appeal by a man with mental problems against a conviction for manslaughter should be heard under reporting restrictions because of his vulnerability and the effect publicity would have on him. He had been held under the Mental Health Act since his conviction. The Court of Appeal held that no one should suffer the risk of physical or mental harm in exercising his legal right of access to the court but embarrassment or distress resulting from publicity was not sufficient reason.

A practice direction has been issued that the crown court should normally sit in public when hearing an application to strike out, on the grounds of insufficient evidence, an indictable-only charge sent for trial by magistrates. Reporting is restricted however under the Crime and Disorder Act 1998. (See chapter 5, 'Reporting restrictions on applications to strike out'.)

Magistrates courts

Magistrates courts, like other courts, are required to conform to the provisions of Art 6 of the European Convention on Human Rights that everyone is entitled to fair and public hearing.

Exceptions to the general rule exist specifically for adoption proceedings and sometimes for family proceedings and for evidence given in Official Secrets Act cases (see later this chapter).

The introduction to the guidelines booklet, *Reporting Restrictions in the Magistrates' Courts*, issued by the Judicial Studies Board in 2001, emphasises the general rule that the administration of justice must be done in public.

> The media is in court to report the proceedings to the public, the majority of whom will be unable to be there in person but who have the right to be informed as to what has occurred. Accordingly, unless there is good and lawful reason, nothing should be done to prevent the publication to the wider public of fair and accurate reports of proceedings by the media.

The booklet says the open justice principle is clearly recognised by the courts and by Parliament and the common law has been supplemented in this respect by statute. 'Statutory defences in libel and contempt are available for fair, accurate and contemporaneous reports of proceedings. Statutory rights have been provided to make representations against the imposition of restrictions on reporting or public access to the proceedings. The role of the media is recognised in case law under the European Convention on Human Rights'.

It says that the common law and statutory restrictions enable the courts to exclude the public and the media and to impose temporary or permanent restrictions on media reports of court proceedings by making an order but it encourages the courts to exercise their discretion to hear media representatives at the time of considering imposition of an order and to hear them on the lifting of restrictions to permit contemporaneous reporting of the proceedings.

> Such discretion should be exercised in addition to any formal rights which the media might have for appeal or review of such orders or to apply for the lifting of automatic reporting restrictions. This often ensures that problems are quickly resolved.
>
> The law provides particular protection to contemporaneous reports of court proceedings and has recognised the perishable nature of news and courts have acknowledged the importance of hearing and resolving issues relating to reporting as soon as possible.
>
> A clear understanding of the legal basis for the imposition of restrictions is necessary by magistrates, court staff and the media.

The Magistrates' Courts Act 1980, section 121 stipulates that magistrates must sit in open court when trying a case or imposing prison sentences in default of fines etc.

Where a juvenile is a witness in a case involving indecency, any court can exclude the public under section 37 of the Children and Young Persons Act 1933. The section goes on to say however: 'Nothing in this section shall authorise the exclusion of bona fide represen-tatives of a news gathering or reporting organisation.' A magistrates court may sit in private however, under section 25 of the Youth Justice and Criminal Evidence Act 1999, to hear vulnerable witnesses in sex cases or where there are reasonable grounds for believing that persons other than the accused may intimidate a witness. But one member of the press must be allowed to remain (see 'Evidence in private in criminal courts', earlier this chapter).

When magistrates are sitting as examining justices (at committal for trial, sending for trial, or proceedings leading up to either), they are required by section 4 of the Magis-trates' Courts Act 1980 to sit in open court except where in the whole or any part of committal proceedings the ends of justice would not be served.

When magistrates hear an application under the Crime and Disorder Act 1998 for a child safety order, for an anti-social behaviour order, or for a sex offender order, there is no statutory provision for any of the application to be heard other than in open court. (see chapter 9, 'Child safety, anti-social behaviour and sex offender orders').

Magistrates court information

The Queen's Bench Divisional Court held in 1987 that the names of magistrates dealing with a case must be made known to press and public. Lord Justice Watkins said any attempt to preserve anonymity was inimical to the proper administration of justice (*R v Felixstowe Justices, ex p Leigh* [1987] QB 582, [1987] 1 All ER 551).

Two circulars from the Home Office, which formerly had oversight of magistrates courts, urged in 1967 and 1989 that names, addresses, charges, and occupations should be made available to the press (see chapter 4, 'Court lists'). The 1989 circular encouraged courts to provide local newspapers with a copy of the court register when it is prepared.

The Department of Constitutional Affairs announced in 2004 that a register of High Court judgments, and fines in the magistrates courts, with name, date of birth and address would become available during 2005. A 'keeper and developer' of the register would be appointed, on similar lines to that provided for county court judgments (see 'County court', earlier this chapter).

Addresses of defendants

Judge David Clarke, Honorary Recorder of Liverpool, in 2000 rejected an application for an order banning publication of the addresses of three defendants on child abuse charges on the grounds that they would be at risk of attack. Their lawyers had cited article 8 (right to privacy) of the European Convention on Human Rights but Judge Clarke said he was not able to find any special factors justifying an exception to the normal rule that court proceedings were open and could be reported. He said:

> I do not overlook that these men are presumed innocent unless and until proved guilty. But their position in this respect is no different from that of anyone facing any criminal charge. Unless and until some statutory prohibition is enacted I do not consider there is any warrant for prohibiting publication of their addresses, as these defendants seek.
>
> It is important to remember that if a name is published without an address, a reader might be misled in the belief that another person with same name is involved rather than the true defendant. This is a real danger, particularly where the defendants bear common names such as my own.

The judge said freedom of expression (article 10) was properly regarded as one of the most fundamental elements in the European Convention. There was no dispute that this could be overridden in appropriate circumstances but the articles of the convention taken together did not increase the number of situations in which a restriction was appropriate. (*R v Thomas Carroll*, Media Lawyer Newsletter, January 2001).

See also chapter 12, 'Challenging the courts'.

The Queen's Bench Divisional Court held in 1988 that a defendant's address should normally be stated in court. A newspaper company successfully brought an action for judicial review against the magistrates' decision to allow a defendant to conceal his address because he feared harassment from his ex-wife. Lord Justice Watkins said: 'While no statutory provision lays down that a defendant's address has publicly to be given in court, it is well established practice that, save for a justifiable reason, it must be' (*R v Evesham Justices, ex p McDonagh* [1988] QB 553, [1988] 1 All ER 371).

Warrant for further detention

Where police wish to continue to detain a suspect before charging him, their application must, under section 45 of the Police and Criminal Evidence Act 1984, be heard by at least two magistrates not sitting in open court (see chapter 2).

Youth courts

Only certain persons have the right by law to be present. Among them are bona fide representatives of news gathering or reporting organisations (section 47, Children and Young Persons Act 1933, as amended).

Family proceedings in magistrates courts

Representatives of newspapers and news agencies may attend under section 69 of the Magistrates' Courts Act 1980 although reporting is restricted both under section 71 of that Act and section 97 of the Children Act 1989 (see chapter 9, 'Family proceedings'). Magistrates courts rules, made under the Children Act, allow magistrates to sit in private when exercising powers under the Children Act in relation to a child under 18. Section 69 of the 1980 Act allows magistrates at their discretion to exclude the press from family proceedings during the taking of indecent evidence, in the interests of the administration of justice or of public decency, and rules out the attendance of the press in any proceedings under the Adoption Act 1976 (see chapter 6, 'Adoption of children').

Divorce

Under rule 48 of the Matrimonial Causes Rules 1977, any person may, within 14 days of a decree nisi being pronounced, inspect the certificate and any affidavit and corroborative evidence filed in support of the petition. Copies may be obtained within 14 days on payment of a fee.

A direction of the senior registrar dated 21 June 1972, says: 'If a matrimonial case is reported it is essential that names and addresses should be reported accurately. In many cases this is not possible unless the associate or court clerk co-operates with the reporter to the extent of confirming the details from the court file.' The direction said the same applied to other matters which were of public record and not confidential, such as the date and place of marriage, the order made by the court and, in the case of divisional court appeals, details of the order appealed from. Though pleadings and other documents should not be shown to reporters, there was no objection to the details referred to being given to them on request.

Official Secrets Act

The public and press may be excluded when evidence would be prejudicial to national security (section 8, Official Secrets Act 1920).

Inquests

Rule 17 of the Coroners Rules states that every inquest shall be held in public save that an inquest or part of an inquest may be in private in the interests of national security.

However, rule 37 allows a coroner to take documentary evidence from any witness where such evidence is likely to be undisputed. It states that the coroner must announce publicly at the inquest the name of the person giving documentary evidence and must read aloud such evidence unless he otherwise directs (see chapter 15).

Court information and data protection

This subject is dealt with in chapter 33, 'Data Protection Acts'.

Employment (formerly industrial) tribunals

Under reg 8 of the Employment Tribunals (Constitution and Rules of Procedure) Regulations 2004, an employment tribunal may sit in private for hearing evidence where it would be against the interests of national security to allow the evidence to be heard in public, or for hearing evidence which in the opinion of the tribunal is likely to consist of

(1) information which a witness could not disclose without contravening a prohibition imposed under any Act of Parliament; (2) information communicated to a witness in confidence or obtained in consequence of the confidence placed in him by another person; (3) information the disclosure of which would cause substantial injury to any undertaking of the witness, or any undertaking in which he works, for reasons other than its effect on negotiations over pay and conditions.

The Queen's Bench Divisional Court held that the decision of a tribunal at Southampton to exclude press and public from hearing salacious or sensitive evidence in a sexual harassment case was unlawful. Mr Justice Brooke said under the rules of procedure tribunal hearings must be in public except in limited circumstances which did not apply in this case. The existence of reg 8 precluded a tribunal from sitting in private in situations other than those in the rule (*R v Southampton Industrial Tribunal, ex p INS News Group* [1995] IRLR 247).

The Court of Appeal held in 2000 that a tribunal hearing conducted in the office of the regional chairman within a secure area protected by a locked door which carried a notice 'Private. No admittance to the public beyond this point' was not a public hearing. The test of whether a hearing was in public was not whether any member of the public was prevented from attending the hearing but whether he would have been able to enter had he wished to do so. The chairman had acted beyond his jurisdiction (*Storer v British Gas* [2000] 2 All ER 440, [2000] 1 WLR 1237, CA).

Challenging the courts

The court reporter of today needs to know considerably more of the law on reporting restrictions than his predecessors

This situation has arisen not only because of the growth of legislation regulating court reporting, as year by year Parliament passes new Acts which include restrictions. It arises also because of the tendency of some courts to exercise their discretionary powers unreasonably, often contrary to rulings from the higher courts. There has been an increasing tendency too for defence lawyers to dredge up any possible statute they believe might be used to restrict publicity for their clients and some courts have been easily swayed by these lawyers without giving due consideration to the law. In the crown courts counsel have on occasions ignored the duty placed on crown counsel by the Court of Appeal in *Ex Parte News Group Newspapers* ([2002] EMLR 9) to act in an unpartisan and objective spirit and give the court such assistance as he or she could on the proper principles to be applied.

Many successful challenges have been made by journalists however, on the grounds that the order made was either unreasonable or was not within the court's powers.

Lord Steyn said in a case before the law lords 2004 that Parliament had created numerous statutory exceptions to the ordinary rule of open court proceedings in the interest of justice:

> Given the number of statutory exceptions it needs to be said clearly and unambiguously that the court has no power to create by a process of analogy, except in the most compelling circumstances, further exceptions to the general principle of open justice. (*Re S (A Child) (Identification: Restrictions on Publication*) [2004])

(See chapter 6, 'Guidelines on injunctions').

The High Court has continued to stress that it is important that the administration of justice should be subject to the spotlight of public scrutiny through reporting of

proceedings in the press (see also chapter 11). It has continued to emphasise the principles of open justice set out in *A-G v Leveller Magazine* [1979] AC 440 at p 450. Lord
Diplock said in that case that the principle could be departed from only:

> where the nature and circumstances of the particular proceedings are such that the
> application of the general rule in its entirety would frustrate or render impracticable the
> administration of justice.

It was also held in *A-G v Leveller Magazine* that a mere request not to publish matter is not
to be regarded as a court order (at p 473).

Senior judges, the Home Office, and the Lord Chancellor's Department have urged that
defendants' addresses should be easily available but editors and their staffs have often
had to challenge orders that have been in conflict with the principle of open justice in *A-G
v Leveller Magazine*.

After persuading Norwich Crown Court in 1999 to withdraw an invalid order prohibiting
the identification of a man accused of indecent assault, a Norwich *Evening News* reporter,
Grizelda Graham, neatly summed up the situation when she said: 'It seems that some
lawyers are trying it on and getting away with it because some courts do not fully know the
law relating to the reporting of cases.'

After eight people died in a house fire at Huddersfield, West Yorkshire, in 2002, magistrates acceded to a defence request to make orders under section 11 of the Contempt of
Court Act, conferring anonymity on two of those accused in connection with the fire.
Magistrates gave among their reasons that publication of a defendant's name and address
might inadvertently prejudice witnesses as yet unidentified. The anonymity orders were
overturned by crown courts after representations from the Press Association. Mr Justice
Henriques said at Leeds Crown Court: 'The ability of the press to report matters of public
interest is critical. Once the important cases cannot be reported, the public and the press
have a real grievance.' (See later this chapter, 'Section 11 orders'.)

Numerous attempts in dubious circumstances have been made by defence lawyers to
seek orders under section 11, sometimes simply on the grounds that the defendant is a
police or prison officer. These applications have sometimes been granted initially but usually overturned later after the legality has been questioned by an editor or reporter. Sometimes the courts have confused banning orders under section 11 with postponement
orders under section 4.

A district judge at Birmingham overturned orders under sections 4 and 11 of the
Contempt Act made by lay magistrates in 2004 to prevent reporting of the case of a
police constable accused of careless driving in an unmarked police car on his way to the

scene of an armed robbery. A 12-year-old girl was knocked down and lost a leg in the accident.

Lawyers defending the constable said that reporting of the case would put his life in danger because he was due to be a witness in a murder trial. It also would prejudice the administration of justice in the trial. District Judge Robert Zara rejected the argument. He said although the constable might have some subjective fear for his life, he had not established an objective basis for that fear. He did not believe that naming the constable would put him at risk. There was no connection between the careless driving proceedings and the murder trial.

European Convention on Human Rights

In seeking to persuade the court to impose reporting restrictions, defence lawyers now often quote articles 6 (right to a fair trial) and 8 (privacy) of the European Convention on Human Rights. Usually these lawyers are silent on article 10 (right of freedom of expression and to impart information).

Article 6 provides that everyone is entitled to a fair and public hearing by an independent and impartial tribunal established by law. It says that judgment shall be pronounced publicly but the press may be excluded from the whole or part of a trial in the interest of morals, public order or national security, where the interests of juveniles or the protection of the private lives of the parties so require, or to the extent strictly necessary in the opinion of the court in special circumstances where publicity would prejudice the interests of justice.

In the House of Lords in 2000, Lord Bingham said the right to a fair trial was absolute but the subsidiary rights within article 6 were not, and it was always necessary to consider all the facts and the whole history of the proceedings in a particular case to judge whether a defendant's right to fair trial had been infringed. (*R v Forbes (Anthony Leroy)* (1999) Times, 19 December).

Article 8 provides that everyone has the right to respect for his private and family life, his home and correspondence.

Article 10 says the right to freedom of expression shall include the right to hold opinions and to receive and impart information. It adds that the exercise of these freedoms may be subject to such conditions prescribed by law and necessary in a democratic society for the protection of the rights of others, for preventing the disclosure of information derived in confidence or for maintaining the authority and impartiality of the judiciary.

Mrs Justice Bracewell said in 2000 that a judge's job was not to carry out a balancing exercise between freedom of expression and other interests. On the contrary, she said, the scales were weighted at the beginning so that article 10 prevailed unless one of the exceptions applied when given a narrow interpretation (*Richmond-upon-Thames London Borough Council v Holmes* (2000) Times, 20 October). See also chapter 30, 'Human Rights Act 1998'.

Judge David Clarke, Recorder of Liverpool, said at Liverpool Crown Court in the same year that freedom of expression was properly regarded as one of the most fundamental elements in the European Convention. There was no dispute that this could be overridden in appropriate circumstances but the articles of the Convention taken together did not increase the number of situations in which a restriction was appropriate. Three defendants on child abuse charges unsuccessfully applied for a ban on publication of their addresses as they would otherwise be at risk of attack. Their lawyers had cited article 8 of the Convention (right to privacy) (*R v Carroll* (*Media Lawyer* newsletter, January 2001)). See also chapter 11, 'Addresses of defendants'.

See also chapter 6, 'Juveniles and the European Convention on Human Rights'.

What the newspaper can do

This book attempts in various chapters to assess the limits of the courts' power to restrict reporting. Court reporters should know these limits well enough in most cases to recognise where the court has made an order of dubious legality and to challenge the order as soon as possible. (See also chapter 17, 'Media could be ordered pay costs').

Approach by the reporter in court

Details are given in the following pages of High Court decisions on reporting restrictions and where possible case references are provided so that these can be drawn to the attention of the court. Attention is also drawn to the guidelines on reporting restrictions, issued by the Judicial Studies Board, to crown courts in 2000 and to magistrates courts in 2001.

In some cases, however all that is needed is for the reporter to make an informal request asking the court to state under which section of which Act the order has been made, and the court will reconsider the matter. On other occasions, the editor or news editor may have to write to the clerk or to the justices or the judge to achieve the desired result.

Lord Bingham, then Lord Chief Justice, said in the Queen's Bench Divisional Court in

2000, referring to a youth court's power to lift anonymity on offenders, that there was nothing which precluded the magistrates from hearing a representative of the press. It was likely if such a matter fell for consideration at all, that they would wish to hear from the press either orally or in writing. It seemed entirely proper for youth court magistrates to have asked the reporter present in court if he wished to say anything. 'Of course a reporter in that position does not enjoy formal rights of audience but it is within the experience of this court, and of other judges in other courts, that on occasion the observations of the press are invited, and that can be a valuable process since a reporter may well have a legitimate point to make and one which will save the court from falling into error.' (*McKerry v Teesdale and Wear Valley Justices* (2000) 164 JP 355, [2000] Crim LR 594). See also chapter 6, 'When youth court anonymity may be lifted'.

Wasted costs

Under the Courts Act 2003 the Lord Chancellor made regulations in 2004 allowing a magistrates court, a crown court and the Court of Appeal, to order a third party to pay costs where there has been serious misconduct, whether or not constituting contempt of court (Costs in Criminal Cases (General) (Amendment) Regulations 2004).

Even before the regulations were made, Mr Justice Sumner said in *A v Times Newspapers* in the Family Division ([2002] EWHC 2444 (Fam), [2003] 1 All ER 587) that if the media knew in advance that a hearing would be subject to restrictions but delayed applying for the restrictions to be lifted until after the hearing was started, thereby causing disruption, they risked an order for costs being made against them whether the application was successful or not. They were unlikely to incur the risk of adverse costs on such a prior application if they presented an arguable, though unsuccessful, case.

See also chapter 17, 'Media could be ordered to pay costs'.

Judicial review

If approaches to the court fail, a newspaper can itself initiate proceedings to challenge a court decision, although this can be costly.

Magistrates court orders, especially those made under sections 4 or 11 of the Contempt of Court Act 1981, have been challenged successfully in the Queen's Bench Divisional Court, which has power of judicial review over the actions of all inferior courts.

Section 159 appeal

Until 1989, orders made by crown courts to restrict reporting could not be challenged in a higher court.

Section 159 of the Criminal Justice Act 1988 provides a right of appeal to the Court of Appeal against a judge's decision to grant or refuse an application either to exclude the press and public at any time or to restrict reporting of a trial on indictment of any related ancillary proceedings.

'Any person aggrieved' (which includes newspapers) may appeal against an order made by a crown court judge:

(1) under sections 4 or 11 of the Contempt of Court Act 1981;

(2) restricting admission of the public to the proceedings or any part of the proceedings;

(3) restricting the reporting of the proceedings or part of the proceedings (eg orders under section 39 of the Children and Young Persons Act 1933).

Earlier, after an approach by Tim Crook, a journalist, and others, the European Commission on Human Rights had expressed the view that the lack of a method of appeal against a judge's secrecy order was a potential breach of human rights.

When section 159 came into force, however, it became apparent that it was not as big a step forward towards a more open system of justice as had been thought. The rules of procedure restrict the scope of any appeal.

Any challenge to a judge's ban on reporting must be by way of written representation. The press has no right to appear and argue its case. Leave to make the appeal must first be given by a single judge. The Queen's Bench Divisional Court held in 1993 that leave to appeal or the appeal itself would be decided by the Court of Appeal without a hearing.

The rules give the court, in these appeals, power to restrict the identification of a witness or any other person.

Another drawback is that by the time the Court of Appeal reaches its decision the trial may have finished, although the court does have the power to stop the trial until the appeal is decided. Even if the appeal is successful the newspaper will no longer get its costs. Formerly the Court of Appeal or the Queen's Bench Divisional Court had discretionary power to award costs out of central funds to successful appellants. In 1993 however the House of Lords ruled that there must be specific authority by Act of Parliament; discretionary powers were insufficient.

When the Queen's Bench Divisional Court held in 1995 in the course of judicial review that an industrial tribunal at Southampton had exceeded its powers in excluding reporters from a sexual harassment case, the INS agency and Express Newspapers, who had brought the case, were not awarded their costs, estimated at £10,000 (see chapter 11).

Invalid orders

Section 4 of the Contempt of Court Act 1981 allows courts to order the postponement of reports if this is necessary to avoid the substantial risk of prejudice (the *postponement* order). The High Court has emphasised that the risk must be substantial to justify an order being made (see below).

Section 11 gives power to the courts, when they withhold a name or other matter from being mentioned in public in their proceedings, to direct that the name or other matter should not be published (the *banning* order).

(See chapter 17, where the sections are explained, and the full wording of section 4 given.)

Where a court makes an order, the newspaper is under a duty to conform to it unless the court can be persuaded to lift or relax it. Mr Justice Eady said in 2002 that it was the plain and unqualified obligation of every person against, or in respect of whom, an order was made by a court of competent jurisdiction, to obey it unless and until that order was discharged. The uncompromising nature of this obligation was shown by the fact that it extended even to cases where the person affected believed it to be irregular, or even void. A person who knew of an order, whether null and void, regular or irregular, could not be permitted to disobey it. He should come to the court and not take it upon himself to determine such a question. As long as the order existed it must not be disobeyed (*Lakah Group and Ramy Lakah v Al Jazeera Satellite Channel* [2002] EWHC 2500, [2002] All ER (D) 383 (Nov) (QB)).

In 2004 the Judicial Committee of the Privy Council warned that regardless of the legality of an order, publication of matter likely to prejudice the administration of justice, particularly where a warning had been given in court, could still give rise to a contempt of court (*Independent Publishing Co Ltd v Attorney-General of Trindidad and Tobago* ((2004) Times, 24 June).

Section 4 orders

Lord Bingham, then Lord Chief Justice, said in 1999:

> Counsel has drawn attention to what the court accepts is a serious problem in some parts of the country: that orders restricting publication are made in situations where they should not be made. The problem is exacerbated in the ordinary run of cases where the story itself, although something which a local newspaper would wish to publish, is not the sort of story of the highest public interest such as to justify the expense by the newspaper of seeking to have the order rectified.

Lord Bingham stressed the necessity of very serious consideration being given before a section 4 order was made. (*Ex p News Group Newspapers* ([2002] EMLR 160.)

The Judicial Studies Board guidelines for magistrates say the court should exercise its discretion to make a section 4 order only after weighing the competing interests of open justice and fair trial. It should be slow to do so where the automatic restrictions under section 8 of the Magistrates' Courts Act 1980 apply.

Mr Justice (later Lord Chief Justice) Taylor in 1988 accepted that he had been wrong in making a section 4 order at Newcastle Crown Court *banning*, rather than postponing, publication of an allegation that a father accused of murdering his daughter's teacher had himself made sexual advances to the girl. The father was said to have believed that the teacher had been his daughter's lover. Counsel for the *Sun* newspaper said: 'It is plain that your lordship has made an order that is a prohibition—not a postponement—and that is not within your jurisdiction.'

The Queen's Bench Divisional Court held in 1992 that any court, including a magistrates court, had discretionary power to hear representations from the press when the court was considering making or continuing a section 4 order. It was implicit in section 4 that a court contemplating its use should be enabled to receive assistance from those who would, if there was no order, enjoy the right of reporting the proceedings. The media were the best qualified to represent the public interest in publicity, which the court had to take into account when performing any balancing exercise in weighing the public interest in open trial against the substantial risk of prejudice (*R v Clerkenwell Metropolitan Stipendiary Magistrates, ex p Telegraph plc* [1993] QB 462, [1993] 2 All ER 183).

Deciding if a section 4 order is necessary

Guidelines to crown court judges issued by the Judicial Studies Board in 2000 say: 'The court should exercise its discretion to make an order only after weighing the competing interests of open justice and fair trial.'

Lord Denning, Master of the Rolls, said of section 4 orders in 1982:

> At a trial judges are not influenced by what they may read in newspapers nor are the ordinary folk who sit on juries. They are good sensible people. They go by the evidence that is adduced before them and not by what they may have read in newspapers. The risk of their being influenced is so slight that it can usually be disregarded as insubstantial and therefore not the subject of an order. (*R v Horsham Justices, ex p Farquharson* [1982] QB 762, 794)

The Court of Appeal set out three principles on section 4 orders in *Ex p Telegraph Group* [2001] EWCA Crim 1075, [2001] 1 WLR 1983:

(1) Unless the perceived risk of prejudice is demonstrated no order should be made.

(2) The question has to be addressed of whether an order is necessary under the European Convention on Human Rights. Sometimes wider considerations of public policy will come into play to justify the refusal of a banning order even though there is no other way of eliminating the prejudice anticipated.

(3) Applications for postponement orders should be approached as follows: i) Whether reporting would give rise to a not insubstantial risk of prejudice. If not, that will be the end of the matter; ii) If such a risk is perceived to exist, would an order eliminate it? If not, obviously there can be no necessity to impose such a ban. However even if the judge is satisfied that an order would achieve the objective, he will have to consider whether the risk can satisfactorily be overcome by less restrictive means; iii) The judge might still have to ask whether the degree of risk contemplated should be regarded as tolerable in the sense of being the lesser of two evils.

In 1993 in the Court of Appeal the Lord Chief Justice said in determining whether publication of matter would cause a substantial risk of prejudice to a future trial, a court should credit the jury with the will and ability to abide by the judge's direction to decide the case only on the evidence before them. The court should also bear in mind that the staying power and detail of publicity, even in cases of notoriety, were limited and that the nature of a trial was to focus the jury's minds on the evidence put before them rather than on matters outside the courtroom (*Ex p Telegraph plc* [1993] 1 WLR 980 at 981 and 987, CA).

Lord Justice Farquharson said in 1991 that the fact that an accused expected to face a second indictment after the hearing of the first one did not in itself justify the making of a section 4 order. It depended on all the circumstances, including the nature of the charges, the timing of the second trial, and the place where that second trial was to be heard. If by an extension of the period between trials, or by the transfer to another court, substantial prejudice to the accused could be avoided then that course should be taken.

Later, Lord Justice Farquharson said if a judge's intention to make a section 4 order was announced suddenly, the press was not generally in a position to make any representations to the judge. The best course was for the judge to make a limited order under section 4 for, say, two days, and thus give the press time to make representations (*R v Beck, ex p Daily Telegraph* [1993] 2 All ER 177, 181).

Where a court fears that the jury in the current trial would be prejudiced by access to reports of the case which they are hearing, the court should be made aware that the Court of Appeal has acknowledged that there is an *insubstantial* risk of prejudice of a jury by media reports of the day's proceedings (*R v Horsham Justices, ex p Farquharson* [1982] QB 762).

In 1994 Mr Justice Lindsay refused to make a section 4 order postponing reporting of civil cases involving Maxwell pension funds to avoid prejudice to future criminal proceedings. He said: 'By framing (section 4) as it did, the legislature contemplated that a risk of prejudice which could not be described as substantial had to be tolerated as the price of an open press and that if the risk was properly to be described as substantial, a postponement order did not automatically follow' (*MGN Pension Trustees Ltd v Bank of America* [1995] 2 All ER 355 Ch D).

Section 4 cannot be used to restrict reports of events outside the courtroom, it was held in *R v Rhuddlan Justices, ex p HTV Ltd* [1986] Crim LR 329. The court held that the magistrates had acted outside their jurisdiction in making an order restraining a television programme about drug trafficking which showed a man being arrested. Lord Justice Watkins said the appropriate route where it was anticipated contempt by media publication was likely was an injunction to restrain the contempt. (See also chapter 17, 'Appeal. being lodged'.)

Practice direction

The Lord Chief Justice in a practice direction in 1982 said that a section 4 order must state the precise scope, the time at which it ceased to have effect, and the specific purpose of making the order. Precise written records must be kept of both section 4 and section 11 orders (*Practice Direction (Contempt of Court Act: Report of Proceedings: Postponement Orders)* [1983] 1 WLR 1475.)

The practice direction also said courts would normally give notice to the press that an order had been made and court staff should be prepared to answer any inquiry about a specific case. It would, however, remain the responsibility of reporters and their editors to avoid a breach of an order and to make inquiry in case of doubt. This guidance was repeated in 1990 in the Court of Appeal.

Many magistrates courts, purporting to make orders restricting reports, appear to have been unaware of the Lord Chief Justice's direction.

The reporter who is in any doubt should, as stated, try to find out from the court under which section of the Act an order has been made, and should then report the matter to his editor so that the validity of the order can be examined.

Section 11 orders

Orders under this section have often been made unnecessarily and judges and magistrates have sometimes acceded to applications by the press to lift or relax orders. The Queen's Bench Divisional Court held in 1985 that it was an essential part of British justice that cases should be tried in public and this consideration had to outweigh the individual interests of particular persons (*R v Central Criminal Court, ex p Crook* (1985) Times, 8 November). The Judicial Studies Board guidelines of 2001 to magistrates say sympathy for the accused or protection of his business interests are not good grounds. Similar guidelines for crown court judges, issued in 2000, say the court has discretion to hear representatives from the media or their legal representatives as to the making, variation or lifting of a section 11 order, and that a copy of the order should be available for inspection.

Has the name or address been withheld in the proceedings?

The first point on challenging a section 11 order may rest on whether the name or address has actually been available in the proceedings. Professor CJ Miller in *Contempt of Court* (3rd edn) says that if it has been available it is difficult to see how such an order can be anything other than a nullity.

In 1985 the divisional court held that a court had no power to make a section 11 order unless it first allowed the name to be withheld from the public during court proceedings. Reporting restrictions imposed by magistrates under section 11 were quashed because the name had been mentioned in open court (*R v Arundel Justices, ex p Westminster Press* [1985] 2 All ER 390, [1985] 1 WLR 708).

When the prosecution at Southwark Crown Court in 1999 of a man accused of theft from a prostitute applied for an order prohibiting publication of his name, address, and photograph, the application was successfully opposed by a barrister instructed by News Group Newspapers. He referred to the decision in *R v Arundel Justices*, mentioned earlier, and said the name and address had already been given in open court and were in the public domain. He said members of the public who received news of what happened in the courts through the media had equal rights with those members of the public able to attend court hearings. The recorder, refusing the order, said even if no one had been present in either the press box or the public gallery she would still have made the decision; all that mattered was that the name had been given in open court.

Lord Justice Watkins said in *R v Central Criminal Court*, mentioned earlier, that it was wholly illogical for an order to be made when a name was freely used in a public hearing.

Is the order necessary?

Lord Woolf, then Master of the Rolls, said in 1998 that any interference with the public nature of court proceedings was to be avoided unless justice required it. The foundation for exceptions was the need to avoid frustrating the ability of the courts to do justice. A witness who had no interest in the proceedings had the strongest claim to be protected by the court if he or she would be prejudiced by publicity since the courts might depend on his co-operation. A party could not be allowed to achieve anonymity by insisting upon it as a condition for being involved in the proceedings.

Disclosure of identity

Lord Woolf was speaking in a case in which a London firm of solicitors appealed against a judge's refusal to make a section 11 order forbidding disclosure of its identity when applying for judicial review of the Legal Aid Board's termination of its legal aid franchise. The Court of Appeal refused to allow a section 11 order and held there was no justification for singling out the legal profession for special treatment (*R v Legal Aid Board, ex p Kaim Todner* [1999] QB 966, [1998] 3 All ER 541, CA).

Defendant's address

In 1987 the divisional court held that, having regard to the principle of open justice, a court was not entitled to make a section 11 order preventing the publication of a defendant's address where the administration of justice did not require such confidentiality. The divisional court granted a declaration that Evesham justices were acting contrary to law in prohibiting the publication of a defendant's address because they felt he might be harassed again by his former wife. Lord Justice Watkins said there were many people facing criminal charges who for all manner of reasons would like to keep their identity unrevealed, their home address in particular. In the vast majority of cases, in magistrates courts anyway, defendants would like their identity unrevealed and would be capable of advancing seemingly plausible reasons why that should be so. Section 11 however was not enacted for the benefit of the comfort and feelings of defendants. He said that the general rule of open justice could be departed from only if, in the phrase used in *A-G v Leveller Magazine* mentioned earlier in this chapter, 'its application would frustrate or render impracticable the administration of justice' (*R v Evesham Justices, ex p McDonagh* [1988] QB 553, 562).

Risk to defendant

In 1997, the Queen's Bench Divisional Court in Belfast overturned a magistrate's order preventing the publication of the name and address of a man charged with indecent assault on the grounds that publication might put him at risk. Lord Justice McCollum said: 'A possible attack on the defendant by ill-intentioned persons cannot be regarded as a consequence of the publication of the proceedings of the court which should influence the court in its deliberations and the danger of its occurrence should not cause the court to depart from well-established principles' (*Re Belfast Telegraph Newspapers' Application* [1997] NI 309). See also chapter 11, 'Addresses of defendants' and chapter 35, 'Northern Ireland'.

Prevention of financial damage

The Queen's Bench Divisional Court held in 1990 that financial damage or damage to reputation or goodwill did not amount to special circumstances entitling a court to restrict press reporting. The court ruled that Dover magistrates had acted wrongly in making a section 11 order prohibiting publication of the identity of a person charged with public health offences (*R v Dover Justices, ex p Dover District Council and Wells* (1991) 156 JP 433).

Protection of vulnerable parties

In a few cases, the courts have held that embarrassment or other inhibitions arising out of medical conditions justified anonymity (*H v Ministry of Defence* [1991] 2 QB 103, [1991] 2 All ER 834 and *R v Criminal Injuries Compensation Board, ex p A* [1992] COD 379). In *H v Ministry of Defence*, the then Master of the Rolls, Lord Donaldson, said that in order that citizens be not deterred from seeking access to justice it was occasionally necessary to protect them from the consequences of public scrutiny of evidence and in particular medical evidence where scrutiny would prove not only embarrassing but positively damaging.

In 2003 the Court of Appeal exercised a general jurisdiction to restrict reporting on a new ground, based on the individual's personal protection and his right of access to the court. It ordered that the appeal of a man with mental problems against his conviction for manslaughter should be heard under reporting restrictions on the grounds of his vulnerability and the effect publicity would have on him. The court held that it was established law that no one should suffer the risk of physical or mental harm in exercising his legal right of access to court. Embarrassment or distress resulting from publicity was not a sufficient reason however. (*Re JCA* (13 November 2003, unreported)).

See also later this chapter, 'Obstructive courts', and chapter 35, 'Northern Ireland, identifying defendants'.

Exclusion orders

The powers of the various courts to exclude the press and public are explained in detail in chapter 11, 'Admission to the courts'.

In the first appeals in November 1989 under the section 159 procedure, journalist Tim Crook appealed against decisions by judges in two cases at the Old Bailey to exclude the public during submissions by counsel that the judge should make orders restricting the reporting of the trial itself.

The appeals were dismissed. The Lord Chief Justice said it was wholly appropriate for a judge to sit in private to receive information on a procedural matter.

Juveniles in adult courts

Under section 39 of the Children and Young Persons Act 1933 courts have the power to impose a ban on the identification of a juvenile under 18 'concerned in' proceedings in adult courts 'either as being the person by or against or in respect of whom the proceedings are taken, or as being a witness therein' (see chapter 6). Unlawful or unreasonable orders should be challenged.

In the criminal courts this power would be replaced by orders under section 45 of the Youth Justice and Criminal Evidence Act should the section be implemented. The section gives the court the power to prohibit publication while he is still under 18 of the name, address, school, or other educational establishment or workplace, or other matter leading to the identification of a minor under 18 involved in the proceedings, as being the person by or against or in respect of whom proceedings are being taken, or as being a witness, nor shall any picture of or including the person be published.

Section 39 orders would continue to be available to civil courts.

Some courts tend to make orders almost automatically when a juvenile is involved and fail to take notice of the guidelines on reporting restrictions issued by the Judicial Studies Board in 2001 which say that there must be a good reason for making a section 39 order. Other courts however have been open to persuasion such as where the offence is a serious one or where a youth almost 18 years of age is jointly charged with an older person with the same offence.

The main complaints have been about orders made when the child is dead, orders made prohibiting the identification of an adult—both of which are unlawful—and orders made in respect of children whose identity is already well known because of previous publicity, which is probably an unreasonable exercise of the court's discretion. (See also chapter 6, 'Offenders who attain their 18th birthday').

Lifting a section 39 order

Magistrates have sometimes said they do not have power to revoke or relax a section 39 order but the legality of lifting an order has been implicitly recognised by the higher courts in a number of cases in the Queen's Bench Divisional Court, such as *R v Central Criminal Court, ex p Simpkins* in 1998 (1998) Times, 26 October and *R v Crown Court at Manchester, ex p H* in 1999, [2000] 2 All ER 166, where the power to lift a section 39 order was not questioned.

Seven principles for section 39 orders

Lord Justice Simon Brown in *R v Crown Court at Winchester, ex p B* [2000] 1 Cr App Rep 11 identified seven principles to be considered when deciding whether to make a section 39 order. He said:

> The principles to be distilled from the various authorities can, I think, be fairly be summarised in this way (and substantially I use the language of other judgments):
>
> (1) In deciding whether to impose or to lift reporting restrictions, the court will consider whether there are good reasons for naming the defendant.
>
> (2) In reaching that decision, the court will give considerable weight to the age of the offender and the potential damage to the child or young person of public identification as a criminal before the offender has the benefit or burden of adulthood.
>
> (3) By virtue of section 44 of the Children and Young Persons Act 1933, the court must have regard to the welfare of the child or young person.
>
> (4) The prospect of being named in court with the accompanying disgrace is a power-

ful deterrent and the naming of the defendant in the context of his punishment serves as a deterrent to others. These deterrents are proper objectives for the court to seek.

(5) There is a strong public interest in open justice and in the public knowing as much as possible about what has happened in court, including the identity of those who have committed crime.

(6) The weight to be attributed to the different factors may shift at different stages of the proceedings, and, in particular, after the defendant has been found, or pleads, guilty and is sentenced. It may then be appropriate to place greater weight on the interest of the public in knowing the identity of those who have committed crimes, particularly serious and detestable crimes.

(7) The fact that an appeal has been made may be a material consideration.

Lord Justice Laws said in the Queen's Bench Divisional Court in 2001:

> If the order as drawn does not tell the journalist all that he is prohibited from doing, then the consequence must surely be that the order is altogether ineffective. To be sufficiently clear and unambiguous the order must leave no doubt in the mind of a reasonable reader or recipient as to precisely what is prohibited . . . Such orders constitute a significant curtailment of press freedom and courts have to be vigilant to see that they are justified and if made are clear and unambiguous.

Mr Justice Newman, concurring, said in the same case: 'In my own experience rarely (if ever) has a draft order been produced by the parties seeking such an order. A draft should be available for the court in every case. There will then be an opportunity to consider the ambit of the application the terms or the order and whether a pressing social need exists.' (*(1) Briffett (2) Bradshaw v DPP* [2001] EWHC Admin 841, (2001) 166 JP 66.)

Guidelines for crown court judges issued by the Judicial Studies Board in 2000 state: 'The power should not be exercised as a matter of routine but the court should balance the general requirement for open justice with the need to protect young people involved in the proceedings.'

See also chapter 6, 'Juveniles in adult courts'.

Court must have a good reason for making an order

In a judgment in the Queen's Bench Divisional Court in 1998 (*R v Central Criminal Court, ex p Simpkins*) Mr Justice Sullivan said previous cases were authorities for the fact that there must be a good reason for making an order and that in deciding that, the court would give considerable weight to the age of the offender. The divisional court upheld a decision by Judge Ann Goddard to lift, at the request of the South London Press, an order banning identification of three youths accused of indecent assault and rape. She had emphasised the potential deterrent effect on the defendants' peers of publication of their names.

Mr Justice Sullivan said he approved the approach in *R v Lee* ([1993] 2 All ER 170, [1993] 1 WLR 103, CA) when Lord Justice Lloyd, saying such orders should not be made automatically, added: 'There must be a good reason for making an order under section 39 . . . If the discretion under section 39 is too narrowly confined, we will be in danger of blurring the distinction between proceedings in the juvenile (now youth) court and proceedings in the crown court, a distinction which Parliament clearly intended to preserve.'

Mr Justice Sullivan rejected the contention in 1992 of Lord Justice Watkins who said that although reports should not be restricted unless there were reasons outweighing the legitimate interest in knowing the identity of those guilty of criminal conduct, the mere fact that a person before the court was a child or young person would normally be a good reason for the restriction and it would only be in rare and exceptional cases that the restriction would not be imposed (*R v Leicester Crown Court, ex p S* (1991) 94 Cr App Rep 153, 156). Mr Justice Sullivan said this reference to rare and exceptional cases placed unwarranted gloss on the requirements of the statute. There was a clear distinction between the position in the youth court where identification was prohibited and that of other courts where it was a matter of the court's discretion.

Lord Justice Rose in 2000 reasserted the importance of the difference between the youth court, with its presumption of anonymity, and other courts, where good reasons had to be shown for imposing restrictions. The Queen's Bench Divisional Court rejected appeals against Judge Ann Goddard's decision at the Old Bailey to lift a section 39 order giving anonymity to three young people who murdered a student by throwing him into the River Thames. Lord Justice Rose said: 'It is to my mind a matter of high materiality that Parliament has distinguished between youth courts on the one hand, in section 49, and courts more generally under section 39. This is a matter to which this court should have regard.' (*R v Central Criminal Court, ex p W, B and C* [2001] 1 Cr App Rep 7).

In the Court of Appeal case *R v Lee*, referred to above, the court gave its approval to the refusal of Judge Michael Coombe at the Old Bailey to continue a section 39 order in relation to a 14-year-old boy who took part in a robbery while on bail on a rape charge. Judge Coombe had said he could see no harm to the boy, and a powerful deterrent effect on his contemporaries, if his name and photograph were published. The public interest in knowing the identity of the boy outweighed any harm to the boy (*R v Lee* [1993] 2 All ER 170, [1993] 1 WLR 103).

In 1993, the Queen's Bench Divisional Court upheld a judge's refusal to continue a section 39 order. It was held that in a very serious case the naming of the offender in the context of the punishment inflicted on him should serve as a deterrent to others and this was a proper objective for the court. Considerable weight should also be given to the age of the offender and the potential damage to him of identification before he had the benefit or burden of adulthood. If a court did take all these considerations into account, the divisional court was unlikely to interfere with the decision to make or to decline to make an order ((1995) Times, 7 August).

Effect on relatives of juvenile

The effect of publicity on relatives of a juvenile in court was considered by Mr Justice Elias in the Queen's Bench Division administrative court in 2000. He said:

> It would be relevant to look at the effect on members of the family to the extent that it may exceptionally impact on the rehabilitation of the defendant himself. It seems to me however that in general it will not be appropriate to have regard to such considerations. Sadly, in any case where someone is caught up in the criminal process other members of the family who are wholly innocent of wrongdoing will be innocent casualties in the drama. They may suffer in all sorts of ways from the publicity given to another family member. But I do not consider that in the normal case that is a relevant factor or a good reason for granting a direction under section 39. I would not say categorically that it could never be factor. It may be that in a very exceptional case indeed it could be shown that there was some extremely damaging consequence to a member of the family, perhaps affecting their emotional or psychological well being beyond that which is the normal consequence of being connected with someone whose criminal activities are made public. .... There would in my judgment have to be very clear evidence of other considerations which the court would have to take into account. (*Chief Constable of Surrey v JHG and DHG* [2002] EWHC 1129 (Admin), [2002] All ER (D) 308 (May))

In 2002 Judge Ann Goddard sitting at the Old Bailey lifted a section 39 order on a 17-year-old youth who had been convicted of murder, after receiving a letter from Rachel Clifford, a reporter on the *Surrey Comet* newspaper. Judge Goddard said she was lifting the restriction not because it would act as further punishment but so that justice was seen to be carried out in the open. Doing so would act as a deterrent to others from making the same mistakes. She rejected a plea from the youth's mother to continue the order to shield the younger children of the youth's family.

Unreasonable orders

Sometimes the making of an order banning identification of minors under 18 has bordered on the absurd. In one case in 1994, after a woman had given a newspaper a story about her 14-year-old son being wrongly served with a summons to appear in court for not paying council tax, Birmingham magistrates made an order forbidding his identification in a report of the summons being withdrawn in court.

In 1996 Anne Rothwell, then editor of the *Lancaster Guardian*, persuaded a judge at Preston Crown Court to lift a section 39 order banning identification of a 13-year-old girl who had been attacked by a man wielding a rock and who had been named in news stories before her assailant was arrested. After the editor made representations, a court clerk told a reporter that the paper was free to name the girl, but the editor sought, and obtained, a formal lifting of the section 39 order in open court.

Often lawyers representing adult defendants request an order for their children when the motive is to protect the defendant from publicity. Newspapers have sometimes been able to persuade the bench that imposing such an order would merely protect the adult defendant. Paul Napier, editor of the *Banbury Guardian*, persuaded magistrates in 2000 to lift a section 39 order banning the identification of an 18-month-old child. He argued that the order would have protected only the defendant, the child's father who had pleaded guilty to being drunk in charge of a child. The chairman of the magistrates said: 'In our consideration a child at 18 months is too young and will not be prejudiced.' After Rachel Campey, then editor of the *Express and Echo*, Exeter, had successfully asked for such an order to be lifted in 1993, a court in the area later refused a prosecution application for a section 39 order in a case involving a man charged with assaulting his six-month-old son. The chairman of the bench said: 'A six-month-old baby cannot be affected by publicity. We would be protecting the defendant by stopping names going into the paper.'

Crown court judges may be even more open to persuasion. Judge Terence Maher at Aylesbury Crown Court in 2004 lifted a section 39 order banning identification of six-week-old baby whose father had thrown him against a wall. Daniel Jones, a *Milton Keynes News* reporter, wrote to the judge pointing out that a baby of that age could not be aware of the publicity and the order would serve only to protect the defendant. Judge Suzan Matthews at in 2004 rescinded an order she had made at Reading Crown Court banning the naming of an 18-month-old girl left blind and disabled by her father and said the order had been wrong in principle. The order had been challenged by Anita Howells, a reporter for the INS News Group, who had said the baby could not be affected by publicity at her age and the order was effectively giving anonymity to the accused.

The *Express and Star*, Wolverhampton, in 1993, challenged an order made in the case of a woman who admitted causing grievous bodily harm to her eight-month-old baby. Judge Richard Gibbs lifted the order he had made and said it was doubtful if a report carrying the woman's name would lead to the detriment of the child in the long term.

In 1994, a man was found in a fume-filled car with his two young sons. When he appeared in court at Tavistock in Devon, charged with the attempted murder of his sons, magistrates made a section 39 order forbidding identification of the boys, thus giving anonymity to the accused. At Plymouth Crown Court, however, the judge refused to renew the section 39 order after representations had been made by newspaper and broadcasting organisations. The mother of the boys had also opposed the order, so that the father did not escape publicity.

The guidelines issued by the Judicial Studies Board in 2001 say: 'Age alone is insufficient to justify the order. Courts have accepted that very young children cannot be harmed by publicity of which they will be unaware and therefore section 39 orders are unnecessary'. Later the guidelines say: 'Any adverse publicity is likely to have been a thing of the past before the child would even be aware of it.'

Unlawful orders

Dead children

Courts sometimes make section 39 orders attempting to ban the identification of dead children. In many cases, such a ban would prevent the reporter from covering the case adequately. But over the years several High Court judges have said the courts do not have this power. The guidelines issued to magistrates courts by the Judicial Studies Board say it has been held that orders cannot be made in respect of dead children.

Judge Grigson, imposing a section 39 order at the Old Bailey in 1994, said: 'The order I have made refers specifically to those children who are alive. I have no power to protect the dead and no power to prevent the publication of names of defendants.' The Court of Appeal later rejected a submission that Judge Grigson should not have made a section 39 order on living children because it would prevent the accused parents from being identified but did not challenge Judge Grigson's statement of the law on dead children (*Ex p Crook* [1995] 1 All ER 537, [1995] 1 WLR 139).

Sarah Leese, a reporter on the *Evening Chronicle*, Newcastle, in 2002 successfully challenged a section 39 order imposed by the North Tyneside Coroner on a 13-month-old baby who had died after allegations of neglect. The coroner had made the order ostensibly to protect the identity of a child in the family who was still living.

Mr Justice Bristow said at Warwick Crown Court in 1973: 'In my judgment, it (section 39) means that while you can order that the name should not be published if the child who is a victim of an attack is still alive, when the child is dead it does not apply.'

A court however may give *guidance* that publication of the name of a dead child could infringe a section 39 order made to protect living siblings, such as where parents are accused of further charges of cruelty.

Adult defendant

In 1991 the Court of Appeal held that section 39 orders could not be used to prohibit the publication of the name of an adult defendant. Lord Justice Glidewell said: 'In our view, section 39 as a matter of law does not empower a court to order in terms that the names of defendants should not be published. It may be that on occasions judges will think it helpful to have some discussion about the identification of particular details and give advice . . . In our view the order itself must be restricted to the terms of section 39(1), either specifically using these terms or using words to the like effect and no more. If the inevitable effect of making an order is that it is apparent that some details, including names of defendants, may not be published because publication would breach the order, that is the practical application of the order; it is not a part of the terms of the order itself' (*R v Southwark Crown Court, ex p Godwin* [1992] QB 190, [1991] 3 All ER 818). The guidelines issued by the Judicial Studies Board in 2001 say there is no power to impose restrictions to prevent the identification of adults involved in the proceedings, eg as defendants charged with, or witnesses of, offences against their own children, or witnessed by their children.

'Concerned in the proceedings'

Some courts have made orders purporting to ban the identification of children who were not 'concerned in the proceedings' as defined in section 39. In 1998 magistrates at Bingley, West Yorkshire, imposed a ban on the naming of a 14-year-old boy who was the subject of a row between his mother and his father's girlfriend. During the row the girlfriend punched the wife in the face. Magistrates rescinded the order when the editor of the *Bingley News*, Malcolm Hoddy, contacted the chief clerk.

Courts covered by an order

In *R v Lee* Lord Justice Lloyd said the words 'any proceedings' in section 39 must mean the proceedings in the court making the order and not any proceedings anywhere. His statement indicates that a section 39 order made in the magistrates court does not apply to reports of the case when it reaches crown court. A judge at crown court can make his own section 39 order however.

Procedure for making order

Procedures which the courts should follow when making orders were suggested by Lord Justice Glidewell in 1994 (*R v Central Criminal Court, ex p Godwin and Crook* [1995] 1 FLR 132).

He laid down three guidelines:

(1) The court should make it clear what the terms of the order are. If there is any possible doubt as to which child or children the order relates to, the judge or magistrate should identify the relevant child or children with clarity.

(2) A written copy of the order should be drawn up as soon as possible after the judge or magistrate has made it orally. A copy of the order should then be available in the court office for reporters to inspect.

(3) The fact that an order has been made should be communicated to those not present when it is made. For this purpose, court lists should include a reference to the order having been made at an earlier hearing.

Lord Justice Glidewell said a judge had complete discretion to allow those parties with a legitimate interest in the making of, or opposing the making of an order to make representations to him about it before he made it.

Lord Justice Lloyd said in the Court of Appeal in 1993 in *R v Lee* mentioned earlier that a member of the press who is aggrieved by a section 39 order should go back to the crown court in the event of any changes in circumstances.

Anti-social behaviour orders (Asbos)

There are two types of Asbo. An order prohibits repetition of objectionable conduct and can be made against anyone over 10 years of age.

Where the order is imposed by magistrates sitting in civil proceedings there is no automatic ban identifying juveniles involved, although one can be imposed under section 39 of the Children and Young Persons Act 1933.

Where the Asbo is imposed at youth court at the conclusion of proceedings at which the juvenile has been convicted of a criminal offence (known as a 'bolt-on' Asbo) there is also no ban on identifying the juvenile in the Asbo context, in the absence of a section 39 order. However the usual identity ban applies in reporting the preceding criminal proceedings, unless the youth court lifts the ban in the public interest, as it is permitted to under the amended section 49 of the Act (see chapter 6, 'When youth court anonymity may be lifted'). The party seeking the 'bolt-on' Asbo, such as the police or the local authority, may choose to repeat information given in the preceding criminal proceedings in saying why the order is necessary. However, unless anonymity is lifted it may be impossible to publish a complete report with names of the juvenile and a description of his criminal offence and of the misconduct that has given rise to the order.

The Minister of State at the Home Office, Hazel Blears, said in 2003: 'The purpose of publicising an Asbo is to enable victims, witnesses and the local community to assist local agencies to monitor compliance with the order. We recognise and appreciate the vital role the media can play in this.'

A regional editor who wrote to the Home Office in October 2004 about the difficulty in giving adequate publicity to a 'bolt-on' Asbo was told that legislation would be required to remedy the situation. The letter added: 'We are looking to introduce new legislation as soon as parliamentary time allows.' Disappointingly the Serious Organised Crime and Police Act makes no provision for the reporting of bolt-on Asbos.

Breach of the order is a criminal offence, usually dealt with at youth court and subject to the normal restrictions, unless they are lifted. However, under the Serious Organised Crime and Police Act the automatic anonymity does not apply to a breach of an Asbo dealt with in the youth court although it is open to the youth court to impose anonymity through an order under section 39 of the Children and Young Persons Act 1933. When the court does make a section 39 order, it is required to state its reasons.

When Asbos have been imposed in civil proceedings, newspapers, sometimes supported by the police, have asked the magistrates in civil proceedings not to make a section 39 order, in that it was in the public interest that the identity of the juvenile should be known in his neighbourhood. In 2000 a stipendiary magistrate (now district judge) at Norwich accepted a submission in behalf of the *Eastern Daily Press* that he should not impose a section 39 order on four juveniles who were the subject of an anti-social behaviour order, on the grounds that it was in the public interest not to do so.

Mr Justice Elias said in 2002 in *Chief Constable of Surrey v JHG and DHG* (see earlier this chapter: Effect on relatives of juvenile) that when a court was considering whether to impose or lift a section 39 order the general public interest in the public disclosure of court proceedings was reinforced, in some cases strongly reinforced, by the fact that the juvenile was subject to an Asbo.

There were, he said, two reasons for this. First, disclosure of the identity of the individuals might well assist in making an order efficacious. If people in the community were aware that the order had been made against individuals then it must improve the prospect of that order being effectively enforced. Any subsequent breach was more likely to be reported back to the authorities. Secondly, the very purpose of these orders was to protect the public from individuals who had committed conduct or behaviour that was wholly unacceptable and of an anti-social nature.

The public had a particular interest in knowing who in its midst had been responsible for such outrageous behaviour. This second factor did not in his view constitute simply 'naming and shaming' which Lord Bingham, then Lord Chief Justice, said would be difficult to justify in *McKerry v Teesdale and Wear Valley Justices* (see chapter 6, 'Public interest').

Mr Justice Wilson said in the Family Division in 2001 that in most cases it would be inappropriate for the magistrates court to ban identification by the press of a child who was the subject of an ASBO, as the efficacy of such orders would often depend upon the awareness of the local community of the identity of the person against whom the order had been made (*Medway Council v BBC* [2002] 1 FLR 104).

The guidelines issued by the Judicial Studies Board in 2001, referred to earlier, state: 'Unless the nuisance is extremely localised, enforcement of the order will normally depend upon the general public being aware of the order and of the identity of the person against whom the order is made.'

The Judicial Studies Board guidelines say that the Home Office and the Lord Chancellor's Department have encouraged the youth courts to use the power to enable media reports to identify young persons and children in appropriate circumstances and the Home Secretary has encouraged the media to make applications for its use (see Home Office/ Lord Chancellor's Department Joint Circular June 1998: *Opening up Youth Court Proceedings* and *The Youth Court 2001—the Changing Culture of the Youth Court: Good Practice Guide* issued by the Home Office and the Lord Chancellor's Department—March 2001).

Asbos and the Human Rights Act

The Queen's Bench Divisional Court in 2004 dismissed applications for a judicial review brought by six youths who claimed their rights to privacy had been breached by their identities being published when Asbos were made against them. Leaflets with their names and photographs, prepared by Brent Council in conjunction with the police, had been pushed through letterboxes of houses on two estates which the youths had terrorised with violence and intimidation. Lord Justice Kennedy said that a report in the local publication of the orders been made was intended to provide information and reassurance to all of the authority's tenants. The use of the this third medium for publicity could not be criticised.

Lord Justice Kennedy said in considering publicity for anti-social behaviour orders there was a need to have in mind the rights under the European Convention on Human Rights of those against whom orders were and the rights of the wider public including past and potential victims of anti-social behaviour. He added: 'Whether publicity is intended to inform, to reassure, to assist in enforcing the existing orders by policing, to inhibit the behaviour against whom the orders have been made, or to deter others, it is unlikely to be effective unless it includes photographs, names and at least partial addresses.' (*R (Stanley) v Commissioner of Police of the Metropolitan* (2004) Times, 22 October).

See also chapter 6, 'Anti-social behaviour orders against juveniles' and chapter 9.

Sexual offences

As detailed in chapter 8, the Sexual Offences (Amendment) Act 1992 prohibits the identification of complainants during their lifetime in most sexual offences, subject to some exceptions. The Act does not give a court power to impose any further restriction on reporting, such as an order prohibiting the identification of the defendant. Such an order purporting to have been made under the Act appears to be invalid. The newspaper is merely obliged to avoid publication of anything that identifies the complainant. Restrictions in the Act were widened by the Sexual Offences Act 2003 and by the implementation in 2004 of part of the Youth Justice and Criminal Evidence Act 1999, but neither Act gives power for any additional, discretionary, prohibition.

Mr Justice Aikens emphasised this at Maidstone crown court in 2004 when he said: 'The position in sexual offences is that defendants have no right of anonymity, even when they have been completely acquitted of the allegations.' (*R v Praill* [2004] *Media Lawyer* newsletter, November 2004).

He overturned an order by West Kent magistrates which had been confirmed by Judge Anthony Balston at crown court, to give anonymity to the chief executive of a charity who appeared one charge of rape and eight of indecent assault.

When the trial was reached, Mr Justice Aikens said it had been submitted that magistrates were entitled to make the order to protect the anonymity of the two complainants. He said he had received a very helpful letter and some oral submissions from Keith Hunt, a reporter with the *Kent Messenger* group, objecting to the order. The judge said he was satisfied the complainants' anonymity could be protected without an order being made which prevented the identification of the defendant or other details concerning him, or his place of work or the nature of his work: 'In my view the public has a right to know what went on in this trial, so long as the complainants' position is protected.' (See also *Re S (A Child) (Identification: Restrictions on Publication)* [2004] earlier this chapter.)

In another case, Mr Justice Aikens said Parliament had expressly provided in section 1(4) of the 1992 Act that there may be publication of a report of a trial in which the accused is charged with a sexual offence. This meant that while Parliament had forbidden the public from knowing the identity of the complainant, it had not placed any general reporting restrictions on trials of sexual offences. Parliament had not said there should be general restriction on reporting of intimate matters of evidence (*R v Burrell*, Central Criminal Court, 20 December 2004).

Also in 2004, a district judge at Cardiff magistrates court rejected a defence solicitor's attempt to get anonymity for a teacher charged with sexual offences against girls on the grounds that otherwise the girls would automatically be identified. District Judge Richard Williams said he had no power to make any order unless there was some justification. It was a matter of judgment for an editor as to whether to publish details of the defendants. The risk of identifying victims was higher in domestic cases than others. 'Those who publish are well aware of their statutory responsibilities. If they do something which falls foul of the Act there are criminal sanctions.'

The Act gives anonymity only during the complainant's lifetime, and where a person is accused of rape and murder the victim may be named. There is no power under the Act for the court to prohibit publication of the identification of the dead person.

Wards of court

The Court of Appeal in 1991 gave guidance to judges on how far injunctions should go in restricting publicity for wards of court. Lord Justice Neill said a distinction could be drawn between cases of mere curiosity and cases where the press was giving information or comment about matters of genuine public interest.

In almost every case, he said, the public interest in favour of publication could be satisfied without any identification of the child to persons other than those who already knew the facts. The injunction had to be in clear terms and had to be no wider than was necessary to achieve the purpose for which it was imposed (*Re M and N (Minors) (Wardship) (Publication of Information)* [1990] Fam 211, [1990] 1 All ER 205).

In 1989, a weekly newspaper, the *Rutland and Stamford Mercury*, successfully challenged the decision by a High Court judge not to lift an injunction restraining the paper from publishing an interview with a foster mother who had looked after two children since they were babies.

Kensington and Chelsea Borough Council had earlier obtained an injunction to stop the interview being used after social workers had removed the children from the woman and her husband without warning or explanation. Dame Elizabeth Butler-Sloss said the interest of the newspaper was not curiosity but public interest in the exercise of the power of a local authority.

The Court of Appeal ordered that the injunction be reworded so that the story could be used as long as the children, their school, and the family were not identified.

The Court of Appeal urged courts to ban publication of information concerning children only when necessary, to use precise terms, and give decisions in open court when possible. The Human Rights Act provides that if the journalist is not present when the application is made, the court must not grant the injunction unless it is satisfied either that the person seeking the injunction has taken all practicable steps to notify the journalist or that there are compelling reasons why the journalist should not be notified.

Central Television in 1994 successfully appealed in the Court of Appeal against an injunction banning the broadcast, without changes, of a programme on the work of the Obscene Publications Squad. The programme included pictures of a man who had been jailed for offences against boys. The mother of the man's child said this would identify her and the child. Lord Justice Neill said the balancing act between freedom of speech and the interests of the child became necessary only where the threatened publication touched matters which were of direct concern to the court in its supervisory role over the care and upbringing of the child. The press and broadcasters were entitled to publish the result of criminal proceedings. What should be left out was mainly an editorial decision.

The court should not restrain publication which was in no way concerned with the upbringing or care of a child but merely affected her indirectly. In the same case, Lord Justice Hoffmann said there was an inevitable tendency for a Family Division judge of the first instance to give too much weight to welfare and too little to freedom of speech and this was reflected in a number of successful appeals (*R v Central Independent Television* [1994] Fam 192, [1994] 3 All ER 641, CA).

In 2000, Mr Justice Munby held in the Family Division that the media did not require the leave of the court either to interview a ward of court or to publish such an interview. In publishing, the media would have to take care to avoid any breach of the other restraints (see above) but as long as they did that there was no contempt in interviewing a child known to be a ward of court (*Kelly v BBC* [2001] Fam 59, [2001] 1 All ER 323). In the same case, he said that in his opinion reports of wardship proceedings were subject to restrictions under the Children Act and the ward could not be identified except by permission of the court (see also chapter 6, 'Children in civil proceedings').

Obstructive courts

The court reporter's essential role can be made difficult and sometimes almost impossible if he does not receive minimum co-operation from court officials.

Magistrates courts

In 1989, the Home Office wrote to justices' clerks commending the practice of making available to the press court lists and, where they are prepared, provisional lists on the day of the hearing. For the details of the circular see chapter 4, 'Court lists'. The circular also recommended that courts supply local newspapers with copies of the court register, when prepared. The circular recommends that papers should be charged the full cost.

Crown courts

In 1989 also, the Lord Chancellor agreed that it was reasonable for the crown court to supply details of a defendant's address if it was available from the court record.

Chief clerks were instructed that where a defendant's address was given in open court the court clerk should note it in the file so that any request for the address, or to confirm it, could be readily dealt with.

Where the address was not given in open court, particular care had to be taken to ensure that it might properly be released, bearing in mind a number of factors. These included whether there was any order restricting reporting, whether the address was readily available, and whether there was confirmation that the address was current. (Reference CS3 (A) DL49/98/01.)

Court information and data protection

This subject is dealt with in chapter 33, 'Data Protection Acts'.

13

Divorce

Only a small percentage of divorce actions take place in open court, although the decree is pronounced in open court and may be reported.

When cases are heard in public there are restrictions on what the media may report (see the end of this chapter).

The spouse starting the proceedings is known as the petitioner. The petition is served on the other spouse, known as the respondent, who is required to state whether he or she intends to defend. If so, the respondent must file an answer.

Decree nisi

Divorce actions begin with either the wife or the husband lodging a petition at a county court after one year's marriage.

Later a list of petitioners granted a decree nisi (provisional decree of divorce) will be read out in court.

In the few cases where a divorce petition is contested, the action will normally be heard at a designated county court. Defended divorce cases are seldom tried in the High Court.

A decree nisi does not allow the parties to remarry. They can do this after the decree is made absolute (usually after six weeks) and the marriage is legally dissolved.

Any person may within 14 days of a decree nisi being pronounced inspect the certificate etc (see chapter 11).

Other decrees which can be awarded by the Family Division of the High Court are listed below.

Decree of nullity

This is awarded where the court rules there has been no valid marriage and for that reason there cannot be a divorce. A nullity decree may be awarded where there is inability or refusal to consummate the marriage; when a marriage has taken place without the real consent of either party, eg under duress; or when at the time of marriage either party was suffering from a venereal disease in a communicable form; or the wife was pregnant by another man and this was unknown to the petitioner at the time of the marriage.

Decree of judicial separation

This is usually sought where a man or woman for religious reasons feels there is a stigma in an actual divorce. It does not allow the parties to remarry, but can be granted only on proof of the same facts as a divorce would be. However it is necessary to wait until one year has elapsed from the marriage before filing a petition for judicial separation.

Decree of presumption of death

This is granted where either side has been absent for seven years or more and adequate efforts to trace him or her have failed. It is also more likely to be sought by those who feel divorce a stigma. If the other party reappears later, the decree still holds good.

The reporting restrictions

Under the Judicial Proceedings (Regulation of Reports) Act 1926, media reports of actions for divorce, nullity, or judicial separation have had to be confined to four points.
They are:

(1)   names, addresses, and occupations of the parties and witnesses;

(2)   a concise statement of the charges, the defence, and counter-charges in support of which evidence has been given (ie not abandoned charges or counter-charges);

(3)   submissions on any point of law arising in the course of the proceedings and the decision of the court; and

(4) the judgment of the court, and the observations of the judge.

No report can be published until all the evidence has been given in order to comply with (2) above, but once evidence is complete in defended cases, it is possible to publish a report within the restrictions.

Newspaper stories of the few defended divorce actions that take place are usually based on (4)—what is said by the judge—but reports of his remarks must be confined to what he says in giving judgment, rather than what is said during the hearing.

The Act of 1926 also imposed restrictions on what may be reported of indecent matter in any type of court. No report of any judicial proceedings may include any indecent matter, or indecent medical, surgical, or physiological details, the publication of which would be calculated to injure public morals.

What would injure public morals in 1926 might not necessarily be held to do so today, were there to be any prosecution.

The Attorney-General must give consent before there can be any prosecution.

In 1999, five Scottish newspapers were prosecuted for their reports of a divorce court action. The reports were said to contain particulars other than those permitted under the Act. The prosecution was the first in the United Kingdom under the Act. The reports contained lurid allegations from documents lodged in court, including claims of homosexual encounters, violence and theft. The charges were dismissed at Paisley Sheriffs Court on the technical grounds that publication had not taken place in the Paisley area but at the point where copies had been made available to wholesalers, and the offences had therefore taken place outside the court's jurisdiction.

Bankruptcy and company liquidation

Many bankruptcies are small affairs of limited news value. Others, however, are stories of wild extravagance at the expense of creditors or the accumulation of large bills for unpaid tax and some may involve criminal conduct, although there can be no prosecution for debt alone.

The Enterprise Act 2002 introduced what has been described as a more lenient regime for those made bankrupt. These changes came into effect on 1 April 2004 and, according to figures released by the Department of Trade and Industry's Insolvency Service, saw almost 12,000 people declare themselves bankrupt in the three months to the end of September 2004. This was a 31 per cent increase on the same period the previous year, although some of that increase was attributed to those who had waited for the new regime to come in before filing for bankruptcy.

Questions put in the public examination in bankruptcy (sometimes referred to as the bankruptcy court) of Mr John Poulson in 1972 led to the first substantial disclosures of corruption in the affairs of local councils and other public bodies, ending in jail sentences for several men.

Now, a public examination in bankruptcy is not held automatically. A public examination may be held however to give the creditors an opportunity to question the debtor, which they do not have at the meeting of creditors, held earlier.

Reporters should note the different procedures for companies and for individuals who are insolvent. Companies go into liquidation (see later in this chapter) while individuals become bankrupt.

A useful source of information on bankruptcy and insolvency for journalists is the website of the Department of Trade and Industry's Insolvency Service—http://www.insolvency.gov.uk/home.htm

Bankruptcy

In the case of an individual, either he, or his creditors, can file a petition at the county court for a bankruptcy order to be made by the district judge (formerly known as the registrar) if at least £750 is owed in unsecured debts. The Department of Trade has power to raise this figure at any time.

A bankruptcy order will then be granted by the district judge unless the debtor has made an offer which has been unreasonably refused. In place of a bankruptcy order, an individual voluntary arrangement may be made, where the debtor has assets exceeding £2,000 and debts not exceeding £20,000. In this case, the district judge may make only an interim bankruptcy order and may refer the matter to a licensed insolvency practitioner from a firm of accountants in the hope of avoiding bankruptcy through voluntary arrangements for a schedule for payment if the creditors agree.

Otherwise, after a bankruptcy order the official receiver (an officer of the Department of Trade and not of the court) takes over the legal control of all the debtor's property.

With his assistance, the debtor must within 21 days submit a statement of affairs setting out the assets, liabilities, and deficiency. When the prospects of the creditors getting a substantial proportion of what is owed to them are fairly bright, the creditors will appoint a licensed accountant as the trustee in bankruptcy who is responsible to the court for the management of the debtor's affairs. In this case, he and not the official receiver supervises the sale of any assets and the process of repayment.

Imputations of insolvency may be regarded as defamatory (see chapter 18: What is defamatory) and it is not safe for a newspaper to report the filing of a petition for a bankruptcy order (because of the danger of a libel action should the debtor be found to be solvent). The only exceptions to this occur when the debtor files his own petition, or when a bankruptcy order has been made and is open to public inspection (see chapter 11, 'Bankruptcy'), or when the newspaper quotes an announcement in the *London Gazette* that a bankruptcy order has been made, all of which would be protected by qualified privilege.

A creditors' meeting may be held. There is no statutory right for the press to attend. They can be admitted if the official receiver so rules, but the meeting can be a tricky one to report because it is not privileged.

Reporting bankruptcy court

A public examination in bankruptcy, which, as its name implies, can be attended by anyone, may be held next. The purpose of this is to satisfy the court that the full extent of the debtor's assets and liabilities are known, to establish the causes of his failure, to discover whether there has been any criminal offence, and to establish whether any assets transferred to another person ought to be recovered. However, as explained below under 'Discharge from bankruptcy', the changes of the Enterprise Act 2002 relaxed the obligations placed on the Official Receiver in this area.

Any transaction in the preceding two years can be declared void, unless it is a normal trading transaction. This can be extended to the preceding 10 years, if intention to deprive the creditors of their money is proved.

The examination usually takes place before the district judge. The debtor is examined by the official receiver or his assistant. If there is a trustee in a bankruptcy, he, or a lawyer representing him, may also ask questions. Otherwise any proven creditor may question the debtor.

Figures reflecting the size of the bankruptcy will emerge during the hearing—the liabilities, the assets, and, most important of all, the deficiency. The liabilities will usually include those due to employees who as preferential creditors are paid first out of any assets.

It may also be mentioned in the hearing that there are secured creditors, eg banks who have lent money on the strength of security, or those who have provided mortgages on property.

A public examination in bankruptcy may also take place after a judge has made an order following the conviction of a criminal. The purpose of this is to distribute the criminal's assets fairly among the victims of his theft or fraud. Examinations after criminal bankruptcy orders may take place in prison for security reasons.

Normally a public examination is closed, subject to the signing of the shorthand notes (a formality). It may, however, be adjourned for the result of further inquiries. Either way, the outcome at the end of the day is more important in a newspaper story than saying that the debtor was declared bankrupt, as in law he was bankrupt much earlier when the bankruptcy order was made.

A fair and accurate report of a public examination is protected by absolute privilege.

See also chapter 11, 'Bankruptcy'.

Effects of bankruptcy

These include the power of the official receiver to assume legal control over all the debtor's property, apart from basic domestic necessities and tools and other items necessary for his work.

The debtor cannot obtain credit for more than £250 without disclosing his bankruptcy, nor trade under any name other than that in which he went into bankruptcy without disclosing it. A bankrupt is not allowed to open new bank accounts. He cannot act as a company director nor take part in the management of any company without the leave of the court.

He cannot sit in Parliament or on a local authority, nor take any public office.

Discharge from bankruptcy

It is in this area that the changes introduced by the Enterprise Act 2002 have had the greatest effect. One of the aims of the legislation was to reduce the stigma attached to bankruptcy for those who were making a genuine effort to clear their debts.

Whereas in the past a bankruptcy would be discharged only after three years, as a result of the change in the law that period was reduced to 12 months. The effects of bankruptcy, listed above, remain the same, but end with the automatic discharge of the bankruptcy.

The new regime also relaxes the obligations placed on the official receiver to investigate a bankrupt's behaviour. A bankrupt can in some circumstances be discharged earlier than 12 months, if the official receiver files a certificate to the court saying the inquiry into the bankrupt's affairs has been concluded, or is unnecessary. As soon as the court receives such a certificate, the bankruptcy is discharged.

One effect of the changes in the law was that heavily-indebted students were able to use bankruptcy as a means of avoiding repayment of their student loans, including those owed to the Student Loans Company. This was a loophole closed by the Higher Education Act 2004, which the Department for Education and Skills said reflected the 'non-commercial nature of the debt.'

So those who behave responsibly and co-operate with the official receiver can have their bankruptcy discharged a lot earlier than in the past. On the other hand those who have recklessly incurred debt face severe penalties.

Someone who spends large amounts of money oblivious to the debts incurred could find himself the subject of a Bankruptcy Restriction Order. A Bro lasts anywhere between two and fifteen years and its effects include preventing a person subject to it obtaining more than £500 credit or becoming a company director. For example, if a debtor were to make excessive contributions into a pension scheme, in the knowledge that there was an impending bankruptcy, they might be likely to face a Bro, because the pension contributions might otherwise have been used to pay creditors.

Company liquidation

In reporting that a limited company has gone into liquidation, care should be taken to make the circumstances clear.

(1) A *members' voluntary liquidation* takes place where the company is solvent, but the directors decide to close down, possibly in the case of a small firm because of impending retirement, or because of a merger. To imply that such a company is in financial difficulties in this case is clearly defamatory.

(2) A *creditors' voluntary liquidation* takes place for the voluntary winding up to proceed under the supervision of a liquidator.

(3) A *compulsory liquidation* follows a hearing in public in the High Court or county court of a petition to wind up the company. This is usually because a creditor claims that the company is insolvent, but technically can also arise where a company fails to file its statutory report or hold its statutory meeting on being set up; where it does not start, or suspends, business; or where members of the company are reduced to below the number required in law. Once a winding-up order is made, a liquidator is appointed to collect the assets and pay off the creditors.

15

Inquests

The office of coroner is one of the most ancient in English law. A coroner must be a barrister, solicitor, or doctor of at least five years' standing.

Although proposals have often been made to reduce the scope of coroners' inquests—see later in this chapter for proposed reform—they continue to be held to inquire into violent, unnatural, or sudden deaths, or into deaths which take place in some forms of custody.

A coroner decides, after an investigation and a post-mortem examination, whether an inquest should be held into a sudden or unnatural death or death due to an unknown cause. He decides which witnesses are to appear and what questions should be asked of them by him or by others. He may dispense with an inquest if an autopsy shows that a sudden death was due to natural causes. About 200,000 deaths per year are reported to coroners: 120,000 of those deaths require post mortems and 20,000 require an inquest hearing.

A coroner has the right at common law to take possession of a body until after his inquest has been completed.

An inquest is inquisitorial in its procedure—unlike the criminal court, where the process is accusatorial and is therefore subject to strict rules in the interests of justice. The coroner will lead witnesses through their evidence, unlike a criminal trial where leading witnesses is usually forbidden. The inquisitorial nature of proceedings also manifests itself when coroners often allow family members and other interested parties, although not reporters, to ask questions of witnesses at the end of their evidence.

The Coroners Rules 1984 regulate proceedings at inquests to some extent.

The purpose of an inquest is to find out:

(1) who the deceased was;

(2) how, when, and where he met his death;

(3) the particulars to be registered.

A coroner's jury may not return a verdict of murder, manslaughter, or infanticide against a named person. The Coroners Rules also forbid a rider to the jury's verdict which appears to determine liability in civil law or in criminal law. In 1994 the Court of Appeal ruled that it was not the function of an inquest jury to attribute blame or to express judgment or opinion. To do so would be unfair to those who might face criminal proceedings. However in 2002 the Court of Appeal held that the rules did not prevent a jury finding neglect if that identified a failure in the system and reduced the risk of repetition. The rules only prevented an individual being named.

However, in the cases of *R (Middleton) v West Somerset Coroner* ([2004] UKHL 10) and *R (Sacker) v West Yorkshire Coroner* ([2004] UKHL 11) it was ruled that an inquest should allow a jury to express a brief conclusion of the disputed facts at the centre of the case. This change of interpretation was required to comply with article 2 of the European Convention on Human Rights—right to life. So a jury is able to decide not just 'by what means' a person died but 'in what circumstances' as well.

Where a person is suspected of crime in connection with a death, an inquest is usually opened simply to obtain evidence of identity and cause of death, and is adjourned until after these proceedings have been completed. However, it is sometimes the case that an inquest may precede court proceedings. In such an event, in the absence of an order made by the coroner restricting reports, the media may report such proceedings, irrespective of their impact on any subsequent trial, free from fear of an action for contempt of court. However, see also chapter 17, 'Media could be ordered to pay costs'. If a trial had to be relocated as a result of a report of an inquest, even though such a report, in the absence of a postponement order could not be in contempt of court, it is possible a paper could be ordered to pay wasted costs.

If a public inquiry conducted by a judge (usually into a disaster involving a number of deaths) is to be held, the Lord Chancellor may direct under the Access to Justice Act 1999 that the inquest should be adjourned. It will not be reopened unless there are special reasons.

The Court of Appeal held in 1982 that a coroner must hold an inquest where it was believed that a person had died a violent or unnatural death abroad and the body had been brought back to that coroner's territory.

A jury of at least seven and not more than eleven may sit at inquests. Under the Coroners Act 1988, a jury must be summoned when there is reason to suspect that death occurred in circumstances the continuance or possible recurrence of which is prejudicial to the health or safety of the public. A jury is not compulsory for a road accident inquest.

It has become the convention to report that a coroner's jury *returns* a verdict and that a coroner sitting without a jury *records* a verdict.

Whereas in the past short verdicts of suicide, misadventure, unlawful killing and so on have been returned or recorded, it is now open for a coroner or jury to record or return a 'narrative verdict'. This will be a short statement detailing the circumstances in which a person died.

Fair, accurate, and contemporaneous reports of inquest proceedings held in public are protected by absolute privilege.

Rule 17 of the Coroners Rules says that every inquest should be held in public save that any inquest or part of an inquest may be held in private in the interests of national security. The Queen's Bench Divisional Court held in 1998 that an inquest remained public even when a member of a police armed response unit was allowed to give evidence behind a screen (*R v Newcastle-upon-Tyne Coroner, ex p A* (1998) Times, 19 January).

Another rule, rule 37, allows a coroner to take documentary rather than oral evidence from any witness where such evidence is unlikely to be disputed. The rule provides that the coroner must announce publicly at the inquest the name of the person giving documentary evidence and must, unless he otherwise directs, read aloud such evidence. The effect of this is that a coroner who is so minded can lawfully prevent the press and public from learning the contents of that evidence.

It has been the custom of coroners not to read out suicide notes and psychiatric reports. However, there have been cases where mobile phone text messages sent by people shortly before they took their own life were read out at their inquest. In an inquest held in Louth in 2004 a series of text messages sent by a woman to her ex-lover and relatives before she drove her car into a lorry were used as proof of her intent to take her own life.

A Home Office circular in May 1980 urged coroners to make arrangements to ensure that the press were properly informed of all inquests. A reminder was sent out in 1987. This duty often falls to the coroner's officer—a police officer attached to the coroner's office on a full or, occasionally, part-time basis. It is worthwhile for journalists to make contact with these officers on a regular basis as they can render great assistance in finding out timings of inquests.

However, in 2003 the actress Laura Sadler, one of the stars of the BBC series *Holby City*, fell to her death from the balcony of a flat. The inquest was held by way of reference to documentation only and no witnesses were summoned and no representatives of the media were present, having not been notified that the inquest was taking place. This was claimed to have been an oversight. A verdict of accidental death was recorded.

Subsequent inquiries by newspapers resulted in a statement from Hammersmith and Fulham Council, where the inquest was held, which revealed that post mortem tests had found traces of alcohol, cocaine derivatives and diazepam in her body.

While the Home Office circular is clear, it is advisable for journalists interested in particular deaths to make regular calls to coroners' officers in order to keep track of when the full hearing is likely to take place.

Contempt of coroner's court

In 1985, six police officers obtained an injunction to restrain London Weekend Television from broadcasting a filmed reconstruction of events surrounding the arrest and sub-sequent death in police custody of a Hell's Angel. The injunction was granted on the ground that the broadcast would amount to contempt of an inquest, due to be resumed. In rejecting the television company's appeal against the injunction, the Court of Appeal held that proceedings become active for contempt purposes as soon as a coroner has opened an inquest (see chapter 17).

Judicial review

There is no direct right of appeal from a verdict at an inquest into a death, but an applica-tion may be made to the High Court for an order to quash a verdict and to order a fresh inquest where it is necessary or desirable in the interests of justice. This application is sometimes made by relatives aggrieved by a verdict that the deceased took his own life. The consent of the Attorney-General must be obtained before such a request can be made.

Reform

Following the mass murders of the GP Harold Shipman—who was able to certify the deaths of his victims himself, thus avoiding an inquest—weaknesses were perceived in the current system for certifying deaths and conducting inquests. In March 2004 the Home Office published a position paper outlining proposals for reform of the service. The proposed new system would have legally-qualified coroners, supported by appropriate medical expertise, and death certification would be subject to increased medical scrutiny.

Under the proposed reforms all deaths would be reported to the coroner service and would be examined by a medical team.

The reforms suggested in the paper include:

- the creation of one jurisdiction for England and Wales, sub-divided into local coroner areas, with each area staffed by a full-time coroner, medical examiner and coroners' officers;

- a reduction in the number of coroners from 127 to between 40 and 60;

- the appointment of a chief coroner, answerable to the courts, with responsibility for deployment of coroners, standards and oversight of complex inquests;

- increased powers of coroners to enter premises and seize documents;

- a reduction in the maximum size of a coroner's jury from 11 to nine;

- the system of narrative verdicts mentioned earlier in the chapter should replace the old system of short verdicts.

The position paper says that inquests should remain a public hearing, and that the suggestion that certain inquests should not be held in public is difficult to reconcile with the principle of open justice. However, the Home Office has said it would welcome further views on what it regards as a 'finely-balanced issue.' The Coroners' Society of England and Wales said it would welcome the opportunity for coroners to order greater privacy in order to protect grieving families, or to enable greater publicity for families wanting more openness. The Society also called for deaths by suicide not to be routinely made subject of an inquest in order to protect the privacy of the bereaved.

The discussion paper proposed a white paper and draft bill within a year.

Treasure trove

Inquests are sometimes held into findings of objects at least 300 years old containing a substantial proportion of gold and silver or of other valuables where the owner or his known dependants cannot be traced. This function dates back to the coroner's oldest responsibilities as a representative of the crown. Under the Treasure Act 1996, finders of such coins and other objects must report the finding to the coroner for the district within 14 days. The coroner will normally ask the finder to take the objects to a local museum, which is then required to inform the British Museum or the National Museum and Galleries of Wales. If the museum wishes to acquire all or part of the find (at full market value), the coroner will hold an inquest to decide whether it is treasure. The finder will receive a reward and landowners and occupiers of land may also be eligible for rewards. If no museum wishes to acquire the find, the coroner returns the objects to the finders.

However, under the reforms mentioned above it was said that the responsibility for investigating treasure 'sits uneasily' with the investigation of deaths. Options for change suggested include a small number of coroners dealing specifically with treasure cases; another judicial officer or organisation dealing with them, or a single coroner conducting all treasure inquests on a national basis.

Tribunals and inquiries

We must now look at the functions of administrative tribunals and ministerial inquiries, and the relationship of the press to them.

Tribunals

Tribunals are bodies, other than the normal courts we have already studied, that adjudicate in disputes or determine legal rights.

There are about 78 types of tribunals, and about 2,000 tribunals, and the tendency is for them to multiply and to become more important. Indeed, Lord Falconer, when addressing the annual conference of the Council on Tribunals, shortly after planned reforms to the system were announced in the Queen's Speech in 2004, made the point that there were probably more hearings in tribunals than there are in courts. The ordinary courts often do not have the specialised experience to deal adequately with disputes that arise as a result of developments in the law. Parliament also considers that tribunals can be cheaper, quicker, and less formal.

Tribunals are concerned with a wide variety of matters, including industrial disputes, land and property, national insurance, income support, the National Health Service, transport, and taxation. They vary so much it is difficult to classify them.

Most have an uneven number of members, so that a majority decision can be reached.

Most members are appointed by the minister concerned with the subject, but where a lawyer chairman or member is required the Lord Chancellor generally makes the appointment.

In most cases, members hold office for a specified period.

There is a right of appeal, at least on a point of law, from the most important tribunals to the Divisional Court or Court of Appeal. This enables the individual to challenge ministerial and tribunal decisions in the courts.

In exceptional circumstances, the Divisional Court or Court of Appeal decisions may be challenged in the House of Lords.

An appeal may also be made to a specially constructed appeal tribunal, to a Minister of the Crown, or to an independent referee (depending upon the standing and the function of the tribunal).

The Council on Tribunals, a permanent body appointed by the Lord Chancellor and the Lord Advocate for Scotland, exercises general supervision over tribunals and reports on particular matters. It was set up by Act of Parliament in 1958 and is now governed by the Tribunals and Inquiries Act 1992, passed to consolidate a series of changes to earlier legislation.

Under the Act, a tribunal must, if requested, furnish a statement of the reasons for the decision reached.

Most tribunals are set up by an Act of Parliament or under a statutory instrument. As a result, a fair and accurate account of the proceedings of those tribunals, even if it contains defamatory statements, enjoys the protection of qualified privilege, subject to a statement by way of explanation or contradiction (see chapter 20, 'Qualified privilege').

A characteristic of most tribunals is informality. The chairman might not be a lawyer, and the parties might not be represented. As a result, many things might be said during fierce exchanges between the parties that are not strictly relevant to the decision being made and that would not be allowed in an ordinary court.

It is therefore important to remember, when covering the proceedings of tribunals, that qualified privilege does not extend to 'any matter which is not of public concern and the publication of which is not for the public benefit'.

The reporting of some tribunals may be covered by absolute privilege. The Defamation Act 1996 provides absolute privilege for a fair, accurate, and contemporaneous account of proceedings in public of 'any tribunal or body exercising the judicial power of the state'.

What of contempt of court? Is it possible for a newspaper to be in contempt as a result of publishing matter that might prejudice proceedings in a tribunal? The question is a difficult one, for judges as well as journalists. The Contempt of Court Act 1981 states that a 'court', for the purposes of the Act, includes any tribunal or body exercising the judicial power of the state.

In *A-G v BBC* [1981] AC 303, the House of Lords agreed that a local valuation court could not be protected in this way. Although it was called a 'court', its functions were essentially administrative, and it was not a court of law established to exercise judicial power.

Another tribunal that is not a court, but for a different reason, is the professional conduct committee of the General Medical Council. In *General Medical Council v BBC* [1998] 3 All ER 426 the Court of Appeal said the committee was exercising a sort of judicial power, but it was not the judicial power of the state.

In *Pickering v Liverpool Daily Post* [1991] 2 AC 370, the Court of Appeal agreed that a mental health review tribunal was a court.

Lord Donaldson, Master of the Rolls, said the power of the tribunal to restore a person to liberty was a classic exercise of judicial power.

In *Peach Grey & Co v Sommers* [1995] 2 All ER 513 the Queen's Bench Divisional Court decided it had the power to punish contempt of an industrial tribunal—now called 'employment tribunal'—which, Lord Justice Rose said, appeared to exercise a 'judicial function'.

Suppose information is disclosed at a tribunal hearing and the publication of that information in a newspaper would prejudice a trial or an inquest. If the tribunal is a 'court' under the terms of the 1981 Act it must make a section 4 order, to postpone reporting of that information. Otherwise the journalist is free to report – provided he does so in good faith. If the tribunal is not a court it has no power to make a section 4 order, but the journalist risks prosecution if he publishes prejudicial matter (see chapter 17).

The journalist should distinguish between an ordinary tribunal and a tribunal of inquiry set up—though this is rare—under the Tribunals of Inquiry (Evidence) Act 1921. In the latter case, newspaper conduct likely to prejudice the inquiry can lead to contempt proceedings (see chapter 24; references to the Vassall tribunal and Bloody Sunday tribunal).

We mention below some of the more important tribunals the reporter may have to attend. In all cases mentioned, a fair and accurate report has privilege, certainly qualified and perhaps absolute.

Employment tribunals provide a large number of good stories relating to such matters as complaints of unfair dismissal, sexual or racial discrimination at work, or exclusion from a trade union; disputes over contracts of employment, redundancy payments, or health and safety at work; and claims to equal pay. The difficulties involved in covering these tribunals are common to many tribunals.

Tribunals sit at 24 permanent centres in England and Wales, or in hired accommodation. About 50 tribunals sit each working day.

It seems likely, in view of the case of *Peach Grey* mentioned above, that a fair, accurate and contemporaneous report of an employment tribunal will be covered by absolute privilege. But 'judicial function' is not necessarily the same as the 'judicial power of the state', the requirement of the 1996 Defamation Act.

Procedure The hearings at employment tribunals tend to be informal and vary according to the chairman. Some chairmen announce at the start of the hearing the details of the claim and then establish the essential facts, but others plunge straight into matters of detail.

Many fail to ask such basic details as the applicant's first name, age, and address, and sometimes do not read out relevant documents. These details have to be obtained from court officials, who are generally helpful (see 'Access to information', below), or the parties themselves. It is normal practice for witnesses to confirm their names and addresses before giving evidence.

Sometimes there is an opening speech, similar to that given in a court of law. Note, however, that the case is not necessarily opened by the claimant (or applicant), as it is in a civil law action. In unfair dismissal claims where dismissal is admitted, it is usually up to the employer to prove the dismissal was fair and thus to present his case first. Where the dismissal is denied, the employee usually starts first—although which course is taken is within the discretion of the tribunal.

At the end of the hearing the three tribunal members can either:

(1) reserve their decision and publish it later;

(2) give a decision with basic reasons and publish a full reasoned decision later;

(3) give their decision and reasons in public at once.

Many employers are represented by solicitors or counsel, or possibly by a senior executive. Many applicants bring their cases with the help of their trade union and have their case presented by union officials or solicitors.

There is often considerable bitterness and applicants are sometimes extremely suspicious of the press. Because the parties sometimes have to be approached for follow-up details, reporters may encounter hostility from applicants who think that because they have seen the reporter talking to the employers' representatives he is 'on their side'.

Reports are read with the greatest suspicion and complaints may be made stemming partly from the parties' ignorance of court procedure. For example, where a case has been adjourned and it has been possible to report only one side because only that side has been heard, a complaint may be made that the report was 'one-sided'. Similarly, a small discrepancy in the name of a company (this can arise easily where there is a network of subsidiaries) is pounced upon by the employers.

The safeguard against complaint is, as always, a good shorthand note of the proceedings, accurate transcription of names from lists and from informants when checking, and care in writing.

The tribunal can require a party to provide a written answer to any question.

A tribunal may hold pre-hearing reviews in some cases and if the tribunal considers the arguments of any party have no reasonable prospect of success it may order that party to pay a deposit of up to £150 as a condition of being allowed to bring or to continue to contest the proceedings.

Admission Employment tribunals must normally sit in public, but there are exceptions (see chapter 11, 'Employment tribunals').

Tribunals have sat in private where details about a burglar alarm installation would have to be given and where evidence about police reports was necessary.

(See chapter 11 for an example of a tribunal hearing that a court decided was *not* held in public when it should have been.)

Access to information During 1984, instructions were issued to the staff of industrial tribunals (as they were then called) restricting the information they were allowed to give to the press. After representations by media bodies these instructions were amended to provide for staff to give full addresses to a reporter on request on the day of the hearing; and to issue a reserved decision of a tribunal on application by a reporter in respect of a specific case whether or not the reporter was present at the hearing.

In 2004 changes were made to the details recorded on the register of applications, appeals and decisions at the central office of the employment tribunals. Until October of that year it was a requirement that they must contain the name of the applicant, the name of the respondent, the date the application was made and received, the relief sought, and a summary of each of the grounds of the claim which would be sufficient to enable any member of the public exercising the right of inspection to identify the gist of those grounds (*R v Secretary of the Central Office of the Employment Tribunals (England and Wales), ex p Public Concern at Work* [2000] IRLR 658).

However, following consultation by the Department of Trade and Industry, details of applications to employment tribunals have been taken off the public register. Details of claims and responses to those claims have been removed. Where parties have reached a settlement before a tribunal announces its decision the details of the settlement will also not appear on the register.

Among the reasons given for this change were that individuals were receiving approaches from 'ambulance-chasers'. Furthermore, unions consulted were concerned that the register was being used for blacklist purposes.

The DTI has said that although the details are not on the public register, journalists would be able to obtain them once a case had been listed for hearing.

The Society of Editors expressed concern at this change, coming as it did just three months before the implementation of the Freedom of Information Act. The Society pointed out that while it might not stop reporting of tribunals, it would make it more difficult and increase the risk of mistakes.

Cases involving sexual misconduct Under the Trade Union Reform and Employment Rights Act 1993, employment tribunals have the power to impose temporary anonymity orders (known as restricted reporting orders) in cases involving allegations of sexual misconduct.

Sexual misconduct includes sexual offences, defined in accordance with the Sexual Offences (Amendment) Act 1976 (rape offences) and the Sexual Offences (Amendment) Act 1992 (other sexual offences) and also sexual harassment or other adverse conduct (of whatever nature) related to sex.

An order can be made on an application by a party or on the tribunal's own initiative. It can be made at any time before promulgation of its decision (the date the notice announcing the tribunal's decision is sent to the parties).

The tribunal must give 'each party' an opportunity to speak on such an application, but the press has no right to speak and if it wishes to do so must rely on the tribunal's discretion. In 1997, in a case where a policewoman accused a male officer of sexual harassment, the press was banned from identifying the accused, the accuser, and the witnesses. The tribunal at first declined to allow the press to challenge the order, but later heard counsel for the *Yorkshire Evening Post* and agreed that some of the witnesses could be named.

In 1997 also the Court of Appeal said it was important that tribunals should recognise that their power to make such orders was not to be exercised automatically at the request of one party, or even at the request of both parties (*Kearney v Smith New Court Securities*). 'The employment tribunal still has to consider whether it is in the public interest that the press should be deprived of the right to communicate information to the public if it becomes available. It is not a matter which is to be dealt with on the nod, so to speak.'

In some cases a tribunal has taken account of previous publicity in refusing to make a restricted reporting order. In 2000 a Glasgow employment tribunal refused to make such an order in a case of a businessman accused of sexual harassment. Both parties wanted the order to be placed, but the Daily Record successfully argued that both parties had previously willingly given information to the press. The tribunal's decision was later confirmed by the Employment Appeals Tribunal

The order must specify the people who must not be identified, who can include any person affected by or making the allegations (which can include alleged perpetrators, witnesses and complainants).

The order remains in force until the promulgation of the decision unless the tribunal has revoked the order earlier. Promulgation can be weeks or months after the decision is reached.

This can give rise to a situation that was the subject of a challenge by the National Union of Journalists (NUJ) in 2004 in a case where a woman was claiming sexual harassment by her employers. Where a restricted reporting order is placed on a tribunal but a settlement is reached before the full hearing the reporting restriction will remain in place indefinitely. This is unless, as was the case here, the tribunal lifts the restriction upon application by the press, or it treats the settlement as its promulgated decision.

It is a criminal offence to breach a restricted reporting order, and a publisher who committed such a breach could be fined up to £5,000.

The NUJ has made representations to the DTI that, where a case was settled, that settlement should be deemed to be the decision, automatically lifting the restrictions.

A notice must be displayed indicating the making of the order and placed on the tribunal's notice board and on the door of the room in which the tribunal is being conducted.

Suppose a woman suing for unfair dismissal claims she was indecently assaulted by her employer. The tribunal makes a restricted reporting order prohibiting identification of the woman or her employer. After the promulgation order you can lawfully identify the employer, but remember that you still cannot identify the complainant because she is protected by the Sexual Offences (Amendment) Act 1992, unless she gives her written consent to be named.

Breach of an order will be a summary offence punishable by a fine.

In addition, in cases that involve sexual offences, tribunals will be able to remove permanently from the documents available to the public any information that would identify any person making or affected by the allegations.

Cases involving disability Employment tribunals can make broadly similar banning orders when considering complaints in respect of unlawful discrimination in employment on disability grounds. The Disability Discrimination Act 1995 says a disability is a physical or mental impairment which has a substantial and long-term effect.

The tribunal can make an order in proceedings in which 'evidence of a personal nature' is likely to be heard, and that means 'any evidence of a medical, or other intimate, nature which might reasonably be assumed to be likely to cause significant embarrassment to the complainant if reported'.

The tribunal can make an order either if the complainant applies for one or on its own initiative. By contrast with cases involving sexual misconduct, in these cases the person or company against whom the complaint is being made cannot apply for an order to be made, but the tribunal has unlimited discretion as to the people it names in the order.

Where the tribunal makes a restricted reporting order and that complaint is being dealt with together with any other proceedings, the tribunal may direct that the order applies also in relation to those other proceedings.

As with cases involving sexual misconduct, the parties must be allowed to make representations before an order is made, but again the press has no right to be heard. The order remains in force until the decision is promulgated.

Appeals Appeals from employment tribunals are heard by the Employment Appeal Tribunal, which sits in London. There are often three 'courts' sitting, each presided over by a High Court judge sitting with lay judges from both sides of industry.

Although still informal compared with a normal court of law, the appeal tribunal hearings are more set in procedure, and parties are more likely to be represented. The court gives reasons for its decisions.

Appeal tribunals frequently produce interesting stories, because the cases tend to be ones regarded as important or difficult.

Under the Employment Protection Act 1975, Schedule 6, the appeal tribunal can sit in private in the same circumstances as employment tribunals (see chapter 11, 'Employment tribunals').

Rent assessment committees hear appeals against fair rents fixed by a rent officer for regulated tenancies and can determine a market rent in certain circumstances for assured and assured short-hold tenancies. Regulated tenancies are, broadly speaking, those lettings by non-resident private landlords that began before 15 January 1989. Assured and assured short-hold tenancies are such lettings that began on or after that date. Hearings are open to the public unless for 'special reasons'—which are not defined—the committee decides otherwise.

Rent tribunals register reasonable rents for restricted contract lettings. These are, broadly, lettings by private landlords living on the same premises as the tenant that were created before 15 January 1989. If the tribunal is asked by one of the parties to sit in public, it has discretion whether or not to do so.

Valuation tribunals hear appeals against the valuation of non-domestic property assessed by valuation officers and against the valuation of domestic property by listing officers—the same people wearing different hats. Upon these valuations are based payments to the local authorities. People may appeal if they believe that their property has been wrongly valued, that they are not liable to pay, that their property should not give rise to council tax, that discounts have been calculated wrongly, or that they have been wrongly penalised by their local authority. These tribunals must sit in public unless satisfied that a party's interests would thereby be prejudiced.

Social security appeal tribunals (SSATs) consider cases relating to national insurance, income support, and family credit. They decide appeals against decisions given by adjudication officers (AOs). They also decide claims and questions referred to them by AOs. Hearings are in public, unless the claimant requests a private hearing or the chairman is satisfied that intimate personal or financial circumstances may have to be disclosed or that considerations of public security are involved. A tribunal can exclude the public while it is deliberating on its decision or discussing any questions of procedure.

Medical appeal tribunals and disability appeal tribunals decide appeals on medical questions from medical boards on claims for mobility allowance and industrial injuries and industrial disablement benefits. The rule on open hearings is the same as for SSATs.

Attendance allowance boards hear questions referred from adjudicating officers. The rule on open hearings is the same as for SSATs.

Pensions appeal tribunals determine appeals from decisions by the Secretary of State for Social Services on claims to pensions in respect of war service injuries suffered in the Second World War, war injuries suffered by civilians in the Second World War, and service injuries since the Second World War. The hearing is held in public unless the chairman directs otherwise.

Family health services committees are set up by family practitioner committees to handle complaints about self-employed health practitioners who are accused of breaking the terms of their contracts with the National Health Service. Proceedings must be in private.

National Health Service tribunals hear representations from the service committees (see above) if a committee decides that the practitioner should no longer be included on the NHS approved list. Proceedings are in private unless the practitioner applies for the inquiry to be in public.

Mental health review tribunals hear applications for discharge from patients detained under the Mental Health Act 1983. Proceedings are in private unless a patient requests a hearing in public and the tribunal is satisfied this would not be contrary to the interests of the patient. In the case of *R (IH) v Secretary of State for Home Department, ex p (IH)* [2003] UKHL, it was said that a mental health review tribunal does have sufficient coercive power to make it a court.

General Medical Council decides matters relating to complaints against doctors. The professional conduct committee sits in public but can exclude the public if it considers this is in the interest of justice, or desirable having regard to the nature of the case or the evidence. It must, however, give its decision in public.

Solicitors' disciplinary tribunals must, in general, hear allegations of professional misconduct in public. But the tribunal may exclude the public from all or any part of the hearing if it appears that 'any person would suffer undue prejudice from a public hearing or that for any reason the circumstances and nature of the case make a public hearing undesirable'.

Bar Council hears allegations against barristers in private unless the barrister asks for a public hearing. The decision must be announced publicly.

Local inquiries

Local inquiries ordered by ministers are comparable to administrative tribunals. Some acts of Parliament provide that a public inquiry must be held, and objections heard, before a minister makes a decision affecting the rights of individuals or of other public authorities.

An inquiry might be held, for example, before land is compulsorily acquired for redevelopment or the building of a housing estate and also before planning schemes are approved.

An inquiry is conducted by an inspector on behalf of the minister. In some cases, the inspector decides the matter at issue. In others he must report to the minister, who subsequently announces his decision and the reasons for it.

Some statutes under which inquiries, local or otherwise, may be held stipulate that they must be held in public. In others, this is discretionary.

By the Planning Inquiries (Attendance of Public) Act 1982, evidence at planning inquiries held under the Town and Country Planning Act 1971 must be given in public. But the Secretary of State can direct that evidence shall not be heard in public if this would result in the disclosure of matters relating to national security or measures taken to ensure the security of property, and if that disclosure would be contrary to the national interest.

Proceedings are, again, not so formal as in an ordinary court of law. Qualified privilege is available as a defence for a fair and accurate report.

The findings of a public inquiry are usually made available to the press.

As *McNae* went to press the Inquiries Bill was making its way through Parliament. It would cover the establishment of ministerial inquiries; the membership of their panels; their procedures and powers and their publication of reports.

The Bill's intent is to provide a single framework for the calling of inquiries, where at the moment there are various pieces of legislation which sometimes do not cover situations where an inquiry is needed.

The new framework would also be used by devolved administrations in Wales, Scotland and Northern Ireland.

17

Contempt of court

The main concern of the law of contempt of court is to preserve the integrity of the legal process rather than to safeguard the dignity of the court.

A journalist can fall foul of the law of contempt in a number of ways. The greatest risk is in the publication of material which might prejudice a fair trial, such as extraneous information that might tend to sway a juror's mind.

The journalist can also be in contempt by publication of anything which interferes with the course of justice generally (for example, by naming a blackmail victim at the end of the trial, which would deter future blackmail victims from coming forward, or by vilifying a person for having acted as a witness at a trial, which might deter future potential witnesses).

An editor and a newspaper company can also be in contempt if material is published in breach of an undertaking given to a court, or in breach of an order of the court (although breaches of orders made by magistrates courts under an Act of Parliament are usually treated as a breach of that Act rather than contempt. (See chapter 8, 'Effect of contravening restrictions').

Another way in which a journalist can be in contempt is by conduct other than publication. An example of this would be seeking to find out about the discussions that had gone on in the privacy of the jury room while a verdict was being reached (see chapter 7). A further example would be if a journalist were to pay or offer to pay a person, due to be a witness in a coming trial, for information to go into a background article for use after the trial, and the amount of that payment were to vary according to whether the accused was eventually found guilty or acquitted. This matter is also dealt with in the PCC code (see chapter 31, 'Payment for articles').

There has been an offence of contempt of court for centuries, but until 1981 it was almost entirely governed by the common law, that is by rules made by the judges rather than Acts of Parliament.

At common law, a newspaper was always at risk of being in contempt when proceedings were 'pending or imminent'.

Until 1981, the common law had regarded contempt by publication as an offence of *strict liability*.

This meant the prosecution had to establish only that the contempt had been committed. It was not necessary for the prosecution to prove that there had been an intent to commit the offence, as is usual in the criminal law.

Now however section 2 of the Contempt of Court Act 1981 provides that a person can be guilty of contempt by publication under the strict liability rule, that is regardless of his intent, only in cases where:

(1) the publication creates a substantial risk of serious prejudice or impediment to particular proceedings; and

(2) proceedings are active.

Human Rights Act

Courts dealing with contempt issues sometimes have to balance the competing interests of the right to a fair trial and the need to protect freedom of speech—both of which are included in the European Convention on Human Rights, now part of British law under the Human Rights Act 1998, which came into force in October 2000. However, in the *Sunday Times* action arising out of publication of information about the marketing of the drug thalidomide (see Discussion of public affairs later in this chapter), the European Court of Human Rights declared: 'The court is not faced with a choice between two conflicting principles, but with a principle of freedom of expression that is subject to a number of exceptions which must be narrowly interpreted' (*Sunday Times v United Kingdom* (1979) 2 EHRR 245, 281).

Lord Rodger of Earlsferry, Lord Justice General, said in the High Court in Edinburgh in 1998 that the due course of justice was only one of the values concerned in the Contempt of Court Act 1981. The other value was freedom of expression under article 10 of the European Convention (*Cox and Griffiths petitioners* 1998 JC 267).

The necessity to protect freedom of speech under article 10 was also reviewed by the Queen's Bench Divisional Court in 1999 when *The Observer* was cleared of contempt over its publication of an article about an artist during his trial for stealing human body parts from the Royal College of Surgeons. Lord Justice Sedley said he had concluded, not without anxiety, that it was simply not possible to be sure that the risk the article created was substantial (*A-G v Guardian Newspapers* [1999] EMLR 904).

Three Scottish judges all agreed in 1999 that the 1981 Act represented a distinct shift towards freedom of expression as interpreted by the European Court of Human Rights. They dismissed a petition that the *Sunday Times* be held in contempt for an article and leader and held that the newspaper did not assume the guilt of two Libyans accused of the Lockerbie bombing (*Al Megrahi v Times Newspapers* 1999 SCCR 824).

Judge David Clarke, then Recorder of Liverpool, said in 2000 that freedom of expression was properly regarded as one of the most fundamental elements in the European Convention. There was no dispute that this could be overridden in appropriate circumstances but the articles of the convention taken together did not increase the number of situations in which a restriction was appropriate. Three defendants on child abuse charges unsuccessfully applied for a ban on publication of their addresses as they would otherwise be at risk of attack. Their lawyers had cited article 8 of the Convention (right to privacy). (*R v Thomas Carroll*, *Media Lawyer* newsletter, January 2001). See also chapter 11, 'Addresses of defendants', and chapter 12, 'Challenging the courts'.

Common law

A contempt prosecution for a prejudicial publication may still be possible at *common law* outside the two conditions for strict liability set out in section 2, for example if proceedings are not active. But specific intent to prejudice proceedings must be proved beyond all reasonable doubt.

The subject is further dealt with later in this chapter (Contempt at common law).

The 1981 Act

The Act defines publication as any writing, speech, broadcast, or other communication addressed to any section of the public.

Proceedings for contempt under the strict liability rule can be taken only by a crown court or higher court, by the Attorney-General, or by some other person with his consent.

Magistrates do not have power to punish contempt of court by publication.

They can however jail for a month or impose a fine of £2,500 on anyone insulting them, or any witness, lawyer, or officer of the court, or on anyone who interrupts the proceedings.

Any contempt of a magistrates court by prejudicial publication (although none appears to have been recorded) would have to be dealt with by the High Court.

A judge trying a case has inherent power to deal with contempt arising during the proceedings but in 1997 the Court of Appeal affirmed that only in exceptional circumstances should trial judges deal with alleged contempt themselves. When the contempt allegation was considered by a different court, the evidence could be weighed up more dispassionately (*R v Tyne Tees Television* (1997) Times, 20 October, CA). (See chapter 8, 'Effect of contravening restrictions'.)

Under the Courts Act 2003, the Lord Chancellor made regulations in 2004 allowing a court to order a third party to pay costs where misconduct, whether contempt or not, had caused serious delay to a trial. (See later this chapter, 'Media could be ordered to pay costs').

Substantial risk

The first criterion, 'substantial risk of serious impediment or prejudice', has been found to give a little more latitude to journalists than was previously the case, especially for material published either months before a trial or distributed in parts of the country far away from the jury catchment area of the court of trial.

The Attorney-General, addressing a London seminar, said in 2004 that it would be unrealistic not to recognise that there had been an important shift of emphasis by the courts in recognising more than it did that the passage of time might dent or remove the recollection of prejudicial reporting to the point where it no longer put in jeopardy the fairness of the trial. This was especially so when combined with appropriate directions to the jury and the focusing effect of listening over a prolonged period to the evidence. However, where archived material was left on newspaper websites there was a real risk that it could be found by the jury. Sensational reporting of high-profile cases was likely to stay in the mind of potential jurors for much longer than mundane events.

The Attorney-General added that the closer to the trial reports appeared, the higher the risk of serious prejudice arising.

Arlidge, Eady and Smith on Contempt (1999) observes:

> A long gap between publication and the anticipated trial date may significantly reduce any risk of contamination . . . On the other hand, some facts are so striking, even when published some time in advance of the hearing, as to render it impossible to be confident that the conscientiousness of jurors, or the directions of a trial judge, would prevent a

substantial risk that the course of justice in the trial would be seriously impeded or prejudiced. Such factors may arise because of the memorable facts of the case itself or because the facts disclosed in media coverage itself about the accused will themselves stay in the mind. This is especially so in the case of the revelation of a criminal record.

Contempt is therefore still possible even at an early stage, especially in assuming the guilt of the accused (see the *Daily Mail* and Manchester *Evening News* case later this chapter), in disclosing his previous convictions or other information derogatory of him, or in the publication of a photograph or other description of him if identity is likely to be an issue at his trial or at a police identity parade.

The Queen's Bench Divisional Court held in 2004 that a newspaper article revealing the identities of two well-known Premier League footballers being questioned by police over allegations of gang rape at a London hotel created a substantial risk of serious prejudice because the identities of the alleged attackers was at issue at the time. The *Daily Star* was fined £60,000, with costs, for contempt. Lord Justice Rose said the article had created a real, substantial, more than remote risk that the course of justice would be seriously impeded or prejudiced. The aggravating feature of the case was that the media had been repeatedly told not to name or carry photographs of the players. There was he said, no evidence that the girl alleging rape knew the men's identities before the article appeared. The Crown Prosecution Service eventually said there was insufficient evidence to prosecute the footballers. See also 'Pictures', later this chapter.

However, most judges in England and Wales have accepted that pre-trial publicity which is merely prejudicial, rather than meeting the higher test of a substantial risk of serious prejudice, is therefore not contempt at all under the strict liability rule. The Court of Appeal held in 2003 that defendants who have been the subject of adverse publicity can nevertheless received a fair trial as long as the judge explained to the jury how they should approach their task. The Court of Appeal upheld the rejection by the trial judge of a submission that to proceed would be an abuse of process in the case of two former suspects in the Stephen Lawrence murder inquiry charged with a racist attack on a black police officer. The defence argued that both men had been subject to widespread publicity following the Stephen Lawrence inquiry and abortive criminal proceedings right up to the date of their trial. The trial judge said the process was designed to ensure a fair trial notwithstanding publicity. He would give clear directions to the jury and he was confident that neither applicant would be disadvantaged. The Appeal Court ruled that the judge's summing up to the jury could not be faulted (*R v Acourt and Norris* [2003] EWCA Crim 929).

There is a particular danger of contempt arising from the publication of matter which might be said to interfere with the course of justice while a trial is actually in progress and the jury is thus more vulnerable to outside influences (see later in this chapter).

Media could be ordered to pay costs

Whether or not a contempt of court is alleged a third party can be ordered to pay costs which have been wasted in a criminal trial such as might occur through publication which is said to have prejudiced the course of justice. Under the Courts Act 2003 the Lord Chancellor, Lord Falconer, made regulations in 2004 allowing a magistrates court, a crown court or the Court of Appeal, to order a third party to pay costs where there has been serious misconduct (Costs in Criminal Cases (General) (Amendment) Regulations 2004). The test of 'serious misconduct' falls short of the statutory test for strict liability for contempt of court—substantial risk of serious prejudice.

Regulation 3F(4) says that the court must allow the third party against whom the order is sought to make representations, and may hear evidence. An order can be made only at the end of a trial, unless there are good reasons to do otherwise. An appeal against an order in the magistrates court may be made to crown court and an appeal against a crown court order may be heard in the Court of Appeal. There is no appeal against an order made in the Court of Appeal.

The Lord Chancellor said: 'This fires a warning shot to anyone who risks causing criminal proceedings to collapse through serious misconduct, such as prejudicial reporting.' Welcoming the new regulation, the Lord Chief Justice, Lord Woolf said: 'Like many of the court's existing powers, it will need to be used with discretion to ensure it is used only to further the achievement of justice and not used in an indiscriminate manner. The power to make an order will be in the hands of a judge who will hear the parties and be aware of all the circumstances.'

When the regulations came into force, the Department for Constitutional Affairs gave as an example of criminal proceedings that had collapsed because of prejudicial media reporting a serious fraud trial at an unnamed crown court in the south of England. As the trial was due to commence, the DCA said, a daily newspaper published an article that was unfair, inaccurate and prejudicial, and repeated the errors the following day with an inflammatory headline. The judge was forced to stop the trial which had to be rescheduled six months later at another crown court where jurors were unlikely to have heard about the case. The judge said: 'I must consider the extent to which publicity has created a risk of prejudice ion this trial so grave that no direction by me (to the jury) could reasonably be expected to remove it.' An explanatory memorandum from the Department of

Constitutional Affairs said the new measure was largely inspired by the abandonment, following a *Sunday Mirror* article, of the trial in the Leeds footballers case (see later this chapter), wasting costs of about £1 million.

Mr Justice Sumner said in *A v Times Newspapers* in the Family Division ([2002] EWHC 2444 (Fam), [2003] 1 All ER 587) that if the media knew in advance that a hearing would be subject to restrictions but delayed applying for the restrictions to be lifted until after the hearing was started, thereby causing disruption, they risked an order for costs being made against them whether the application was successful or not. They were unlikely to incur the risk of adverse costs on such a prior application if they presented an arguable, though unsuccessful, case.

It seems likely that an order to pay wasted costs can be made if the 'serious misconduct' arises in the course of reporting a running trial where the newspaper reports, before the end of the trial, matter heard in the absence of a jury, or before the jury is brought into court. This could arise even though the newspaper might have a defence against a charge of contempt if no order postponing such reporting is made under section 4(2) of the Contempt of Court Act (see later this chapter, 'Contempt in court reporting, section 4 orders').

It has been suggested that the new regulation, in the form in which it was drafted, is not compatible with article 10 (freedom of expression and the right to impart information) of the European Convention on Human Rights. It is argued that the undefined phrase 'serious misconduct' is too vague, that legal certainty is necessary to ensure that the discretion of the lower criminal courts is exercised compatibly with article 10, that the media have no right to know how the wasted costs had been calculated and the risk of abuse of the regulation is sufficiently strong to have a serious chilling effect on freedom of expression.

Power to issue injunction to prevent contempt

A High Court judge held in 2000 that although a crown court had no general power to grant injunctions it had power to do so under the Supreme Court Act 1981 to stop a threatened contempt of court. Mr Justice Aikens said the court must take into account Article 10 (freedom of expression) in the European Convention on Human Rights and must injunct only to the minimum necessary. Such cases would be rare. The media should be ready to challenge orders which appeared more than necessary or proportionate. Crown court judges and recorders would always have to consider very carefully whether the stringent conditions had been met before exercising this draconian power. He issued an injunction to prevent HTV Wales from interviewing witnesses in a murder trial for a documentary, to be broadcast after the jury had returned its verdict. He said such an approach could alter witnesses' view of the evidence they had given in the trial and at least one prosecution witness would have to be recalled before the crown closed its case. He said the injunction was necessary to restrain HTV but only while evidence was being completed and it was one of those rare cases where it was appropriate to grant an injunction to restrain a threatened contempt (*Ex p HTV Cymru (Wales) Ltd, Crown Court at Cardiff* (Aikens J) [2002] EMLR 184).

Effect on the jury

As long ago as 1969, Mr Justice (later Lord Justice) Lawton said: 'I have enough confidence in my fellow-countrymen to think that they have got newspapers sized up . . . and they are capable in normal circumstances of looking at a matter fairly and without prejudice even though they have to disregard what they have read in a newspaper. . . . It is a matter of human experience and certainly a matter of experience for those who practise in the criminal courts first that the public's recollection is short, and secondly, that the drama, if I may use that term, of a trial almost always has the effect of excluding from recollection that which went before' (*R v Kray* (1969) 53 Cr App Rep 412).

More recently, some senior judges have taken the view that a jury when instructed by the judge is capable of looking at the evidence fairly, even though they may have to disregard what they have read or heard.

The Court of Appeal in April 1996 dismissed an appeal by Rosemary West against her convictions for murder. One of the grounds of the appeal was that adverse press coverage about West and her husband, Fred, meant that she could no longer get a fair trial. The Lord Chief Justice, Lord Taylor, rejected this argument. He said that to hold that view would mean that if allegations of murder were sufficiently horrendous as to shock the nation, the accused could not be tried. That would be absurd. 'Moreover provided the judge effectively warns the jury to act only on the evidence given in court, there is no reason to believe that they would do otherwise,' he said.

Three months later the Queen's Bench Divisional Court refused to hold five national newspapers in contempt through reports they had carried after the arrest of Geoff Knights on a charge of wounding a cab driver. Knights' trial at Harrow Crown Court had been abandoned in October 1995 by Judge Roger Sanders, who accepted submissions that Knights could not get a fair trial.

Lord Justice Schiemann gave the Queen's Bench Divisional Court's reasons for not finding the newspapers in contempt (*A-G v MGN Ltd* [1997] 1 All ER 456). He said it was difficult to see how any of the articles complained of created any greater risk of serious prejudice than that which had already been created by publicity about Knights before the incident with the cab driver. However, he accepted that there could be circumstances where it was proper to stay a trial on the grounds of prejudice even though no individual was guilty of contempt.

When Tracy Andrews, who was jailed for life for murdering her fiancé after claiming he had been the victim of a road rage attack, appealed in 1998 against her conviction because of pre-trial publicity, the Court of Appeal rejected the appeal. Lord Justice Roche said the reporting was not one-sided nor a blaze of adverse publicity. The court did not consider that the jury at her trial could have been prevented from reaching a proper verdict by reporting in the media about the issues it had to decide (*Daily Telegraph*, 15 October 1998).

Principles of the strict liability rule

Lord Justice Schiemann in *A-G v MGN Ltd*, mentioned above, set out the principles for the application of the strict liability rule. He said each case must be decided on its own merits and the court would test matters as they were at the time of publication. The mere fact that by reason of earlier publications there was already some risk of prejudice did not in itself prevent a finding that the latest publication had created a further risk. The court would not convict of contempt unless it was sure that the publication in question had created some substantial risk that the course of justice would not only be impeded or prejudiced but seriously so. In assessing this, the court would consider the likelihood of the publication coming to the attention of a potential juror, the likely impact on an ordinary reader, and, crucially, the residual impact on a notional juror at the time of the trial.

In assessing substantial risk a small risk multiplied by a small risk resulted in an even smaller risk, as when the long odds against a potential juror reading the publication was multiplied by the long odds of any reader remembering it.

Risk less than substantial

In 1994, Mr Justice Lindsay giving judgment in the Chancery Court said the legislature contemplated that a risk of prejudice which could not be described as substantial had to be tolerated as the price of an open press (*MGN Pension Trustees v Bank of America National Trust and Savings Association and Credit Suisse* [1995] 2 All ER 355). He said the authorities were almost unanimous in the respect they paid to a jury's ability to put out of mind that which should not be in mind. He quoted Lord Denning, Master of the Rolls, who in 1982 said that the risk of juries being influenced was so slight it could usually be disregarded as insubstantial.

Next he quoted Sir John (later Lord) Donaldson, Lord Denning's successor as Master of the Rolls, who said that trials by their nature served to cause all concerned to become progressively more inward-looking, studying the evidence given and submissions made, to the exclusion of other sources of enlightenment. Finally, Mr Justice Lindsay quoted Lord Taylor, Lord Chief Justice, as saying in 1993 in the Court of Appeal (*Ex p Telegraph* [1993] 1 WLR 980):

> In determining whether publication of matter would cause a substantial risk of prejudice to a future trial, a court should credit the jury with the will and ability to abide by the judge's direction to decide the case only on the evidence before them. The court should also bear in mind that the staying power and detail of publicity, even in cases of notoriety, are limited and that the nature of a trial is to focus the jury's minds on the evidence put before them rather than on matters outside the courtroom.

In May 1994, when prosecutions for contempt against Independent Television News, the *Daily Mail, Daily Express, Today*, and the *Northern Echo* (Darlington) failed, the Queen's Bench Divisional Court decided that there was no more than a remote risk of serious prejudice actually occurring. The court held that no contempt had been established because of the length of time between publication and trial, the limited circulation of copies of the papers which contained the offending material, and the ephemeral nature of a single ITN broadcast.

The material complained of had been used within two days of the arrest of two Irishmen on charges of murdering a special constable and the attempted murder of another police officer.

ITN had said in its early evening news bulletin that one of the arrested men, Paul Magee, was a convicted IRA terrorist who had escaped from prison while serving a life sentence for the murder of an SAS officer. Next day, three national newspapers used similar stories and a fourth gave information about Magee's past without actually mentioning his conviction for murdering the SAS officer.

Lord Justice Leggatt said it was of overriding importance that the lapse of time between the publications and the trial was likely to be nine months, and in the event was.

He was not persuaded that viewers of the ITN broadcast would have retained the information for that time. Different considerations would have applied if the information had been repeated. In the case of the newspapers, the risk of serious prejudice occurring was diminished; in the case of one newspaper, the *Northern Echo*, it was annulled because only 146 copies of the paper were on sale in London where Magee's trial was to take place. Although the possibility of leakage of the previous conviction through a juror having heard about it indirectly by word of mouth did exist, the risk was so slight as to be insubstantial.

The risk of prejudice could never be excluded but the requirement for strict liability contempt was the criminal standard of proof beyond all reasonable doubt. ITN had been extremely careless and the newspapers had behaved erroneously. The broadcast should never have taken place nor the articles been published but, as stated, no contempt had been committed.

Some editors have taken the *Northern Echo* judgment to mean that regional newspapers may be allowed to report more widely on crime which is to be tried at a great distance from their circulation area.

The lapse of time was a factor in assessing the substantial risk of serious prejudice in a contempt case in 1986. The cricketer Ian Botham had issued a writ for libel against a newspaper which had published allegations about his activities during the MCC tour of New Zealand. The libel case was set down for trial not before March 1987, but in 1985 another newspaper, the *News of the World*, published similar allegations linked to a tour in the West Indies. The Court of Appeal held that because of the lapse of time between the publication of the *News of the World* article and the trial due to take place before a jury at least ten months later, the test of a substantial risk of serious prejudice was not satisfied and therefore the *News of the World* was not in contempt of court.

The *Daily Mail* and the Manchester *Evening News*, who had carried stories describing how a home help was caught on video film stealing from an 82-year-old widow, were found not guilty of contempt of court in the Queen's Bench Divisional Court in 1997. Mr Justice Owen said his initial view was that the stories were a plain contempt of court carrying as they did the clearest statements that the home help was guilty, at a time when proceedings against her were active. The key issue was whether the stories created a substantial risk that the criminal proceedings against the home help would be seriously prejudiced. The stories were several months old by the time of the trial however and he had concluded that the allegation of contempt was not made good. Lord Justice Simon Brown said in applying the test of the residual impact on the notional juror at the time of trial, listed by Lord Justice Schiemann in *A-G v MGN Ltd* (mentioned earlier in this chapter) he found that the fade factor in jurors' recollection of the article applied. He warned the media however against taking the view that where a person was caught red-handed there was no possibility of a not guilty plea being entered at trial. In the case of an either-way offence there was always a real chance that an accused however strong the evidence against him would plead not guilty and elect jury trial (*A-G v Unger* [1998] 1 Cr App Rep 308). (See also later this chapter, 'Crime stories'.)

When proceedings are active

A writer, editor, publisher, proprietor, director, or distributor of any publication may be held to be in contempt regardless of intent only if proceedings are active at the time of publication. The Act says criminal proceedings are deemed to be active from the relevant initial step—if a person has been arrested, or a warrant for his arrest has been issued, or a summons has been issued, or if a person has been charged orally.

However, the reporter may not know whether a person who is with the police, after a crime has been committed, has actually been arrested or is merely 'helping the police with their inquiries'. If he is at the police station against his will, he is, in law, under arrest, whether or not the proper arrest procedures have taken place. There are many cases where journalists do not know if a person has willingly gone to the police station and is to go home later, or is to be detained. The Police and Criminal Evidence Act 1984 provides that where a person attends voluntarily at a police station without having been arrested, he is entitled to leave at will unless placed under arrest. (Quite apart from the contempt issue, there may also be a libel risk in naming a person who is helping the police with their inquiries: see chapter 2.)

In some cases, where the police have other suspects in mind, they may not wish to disclose that they have arrested one person.

Often, the press do not know a warrant has been issued. If a journalist is not certain whether proceedings are active or not, he should use extreme caution.

As a result of a case in 1985, proceedings are also active if an inquest has been opened, even if the evidence given was merely formal, and even if the inquest was adjourned, without a date being fixed (see chapter 15).

When proceedings cease to be active

Under the Act proceedings are no longer active when:

(1) the arrested person is released without being charged (except when released on police bail);

(2) no arrest is made within 12 months of the issue of a warrant;

(3) the case is discontinued;

(4) the defendant is acquitted or sentenced; or

(5) he is found unfit to be tried, or unfit to plead, or the court orders the charge to lie on file.

The Act leaves open the possibility that the journalist and his newspaper may be liable for contempt even though a jury has returned a guilty verdict and the defendant is merely awaiting sentence by the judge. In the past, judges have expressed differing views as to whether they could be affected by anything that appeared in a newspaper (for example, background stories about the accused and the crime) once the jury has discharged its duty. When a judge is conducting proceedings without a jury, however, it is considered unlikely that any substantial risk of serious prejudice will arise (see also later this chapter, 'Liability for contempt in civil proceedings'). A carefully-written background article may seem unlikely to prejudice the sentencing process. Additionally it may be protected by the defence of a discussion in good faith of public affairs under section 5 of the Act (see later this chapter).

Appeal being lodged

The Act provides that if an appeal is lodged liability for contempt resumes from the lodging of the appeal and ends again when hearing of the appeal is completed unless a new trial is ordered or the case remitted to a lower court. Thus there is a free-for-all time (the words of Sir Michael Havers when Attorney-General) between sentence and the lodging of any appeal.

Often a lawyer announces at the end of a case that his client will appeal but liability for contempt does not resume until the appeal is lodged formally.

Appeals to the Court of Appeal from crown court trials may be lodged at a crown court office. Appeals on a point of law to the Queen's Bench Divisional Court from a crown court appeal hearing must be lodged at the Royal Courts of Justice in London. Appeals from magistrates court summary trials may be lodged at a local crown court office.

The Queen's Bench Divisional Court in Belfast in 2002 refused to impose an injunction preventing Ulster Television broadcasting a programme containing new material which had not been put before the jury in a trial in which two men had been convicted of murder. The men's lawyers said they intended to appeal and, if they were granted a re-trial, the material could prejudice a new jury, thereby denying them a fair trial under Article 6 of the European Convention on Human Rights. Ulster Television's lawyers said a ban on the broadcast was contrary to Article 10 of the Convention, allowing freedom of expression and the right to impart information. Mr Justice Kerr said the possibility of a re-trial was a matter of speculation and was contingent on a number of imponderables, not least that the men would be successful in overturning the guilty verdict.

Police appeals for press assistance

Sometimes when the police have obtained a warrant for a person's arrest, they seek the help of the press and television in tracing him. Technically, a newspaper publishing a police message which links the wanted man with the crime could be at risk of contempt. But the Attorney-General said in the House of Commons during the debate on the Contempt Bill in 1981:

> It is plainly right that the police should be able to warn the public through the press that a particular suspect is dangerous and should not be tackled, or it may simply be that they issue a photograph or some other identification of the wanted man. The press has nothing whatever to fear from publishing in reasoned terms anything which may assist in the apprehension of a wanted man and I hope that it will continue to perform this public service.

There is no known case of a newspaper being held in contempt after publishing a police appeal, but a judge could still decide it was contempt.

The Attorney-General's comments would not apply to information supplied by the police and published or repeated after an arrest had been made as this could not be said to be information published to assist in tracing a wanted man.

Defence in not knowing proceedings were active

Section 3 of the Act provides a publisher with a defence for contempt of court under the strict liability rule if, at the time of publication, having taken all reasonable care, he did not know and had no reason to suspect that relevant proceedings were active. The burden of proof, however, in establishing that all reasonable care was taken is upon the publisher accused of contempt. To avail his newspaper of this defence, therefore, a journalist reporting a crime story must check with the police to discover what stage their inquiries have reached. He should make a habit of noting the time and the name of the police informant.

Contempt in court reporting

One of the greatest dangers of being in contempt of court through creating prejudice can arise in publication of extraneous matter when a jury has started to try a case. Indeed, before the Contempt of Court Act 1981 came into effect even a fair and accurate report of proceedings in open court, though privileged against an action for defamation (see chapter 2 and chapter 20), could be held to prejudice a fair trial and thus be contempt of court. The Act now provides a possible defence in this situation unless a court has made a specific order, postponing publication (see 'Section 4 orders' below). In the past, judges took a stern view when journalists reported even the actual proceedings in the court before the jury had been brought in. Sometimes, a defendant facing a number of charges will plead guilty to some but deny others, and then the jury will be brought in to try him on the charges he has denied. If a newspaper carrying a report before the end of the trial mentions that the defendant has pleaded guilty to some offences, the judge may feel it necessary to stop the trial and to order a re-trial before a fresh jury in another town at great expense to public funds.

In 1981, before the 1981 Act took effect, four evening newspapers were each fined £500 for contempt of court arising in this way. In no case had the judge indicated to reporters present that they should not report the guilty pleas made before the jury was brought in.

Section 4, detailed below, may also provide a defence for a contempt that could otherwise arise in reporting details of proceedings in open court which take place after the jury is sent out during legal submissions, such as on the admissibility of a witness's evidence or about matters incriminating the defendant. To make it possible for the jury to read such submissions in a newspaper or hear them in a broadcast before the end of the trial would defeat the purpose of the jury being sent out.

The defence would not be available for a newspaper which added extraneous information to a report of an ongoing trial before a jury has reached its verdict.

The *Sunday Mirror* was fined £75,000 in 2002 for the publication of an article which led to the collapse of the first trial of two Leeds United footballers on assault charges. The article was used while the jury was still considering its verdict and had been sent home for the weekend. It contained an interview with the victim's father who said his son was the victim of a racial attack—at variance with a direction which had been given by the trial judge that there was no evidence of a racial motive. In the contempt proceedings, counsel for the Attorney-General estimated the cost of the aborted trial at £1,113,000 and the cost of the subsequent retrial £1,125,000. (See also earlier this chapter, 'Media could be ordered to pay costs'.)

Even information which has previously been in the public domain is not exempt from this. In 1981, the *Guardian* was fined £5,000 for contempt because during a trial it recalled that two of the accused had previously escaped from custody. The jury had not been told of their escape. The trial had to be abandoned and held afresh in the following year.

Section 4 orders

The 1981 Act gives the courts power to rule that some matters should not be reported for the time being. Section 4(2) says:

> The court may, where it appears to be necessary for avoiding a substantial risk of preju-
> dice to the administration of justice in those proceedings, or in any other proceedings,
> pending or imminent, order that the publication of any report of those proceedings or any
> part of those proceedings be postponed for such period as the court thinks necessary for
> that purpose.

Section 4 of the Act also provides that when publication of a report is ordered to be postponed, eventual publication of it will be treated as contemporaneous for purposes of privilege against a libel action if the report is published as soon as is practicable after the order expires.

Where no section 4 order is made, a report of the proceedings is unlikely to be treated as contempt, although it may incur the displeasure of the judge if information is disclosed which the jury ought not to be made aware of before the end of the trial.

Section 4(1) says that subject to any such court order a person is not guilty of contempt of court under the strict liability rule in respect of a fair and accurate report of legal proceedings held in public published contemporaneously and in good faith. It might be assumed from this provision that if a court inadvertently omits to make an order banning immediate publication of statements made in open court which could prejudice a fair trial (eg legal submissions made in the middle of a crown court trial during the absence of the jury), a journalist and his paper would not be in contempt in reporting these statements.

Even in the absence of a section 4 order, it is wise to assume that matters discussed in the absence of the jury ought not to be reported lest publication results in a trial being aborted. It remains possible that liability for contempt could arise if the report of the proceedings failed to meet the requirements of being fair and accurate and it created a substantial risk of serious prejudice under the strict liability rule. A newspaper publishing a report which causes a trial to be abandoned or delayed could also be ordered under the

Courts Act 2003 to pay the cost to public funds of the wasted time whether or not strict liability for contempt arises. See earlier this chapter, 'Media could be ordered to pay costs'.

Dealing with strict liability for contempt, *Halsbury's Laws of England* states: 'It appears that the effect of section 4 is to give complete protection unless a order is made under that provision, and except in cases where there is an intention to interfere with the administration of justice.'

In 2004 the Privy Council, dealing with an appeal from the West Indies, held that that unless power had been conferred by statute, as in the United Kingdom, a court had no power to order postponement of reports of proceedings in public and any such order at common law infringed rights of free speech and freedom of the press (*Independent Publishing Co Ltd v Attorney General of Trinidad and Tobago* (2004) Times, 8 June).

Arlidge, Eady and Smith on Contempt (1999) says:

> Suppose that through oversight or other reason no such order is made. Suppose also that information comes to light in the absence of the jury—guilty pleas, or an inadmissible confession for example—which journalists readily appreciate would be likely to prejudice the jury if they were to find out about it. It may well be in such circumstances that publication of that information would give rise to a substantial risk of serious prejudice, and thus to a prima facie contempt under the strict liability rule. It would seem that in principle, provided the publication took place in good faith, the protection would prevail.
>
> Even if the journalists were conscious of the risk of serious prejudice at the time of publication, it would be difficult to infer any intention on their part to interfere with the administration of justice sufficient to found a common law contempt, since they would presumably (in accordance with the majority view in *R v Horsham Justices, ex p Farquharson* [1982] QB 762) be entitled to assume that the court having the power to order a section 4(2) postponement, knew its own business and had decided on good and sufficient grounds to make no such order.

Media Lawyer newsletter (November/December 2000 issue), noted that it could not recall a single case where a newspaper has been in contempt for including material in a court report in the absence of a section 4 order, and said such a prosecution would be very unlikely.

In February 1985 during the trial of Clive Ponting, a civil servant, on a charge under the Official Secrets Act, the judge discussed with counsel in the absence of the jury the instructions he should give to the jury on their return to court. The *Observer* published a report of these discussions, while the trial was still in progress.

The judge said afterwards that he had not issued a directive under section 4 prohibiting publication because it had never occurred to him that the discussions would be publicised before the end of the trial.

He referred the matter to the Attorney-General who later announced that he had decided not to prosecute the *Observer* for contempt.

It is permissible to indicate in a general way that the jury were excluded during legal submissions and to report anything about the submissions that is said before the jury is sent out of court or what is said after they return.

It is permissible to report details after the defendant has been tried.

It should be noted that the Act empowers any court, for example a magistrates court, to order postponement of a report. A magistrates court can make such an order delaying a report of a preliminary hearing of an indictable offence, or part of it, even if the defendant has chosen to have reporting restrictions lifted under section 8 of the Magistrates' Courts Act 1980. In November 1981 the Queen's Bench Divisional Court ruled that such an order should be no wider than was necessary to prevent the possibility of prejudice. (But see earlier this chapter, 'Media could be ordered to pay costs'.)

Tainted acquittals

If a person is convicted of an offence involving intimidation of a witness and the court believes that a fresh trial may now take place of a person who was acquitted because of that intimidation, a section 4 order may be made postponing reporting of the proceedings against the person guilty of the intimidation offence. Once the court dealing with the intimidation offence grants a certificate as a first step towards a new trial of the person originally acquitted, proceedings for the new trial are treated as if they were pending or imminent for the purposes of making a section 4 order. This provision, in the Criminal Procedure and Investigations Act 1996, makes an inroad into the principle that a person once acquitted by a jury cannot be tried again for the same offence. (see also chapter 7, 'Application for acquittal to be quashed').

Reporting of section 4 orders

Is it permissible to report that a section 4 order has been made and the terms of the order? Lord Justice Mann said in the Queen's Bench Divisional Court in 1992 that if the courts were minded to make orders preventing the public from knowing what was going on in a public court, those orders should be drafted and made public in such a way that it was crystal clear what the press could or could not do.

See also chapter 12, 'Invalid orders'.

Section 11 orders

Section 11 of the Contempt of Court Act also gives power to the courts, when they allow a name or other matter to be withheld from the public, to prohibit the publication of that name or matter in connection with the proceedings, as appears to the court to be necessary for the purpose for which it was withheld. The power is intended to prevent the names of blackmail victims or people involved in national security from being revealed and secret processes from being disclosed.

There has been criticism that the courts have, in many cases, been using both the 'delaying powers' of section 4 and the 'no names' powers of section 11 without good cause. A number of regional papers have successfully challenged in the Queen's Bench Divisional Court orders made in magistrates courts, and orders made at crown court can now be challenged in the Court of Appeal.

See also chapter 11, 'Civil proceedings' and chapter 12, 'Invalid orders'.

Inaccurate reporting of a current jury trial

The BBC was fined £5,000 in the Queen's Bench Divisional Court in 1992 for an inaccurate report of a continuing trial before a jury. It was submitted on behalf of the Attorney-General that critical issues in the trial were affected by erroneous comment and presentation of facts which could easily and wrongly influence members of the jury. It was held that the report contained errors which had created a substantial risk of serious prejudice since it was foreseeable that publication would delay and obstruct the course of justice (*A-G v BBC* [1992] COD 264).

Crime stories

One of the most common situations where a journalist could find himself in contempt of court arises in crime reporting.

It has been argued that the 'substantial risk of serious prejudice' test for strict liability contempt has created a more liberal climate for some stories published at the time of the arrest.

Before proceedings become active because of an arrest, or the issue of a warrant for arrest, there will normally be no danger under the strict liability rule of the 1981 Act, but there is still a (distant) possibility of contempt at common law, as already explained.

Once proceedings become active, the crime can still be reported but the story must be carefully worded lest way that those in police hands are indeed the culprits. Lord Justice Simon Brown, in the unsuccessful contempt prosecution against the *Daily Mail* and the Manchester *Evening News* mentioned earlier, said articles which published as a fact the guilt of a named person after an arrest and before trial were not to be taken lightly. All those in the business of crime reporting should recognise that articles such as these were published at their peril. They should exercise great caution (*A-G v Unger* [1998] 1 Cr App Rep 308).

One can report a post office robbery and say that later a man was arrested, but not *the* man was arrested. It would also be prejudicial after an arrest to describe the appearance of three men who raided a bank as being tall or dark-haired or bearded, lest those arrested answered to that description. To publish such matter would be to curtail the ability of the defence to contest identity.

There are dangers too in publishing interviews with a witness to a crime once an arrest has been made, where the witness makes contentious statements. A witness who sees his account published in a newspaper or on television may be less receptive to questions put in cross-examination or examination-in-chief and feel obliged to stick to his story, even when wrong.

Interviewing witnesses with a view to publication of material after the trial, though probably permissible in most cases, should be handled with care, lest even this might be said to influence a witness in sticking to the account he gave to the journalist when he comes to give evidence. (See earlier this chapter, 'Power to stop witnesses being interviewed'.)

It could also be contempt to publish background material about an accused person. In particular, any statement implying that an arrested man has a previous criminal history is likely to be treated as a serious contempt.

A Scottish daily newspaper was fined £20,000 and its editor £750, in 1979, for contempt of court arising from an article published at the time of the arrest of four people on drugs charges. The article referred to three of the four as having escaped from custody in the Netherlands. It said they set up a registered company and imported chemicals and that a large quantity of drugs was seized from a bungalow they occupied.

Some matter will be common ground, not creating a substantial risk of serious prejudice, and in each case the decision on whether to publish it must be taken in the light of the effect it might have on the mind of a potential juror.

Journalists should also be aware that it is possible to prejudice proceedings in favour of the accused, as well as against him. Newspaper campaigns to secure an acquittal could be held to be contempt.

Discussion of public affairs

Section 5 of the Contempt of Court Act was introduced because of complaints that freedom of expression in the United Kingdom had been unnecessarily restricted by a ruling given in a case in 1974. The *Sunday Times* wanted to publish an article raising important issues of public interest on the way the drug thalidomide had been marketed at a time when civil actions were pending against the manufacturers, Distillers Company (Biochemicals) Ltd, on behalf of children affected by the drug before their birth.

The House of Lords ruled in an appeal that the proposed article would be contempt, because the public interest in the proper administration of justice outweighed the public interest in discussion of the matters raised in the article.

Commenting on the decision, the Government-appointed Phillimore Committee said in 1974:

> At any given moment many thousands of legal proceedings are in progress, a number of which may well raise or reflect such issues (matters of general public interest). If, for example, a general public debate about fire precautions in hotels is in progress, the debate clearly ought not to be brought to a halt simply because a particular hotel is prosecuted for breach of the fire regulations.

The European Court of Human Rights in 1979 held that the Lords' ruling violated article 10 of the European Convention on Human Rights, protecting freedom of expression.

The Government's response to the Phillimore Committee and the Court was to introduce a new defence. It is that a publication made as, or as part of, a discussion in good faith of public affairs is not to be treated as contempt of court under the strict liability rule if the risk of impediment or prejudice to particular legal proceedings is merely incidental to the discussion. The time of liability for contempt in civil proceedings was also changed (see later in this chapter).

Two newspapers were prosecuted in 1981 for contempt arising from comments published during the trial of Dr Leonard Arthur, a paediatrician accused of murdering a Down's Syndrome baby. The *Sunday Express* admitted contempt in an article by John Junor, the editor. The article complained of the trial taking five weeks and said if the Down's Syndrome baby had been allowed to live so long he might have found someone apart from God to love him. The editor was fined £1,000 and Express Newspapers £10,000.

The *Daily Mail*, however, denied contempt. When the case was heard in the Queen's Bench Divisional Court, the court rejected a submission put forward by the *Daily Mail* that its article, by Malcolm Muggeridge, was a discussion in good faith of public affairs under section 5 and that the risk of prejudice was merely incidental.

On appeal, the House of Lords held that the article did create a substantial risk of serious prejudice to the trial of Dr Arthur. But it ruled that the article did meet the criterion of being written in good faith and because it was written in support of a pro-life candidate at a by-election it was a discussion of public affairs.

Lord Diplock said the article made no express mention of the Arthur case and the risk of prejudice would be properly described as merely incidental.

A television company and the proprietors of a free newspaper accused of contempt of court in 1989 failed when they pleaded that the offending item was a discussion in good faith of public affairs, under the terms of section 5.

Lord Justice Lloyd said in the Queen's Bench Divisional Court that one test of section 5 was to look at the subject matter of the discussion and see how closely it related to particular legal proceedings. 'The more closely it relates, the easier it will be for the Attorney-General to show that the risk of prejudice is not merely incidental to the discussion.'

TVS Television Ltd was fined £25,000 and H W Southey £5,000 for carrying reports which caused a trial at Reading Crown Court to be stopped and re-heard later, at an estimated additional cost of £215,000.

TVS had screened an investigation 'The New Rachmans' while one of the landlords identified in the programme was on trial accused of conspiracy to defraud the DSS. The free newspaper carried a story based on a TVS press release.

Lord Justice Lloyd also rejected a submission that the new 'Rachmanism' had been the subject of a public discussion in Reading for many years and therefore did not create a substantial risk of prejudice. The judge said publication in the middle of a trial would have had a very different impact since it dealt with a matter with which the jury were very closely concerned.

Liability for contempt in civil proceedings

The Act says that civil proceedings are deemed to be active for contempt purposes when the case is set down for trial, or when a date is fixed for the case to be heard. 'Setting down for trial' is a technical stage when the case enters a waiting list where it may remain for months. Liability lasts until the case is disposed of, abandoned, discontinued, or withdrawn. Contempt of court by publication is less likely in civil proceedings. Juries are rarely used apart from in actions for defamation, false imprisonment, or malicious prosecution.

Arlidge, Eady and Smith on Contempt (1999) says: 'There will be few occasions when a publication will raise a substantial risk of serious prejudice to a trial to be conducted by a judge alone.' (See also chapter 12, 'Deciding if a section 4 order is necessary'.)

There remains however the possibility that potential witnesses could be affected in that their evidence could be coloured by what they have read in a story that delves deeply into the circumstances behind a claim.

It was decided in a 1925 case that it is possible to be in contempt of civil proceedings through disclosure of a sum paid into court which would not otherwise become known to the jury until they had decided on liability. A contempt could also arise through speculating on the damages a jury might award. Mr Justice Poole, in the High Court at Birmingham in 1999, reminded reporters that civil proceedings remained active until the end of the case. A jury had decided in favour of a man's claim against West Midlands Police for malicious prosecution. Before the jury had decided on the damages to be awarded, the *Birmingham Post* suggested that the claimant was in line for an award of £30,000. The judge said the proceedings were therefore tainted. The claimant then abandoned his case rather than go through a retrial. The judge said: 'I offer a helpful and friendly piece of advice to the press to remember that civil proceedings are not completed until the second stage has taken place.'

Tape recordings

It is contempt of court under section 9 of the 1981 Act to use or take into court for use any tape recorder (except by permission of the court), or to make any recordings.

Tribunals

See chapter 16.

Interviewing jurors

See chapter 7.

Pictures

Publication of a photograph can in general be contempt just as much as an accompanying story.

The rule is that publication of the photograph of a defendant is not likely to be contempt provided there is no argument about his identity. But if the case hinges on witnesses identifying the defendant, in court or at an identity parade, as a man who committed the crime, to use a picture of the man would clearly be contempt.

In 1994, a record fine for contempt of court of £80,000 was imposed by the Queen's Bench Divisional Court on the *Sun* which published a photograph of a man accused of murder. This picture was published six weeks before a police identity parade, in which he was picked out by witnesses. Kelvin MacKenzie, editor at the time of publication, was fined £20,000. Lord Justice Steyn said two witnesses who saw the photograph in the *Sun* and who picked out the accused man at the identity parade were cross-examined at the trial. He said that not surprisingly the defence were able to argue that their identification was unreliable. Kelvin MacKenzie had said that the *Sun* did not know an identity parade was imminent when the photograph was published.

In 2004 the Attorney-General obtained an injunction to stop publication of photographs of suspects arrested as part of counter-terrorist operations where identification was an issue.

Contempt at common law

As stated, it remains possible for a journalist to be prosecuted for common law contempt, outside the provisions of the Contempt of Court Act, eg when proceedings are not yet active.

But the prosecution has to prove beyond all reasonable doubt that the journalist intended to prejudice proceedings. The court can infer intent from all the circumstances, including the foreseeability of the consequences of the conduct.

If an armed man against whom no proceedings were active were in a house holding police at bay, it could be contempt of court to publish or broadcast a list of his previous crimes. It could be argued that the editor must have realised that the eventual proceedings were bound to be prejudiced and the court could infer from this that he intended this result, even if he did not desire it.

In 1988 the *Sun* was fined £75,000 for contempt at common law. The newspaper offered to fund a private prosecution of a doctor on a charge of raping an eight-year-old girl, and then published two articles with details of the allegation.

The newspaper said that at common law no offence was committed unless the proceedings were 'pending or imminent', but Lord Justice Watkins rejected this argument. Contempt could be committed if proceedings were not imminent, he said.

He said intent was proved because the editor must have foreseen that the articles he published and the steps he announced he was taking to assist the mother to prosecute would incur a real risk of prejudicing the fairness of the doctor's trial.

But in 1991 the *Sport* newspaper and its editor were cleared of contempt at common law after they published previous convictions of a rapist being sought by police for questioning about a missing schoolgirl. No warrant had been issued, so the case was not active under the strict liability rule of the 1980 Act.

The editor said he had ignored police requests not to publish because the rapist was 'on the run and a danger to other women'. The court held the Attorney-General had not proved intent beyond reasonable doubt. Lord Justice Bingham (later Lord Bingham of Cornhill, the senior law lord in the House of Lords) said that proof of recklessness was not sufficient.

He and the other judge in the case, Mr Justice Hodgson, disagreed as to whether Lord Justice Watkins was right in saying (above) that contempt could be committed when proceedings were not yet imminent, so the law on this point remains unclear.

In 1987 the *Sunday Times* and the *Independent* were found guilty of contempt of court for publishing material from Peter Wright's book *Spycatcher* at a time when injunctions were in force against the *Observer* and the *Guardian* (see chapter 23).

The injunctions were interim (temporary), intended to prevent publication of confidential information until the issues could be argued at trial, and lawyers said there would be little point having a trial if the confidential material had already been published by other papers and so was no longer confidential. Thus the administration of justice would be impeded.

The cases against the *Observer* and the *Guardian* were not active because they had not been set down for trial.

The strict liability rule of the Act applies only to publications likely to affect particular proceedings. A publication interfering with the course of justice generally without affecting particular proceedings, such as an article after a trial which vilified witnesses for coming forward to give evidence, could not be treated as strict liability contempt. Proceedings would no longer be active and the article would not create prejudice to particular proceedings. Therefore it could be dealt with only at common law.

Appeals

Under section 13 of the Administration of Justice Act 1960, a right of appeal is provided for a person held to be in contempt. Appeals from the High Court (except from the

Divisional Court) and the county court go to the Court of Appeal, and appeals from the Divisional Court and the Court of Appeal go to the House of Lords.

Reports of hearings in private

The fact that proceedings are held in private does not in itself make it a contempt to report what occurs. Section 12 of the 1960 Act provides that publication of information about proceedings held in private or in chambers shall not in itself be contempt. It is however contempt to report proceedings involving mental health, national security, or secret processes; wardship of children, cases under the Children Act 1989, and others relating wholly or mainly to the maintenance or upbringing of children (see chapter 6).

Mr Justice Munby said in the Family Division in 2004, in a case involving a child, that the prohibition in section 12 applied equally whether or not the information from the proceedings was anonymised. It prohibited publication even of summaries of the evidence (*Re B (A Child) (Disclosure)* [2004] EWHC 411 (Fam)). See also chapter 6, 'Children in civil proceedings', and 'Wards of court'.

In *Pickering v Liverpool Daily Post* [1991] 1 All ER 622, a man convicted of a number of sexual attacks and ordered to be detained in a secure mental hospital wanted to prevent the press publishing details of his application to a mental health tribunal for discharge. The House of Lords said the press could report that a named patient had applied to a tribunal. That was not 'information relating to the proceedings' within section 12.

The essential privacy protected by the exceptions in section 12 attached to the substance of the matters that the court had closed its doors to consider. The press could report that the tribunal would sit, was sitting, or had sat on a certain date, time, or place behind closed doors. It could report the decision of the tribunal to discharge, absolutely or conditionally. But it could not report the recorded reasons for the decision because these disclosed the evidence and other material on which it was based.

In *Clibbery v Allan* [2002] EWCA Civ 45, [2002] Fam 261, [2002] 1 FLR 565 the Court of Appeal ruled that it was not unlawful for one of the parties to disclose what went on in chambers when proceedings in relation to money or property (as opposed to children) were heard in the Family Division in chambers. Public disclosure could be made in the absence of: (1) a specific statutory restraint; (2) a lawfully-imposed order of the court; (3) an implied undertaking not to make use of material compulsorily disclosed for the hearing; or (4) any restrictions imposed by the duty of confidentiality. The judge discharged an injunction restraining a woman from disclosing to the *Daily Mail* material placed before the court, during her attempt to obtain an occupation order of the flat she had shared with a millionaire businessman for 15 years. The businessman had sought the injunction to restrain her from disclosing any document or oral evidence or any part of the judgment. Lawyers for the woman had pointed out the importance, if the administration of justice was to be promoted and public confidence in the courts maintained, of justice being administered in public or at least in a manner which enabled its workings to be scrutinised. The Court of Appeal later rejected an appeal against Mr Justice Munby's finding.

The Lord Chief Justice said in 1971, during an espionage trial, that speculation about what had gone on in court while it was sitting in private was potentially contempt of court.

There is nothing to prevent a newspaper reporting the outcome of applications made to a judge in chambers for bail or for a bill of indictment, provided no order has been made under section 4 of the Contempt Act.

Scandalising the court

The courts have often held that the conduct of the judges in court and decisions of the court are matters of legitimate concern, and the press has a right, and even a duty, to criticise in good faith within reasonable limits.

Lord Atkin said in the Appeal Court in 1936: 'Justice is not a cloistered virtue. She must be allowed to suffer the scrutiny and respectful, even though outspoken, comment of ordinary men.' However, that there must be no imputing of improper motives to those administering justice.

What is prohibited is scurrilous abuse of a judge and attacks upon the integrity or impartiality of a judge or court. In 1928, an article in the *New Statesman* saying that Dr Marie Stopes, the birth control pioneer, could apparently not hope for a fair hearing before Mr Justice Avory was held to be a contempt and the magazine was ordered to pay costs.

Today, a newspaper may be more likely to be sued for defamation by a judge whose good faith is questioned than it is to be prosecuted for contempt of court.

Defamation

Dangers of defamation

For the journalist, the publisher and, indeed, for anyone who earns his or her living with words, the law of defamation presents one of the greatest perils.

The law exists to protect the reputation of the individual (both his moral reputation and his professional reputation) from unjustified attack. Such an attack may be dealt with either as a civil or as a criminal matter. In civil law it is a tort—that is, a civil wrong for which monetary damages may be claimed.

The principle is the same as that involved in an action for damages brought by a man who has been physically injured as a result of another's act, whether through negligence or premeditated attack. He may sue for damages and, if successful, will be awarded a sum of money by way of compensation.

'The chilling effect'

As we have seen (in chapter 1), the law of defamation tries to strike a balance between the individual's right to have his reputation protected and freedom of speech, which implies the freedom to expose wrongdoing and thus to damage reputation.

So the law provides certain defences for the person who makes a defamatory statement about another for an acceptable reason.

Newspapers, however, are often reluctant to fight defamation actions even when they seem to have a strong defence. There are various reasons for this.

The first is the uncertainty involved in libel actions. For example, the statement that seems to one person quite innocuous may, equally clearly, be defamatory to another. It is often difficult, therefore, even for lawyers skilled in the law of defamation to be able to forecast the jury's decision (see 'What is defamatory?', next section).

Then even if a journalist and his newspaper are convinced of the truth of his story, he may be unable to prove it in court (see chapter 20, 'Justification').

Because the outcome of a case may be unpredictable, a newspaper has to consider very carefully indeed the money involved if it loses. A substantial award against a publication can cause it great difficulty or even closure. In 2000 the magazine *LM* (formerly *Living Marxism*) went into liquidation and ceased publication after a jury awarded £375,000 damages to two television reporters and the ITN company for an article in the magazine that accused them of sensationalising the image of an emaciated Muslim pictured through barbed wire at a Serb-run detention camp in Bosnia.

Newspapers considering whether to contest a libel action brought against them find it difficult to assess the damages that might be awarded should they lose. In personal injury cases a judge decides the damages to be paid to a successful claimant—that is, the person suing. He can assess the value of a limb, or an eye, or even a life by the application of certain standards, such as a person's age and earning capacity.

In libel cases, however, damages are normally determined by a jury. We do not know how they reach their decision, but there is little doubt that in general they find it a difficult and confusing job and some have awarded huge sums.

As the result of a change in the law in 1990 the Court of Appeal can substitute its own award when a jury award is held to be excessive or inadequate.

In 2002 the court reduced to £30,000 damages of £350,000 awarded by a Liverpool jury to a businessman for a *News of the World* story claiming he was a paedophile. The House of Lords has the same power and, again in 2002, cut to £1 a jury award of £85,000 to Bruce Grobbelaar, the former Liverpool goalkeeper, for a *Sun* story claiming he took bribes for match fixing.

From 1995, judges and counsel in libel actions have been allowed to draw the attention of juries to the level of awards in personal injury cases and can suggest the level of award they consider appropriate in a particular action. In 2002 a leading libel judge said that the ceiling for the most serious defamatory allegations was currently 'reckoned to be of the order of £200,000'. That was the figure he awarded in that year, when trying a case without a jury, to each of two nursery nurses wrongly accused of sexual abuse. He said a report referring to them contained untrue allegations 'of the utmost gravity'.

Many libel actions are against national newspapers and involve stories of sex and scandal. But large sums have also been awarded against small publications and for articles in which the media erred while trying to fulfil their traditional role as the public's watchdog.

The damages award, large as it often is, is frequently exceeded by the legal costs, which are generally met largely by the loser. In 1994 the BBC was ordered to pay an estimated £1.5 million costs in a case where a judge, rather than a jury, had heard the case and awarded £60,000 damages. The libel was contained in a *Panorama* programme, 'The Halcion nightmare', which reported that, long before the sleeping drug was banned in the United Kingdom, evidence existed that it might have had serious adverse side effects.

In 1998 Granada agreed to pay £50,000 damages over a libel contained in a *World in Action* programme which revealed that garments sold by the store company Marks and Spencer and marked 'Made in England' were in fact made by a factory in Morocco employing child labour. Granada also had to pay £600,000 costs.

It is not surprising that, faced with these figures, even the more ardent campaigning papers sometimes decide either not to carry the story or, having carried it, to apologise and settle out of court by payment of damages.

Indeed, the vast majority of libel cases are settled out of court, without any publicity, and for this reason the cost of libel to newspapers is often underestimated.

In the book *Libel and the Media: The Chilling Effect* (1997), the authors argued that the libel law exerted a chilling effect on the media, significantly restricting what the public was able to read and hear. The most obvious manifestation occurred when articles, books or programmes were specifically changed in the light of legal considerations. But the deeper and subtler effect prevented articles being written in the first place. Particular organisations and individuals were considered taboo because of the libel risk; certain subjects were treated as off-limits. The book said:

> Preventive self-censorship seems just as effective in ensuring that journalists and editors
> on these newspapers steer well clear of, for example, investigations of deaths in police
> custody; exploitative employment practices by various large companies operating in the
> United Kingdom; or bribery and other corrupt practices by British companies bidding for
> overseas contracts.

The chilling effect of libel on investigative journalism was increased as a result of the introduction of conditional fee agreements (CFAs), otherwise known as 'no win, no fee' agreements, after their use was extended to defamation cases in 1998 under the Conditional Free Agreements Order.

Legal aid was never available for launching libel actions, but now litigants without the means to sue could do so and be represented by lawyers who would receive nothing if they lost the case but who could claim up to a 100 per cent increase on their fees if they won.

The media argued that a claimant without means could hold a media defendant to ransom by threatening to sue under a CFA. If the claimant lost the case, the media defendant would be unlikely to recover the large sums it had spent in fighting the case. If he won, the media defendant would have to pay not only damages to the claimant but also his lawyer's 'success fees', which might be huge.

In a case considered by the Court of Appeal in 2004, Lord Justice Brooke pointed out that the *Daily Telegraph* would be required to pay 'up to twice the reasonable and proportionate costs' of the claimant if it lost the case and would almost certainly have to bear its own costs (estimated at about £400,000) if it won (*Adam Musa King v Telegraph Group Ltd* [2004] EWCA Civ 613).

Proponents of CFAs argued that they ended the injustice resulting from the fact that previously people of modest means had no way of seeking redress if their reputations were subjected to baseless attacks in the media. They could now get that redress in the courts.

Most journalists believe that the law, in attempting to 'strike a balance' between protecting reputation and allowing freedom of speech, has been tilted historically in favour of claimants.

But in recent years there have been a number of developments that seemed likely to tilt the balance, to a greater or lesser degree, in favour of freedom of expression.

They were:

(1) The Human Rights Act, which took effect on 2 October 2000, requiring courts to pay regard to article 10 of the European Convention on Human Rights, concerned with freedom of expression. The European Court of Human Rights has said that article 10 does not involve a 'choice between two conflicting principles' but 'a freedom of expression that is subject to a number of exceptions which must be narrowly construed'. See chapter 30 on the Human Rights Act and references in this chapter ('What is defamatory?'), chapter 19 ('Introduction', 'Identification', 'Only rumours', and 'Libel and the internet'), chapter 20 ('Introduction'), and 21 ('Introduction').

(2) The decision of the House of Lords in *Reynolds v Times Newspapers* [2001] 2 AC 127, which greatly extended the ambit of the defence of qualified privilege (see chapter 20, 'Qualified privilege').

(3) The Defamation Act 1996, which introduced:

(a) a summary procedure for trying defamation cases, which it was hoped would reduce the cost of smaller-scale libel actions. Under the procedure a judge can fix damages up to a ceiling of £10,000. That was the figure awarded in 2002 to a claimant for what the judge described as a 'serious' libel (*Mawdsley v Guardian Newspapers Ltd* [2002] EWHC 1780 (QB));

(b) a new procedure, the offer to make amends (chapter 20).

What the journalist should do

In the remainder of this chapter, we shall be looking at the classic definitions of defamation, in the next chapter what a claimant has to prove, and in the following chapter defences available to anyone who finds himself facing an action for damages.

But first a word of warning. Because the law of defamation is so complex, this book can provide nothing more than a rough guide, an indication that a newspaper can sometimes go further, in safety, than many journalists suppose, and ought sometimes, in prudence, to stop and reflect before taking a dangerous course of action. In this way it may help to preserve a balance between excessive caution and unreasonable risk.

Beyond this it cannot claim to go. The golden rule for the journalist is that if publication seems likely to bring a threat of libel, take professional advice first.

This does not mean that the editor must necessarily take the lawyer's advice. At some time or other every editor must decide whether to play for safety or to obey his conscience and 'publish and be damned'.

The newspaper's role in exposing wrongs is an extremely important one. As Lord Justice Lawton (then Mr Justice Lawton) said in a case in 1965:

> It is one of the professional tasks of newspapers to unmask the fraudulent and the scandalous. It is in the public interest to do it. It is a job which newspapers have done time and time again in their long history.
>
> It is a job which frequently cannot be done without risk and therefore requires a considerable degree of courage on the part of the journalists involved.

Sometimes, however, publication of the words that cause the problem are not the result of a conscious decision but the result of an innocent error. There will be a solicitor's letter from 'the other side' which may lead eventually to the High Court.

Again, this is the moment to take legal advice. Libel should not be a matter for the editorial office amateur to play with, for the dangers of aggravating the offence by mishandling are too great.

A too fulsome apology can, in certain circumstances, be as dangerous as an inadequate correction. On the other hand, the correct legal steps, taken promptly, can remove the sting from an action and save perhaps thousands of pounds.

If these comments make the subject seem rather alarming, remember that the most common cause of libel actions against newspapers is the journalist's failure to apply professional standards of accuracy and fairness.

The best protection against getting your newspaper involved in an expensive action is to make every effort to get the story right.

What is defamatory?

The law of the United Kingdom recognises in every man a right to have the estimation in which he stands in the opinion of others unaffected by false and defamatory statements and imputations.

Defamatory statements may be made in numerous ways. Broadly speaking, if the statement is written or is in any other permanent form, such as a picture, it is libel; if it is spoken or in any other transient form it is, with two exceptions, slander.

The exceptions are (1) a defamatory statement broadcast on radio or television, or in a cable programme, which by the Broadcasting Act 1990 is treated as libel, (2) a defamatory statement in a public performance of a play, by virtue of the Theatres Act 1968.

The journalist's job in recognising and avoiding libellous statements would be simpler if there were a comprehensive definition of defamation, but no one has yet devised a definition that covers every case.

There are, however, certain definitions that judges often use when they are trying to explain defamation to juries. In a libel case, the judge rules whether the words complained of are capable of bearing a defamatory meaning. If the answer is yes, a jury must decide whether in the circumstances in which they were used the words were in fact defamatory. It is not the job of the judge when sitting with a jury to say whether words complained of were defamatory.

Judges tell juries that a statement about a person is defamatory of him if it tends to do any one of the following:

(1) expose him to hatred, ridicule, or contempt;

(2) cause him to be shunned or avoided;

(3) lower him in the estimation of right-thinking members of society generally; or

(4) disparage him in his business, trade, office, or profession.

Notice the words 'tends to', which are important. The person suing does not have to show that the words actually did expose him to hatred or whatever.

Judges tell juries that in deciding whether statements are defamatory they should use as their measuring stick the standard of intelligence and judgment of a completely hypothetical creature they refer to as the 'reasonable man'.

The test is whether, under the circumstances in which the statement was published, reasonable men and women to whom the publication was made would be likely to understand it in a defamatory sense.

As stated above, even lawyers sometimes find it difficult to decide whether a statement is defamatory or not. And even judges sometimes disagree. A judge decided that the allegation contained in the following story, about the film stars Tom Cruise and his wife, Nicole Kidman, was not capable of bearing a defamatory meaning, and he struck it out from the couple's claim. He said the allegation was 'unpleasant, maybe; defamatory, no'. The story appeared in the magazine section of the *Express on Sunday* 5 October 1997:

'Nicole bans brickies from eyeing her up' said the papers last year. Not much of a story, really: the Cruises had the builders in to do a little work on their LA mansion and Nicole ordered the hapless hodwielders to turn and face the wall as she passed. Quite natural, of course: you and I would do the same thing. They were brickies, after all, so they ought to be facing the wall.

The couple challenged the decision in the Court of Appeal, and the court restored the statement to their claim, saying it was 'very much a matter for the jury to consider'. Their counsel had told the court that to impute arrogance was plainly capable of being defamatory. The incident described in the story was to Ms Kidman's discredit and could affect the way people saw her in 'a whole range of situations, from her employability on a film set teeming with technicians to her work as Australian ambassador to UNICEF'. (The matter never came before a jury because the newspaper settled out of court.)

In definition (3), notice the phrase 'right-thinking members of society generally'. It is not enough for a claimant in a libel action to show that the words of which he complains have lowered him in the estimation of a limited class in the community who may not conform with that standard.

For example, it is not defamatory to say of a member of a club that he gave information to the police, leading to the conviction of officials of the club for keeping an illegal gaming machine on the premises, even if that statement lowers his reputation in the eyes of members of the club. 'Right-thinking members of society' would expect a person to give information to the police in the circumstances.

It is defamatory to say of a person that he is insolvent or in financial difficulties—even though this may impute no blame to him at all. (See chapter 14, 'Bankruptcy and company liquidation'.)

Some lawyers consider it possible that at least one of these definitions could now be challenged on the ground that it is incompatible with the European Convention on Human Rights. In a case in 1997 judges differed over an article by columnist Julie Burchill that actor Steven Berkoff was horrendously ugly.

The Court of Appeal said the statement was capable of being defamatory because it might expose him to ridicule. But one of the appeal court judges, in a dissenting judgment, said the claim was an unwarranted restriction on free speech. It could be argued that it is not 'necessary', within the meaning of article 10(2) of the European Convention, to restrict freedom of expression to prevent a person being ridiculed.

Meaning of words

Many statements are capable of more than one meaning. An apparently innocuous statement may carry an inference that, in the ordinary and natural meaning of the words, is defamatory. The inference is understood by someone without special knowledge who 'reads between the lines in the light of his general knowledge and experience of worldly affairs'.

The test of what the words mean is again the test of the reasonable person. It is not the meaning intended by the person who wrote the words, nor indeed the meaning given to them by the person to whom they were published. The point is illustrated by the following three cases.

In a case in 1988 against *Stationery Trade News*, the Charles Freeman Group, a firm of envelope importers, sued for an article that carried the headline 'Counterfeits—retailers warned'.

The article reported that retailers and wholesalers had been asked to boycott counterfeit stationery products from overseas, which were causing concern among British manufacturers. It gave examples of products imitating well-known brands and illustrated one of the products and the original using the captions 'Impostor' and 'Real thing'.

The last two paragraphs of the article dealt with another issue. They read:

> In the envelope market, there have been similar problems involving foreign envelopes being marketed here under a British-sounding brand name.
>
> The envelope makers' association, EMMSA, recently won an origin marking victory over Charles Freeman which was selling, under its own name, the Great West range of envelopes. These products were not British as the marketing implied, but mainly from

Germany. The company was required by the Trading Standards Office to include the country of origin on the label. 'This is not just a protectionist measure towards a British industry,' said Eric Smith, EMMSA chairman, 'consumers have a right to know what they are buying.'

Charles Freeman said the article, the headline, and the pictures were defamatory. The words meant 'in their natural and ordinary meaning' first that the company was guilty of marketing counterfeit envelopes and that retailers and wholesalers were being asked to boycott the company's products. In addition the company said the article meant it was marketing rubbish and had been dishonestly marketing its products as British.

The magazine denied the article bore any of these meanings—and indeed nowhere in the article can one find any of these specific allegations. However, the jury found for the envelope distributors and awarded £300,000 against the magazine (which had a controlled circulation of fewer than 9,000).

In a case the same year against Radio City, the judge said the meaning of the words was of crucial importance. The Liverpool radio station had put out a one-hour programme in which four local people strongly criticised holidays provided at a site in France by a holiday company run by another local man, David Johnson, and his wife.

The interviewer told Johnson, during the broadcast: 'We have spoken to literally dozens of people who bought holidays off you during the last two years and they have described you as a con man.'

Radio City said the broadcast meant the Johnsons knowingly or recklessly deceived 'some at least of their customers', made promises to them that they could not keep and displayed a callous indifference to the distress that such behaviour caused. And it said those allegations were true.

By contrast Johnson said the broadcast meant he was habitually dishonest or cynical, but the great majority of his customers were well-satisfied. The judge told the jury they must decide whether the words did in fact mean conduct towards 'at least some' customers or whether they meant 'habitual' conduct. The jury found for Johnson and awarded £350,000.

In 1989 £470,000 was awarded against the *Mail on Sunday* for libelling a food retailer and his firm in the course of an award-winning series revealing the extent to which the public was being sold food after the sell-by date. The article read in part:

Backstreet spaghetti mountain!

Eleven thousand cans of spaghetti have been discovered in a backstreet warehouse—yet another example of the thriving trade in secondhand food.

The cans were originally destined for Sainsbury's but somewhere along the complicated chain of food dealers their labels have been ripped off and replaced with the
obscure brand name Samantha . . .

As the law stands it is perfectly legal to deal in secondhand food but health officers
and consumer watchdogs are increasingly concerned about the multi-million pound
business. They are particularly worried about the growth in sales of repackaged food that
is near to or beyond the sell-by date stamped on the products. Food withdrawn from
supermarket shelves is turning up in corner shops repacked and, in some cases, not fit
for human consumption . . .

It was true the spaghetti had been intended originally for Sainsbury's. The *Mail on Sunday*
said the article meant the company sold secondhand food of uncertain origin which was or
might be unfit for human consumption, and it claimed that was true. The company said
the article meant it knowingly repackaged and sold food past its sell-by date. The jury
found for the food wholesalers.

The eminent judge Lord Reid summed up the question of the meaning to be given to
words in this way:

Ordinary men and women have different temperaments and outlooks. Some are
unusually suspicious, and some are unusually naive. One must try to envisage people
between these two extremes and say what is the most damaging meaning they would put
on the words in question.

Dangers of juxtaposition

The words must be read in full and in their context. As a result, a statement that might be
innocuous standing alone can acquire a defamatory meaning as a result of juxtaposition
with other material. Juxtaposition is a constant danger for journalists, and particularly for
sub-editors and those dealing with production.

In the case against the *Mail on Sunday*, the judge reminded the jury the article about
the 'spaghetti mountain' appeared on a page carrying the strapline: 'Exclusive Mail on
Sunday Investigation: The scandal of sell-by food.' Above the article about the spaghetti
was a piece carrying the headline: ' "Change the law" call—shoppers want a binding date
stamp' and there was a rag-out of the front-page article from the previous week's paper
carrying the headline: 'The great food racket—old and unfit to eat, but it's still for sale.'

Referring to the strapline, the judge said: 'There it is at the top of the page with the
black line [a six-point rule] round everything in the page. You may think the sub-editor's

headline . . . provides a setting for everything which appears in the page which is sur-
rounded by that thick black line.'

Bane and antidote

Just as a defamatory meaning may be conveyed by a particular context, so a defamatory
meaning may be removed by the context. A judge said in 1835 that, if in one part of a
publication something disreputable to the claimant was stated that was removed by the
conclusion, 'the bane and the antidote must be taken together'.

The House of Lords applied this rule in 1995 (*Charleston v News Group Newspapers Ltd*
[1995] 2 AC 65), when it dismissed a case in which Ann Charleston and Ian Smith, two
actors from the television serial *Neighbours*, sued the *News of the World* over headlines
and photographs with captions in which their faces had been superimposed on models in
pornographic poses.

The main headline read: 'Strewth! What's Harold up to with our Madge?' The text said:

> What would the Neighbours say . . . strait-laced Harold Bishop starring in a bondage
> session with screen wife Madge. The famous faces from the television soap are the
> unwitting stars of a sordid computer game that is available to their child fans . . . The
> game superimposes stars' heads on near-naked bodies of real porn models. The stars
> knew nothing about it.

The actors' lawyers conceded that a reader who read the whole of the text would realise the
photographs were mock-ups, but said many readers were unlikely to go beyond the photographs and the headlines.

Lord Bridge, one of the judges, said it was often a debatable question, which the jury
must resolve, whether the antidote was effective to neutralise the bane. The answer would
depend not only on the nature of the libel a headline conveyed and the language of the text
that was relied on to neutralise it but also on the manner in which the whole of the material
was set out and balanced. In this case, no reader could possibly have drawn a defamatory
inference if he had read beyond the first paragraph of the text.

Lord Nicholls, another of the law lords, warned that words in the text of an article would
not always be efficacious to 'cure' a defamatory headline. 'It all depends on the context,
one element in which is the layout of the article. Those who print defamatory headlines are
playing with fire.' The ordinary reader might not notice words tucked away low down in an
article.

(Important note: A journalist trying to decide whether, in a story he is about to write, the antidote is sufficient to cure the bane, should read first the section 'Only rumours' in the next chapter.)

Innuendoes

A statement may be innocuous on the surface, but be defamatory to those with special knowledge.

A famous judge once said that there were no words so plain that they might not be published with reference to such circumstances and to persons knowing those circumstances so as to have a meaning very different from that which would be understood by the same words used differently.

For example, for a newspaper to say of Mr Smith that he is a socialist is not obviously defamatory; but if the paper's readers know that he is a member of the Conservative Party such a statement might be held to be defamatory because it imputes he is politically dishonest.

Such a hidden meaning is referred to as an innuendo, from the Latin word meaning to nod to.

The claimant who claims that he has been defamed by an innuendo must show not only that the special facts or circumstances giving rise to the innuendo exist, but also that these facts are known to the people to whom the statement complained of was published.

For example, if Mr Smith wants to sue the newspaper, he must show not only that he is a member of the Conservative Party, but also that some of the newspaper's readers know this. Otherwise, they could not understand the statement in anything other than its innocent sense.

In 1986 Lord Gowrie, a former Cabinet Minister, received 'substantial damages' after suing over a newspaper article which implied that he took drugs.

The previous year he had resigned as Minister for the Arts and the *Star* newspaper, under the headline 'A lordly price to pay', stated:

> There's been much excited chatter as to why dashing poetry-scribbling Minister Lord Gowrie left the Cabinet so suddenly. What expensive habits can he not support on an income of £33,000? I'm sure Gowrie himself would snort at suggestions that he was born with a silver spoon round his neck.

Lord Gowrie's counsel said:

> The reference to Lord Gowrie's expensive habits, the suggestion that he was unable to support those habits on his ministerial salary, the use of the word 'snort' and the

reference to a 'silver spoon around his neck' all bore the plain implication, to all the many familiar with the relevant terminology, that Lord Gowrie was in the habit of taking illegal drugs, in particular cocaine, and had resigned from the Cabinet because his ministerial salary was insufficient to finance the habit.

Changing standards

It might be easier for journalists to cope with the law of libel if the 'reasonable man' was consistent, but the standards of public opinion which this hypothetical individual is supposed to reflect are not fixed and unchangeable, but vary from time to time depending upon public attitudes in the country.

Imputations that were defamatory a hundred years ago may not be defamatory today, and vice versa.

For example, in the reign of Charles II it was held to be actionable to say of a man that he was a papist and went to mass. In the next reign similar statements were held not to be defamatory.

During the 1914–18 war a court decided that it was a libel to write of a man that he was a German.

Is it defamatory to call someone homosexual? It certainly used to be. In the case of *Ashby v Sunday Times* (1995), where a paper claimed an MP shared a double bed with another man, the paper's counsel argued this allegation was no longer defamatory. It is not clear what view a jury would take on that argument, but allegations of homosexuality are dangerous because in such cases the claimant generally argues that the allegation carried other defamatory inferences. Ashby argued the statement meant he was a liar and a hypocrite in denying that he had left his wife because of a homosexual affair. (The jury found for the newspaper.)

Product testing

Can a publication defame a person or a firm by disparaging goods? It is an increasingly important question as product testing becomes commonplace in newspapers and magazines.

The answer is yes. But consider first the statement that any words that disparage a person in the way of his business, trade, office, or profession are defamatory.

To fall within this category it is not sufficient that the statement should simply affect the person adversely in his business; it must impute to him discreditable conduct in his business, or else tend to show that he is ill suited or ill qualified to carry it on because he has some characteristic or lacks some other characteristic.

For example, it is defamatory to write of a businessman that he has been condemned by his trade association or of a bricklayer that he does not know how to lay bricks properly.

It is not defamatory to report incorrectly that a businessman has retired, even though such a report may result in substantial loss to the person referred to. Such a statement does not impute any misconduct or suggest that the person is in any way unsuited to carry on his trade; nor does it reflect upon his reputation in any way. (However, the wronged person may have an action for malicious falsehood: see chapter 21.)

From the above it follows that any statement in disparagement of goods or their quality is defamatory if it reflects on the owner or manufacturer in his character as a person or as a trader. Not all words that criticise a person's goods are defamatory. For example, a motoring correspondent could criticise the performance of a certain make of car without reflecting upon the character either of the manufacturer or the dealer. (Again, the statement might give rise to an action for malicious falsehood: see chapter 21.)

The imputations that give most problems are dishonesty, carelessness, and incompetence.

In a case in 1994 in which a jury awarded £1.485 million damages to the manufacturer of a yacht, Walker Wingsail Systems plc, an article in *Yachting World* contrasted the manufacturer's striking claims for the yacht's performance with the drastically poorer performance of the boat when tested by the journalist. Even the claimant's expert witness, who tested the boat, found the performance figures substantially worse than claimed by the manufacturer.

The article also revealed that the company's claims of impressive sales 'deals' referred to returnable deposits rather than firm contracts.

The manufacturer said the article meant it had deliberately misled the public by its publicity material. The sales director, wife of the managing director, told the court: 'Effectively [the article] called my husband and myself charlatans and liars.' *Yachting World* denied the article meant the manufacturer had been dishonest, but said the firm had made its misleading claims carelessly and irresponsibly, and it said that was true.

In the case, also in 1994, in which the BBC had to pay £60,000 damages (with an estimated £1.5 million costs) to the makers of the drug Halcion (see above, 'Dangers of defamation'), the judge was not asked to adjudicate on the question of the safety of the drug but upon whether there had been intentional concealment of information relating to its safety.

So the journalist must be keenly aware of the dangers in such articles. This does not mean that articles highly critical of products cannot be published. On the contrary, the journalist has a duty to his readers to expose false claims. But he must be sure when doing so that he has protection under one of the defences explained in chapter 20 before going ahead.

One important defence is justification, which means truth (see chapter 20). You must be careful you have your facts right. Bovril, the meat extract, collected damages in 1985 from the publishers of a book that said the product contained sugar. The statement (which was incorrect) implied the company was lying when stating the contents of its product.

The other important defence is fair comment, which allows people to give their honest views on matters of public interest (see chapter 20). The facts upon which the comment is based must be correct. In the *Yachting World* case, the manufacturer claimed the magazine, in making its criticisms, had failed to point out that the boat when tested by the magazine was far heavier than it had been when the manufacturer's performance claims were originally made, and in addition its bottom had become badly fouled. (As stated, we have no means of knowing whether the jury accepted that argument, which the magazine strongly rejected.)

The defence also fails if the person suing can show the journalist was motivated by malice, a legal concept explained in chapter 20. The judge told the jury in the *Yachting World* case that this did not necessarily involve telling lies but it did require the journalist to have an honest belief in his story. He continued:

> If someone publishes defamatory matter by way of comment recklessly, without considering or caring whether it be true or false, that defendant is treated as if he or she knew it was false.

Earlier he had asked the editor of the magazine why, when he realised his journalist's performance figures were so drastically different from the firm's, he did not check back. 'Why not, in the extraordinary circumstances, before sanctioning the publication of the article, pick up the telephone and say, "Hey, this looks extraordinary. Is there any explanation?" '

But the editor said the manufacturer had already had opportunities to explain the discrepancies and the magazine's technical editor said it was policy not to 'enter into negotiations or ask for explanations'. If he did so, pressure would be put upon him and this would strike at the credibility of the magazine. 'Our readers want to see what a fair report says on the day.'

Journalists tend to accept without question the long standing journalistic policy of declining to show copy to the subjects of investigations but this approach appears less than fair to judges and juries and could now prejudice a possible defence under the Reynolds rules (see chapter 20).

Which magazine, publisher of perhaps the greatest number of product tests, always sends the factual results of its tests to the subjects before publication but never the comments. Thus it can be, and is, highly critical of products while minimising the danger that its defence of fair comment will be lost as a result of challenges on facts.

Who can sue?

In addition to individuals, a corporation (see Glossary) can sue for a publication injurious to its trading reputation. And, in general, a corporation, whether trading or non-trading, can sue in libel to protect its reputation—if it has a corporate reputation distinct from that of its members which is capable of being damaged by a defamatory statement.

In the case against *Yachting World*, referred to above, the jury awarded £1 million to the firm, £450,000 to the managing director, and £35,000 to the sales director.

In an important decision in 1993 (*Derbyshire County Council v Times Newspapers* [1993] AC 534), the House of Lords held that institutions of local or central government could not sue for defamation in respect of their 'governmental and administrative functions' because this would place an undesirable fetter on freedom of speech. They can still sue for libels affecting their property, and they can still sue for malicious falsehood over articles concerning their governmental and administrative functions if they can show malice.

Note that it is still possible for individual members or officers of the council to sue. A judge in the House of Lords said:

> A publication attacking the activities of the authority will necessarily be an attack on the body of councillors which represents the controlling party, or on the executives who carry on the day-to-day management of its affairs. If the individual reputation of any of these is wrongly impaired by the publication any of these can himself bring proceedings for defamation.

As a general rule, an association, such as a club, cannot sue unless it is an incorporated body, but words disparaging an association will almost invariably reflect upon the reputations of one or more of the officials who, as individuals, can sue.

Trade unions are not corporate bodies. Can they sue for libel? The leading books differ in their answers to this question. In a case in 1980 a judge held that they cannot sue, and *Carter-Ruck on Libel and Slander* (1997) maintains this is still a correct statement of the law, but *Gatley on Libel and Slander* (2004) doubts whether this decision 'represents the law'. Again, individual officers can sue.

The Bill of Rights 1689 reserved jurisdiction in all matters relating to proceedings in Parliament to Parliament itself, and this had the effect that an MP was unable to sue a newspaper for allegations about his conduct in the House. The Defamation Act 1996, in a provision that took effect in September 1996, allows Parliamentarians to waive their parliamentary privilege in defamation actions and thus sue. The change enabled Neil Hamilton MP to continue an action against *The Guardian* over allegations that he had accepted cash for asking parliamentary questions. In October that year he abandoned his case.

19

What the claimant must prove

To succeed in an action for defamation, a claimant (formerly known as a plaintiff) must prove three things about the statement he is complaining about:

(1) it is defamatory;

(2) it may be reasonably understood to refer to him;

(3) it has been published to a third person.

It is almost as important for the journalist to remember what the defamed person does not have to prove.

Most important of all, he does not have to prove that the statement is false. If a statement is defamatory, the court assumes it is false. If the statement is in fact true *and the journalist can prove it is true* he has a defence.

Secondly, the claimant does not have to prove intention: it is normally no use the journalist saying, 'I didn't mean to discredit him'. (Intent is, however, relevant in the 'offer of amends' defence, under the Defamation Act 1996: see next chapter. It is also relevant upon the issue of damages.)

Thirdly, the claimant does not have to prove that he has been damaged in any way. He needs to show only that the statement *tends to* discredit him. A person may, in fact, sue for libel even though the people to whom the statement was published knew it to be untrue. The court will presume damage.

Some lawyers believe long-standing principles of libel may be susceptible to challenge under the regime established by the Human Rights Act. Compared with the English common law, the European Court of Human Rights has attached greater importance to freedom of expression even when damage to reputation has been the likely consequence of publishing.

It was suggested that the presumption of falsity, referred to above, would be regarded as incompatible with the Convention right to freedom of expression. In several cases, the court has held that a newspaper could publish defamatory factual allegations without proving them.

In one case, the author of articles in an Icelandic newspaper was convicted of criminal libel by a domestic court for allegations that unnamed police officers frequently behaved in a brutal manner.

On appeal, the European Court in 1992 held that these articles dealt with a matter of public concern, the language was not excessive, and the purpose of the criticism was to prompt the minister to set up an inquiry into police brutality. Statements in the articles had an objective basis; one incident was undisputed, while other allegations were based on widespread rumours and stories. It was unreasonable to require the author to prove their truth. The court said his conviction was incompatible with the European Convention (*Thorgeirson v Iceland* (1992) Series A no 239, (1992) 14 EHRR 843).

In a second case, a Norwegian newspaper, under the headline 'Seals flayed alive', repeated allegations by a Ministry of Fisheries inspector that seal hunters had acted cruelly towards seals and broken hunting regulations. The report at that time had been exempted by the ministry from publication, and many of the inspector's more serious allegations were later found to have been inaccurate.

Norwegian courts ruled the factual allegations unproven, and held the newspaper liable to pay compensation. But the European Court, in 2000, disagreed. It held that normally the press should be entitled to rely on the contents of official reports without having to undertake independent research. Before the date when the ministry began to express doubts about the inspector's competence and the quality of his report, it was reasonable for the paper to rely on that report without an independent check on its accuracy (*Bladet Tromsø v Norway* (1999) 29 EHRR 125).

In a third case, the European Court said 'there is no proof that the description of events given in the articles was totally untrue', which suggests that it is for the claimant or state to demonstrate the falsity of factual accusations (*Dalban v Romania* (28 September 1999, unreported)).

But in 2002 the European Court rejected an attempt by author John McVicar to reverse the burden of proof, so that a claimant in a UK court would be obliged to prove that the defamatory allegation was untrue, rather than the defendant having to prove that it was true. McVicar had written an article about the champion sprinter Linford Christie which, Christie alleged, meant that he was a cheat who regularly used banned performance enhancing drugs. The jury found for Christie, after McVicar failed to convince them the allegation was true. The following year the athlete was banned for two years after failing a test for the anabolic steroid nandrolone.

When McVicar appealed to the European Court, the court said proving the allegations as substantially true was a justified restriction on McVicar's freedom of expression in order to protect the reputation and rights of Christie (*McVicar v United Kingdom* [2002] NLJR 759, ECtHR).

Notice however that in the Reynolds defence, developed under the influence of the European Convention and now available to the media, there is a defence in some circumstances for publishing untrue statements without having to prove their truth (see 'The Reynolds Defence', next chapter).

Identification

Under English law, the claimant must be able to prove that the words of which he complains identify him as the person defamed.

Some journalists believe they can play safe by not naming the person about whom they are making the defamatory statement, but such an omission may prove no effective defence.

The test of whether the words identified the person suing is whether they would reasonably lead people acquainted with him to believe that he was the person referred to.

A judge said in 1826: 'It is not necessary that all the world should understand the libel; it is sufficient if those who know the claimant can make out that he is the person meant.' That is still the law today.

During the late 1980s and 1990s the Police Federation, representing junior police officers, made good use of this aspect of the libel law in many actions against newspapers on behalf of their members. During the 33 months to March 1996 the federation fought 95 libel actions, winning all of them and recovering £1,567,000 in damages. (A case the federation did not win, *Bennett v Guardian* (1997), is referred to below and in the next chapter.)

Many of the officers were not named. In a characteristic case, the Burton Mail paid £17,500 compensation plus legal costs to a woman police constable who featured anonymously in a story following a complaint about an arrest. The original complaint was investigated by the Police Complaints Authority, but rejected.

Note well that in this type of case the test of identification is not whether the general reader knew who was referred to, but whether some individuals, such as the officer's colleagues (and family), did.

In *Morgan v Odhams Press Ltd* [1971] 2 All ER 1156, a journalist sued successfully over an article in the *Sun* newspaper which neither named him nor described him. A person reading the article carefully would have noted various details that were inconsistent with a reference to Mr Morgan. However, the court said ordinary people often skimmed through such articles casually, not expecting a high degree of accuracy. If, as a result of such reading, they reached the conclusion that the article referred to the claimant, then identification was proved.

Derogatory comments about an institution can reflect upon the person who heads that institution. For example, many newspapers have had to pay damages to head teachers, who were not named in the paper, for reports that criticised schools. These reports are generally based on complaints by parents.

Accounts of bad teaching and discipline at a school almost inevitably reflect on the head teacher, who is responsible, and imply that he or she is incompetent or negligent. Journalists can generally defend themselves, when challenged over such reports, only by proving the statements are true or fair comment (see next chapter).

It is dangerous to make a half-hearted effort at identification. In *Newstead v London Express Newspapers Ltd* [1940] 1 KB 377, the *Daily Express* reported that 'Harold Newstead, 30-year-old Camberwell man', had been sent to prison for nine months for bigamy.

The paper was successfully sued by another Harold Newstead, who worked in Camberwell, and who claimed that the account had been understood to refer to him.

The claimant claimed that if the words were true of another person, which they were, it was the duty of the paper to give a precise and detailed description of that person, but the paper had 'recklessly struck out' the occupation and address of the person convicted.

And not naming may not protect you. Indeed, greater trouble is often caused by failing to identify properly the person whose reputation is being attacked because another person may say the words referred to him. A newspaper quoted from a report by the district auditor to a local council criticising the council's deputy housing manager. The paper did not name him. But a new deputy manager had taken over, and he issued a writ claiming he was thought to be the offending official.

It is sometimes wrongly assumed that there is safety in generalisations. There seldom is. Again, dangers may be increased.

For example, the statement 'I know of at least one member of Blanktown Council who is there only because of the contracts that come his way' is clearly defamatory of someone. Almost certainly the councillor the writer has in mind will find plenty of friends to identify him as the member concerned, and if there are two or three other members who also have (legitimately) obtained contracts from the council, the paper may face actions for libel by all of them.

It must be stressed, as was illustrated in the Newstead case, that the fact that a defamatory story is true of one person does not give you any protection if your story is understood to refer to someone else.

The principle was illustrated in the case *Bennett v Guardian*, referred to above. In 1992 *The Guardian* newspaper was running stories about an investigation into allegations of corruption at Stoke Newington police station made by people convicted or accused of drug offences. Scotland Yard issued a press statement saying that eight Stoke Newington officers, whom it did not name, had been transferred to other stations, and the paper's crime correspondent wrote two pieces about the transfer of the officers, whom he did not name, together with background material he had accumulated during his investigation.

Five officers sued, saying the story meant they were involved in planting and dealing drugs, a meaning denied by *The Guardian*, which had no idea of the identity of the men when it published the story.

When the case came to court in 1997, five years later, the newspaper sought to show that its story was true, but it was not allowed to bring any evidence of allegations made against police officers other than the five who were suing. (The jury found for the newspaper by a majority.)

Note the *Thorgeirson* case, mentioned in the introduction to this chapter, for the different attitude of the European Court to a story criticising unnamed police officers.

Subject to what we shall learn about the defences of justification and fair comment, it is safer under English law to be specific, and to pin critical comment fairly and squarely on the person meant, by naming him.

Another common danger arises from juxtaposition, mentioned in the previous chapter. A person may be defamed because a reference to him is juxtaposed with other material. The other material may or may not be defamatory, but in combination the two have this effect.

A meat porter collected damages from *Titbits*. He won a meat-carrying race during the Smithfield centenary celebrations and the magazine used the picture to illustrate an article about Christmas thieving. Always consider the implications when using library pictures to illustrate stories and features.

Notice that in the *Stationery Trade News* case described in the previous chapter the magazine accurately reported the counterfeiting of stationery products and named some of those responsible. The company which won huge damages in the case was named in what the magazine considered to be a separate part of the article, dealing with another issue, but the jury found the allegations referred to the claimant company as well.

The copy referring to the envelope manufacturers was sandwiched between the allegations of counterfeiting and the pictures illustrating counterfeiting, and no doubt this additional juxtaposition helped to persuade the jury.

Publication

The claimant must also prove that the statement has been published. With the exception of criminal libel (see chapter 21) there is no defamation if the words complained of, however offensive or untrue, are addressed, in speech or writing, only to the person about whom they are made.

To substantiate defamation, they must have been communicated to at least one other person.

In the case of the media, there is no difficulty in proving this: publication is assumed.

It is important to remember that, as the lawyers put it, every repetition of a libel is a fresh publication and creates a fresh cause of action. This is known as the repetition rule.

Some journalists are reluctant to accept this. If they are told that a statement in their copy is libellous they reply, 'But we are not making that statement: the chairman of the council (or some other important local figure) is.'

Certainly the person who originated the statement may be liable, but also anybody who repeats the allegation may be sued.

Indeed, one of the most common causes of libel actions is repeating statements made by interviewees without being able to prove the truth of the words.

In 1993 the *Western Daily Press* had to pay damages for libellous comments made by the chairman of an NHS hospital trust when commenting upon the resignation of a doctor. (There might well be a defence now under the Reynolds ruling; see next chapter.)

In 1993 and 1994 papers had to pay damages to defendants in the Birmingham Six case, who had been sentenced to prison for terrorism but later cleared on appeal. Former West Midlands police officers were accused of fabricating evidence in the case, but their prosecution was abandoned. After the abandonment of the case, the *Sunday Telegraph* reported one of the three officers as referring to the Birmingham Six and saying: 'In our eyes, their guilt is beyond doubt.' The matter was settled out of court. The paper had to carry a prominent apology and the claimants were reported to have received £250,000.

The *Sun* newspaper published an article based upon the *Sunday Telegraph*'s interviews. It later carried an apology and was reported to have paid £1 million.

In the past it has not even been safe to repeat a defamatory allegation made by a head of state. In 1976 Princess Elizabeth Bagaya of Toro, the former foreign minister of Uganda, collected substantial damages from several publications which had repeated libellous allegations of immoral conduct made about her by General Amin, then dictator of Uganda.

However, under a provision of the Defamation Act 1996 that came into effect in 1999, journalists have privilege for a fair and accurate copy of or extract from matter published by or on the authority of a government anywhere in the world. (The privilege, however, does not apply to publication to the public of matters which are of no public concern and the publication of which is not for the public benefit.)

The repetition rule is particularly important for those responsible for online sites that contain archive material. The rule dates from the 1849 case of the Duke of Brunswick, who sued a newspaper for defamation after sending his butler out to buy an old back copy. Nowadays the duke would be able to call up the archive version on the internet.

It is normally a defence to a libel action that it was not launched until more than a year after the publication (see next chapter, 'Other defences'). But the law takes the view that every time an article in an archive is accessed this amounts to a new publication and can give rise to a new action. So a publisher could find that someone accesses a 10-year-old article in its archive via the internet—and it then faces an action for defamation as a result. In that case the age of the article would mean that the case would be almost impossible to defend, as notebooks would have been discarded, witnesses' memories would have faded, and the author of the piece might be impossible to trace.

In 2001 the Court of Appeal confirmed that 'the rule in the Duke of Brunswick case'' was still the law and applied to the internet. *The Times* had published articles alleging that Grigori Loutchansky, an international businessman, had been involved in criminal activities, and he sued both for the stories in the paper and for those in the paper's archive, available on the internet. The paper argued that the 'single publication' rule should be applied to internet publication so that publication took place only on the day the material was posted.

But the appeal judges, rejecting this argument, said the repetition rule did not impose a restriction on the readiness to maintain and provide access to archives that amounted to a disproportionate restriction on freedom of expression.

In 2002 the Law Commission proposed that newspapers and other organisations which have online archives should be given greater protection from the threat of an action for defamation.

Journalists on local newspapers also need to be alert when handling the bygone days column. A doctor received damages for statements published in 1981 in the 'Looking Back' column of the *Evening Star*, Ipswich. The statements, repeated from an article published 25 years previously, had gone unchallenged then.

'Only rumours'

Suppose a journalist in writing defamatory allegations makes it clear that they are only rumours, or goes further and says he does not believe them? The law takes the view that ordinary people reading the story may take the view there is no smoke without fire.

In 1999 the *Sunday Life, Belfast* had to pay damages to film star Liam Neeson and his actress wife Natasha Richardson for a story headlined: 'Friends deny marriage of Ulster superstar is on the rocks'.

The paper's counsel argued that the claim should be struck out because the article did not adopt the untrue story about the Neesons, but was giving publicity to the denials, and no reasonable person would think the worse of either of them after reading the article.

But the Lord Chief Justice of Northern Ireland said a newspaper could be liable for an article that referred to defamatory rumours even though on its face it was largely directed to denials of the rumours.

Journalists may wonder how this ties in with the statement of the judge, referred to in the last chapter ('Meaning of words'), that, if in one part of a publication something disreputable to the claimant is stated and this is removed by the conclusion, 'the bane and the antidote must be taken together'.

The word 'removed' is important. In the case where the News of the World published pictures of well-known actors whose faces had been superimposed on models in pornographic poses no reasonable person reading the story could have reached the conclusion that the two actors had actually been indulging in pornographic activity; the antidote cured the bane by *removing* the defamatory meaning, the sting. In the case brought by the Neesons, by contrast, readers of the newspaper may or may not have been persuaded by denials.

A judge said in 1996 that the repetition rule did not apply to 'bane and antidote cases', but he added that such cases were rare (Lord Justice Simon Brown in *Stern v Piper* [1997] QB 123).

In 1993 the *New Statesman* paid damages to John Major, the Prime Minister, after the cover of an issue carried the headline 'The curious case of John Major's "mistress" ', and an article within discussed rumours which it said had been circulating. When sued, the magazine said the article was never intended to assert that an affair, let alone an adulterous relationship, had ever taken place.

Notice that the European Court, in the *Thorgeirson* case (above), took a different view from English common law when it found in favour of the newspaper's account of police misconduct on the ground, among others, that its allegations were 'based on widespread rumours'.

Who are the 'publishers'?

A person who has been defamed may sue the reporter, the sub-editor, the editor, the publisher, the printer, the distributor, and the broadcaster. All have participated in the publishing of the defamatory statement and are regarded as 'publishers' at common law.

In John Major's case against the *New Statesman*, referred to above, the damages paid by the magazine were only £1,001, but the Prime Minister and the woman named in the article, who also sued, received £60,000 from the printers and distributors.

The actual cost to the magazine was estimated to be £250,000, including the damages, legal costs, indemnities to printers and distributors, and the cost of the issue containing the words, which had to be withdrawn.

The section 1 defence

Live broadcasts have proved dangerous. In 1996, before passage of the Defamation Act of that year, a member of a television audience made allegations against a vet during a studio discussion. The broadcaster, Anglia TV, accepted that the claims were entirely untrue. The company said it had no prior knowledge of what was to be said, and did nothing to endorse the allegations, but it had to pay damages. The comments made on television were later reported in *Our Dogs* magazine, which also had to pay damages. All three—the member of the audience, the television company, and the magazine—had 'published' the defamatory words.

In the past, a newsvendor or bookseller could usually put forward a defence of innocent dissemination, saying he was merely the conduit for the passage of the words complained of and was thus not responsible for them. But this defence was not available to others, such as distributors and broadcasters.

The Defamation Act 1996, in section 1, extended the defence, and it now applies to anyone who was not the author, editor, or publisher (as defined by the Act) of the statement complained of, who took reasonable care in relation to its publication, and who did not know and had no reason to believe that whatever part he had in the publication caused or contributed to the publication of a defamatory statement.

A court deciding whether a person took reasonable care, or had reason to believe that what he did caused or contributed to the publication of a defamatory statement, shall have regard to:

(1) the extent of his responsibility for the content of the statement or the decision to publish it;

(2) the nature or circumstances of the publication; and

(3) the previous conduct or character of the author, editor, or publisher.

The list of categories of people who are not authors, editors, or publishers for the purposes of the new defence includes broadcasters of live programmes who have no effective control over the maker of the statement complained of.

In 1999 the BBC was sued by the research firm MORI and its head, Bob Worcester, for defamatory remarks made by the controversial politician Sir James Goldsmith during a live radio interview. The BBC said it had a defence under section 1—but could it be said it had taken 'reasonable care'? It was argued it should have known Sir James was likely to say something defamatory and it should at least have used a 'delay button', which imposes a delay of several seconds between the caller to a live show speaking and the words being broadcast, enabling defamatory words to be omitted from the broadcast. The case was settled before the jury could reach its verdict.

Libel and the internet

Another category of people for whom the new defence is available comprises providers of internet services over which the statement complained of is transmitted by a person over whom they have no effective control.

On-line publishers cannot meet this requirement, so they and their journalists will be liable for libel just as if they had published the defamatory allegations in a newspaper.

The defence is available for ISPs (internet service providers), but the restricted nature of the defence was illustrated in a case in 1999. Laurence Godfrey, a lecturer, had complained to the ISP, Demon, that a message being carried on a newsgroup hosted by Demon purported to be written by him, but was in fact a forgery and was defamatory of him.

Demon, however, allowed the message to remain on its server for about 10 days and Godfey sued, restricting his claim to those 10 days.

In court, the judge said that Demon was not the author, editor or publisher of the statement complained of, as defined by section 1. But because it had not removed the defamatory statement when it was drawn to its attention, it could not say it had taken reasonable care in relation to the publication and that it did not know and had no reason to believe that whatever part it had in the publication caused or contributed to the publication of a defamatory statement.

So Demon was unable to use the defence and eventually had to pay Godfrey in an out-of-court settlement (*Godfrey v Demon Internet Ltd* [2001] QB 201).

It seems therefore that ISPs have no defence under section 1 of the Act if they continue to host material after they have received notice it is defamatory, even if they have good reason to believe it is true or in some other way defensible (see chapter 20, 'How much protection?'). The result of the Demon case was that ISPs began to remove defamatory statements from their service as soon as these statements were brought to their attention. Media lawyers took the view that this restriction on freedom was 'disproportionate', and suggested it might not survive a challenge under the Human Rights Act.

20 How much protection?

Though libel holds many perils for journalists the law provides a greater degree of protection than journalists always fully appreciate.

Indeed, if you are just beginning to study the law of defamation you will find it instructive to examine a copy of a daily newspaper and pick out the defamatory material. You will probably be surprised to see how much of what is published is clearly defamatory, within the definitions you have just been studying. How can the papers get away with these stories?

This chapter will answer that question by explaining the various defences available in an action for defamation.

The main defences are:

(1) justification;

(2) fair comment;

(3) privilege;

(4) accord and satisfaction;

(5) offer of amends.

If you have a good knowledge of these defences you can use it to test the safety or otherwise of what you intend to publish and thus work with much greater confidence.

In earlier editions of this book the authors, having listed in the last chapter some matters the claimant did not have to prove, noted in this chapter two defences that did not exist—though many students and some journalists appeared to believe they did.

It was no defence to show that your story was published in the public interest. The previous chapters of this book have referred to several stories in the past publication of which appeared to be clearly in the public interest but which resulted in the payment of damages—in some cases very large damages.

But after the House of Lords decision in 1999 in the *Reynolds* case (see below, 'The Reynolds Defence') English law in effect recognises a public interest defence. The leading media lawyer Lord Lester QC said the Fourth Estate was now to be treated in law as endowed with vital public powers and duties. A new public interest defence of publication of information of public concern might be relied upon, he said, provided the newspaper or broadcaster had exercised its powers fairly and reasonably.

The European Court of Human Rights also is much concerned with the importance of freedom of expression in the discussion of matters of public interest and emphasises that any restriction must be 'necessary' for the protection of the reputation of the claimant. It is doubtful whether any of the European Court cases previously considered would have resulted in a victory for the media under English law, before the *Reynolds* case, and it seems the 'public interest' element in the cases was a key factor for the European judges.

There is still no defence of 'fairness'. Some journalists believe that if they intend to publish a defamatory statement about someone and offer the defamed person the opportunity to reply the resulting report is 'fair' and they have a defence. But if they are sued they will generally have to prove the truth of the allegation.

The preceding paragraph is not of course an argument for not being fair. There are strong ethical and professional reasons impelling journalists to be fair. There are good practical reasons too. People who sue the media tend to be angry; they are less likely to be angry and thus to sue you if they understand that, even if you have the story wrong, you were trying to be fair.

And you will see when you read the sections on privilege that the question of fairness arises. If you are pleading that your story is protected by privilege at common law you may have to show you put it to the subject for his comments.

Justification

It is a complete defence to a libel action (with the limited exception arising under the Rehabilitation of Offenders Act 1974: see chapter 22) to prove that the words complained of are substantially true.

But it is a difficult defence to advance because, as stated previously, in a libel action it is not the task of the claimant to show the words were untrue, but of the defendant to show that they were true. Other reasons why the defence is so difficult are explained below.

The name of the defence is justification, a misleading name because the defendant does not have to show he had any moral or social reason for publishing the defamatory words. It is sufficient if they are true. It has been suggested that the defence should be renamed truth.

Suppose a claimant asks a court to grant him an injunction preventing a newspaper from publishing defamatory material. The court will normally refuse an injunction once a newspaper says it is going to plead the defence of justification (see chapter 30, 'Protection against injunctions').

Facts must be proved true

The defence applies to statements of fact. If the words complained of consist of a statement of fact they must be proved to be true, but if they are an expression of opinion they may be defended as fair comment (see next section).

The journalist must persuade the jury that his story is true 'on the balance of probabilities', which is a lower requirement than 'beyond all reasonable doubt', the standard in criminal cases.

The *Sun* successfully used the defence when sued in 1994 by Gillian Taylforth, the television actress, and her boyfriend after the paper published a front-page splash headlined 'TV Kathy's "sex romp" on A1' saying the couple had indulged in oral sex in a parked car.

The *Sun* obtained confirmation from the police press office that the boyfriend had been cautioned for indecency, and when sued the paper joined the police in the defence, with the result that the main defence witness was the officer who claimed he saw the incident.

Taylforth and her boyfriend denied the story and the court arranged a reconstruction of the event in which the judge, jury, and journalists watched as the couple showed what position they said they had been in and then two *Sun* journalists simulated the paper's version. The jury found for the paper 10–2.

The costs of that case, which Taylforth and her boyfriend had to meet, were estimated at £500,000. Had the paper lost, it would have had to pay the bill, in addition to damages.

Cases can be complex

Cost is not the only factor that makes justification a difficult defence. Cases in which the media plead justification can be extremely complex, as the following examples show.

In 1992 Scottish Television (STV) successfully defended a libel action brought by

Antony Gecas, the former platoon commander of a Lithuanian police battalion under German occupation who settled in Edinburgh after the 1939–45 war. In a 1987 programme called 'Crimes of War' STV accused him of involvement in the murder of thousands of Jews.

When sued, STV was faced with the task of proving its account of events that had happened nearly half a century before. Its researchers visited many countries to find new evidence. Some of the witnesses were too old or fragile to go to Scotland for the trial, so the court sat in Lithuania to hear some of the evidence.

At the end the judge (who heard the case without a jury, as is usually the practice in Scotland) found for STV. He said Gecas had participated in many operations involving the killing of innocent Soviet citizens, including Jews, in particular in Byelorussia during the last three months of 1941, and in doing so committed war crimes against Soviet citizens who included old men, women, and children. The case cost an estimated £1.5 million.

In 1997 *The Guardian* newspaper risked the award of huge libel damages and costs when it defended a case brought against it by the former Conservative cabinet minister Jonathan Aitken. The paper had reported, among other things, that he had allowed an Arab business associate to pay his hotel bill in Paris for the notorious 'Ritz weekend' in breach of ministerial guidelines. Aitken had resigned from the Cabinet in order, he said, to pursue *The Guardian* with 'the sword of truth' and 'the shield of fair play'.

The Guardian embarked on a four-year investigation of monumentally complex proportions, which culminated in the production of vital evidence at a late stage in the trial, as Aitken appeared to be winning, and the former minister dramatically abandoned the case. He faced a costs bill of £2 million, which *The Guardian* would have had to pay, in addition to damages, if it had lost. Aitken was later jailed for perjury.

But such determined defences have been rare.

Inferences must be proved

Another reason that the defence of justification is so difficult is that it entails proving not only the precise truth of each defamatory statement (subject to the exception provided for in the 1952 Defamation Act, mentioned below) but also any reasonable interpretation that may be understood of the words complained of and any innuendoes lying behind them.

An example is provided by the case referred to in chapter 18 in which in 1998 Granada television agreed to pay damages and huge costs over a *World in Action* programme which revealed that garments sold by the store company Marks and Spencer (M & S) and marked 'Made in England' were in fact made in a factory in Morocco which employed child labour.

Investigative reporters visited the factory posing as the sales director and marketing director of a fictitious mail order company. They found girls aged 13 and 14 who said they worked 49-hour weeks in sweltering conditions for 20 pence an hour (later the rate was found to be 10 pence an hour). Pyjamas being made for Marks and Spencer by its supplier carried the M & S 'made in UK' label.

The narrator of the programme said: 'We wondered if M & S's checks were working as well as it claims, and if M & S realised children were being exploited.'

The store said the programme meant it had 'knowingly and deliberately exploited child labour in order to boost its profits' and had misled customers by selling foreign-made garments labelled 'made in UK'. It claimed it was ignorant of the use of child labour and stopped using the supplier at that factory when it found out.

Granada said the programme meant only that M & S fell far short of the high standards it proclaimed for itself in not making adequate checks on its suppliers. The television company settled the case after the jury rejected both meanings and said the words did mean that the company knew exploitation was occurring—a meaning that Granada denied it had intended.

As stated in chapter 18, *Yachting World* was sued for libel over statements in a critical boat test it had published. It claimed that the facts contained were true, and there was no doubt that there was a wide difference between the performance of the boat as claimed in the manufacturer's publicity material and the figures recorded by experts who tested the boat after litigation began. But the manufacturer said the article meant it had deliberately misled the public by its publicity material and the jury found in its favour.

In 1987 Jeffrey Archer, the politician and novelist (later Lord Archer), was awarded £500,000 against the *Star* newspaper, which said that he had paid a prostitute for sexual intercourse. He also sued the *News of the World* for a story headlined 'Tory boss Archer pays off vice girl'. It was true that Archer had paid £2,000 to the prostitute to go abroad to avoid scandal but he claimed the article implied he had had a sexual relationship with her. The paper said it had never intended such a suggestion, but it had to pay Archer £50,000 damages in an agreed settlement. (In 2001 Archer was found guilty of perjury and perverting the course of justice in the libel action and jailed for four years. He repaid the damages to the two papers, and their costs.)

Reporting investigations

In considering reports linking a claimant with criminal or anti-social conduct, the courts recognise three levels of meaning. The report may mean the person is guilty of the offence (a level 1 meaning), or he is reasonably suspected of the offence (level 2), or there are grounds for an investigation (level 3). All three meanings may be defended if they can be proved to be true, but clearly the standard of proof differs according to the meaning of the story, and many libel actions relating to investigations involve disputes over the meaning of the words.

The three categories were set out by Lord Devlin in a case in which two national newspapers stated that the City of London Fraud Squad was inquiring into the affairs of a company. The statement was true, but the claimant said the words meant (by implication) that he and the company were guilty of fraud, or at least were suspected of fraud, and heavy damages were initially awarded against the newspapers. On appeal, the House of Lords ruled that the words were not capable of meaning that fraud had been committed, but they were capable of meaning that the claimants were suspected and that whether they had this meaning or not should be left to a jury. The matter was settled out of court without a new trial (*Lewis v Daily Telegraph*, and *Lewis v Associated Newspapers Ltd* [1964] AC 234).

The reason it is defamatory to say of a person that he is reasonably suspected of an offence is that it implies conduct on the person's part that warranted the suspicion, so if you are to succeed in a plea of justification you must show conduct on the person's part giving rise to the suspicion. It is no use saying other people told you about their suspicions (*Shah v Standard Chartered Bank* [1999] QB 241).

In 2003 the *Sun* newspaper had to pay £100,000 damages to a children's nurse for a story headlined 'Nurse is probed over 18 deaths'. The police had been investigating the circumstances of the deaths of a number of terminally ill children whom she had treated but they concluded (after the *Sun*'s story was published) that there were no grounds to suspect her of an offence.

The newspaper tried to show there were reasonable grounds for suspicion, but the Court of Appeal said the newspaper was relying almost entirely upon the fact that a number of allegations had been made against the nurse to the hospital trust and the police. The only respect in which the newspaper focused upon the nurse's *conduct* concerned an allegation made *after* publication, and the court said that could not be taken into consideration (*Elaine Chase v News Group Newspapers Ltd* [2002] EWCA Civ 1772, [2002] All ER (D) 20 (Dec)).

Courts sometimes find it difficult to decide to which level of meaning a story belongs. The Saudi billionaire Yousef Jameel sued *The Sunday Times* over a story headlined 'Car tycoon "linked" to Bin Laden'. Jameel said the story meant there were reasonable grounds for suspecting that he was associated with Osama Bin Laden and had helped to fund the terrorists who destroyed the twin towers in New York (a level 2 meaning); but a High Court judge rejected that meaning and allowed the case to go ahead on the basis that the story meant only that there were grounds for inquiry or investigation—an allegation which the paper said was true. The Court of Appeal, however, reinstated the stronger claim, and as this edition of *McNae* went to press the trial of the case was awaited (*Yousef Jameel v Times Newspapers Ltd* [2004] EWCA Civ 983).

Avoid implying habitual conduct

To say of A 'He is a thief' may be true in the simple meaning of the words. But if the basis for the assertion is one conviction for stealing a packet of bacon from a self-service store a defence of justification to any action for defamation brought by A might fail.

For A would argue that the words contained the meaning that he was a persistent thief, and was a person whom no one should trust, whereas he was essentially an honest man who had had a single lapse.

A jury might well take the view that A's reputation, though not exemplary, had been made blacker by the description applied to him.

The principle is an important one. Many libel actions result from the journalist implying habitual conduct from a single incident. In the Radio City case referred to in chapter 18 the broadcast company said it was true that the holiday firm's proprietor made promises to holidaymakers that he could not keep and was indifferent to the distress caused. Nineteen witnesses gave evidence in support of the programme.

But the proprietor said the implication was he did this habitually, and he called 21 witnesses who gave glowing or favourable accounts of their holidays with him. The jury found in his favour.

In the libel action in 2001 in which a jury awarded £350,000 damages (later reduced on appeal) to a man described by the *News of the World* as a pervert, the paper had a video film, shot by the claimant himself, showing him involved in sexual activity with a male. The man told the jury this was a 'one-off' event that occurred when he was depressed over the loss of his business.

Sticking to story is expensive

The defence of justification is not only difficult; it is dangerous. If it fails the court will take a critical view of the newspaper's persistence in sticking to a story which it decides is not true, and the jury may award greater damages accordingly.

In the *Archer* case (see above) the *Star* newspaper claimed its story that Archer had sexual relations with the prostitute was true. The case lasted three weeks. The £500,000 damages were awarded after the judge told the jury that the newspaper had carried the case through to the bitter end and if they found in Mr Archer's favour the damages should be sufficiently large to 'send a message to the world that the accusations were false'.

The investigative journalist

The examples given make it clear that the journalist embarking on an investigative story must not only be sure of his facts. He must be able to prove them in court. A number of stories for which newspapers paid damages later proved to be true, but too late to prevent the damage to the paper; as a general rule, courts are very reluctant to overturn decisions or agreed settlements when new facts come to light.

Make sure of your witnesses

If the journalist is relying on a witness to back up his case, it is generally what that witness says, rather than the journalist's account of it, that is likely to be more convincing in a jury's eyes.

Are your witnesses going to be available to give evidence when the case comes to court, which may be years after the events described in the story? The journalist must be sure he keeps track of them, noting their various changes of address.

Are they going to be willing to give evidence?

How convincing will their version of events sound when tested by clever cross-examination? What impression will they make on the jury? In particular, will the jury believe their version of events in preference to the version of the person suing? The libel action that Jeffrey Archer brought against the *Star* (see above) resolved itself into a clash of evidence on whether he had in fact resorted to a prostitute. The jury accepted the account of the leading Conservative politician in preference to that of the prostitute.

English juries are said to be likely to accept the word of a police officer. In the case brought by the TV actress Gillian Taylforth against the *Sun* (see above) the newspaper had the rare experience of having its story backed by police evidence.

Reference has been made (see previous chapter, 'Identification') to the numerous cases brought in recent years on behalf of police officers for allegations of bad conduct such as brutality and harassment. Local editors may see it as their duty to publish such stories in the public interest but they must be aware of the strong likelihood that the jury will accept the denial of the officer rather than the allegation of the source, who, in the nature of things, will often be a person of low social standing, perhaps with a criminal record.

In the case of *Bennett v Guardian*, in 1997 (see previous chapter, 'Identification'), the sources of allegations printed in *The Guardian* included a convicted person (later cleared on appeal); a man who had been charged with drug dealing, but against whom charges had been dropped; and the solicitor of a convicted drug dealer.

Signed statements important

If the journalist is working on a story where he expects his version may be challenged in court, he should persuade his witness to make a signed statement at the time and date it.

This could be a signed statement or tape recording of any witness willing to testify against the claimant. It could be a note written by the journalist in his notebook and signed by the witness.

Better, it could be a statutory declaration from any such witness. That is a more formal statement made before a JP, solicitor, or court officer and it carries greater weight in court.

Best, it could be an affidavit, more formal still and sworn on oath. Both this and a statutory declaration put the deponent at risk of perjury if he is not telling the truth.

If the worst happens and the journalist's vital witness decides when the case comes for trial he does not want to give evidence, but the journalist has a signed statement, the reluctant person can be summoned to court by subpoena and forced to answer questions; if he changes his story, he may be cross-examined.

If the journalist has a statement, whether written or tape recorded, from a witness who dies or goes abroad before the trial the statement itself can be produced in evidence.

The Civil Evidence Act 1995 makes hearsay evidence acceptable in court subject to certain conditions. For practical purposes, where the statement comprises, or is contained in, a document, it must be signed to make it admissible.

What is the value of a photocopy of a document? Suppose, for example, you are running a story about council workmen fiddling their expenses and you derived your facts from the photocopy of a confidential council document that included false expenses claims.

If you can explain why the original is not available, that makes the copy available for evidence. But you would have to persuade the court that the document is authentic—eg by evidence from someone within the council. The libel claimant would no doubt challenge its authenticity.

Make sure you keep the evidence

Often the paper's case is weakened because the journalist himself has failed to observe the basic editorial discipline of keeping his notebook in good order. When the journalist is required to give evidence, a court will attach weight to a shorthand note properly dated.

By contrast, the court may attach significance to the lack of any such note. In the case in which Jeffrey Archer sued the *Star* (see above) the judge asked the jury if they did not find it odd that none of the journalists had produced a note of what they had been told by Archer.

Keeping a good note is particularly important when a newspaper is using the Reynolds defence to contest a libel action. The passage later in this chapter on the Reynolds defence records that the *Sunday Times* and *The Times* both lost libel actions (*Reynolds* and *Loutchansky*) after their reporters failed to produce a written note of vital conversations, but the *Leeds Weekly News* succeeded even though the reporter had lost some of her notes; those she had were in transcribable shorthand, which the judge duly weighed in the paper's favour.

Tape recordings must be kept too. In 1992 Jason Connery, the actor, sued over an article in the *Sun* which carried comments attributed to him and which, he said, meant he would be afraid to fight for his country in the Gulf War. He denied making any such comments.

The journalist, in her evidence, said she had tape recorded a conversation with Connery, but had destroyed the tape after she had taken notes from it to prepare her copy. The jury awarded £35,000 damages.

The time factor is important. Until the law was changed in September 1996 claimants had three years within which to issue their writs, and for tactical reasons their lawyers often delayed. In the 1997 case of *Bennett v Guardian*, referred to above, the writ was issued in 1995 a week before the end of the three-year period.

The Defamation Act 1996 reduced the limitation period to one year (though the court has power to extend the time in some circumstances). But it may still be another year or two before the matter eventually comes to court.

If there is a plea for special damages to compensate for actual loss caused by the damaging publication, the delay may well be necessary for the claimant to accumulate proof.

But for the defendant newspaper, the delay poses enormous difficulties. Witnesses may have died or disappeared: in any event, they can hardly be expected to remember the details. In the *Mail on Sunday* case referred to in chapter 18, the writ was issued in 1984 but the matter did not come to trial until 1989; by that time much of the evidence had been destroyed as a danger to health and journalists' notes had been disposed of.

Section 5 defence

Before the 1952 Defamation Act was passed, to succeed in a plea of justification it was necessary to prove the precise truth of every defamatory statement in the offending article. Now the law says (in section 5 of the Act) that a defence of justification shall not fail merely because the article contains some inaccuracies.

This is the actual wording:

> In an action for libel or slander in respect of words containing two or more distinct charges against the claimant, a defence of justification shall not fail by reason only that the truth of every charge is not proved, if the words not proved to be true do not materially injure the claimant's reputation, having regard to the truth of the remaining charges.

The section 5 defence was used successfully in 1992 in the case mentioned above in which Antony Gecas sued STV. The programme said Gecas used his pistol to 'finish off' Jews and others who had been shot and thrown into pits but were still alive.

The judge said he did not consider STV had proved the allegation but in his opinion the inclusion of the allegation in the programme did not materially injure Gecas's reputation over and above the injury to his reputation arising from the allegations that had been proved.

Fair comment

Newspapers faced with an action for defamation rely much more frequently on the defence of fair comment made honestly on a matter of public interest.

Only comment

Notice that the defence applies only to comment. It does not provide a defence for the publication of defamatory facts. The comment must be based upon facts that are either stated or indicated in the story complained of. These facts must be true and the burden of proving their truth is on the publisher.

A judge gave an example of fair comment. He said that if you accurately report what some public man has done and then say 'Such conduct is disgraceful', that is merely an expression of your opinion, your comment on the person's conduct.

So also if, without reporting the man's action, you identify the conduct by a reference to it that readers will understand. In either case, you enable your readers to judge for themselves how far your opinion is well founded.

But, the judge said, if you assert that the man has been guilty of disgraceful conduct and do not state what that conduct was, this is an allegation of fact for which there is no defence other than truth or privilege (see next section).

It is no use going to court and saying: 'This comment would have been fair if we had not been misinformed.' The only acceptable defence is: 'The facts are true and the comment upon those facts is fair.'

Sub-editors need to take special care if they introduce comment into headlines on news stories. In 2003 *The Daily Telegraph* published news stories and leading articles making allegations about the left-wing Labour MP George Galloway after a reporter was said to have found documents referring to him in the ruins of a government building in Baghdad, soon after the invasion of Iraq by coalition forces. One news story was headlined 'Telegraph reveals damning new evidence on Labour MP'. When sued, the paper did not claim the allegations were true but claimed the headline was an expression of opinion. But the judge said 'damning' had a plain meaning—'that is to say, that the evidence goes beyond a prima facie case and points to guilt'. He said there was no basis upon which the defence of fair comment could succeed. The MP won his case (*George Galloway MP v Telegraph Group Ltd* [2004] EWHC 2786 (QB); for a fuller account of this case, see 'Privilege, Neutral Reportage', later in this chapter).

There is an exception to the rule that comment must be based on true facts. This is where the comment is based on privileged material, such as a report of judicial proceedings. In that case, the defence will still succeed even if the facts mentioned in the privileged report later turn out to be untrue.

The law does not require the 'truth' of the comment itself to be proved; by its nature it cannot be. Comment may be responsible or irresponsible, informed or misinformed, constructive or destructive; but it cannot be true or false.

Nor does the law require that the defendant pleading fair comment should carry the court with him. It is not necessary to persuade either the judge or the jury to share his views.

Honest opinion

What a defendant must do is satisfy the jury that his comment upon established facts represents his honestly held opinion.

The law was expressed by Lord Diplock (then Mr Justice Diplock) in his summing up to the jury in a case in which Lord Silkin unsuccessfully sued Beaverbrook Newspapers for certain statements by 'Cross Bencher' in the *Sunday Express*. He said:

> People are entitled to hold and express strong views on matters of public interest, provided they are honestly held. They may be views which some or all of you think are exaggerated, obstinate, or prejudiced.
>
> The basis of our public life is that the crank and the enthusiast can say what he honestly believes just as much as a reasonable man or woman.
>
> It would be a sad day for freedom of speech in this country if a jury were to apply the test of whether it agrees with a comment, instead of applying the true test of whether this opinion, however exaggerated, obstinate, or prejudiced, was honestly held.

The name of this defence does not help the young journalist to understand its nature; indeed the Faulks Committee on Defamation described it in 1975 as 'seriously misleading having regard to the actual nature of the defence, which in reality protects unfair comment'.

Clearly, the opinion of a person with prejudiced or exaggerated views may be extremely unfair if viewed objectively by a balanced person. It is better to emphasise that the comment must be honest. The committee recommended that the defence should be renamed simply 'comment'.

Without malice

If the defence is to succeed, it is essential that the defamatory statement was made without malice. The word malice has a special meaning in the law and, to make things more complicated, has a different meaning depending upon whether you are considering fair comment or privilege, as a defence.

The leading judge Lord Nicholls explained in a case in 2000 that, when considering comment as a defence, 'malice covers the case of the defendant who does not genuinely hold the view he expressed. In other words, when making the defamatory comment, the defendant acted dishonestly. He put forward as his view something which, in truth, was not his view. It was a pretence. The law does not protect such statements' (*Tse Wai Chun Paul v Albert Cheng*, Court of Final Appeal, Hong Kong [2001] EMLR 777).

In previous editions *McNae*, like other books on the law, has said that the free speech made possible by the fair comment defence must not be abused by people for the wrong reasons. 'For example, if it could be shown that the editor of a newspaper had published critical comment to discredit a public figure because of a personal grudge this would constitute malice, and the defence of fair comment would fail. The defence would probably fail also if the editor had launched a sensational attack, couched in immoderate terms, merely in the hope of increasing his paper's circulation.'

But Lord Nicholls, in the case referred to above, said that the defence is not defeated by the fact that the writer is actuated by spite, animosity, intent to injure, intent to arouse controversy or other motivation even if that is the dominant or sole motive. He added, however, that proof of such motivation might be evidence from which a jury could infer lack of genuine belief in the view expressed.

Lord Nicholls said 'critics need no longer be mealy-mouthed in denouncing what they disagree with', provided the 'objective limits' of the fair comment defence were established—that is, that the issue was one of public interest, that the comment was readily recognisable as such and based on facts which were probably true or protected by privilege, that it explicitly indicated what were the relevant facts, and was a comment which could have been made by an honest person, no matter how prejudiced or obstinate.

Lawyer Antony Whitaker, commenting on the case, described the judge's ruling as 'a brave step forward . . . Journalists can now sharpen their arrows and, within the limits of what they honestly believe on matters of public interest, vent rage, spite and spleen on their favourite targets.'

Imputing improper motives

Ealier editions of *McNae* warned that an important limitation of the defence occurred where the journalist not only criticised a person's actions, but also imputed corrupt or dishonourable motives to him. A judge said in 1885 that 'The state of a man's mind is as much a matter of fact as the state of his digestion' (Lord Justice Bowen in *Edgington v Fitzmaurice* (1885) 29 Ch D 459), from which it followed that normally only the claimant in a libel action could state exactly what his motives were so a defence of fair comment would not be available.

The imputation of improper motives has been a frequent cause of libel actions. Notice how this applies to some of the cases we have considered, for example the cases involving *Yachting World* and the drug Halcion in chapter 18.

But judges in the Court of Appeal took a more helpful view in a case in 2001 in a libel action brought by the entrepreneur Richard Branson against his biographer Tom Bower (*Branson v Bower* [2001] EWCA Civ 791, [2001] EMLR 800). Bower, commenting on the attempt by Branson to run the national lottery, said: 'Sceptics will inevitably whisper that Branson's motive is self-glorification.' When sued, Bower claimed this was fair comment but Branson said it was a factual allegation (that he had a questionable intention in bidding for the national lottery) and that this was untrue.

Lord Justice Latham, giving the judgment of the Court of Appeal, said that comment was 'something which is or can reasonably be inferred to be a deduction, inference, conclusion, criticism, remark, observation'.

He said that an assertion as to motive might be capable of amounting to an assertion of fact, but that depended on its context and in this case the judge in the lower court had been fully entitled to come to the conclusion that Bower was expressing a series of opinions about Branson's motives in a way that would leave the reader in no doubt that they were inferences drawn by Bower from the facts set out in the article.

Privilege

The law recognises that there are occasions when the public interest demands that there shall be complete freedom of speech without any risk of proceedings for defamation, even if the statements are defamatory and even if they are untrue. We say that these occasions are privileged.

Privilege exists under the common law (see 'Privilege at common law', later in this chapter). But journalists in most cases rely on privilege granted by Parliament—that is, statutory privilege.

Absolute privilege

Absolute privilege, where it is applicable, is a complete answer and bar to any action for defamation. It does not matter whether the words are true or false. It does not matter that they were spoken maliciously (for the meaning of 'malicious' in this context, see below). If they are protected by absolute privilege, that is a complete bar to any action.

But though a journalist may be reporting what is said on an occasion that is protected by absolute privilege it does not follow that his report is similarly protected.

Take the proceedings of Parliament. These enjoy absolute privilege under the common law. A Member may say whatever he wishes in the House of Commons without fear of an action for defamation. But the reports of parliamentary debates published in a newspaper enjoy only qualified privilege which, as we shall see later in this chapter, introduces a question of the motive in publication.

The official daily reports of parliamentary proceedings (in *Hansard*) have absolute privilege; so have reports published by order of Parliament (such as White Papers). But their publication in a newspaper, in full or in part, enjoys only qualified privilege.

The only time journalists enjoy absolute privilege is when they are reporting the courts. This defence is available for a fair and accurate report of judicial proceedings in open court within the United Kingdom, published contemporaneously.

There was some doubt whether the protection for such a report was absolute or qualified, but a section of the Defamation Act 1996 removed any doubt. The Act also extended the protection to reports of the European Court of Justice, or any court attached to that court, the European Court of Human Rights, and any international criminal tribunal (a war crimes tribunal) established by the Security Council of the United Nations or by an international agreement to which the United Kingdom is a party.

Privilege for court reports constitutes a most valuable protection for newspapers because what is said in court (especially a criminal court) is often highly defamatory.

Without such protection, court reporting as we know it would be impossible, and the protection is given because the law recognises the vital part that newspapers must play in the administration of justice.

Reports must be fair

However, there are still precautions that must be taken if it is not to be forfeited.

The law specifies that the report must be 'fair and accurate'. This does not mean that the proceedings must be reported verbatim; however abbreviated the report, it will still be 'fair and accurate' if it presents a summary of both sides, contains no inaccuracies, and avoids giving disproportionate weight to one side or the other.

The unfair or inaccurate report, however, forfeits the protection of privilege. Should this happen, the newspaper is in a dangerous position, for it may be that there is no other defence available to it.

In 1993 the *Daily Sport* paid substantial damages to a police officer acquitted of indecent assault. The paper reported the opening of the case by the prosecution and the main evidence of the alleged victim, but did not include her cross-examination by the defence, which began on the same day.

Later the paper briefly reported the officer's acquittal. The officer's solicitor said the alleged victim made a number of admissions under cross-examination that weakened the evidence-in-chief given by her.

Trials may last for days, weeks, or months and statements made by the prosecution in criminal cases or by the claimant in civil cases may subsequently be shown by the defendant to be wrong. However, it is established that where a trial lasts more than one day the proceedings of each day may be published separately at the time.

Evening papers and broadcasters regularly publish accounts of that part of a day's trial that has been heard by their time of publication. Had the *Daily Sport* case gone to court the outcome is uncertain. It may have been in a less strong position than an evening paper because it had ample time to publish details of the cross-examination in its report of the day's hearing.

The safest journalistic practice is that if the newspaper has reported allegations made by the prosecutor that are later rebutted those rebuttals also should be carried.

Reports must be accurate

Turning to accuracy, all allegations in court reports must be attributed because a report that presents an allegation as if it were a proved fact is inaccurate. Do not write 'Brown had a gun in his hand' but 'Smith said Brown had a gun in his hand'.

A newspaper is left with no protection at all if, whether or not by carelessness, it identifies as the defendant someone who is only a witness or unconnected with the case. This may happen because of similarities of name and address. In county court cases reporters sometimes confuse the names of the claimant and the defendant.

Newspapers must avoid wrongly reporting that the defendant has been convicted when he has in fact been acquitted. In 1993 the *Hendon and Finchley Times* had to pay substantial damages to a man acquitted of conspiring to smuggle drugs. The man's solicitor told the court that although the story reported the man had been acquitted, it did so in terms that conveyed the impression he was in fact guilty as charged and ought not to have been cleared.

Other mistakes that the court reporter can make include wrongly reporting the defendant has been found guilty of a more serious offence than the correct one, and giving the wrong address for the defendant—which can lead to a complaint by the person living at that address.

Reports must be contemporaneous

The law also requires, for absolute statutory privilege to attach, that the report should be published contemporaneously with the proceedings. For all practical purposes this means publication in the first issue of the paper following the hearing, or while the hearing is proceeding.

An evening paper might begin reporting a case in its early editions, continue to add to its report as later editions appear, and perhaps conclude it the following day.

However, care should be taken in 'holding over' court matter from one issue to another, as weekly newspapers sometimes do.

Sometimes the report of court proceedings has to be postponed in accordance with the law. In that case, says the Defamation Act 1996, the story is treated as if it were published contemporaneously if it is published 'as soon as practicable after publication is permitted'.

Even if the report is not contemporaneous, it will still attract qualified privilege under statute and under common law (see 'Qualified privilege by statute', 'Statements having qualified privilege', and 'Privilege at common law, Reports of judicial and parliamentary proceedings', later in this chapter).

Protection only for reports of proceedings

In general, privilege extends only to the actual report of the proceedings, held in open court. It does not protect defamatory matter shouted out in court which is not part of the proceedings. Nor does it protect matter gleaned from documents presented to the bench but not read out in open court.

The Defamation Act 1996 extended qualified privilege to a fair and accurate copy of or extract from a document made available by a court and this may for the first time give protection to information from court lists; may rather than will because it is not clear what meaning courts will attach to the words 'made available by a court'. Previously, such information had not been privileged unless read out during the proceedings. The leading libel lawyer, the late Peter Carter-Ruck, believed such a publication would be privileged.

Headlines and introductions lead to many complaints. Particular care should be used in writing them to avoid any misrepresentation or exaggeration.

Qualified privilege

Qualified privilege is available as a defence to the journalist in circumstances where it is considered important that the facts should be freely known in the public interest. There is privilege at common law for the publication of defamatory statements in certain circumstances (see later in this chapter). But the journalist has traditionally relied in his everyday work not upon the common law but upon statute. The Defamation Act 1952 listed categories of circumstances in which statutory protection applied and the Defamation Act 1996, in a provision that came into effect in 1999, considerably extended the categories.

Qualified privilege by statute

In general, qualified privilege affords just as much protection to a newspaper as absolute privilege, provided certain conditions are observed.

These are that the report is:

(1) fair and accurate; and (unlike absolute privilege);

(2) published without malice.

Malice in this context has a different meaning from malice in the context of fair comment (see earlier this chapter). It means ill-will or spite towards the claimant or any indirect or improper motive in the defendant's mind. Lord Nicholls explained in the *Cheng* case that the purpose of the defence of qualified privilege is to allow a person who has a duty to perform, or an interest to protect, to provide information without the risk of being sued. If a person's dominant motive is not to perform this duty or protect this interest, he cannot use the defence.

Qualified privilege (again, unlike absolute privilege) does not protect the publication in a newspaper of matter which is not of public concern and the publication of which is not for the public benefit.

The protection applies only to reports of the actual proceedings or other matters listed below. Just as the court reporter must take care not to lose his privilege by reporting matter which is not part of the proceedings, so the reporter who has attended, say, a council meeting must be careful not to hazard the protection which the law allows to that report by including matter which is not privileged.

For example, there is no privilege for a report of defamatory statements made by a councillor after the meeting when he is asked to expand on statements made during the meeting.

An official police statement may be reported safely. Even so, journalists must be very careful in straying outside the strict wording of the statement. In the case *Bennett v Guardian* (referred to in the previous chapter, 'Identification'), the paper's story was based upon a Scotland Yard press statement saying that eight Stoke Newington officers, whom it did not name, had been transferred to other stations.

The paper's crime correspondent accurately reported the statement, but added background material he had accumulated during his investigation. Five officers sued. As stated, the jury found for the newspaper by a majority. Had they not done so the paper would have faced huge damages and costs.

Statements subject to explanation

The Schedule to the 1996 Act gives in Part I a list of statements having qualified privilege and in Part II a list of statements privileged 'subject to explanation or contradiction'.

This means that, if required to do so, an editor who has published a defamatory statement upon an occasion mentioned in Part II must publish a 'reasonable letter or statement by way of explanation or contradiction'.

Failure to publish such a statement, or failure to do so in 'an adequate or reasonable manner having regard to the circumstances', would destroy the defence of qualified privilege.

Legal advice should be taken if any statement that the complainer asks to be published gives rise to any difficulty, such as the risk of libelling another person by contradicting what he has been reported as saying.

Public meeting defined

The Schedule to the 1996 Act is reproduced below. Reference to it will show what action is appropriate in any particular circumstances. Attention is drawn particularly to paragraph 12 of the Schedule, which provides a legal definition of a 'public meeting'.

It is very wide, covering almost any kind of meeting that a reporter will be required to attend. Note that it refers to a lawful meeting held for the furtherance or discussion of a matter of public concern, whether admission to the meeting is general or restricted.

The House of Lords ruled in 2000 that a press conference is a public meeting, an important decision for journalists and the media generally. *The Times* had been sued over its report of a press conference called by a group of people campaigning for the release of a soldier convicted of murdering a joyrider.

During the press conference defamatory comments were made about the solicitors who had represented him, and these were reported by the paper. A jury awarded £145,000 damages. But on appeal, Lord Bingham, the senior law lord, said that press representatives could either be regarded as members of the public themselves or as 'the eyes and ears of the public, to whom they report'.

The court also ruled that a written press release, handed out at the meeting but not read aloud, and reported by the paper, was still part of the proceedings because it was taken as read.

Whether a meeting is 'lawful' within the meaning of this Act is a matter for the judge to decide if the matter goes to court.

Note also that paragraph 11 of the Schedule covers meetings held in public by local authorities or by justices of the peace 'acting otherwise than as a court exercising judicial authority'.

'Findings' but not proceedings

Paragraph 14 of the Schedule gives protection to reports of findings or decisions of a wide variety of bodies. Many of these matters were covered by the 1952 Act, but the 1996 Act extends the protection to reports of the findings or decisions of associations formed to promote charitable objects 'or other objects beneficial to the community'. Note the protection does not apply to a report of the *proceedings* of such bodies.

Privilege for sub-committees

Under the previous law there was no statutory qualified privilege for reports of the sub-committees of minor local authorities, notably town councils. This omission was remedied by paragraph 11 of the 1996 Act, which includes in its definition of local authorities any authority or body to which the Public Bodies (Admission to Meetings) Act 1960 applies (see chapter 27).

Important protection restricted

Paragraph 12 of the 1952 Schedule was a very important protection for journalists. It gave protection for a copy or fair and accurate report or summary of any notice or other matter issued for the information of the public by or on behalf of any government department, officer of state, local authority, or chief officer of police.

In a case in 1966 the broadcasters of *Police 5* were protected by qualified privilege in relation to a broadcast concerning a suspected theft of pigs, in which the claimant had been mistakenly identified as a suspect.

The term 'local authority' was defined by a later Act to include health authorities.

Paragraph 9 of the 1996 Act, which came into effect in 1999, covers a more extensive list of privileged matter but gives privilege, subject to explanation or contradiction, only to 'a fair and accurate copy of or extract from' a notice or other matter. A 'report or summary' of the notice is no longer within the privilege.

The leading law books differed on the significance of the change but *Carter-Ruck on Libel and Slander* (1997), said: 'It is submitted that it will be a foolhardy claimant who gambles on a newspaper not enjoying privilege for a report that would successfully have relied on para 12 of the Schedule to the 1952 Act.' It is also suggested in such a case common law privilege might now be available.

The 1996 Act protects a fair and accurate copy of or extract from a notice or other matter issued for the information of the public by or on behalf of:

(1) a legislature in any member state (that means a member of the European Union) or the European Parliament;

(2) the government of any member state, or any authority performing governmental functions in any member state or part of a member state, or the European Commission;

(3) an international organisation or international conference.

Any authority performing governmental functions clearly includes local authorities, and the Act states that the phrase also includes 'police functions'.

There will be many occasions when a reporter will wish to report the misdeeds of a person but may be inhibited by the fear of a libel action. The answer is often to obtain the information in the form of an official statement by a police or local authority spokesman.

But notice that the list in the Schedule is very precise. It is tempting to assume it covers all statements by people in authority, but it does not cover, for example, statements by the spokesmen of NHS hospital trusts, British Telecom, a gas board, a water board, British Rail, London Regional Transport, British Airport Authority or other bodies created by statute that are involved in providing day-to-day services to the public. It seems likely, however, that a fair and accurate account of such a body would now be held to be covered by privilege at common law.

Suppose a reporter telephones the spokesman of one of the bodies mentioned in the Act and puts questions to him: is the report of the spokesman's comments protected? In *Blackshaw v Lord* [1984] QB 1, Lord Justice Stephenson said that it would unduly restrict the privilege contained in paragraph 12 [paragraph 12 of the Schedule to the 1952 Act, now paragraph 9] to confine it to written handouts.

> It may be right to include . . . the kind of answers to telephoned interrogatories which Mr Lord [a *Daily Telegraph* reporter], quite properly in the discharge of his duty to his newspaper, administered to Mr Smith [a government press officer]. To exclude them in every case might unduly restrict the freedom of the press . . . But information which is put out on the initiative of a government department falls more easily within the paragraph than information pulled out of the mouth of an unwilling officer of the department

. . . not every statement of fact made to a journalist by a press officer of a government department is privileged.

In chapter 2 we saw the danger of giving information about people 'helping police with their inquiries', but paragraph 9 of the 1996 Act, as mentioned above, gives protection to a 'copy of or extract from' such a notice issued by the police for the information of the public. Note that the section refers to matter 'issued for the information of the public'. The privilege might not be held to cover a report based on a document leaked to the press.

Stories from some claim forms protected

There is privilege under paragraph 5 of the Schedule for a fair and accurate copy of or extract from, among other things, a document which is required by the law to be open to inspection by the public.

This provision gives protection, for example, to the reporting of defamatory statements that are endorsed on a libel claim form (formerly writ), but the protection does not cover any accompanying documentation.

More categories protected

As stated above, the 1996 Act greatly widens the categories of situations where privilege applies. The 1952 Act did not cover reports of foreign courts, foreign legislatures, or public inquiries appointed by governments (unless they operated within 'Her Majesty's dominions'). But the 1996 Schedule gives privilege to a fair and accurate report of such proceedings in public anywhere in the world.

The 1996 Act also greatly extends qualified privilege with respect to the reporting of company affairs. Until now only reports relating to proceedings at general meetings of public companies carried qualified privilege. The Act extends privilege to documents circulated among shareholders of a UK public company with the authority of the board or the auditors or by any shareholder 'in pursuance of a right conferred by any statutory provision'. Such documents may well be very critical of board members.

The Act gives the Government the power to extend privilege to the reports of statements by bodies, officers, or other people designated by them. This power would enable the Government to extend privilege to quangos and other such non-governmental bodies. This provision had not come into effect when this book went to press in 2005.

Free publications

Until 1996, free publications received much less protection from privilege than paid-for papers, but the Defamation Act 1996 ended the distinction.

Schedule to Defamation Act 1996

Here is the Schedule to the 1996 Act in full.

Statements having qualified privilege

Part I: statements privileged without explanation or contradiction

1 A fair and accurate report of proceedings in public of a legislature anywhere in the world.

2 A fair and accurate report of proceedings in public before a court anywhere in the world.

3 A fair and accurate report of proceedings in public of a person appointed to hold a public inquiry by a government or legislature anywhere in the world.

4 A fair and accurate report of proceedings in public anywhere in the world of an international organisation or an international conference.

5 A fair and accurate copy of or extract from any register or other document required by law to be open to public inspection.

6 A notice or advertisement published by or on the authority of a court, or of a judge or officer of a court, anywhere in the world.

7 A fair and accurate copy of or extract from matter published by or on the authority of a government or legislature anywhere in the world.

8 A fair and accurate copy of or extract from matter published anywhere in the world by an international organisation or an international conference.

Part II: statements privileged subject to explanation or contradiction

9(1) A fair and accurate copy of or extract from a notice or other matter issued for the information of the public by or on behalf of—

(a) a legislature in any member state or the European Parliament;

(b) the government of any member state, or any authority performing governmental functions in any member state or part of a member state, or the European Commission;

(c) an international organisation or international conference.

(2) In this paragraph 'governmental functions' includes police functions.

10 A fair and accurate copy of or extract from a document made available by a court in any member state or the European Court of Justice (or any court attached to that court), or by a judge or officer of any such court.

11(1) A fair and accurate report of proceedings at any public meeting or sitting in the United Kingdom of—

(a) a local authority or local authority committee;

(b) a justice or justices of the peace acting otherwise than as a court exercising judicial authority;

(c) a commission, tribunal, committee or person appointed for the purposes of any inquiry by any statutory provision, by Her Majesty or by a Minister of the Crown or a Northern Ireland Department;

(d) a person appointed by a local authority to hold a local inquiry in pursuance of any statutory provision;

(e) any other tribunal, board, committee or body constituted by or under, and exercising functions under, any statutory provision.

(2) This sub-paragraph defines 'local authority' in England and Wales, Scotland, and Northern Ireland.

(3) A fair and accurate report of any corresponding proceedings in any of the Channel Islands or the Isle of Man or in another member state.

12(1) A fair and accurate report of proceedings at any public meeting held in a member state.

(2) In this paragraph a 'public meeting' means a meeting bona fide and lawfully held for a lawful purpose and for the furtherance or discussion of a matter of public concern, whether admission to the meeting is general or restricted.

13(1) A fair and accurate report of proceedings at a general meeting of a UK public company.

(2) A fair and accurate copy of or extract from any document circulated to members of a UK public company—

(a) by or with the authority of the board of directors of the company,

(b) by the auditors of the company, or

(c) by any member of the company in pursuance of a right conferred by any statutory provision.

(3) A fair and accurate copy of or extract from any document circulated to members of a UK public company which relates to the appointment, resignation, retirement or dismissal of directors of the company.

(4) This sub-paragraph defines 'UK public company'.

(5) A fair and accurate report of proceedings at any corresponding meeting of, or copy of or extract from any corresponding document circulated to members of, a public company formed under the law of any of the Channel Islands or the Isle of Man or of another member state.

14 A fair and accurate report of any finding or decision of any of the following descriptions of association, formed in the United Kingdom or another member state, or of any committee or governing body of such an association—

(a) an association formed for the purpose of promoting or encouraging the exercise of or interest in any art, science, religion or learning, and empowered by its constitution to exercise control over or adjudicate on matters of interest or concern to the association, or the actions or conduct of any persons subject to such control or adjudication;

(b) an association formed for the purpose of promoting or safeguarding the interests of any trade, business, industry or profession, or of the persons carrying on or engaged in any trade, business, industry or profession, and empowered by its constitution to exercise control over or adjudicate upon matters connected with the trade, business, industry or profession, or the actions or conduct of those persons;

(c) an association formed for the purpose of promoting or safeguarding the interests of a game, sport or pastime to the playing or exercise of which members of the public are invited or admitted, and empowered by its constitution to exercise control over or adjudicate upon persons connected with or taking part in the game, sport or pastime;

(d) an association formed for the purpose of promoting charitable objects or other objects beneficial to the community and empowered by its constitution to exercise control over or to adjudicate on matters of interest or concern to the association, or the actions or conduct of any person subject to such control or adjudication.

15(1) A fair and accurate report of, or copy of or extract from, any adjudication, report, statement or notice issued by a body, officer or other person designated for the purposes of this paragraph—

(a) for England and Wales or Northern Ireland, by order of the Lord Chancellor, and

(b) for Scotland, by order of the Secretary of State.

(2) An order under this paragraph shall be made by statutory instrument which shall be subject to annulment in pursuance of a resolution of either House of Parliament.

Privilege at common law

Privilege at common law applies in certain circumstances where the law affords protection to defamatory statements that are untrue for 'the common convenience and welfare of society', as a judge said in 1834.

One such circumstance is where a person makes a defamatory statement in the performance of a legal, moral, or social duty to a person who has a corresponding duty or interest in receiving it.

For example, suppose someone is seeking a job. His potential employer writes to his former employer to ask for a reference. The former employer can reply frankly. He cannot be sued for libel for what he says, even if the facts are wrong, provided he is not motivated by malice.

The Reynolds defence

Journalists believe that they have a duty to tell their readers about matters of public interest and that their readers have an interest in receiving this information, but that general duty had never been recognised by the courts until the *Reynolds* case. In 1998, in *Reynolds v Times Newspapers* ([1998] 3 All ER 961), the Lord Chief Justice, Lord Bingham, said in the Court of Appeal:

> As it is the task of the news media to inform the public and engage in public discussion of matters of public interest, so is that to be recognised as its duty. The cases cited show acceptance of such a duty, even where publication is by a newspaper to the public at large. In modern conditions what we have called the duty test should, in our view, be rather more readily held to be satisfied.

In 1999 the House of Lords ([2000] 2 AC 127) affirmed the principle that the media have such a duty and Lord Nicholls, who gave the judgment of the court, set out a list of 'circumstances' that a judge should take into account in deciding whether the duty and interest tests were met, in which case the media would have a defence.

(1) The seriousness of the allegation. The more serious the charge, the more the public is misinformed and the individual harmed, if the allegation is not true.

(2) The nature of the information, and the extent to which the subject-matter is a matter of public concern.

(3) The source of the information. Some informants have no direct knowledge of the events. Some have their own axes to grind, or are being paid for their stories.

(4) The steps taken to verify the information.

(5) The status of the information. The allegation may have already been the subject of an investigation which commands respect.

(6) The urgency of the matter. News is often a perishable commodity.

(7) Whether comment was sought from the claimant. He may have information others do not possess or have not disclosed. An approach to the claimant will not always be necessary.

(8) Whether the article contained the gist of the claimant's side of the story.

(9) The tone of the article. A newspaper can raise queries or call for an investigation. It need not adopt allegations as statements of fact.

(10) The circumstances of the publication, including the timing.

Judges hearing a case in which a media defendant pleads the Reynolds defence customarily go through the 10 points systematically, attaching weight to these and any other relevant factors according to the case. Lord Nicholls said his list was not exhaustive.

The 'responsible journalist' test

As this edition of *McNae* went to press in 2005 the Reynolds defence was still being developed by the judges, but two decisions by the Court of Appeal, in particular, had strengthened the protection afforded by the defence to responsible journalism.

The *Loutchansky* case in 2001 recognised the Reynolds defence as a new legal doctrine, wholly different from traditional qualified privilege, based on public interest principles, and not defeated even by proof of malice. The court said that the defence, although built upon an orthodox foundation, was 'in reality sui generis'—that is, unique, unlike other forms of common-law privilege.

The court was considering an appeal by *The Times* concerning articles the paper had published about an international businessman Grigori Loutchansky. The stories alleged he controlled a major Russian criminal organisation involved in money-laundering and the smuggling of nuclear weapons. The paper agreed the stories were defamatory, but argued it had a defence of qualified privilege.

The trial judge rejected the defence because he ruled, among other things, it failed the duty-interest test, which he said involved proving that 'a publisher would be open to legitimate criticism if he failed to publish the information in question'.

But the Appeal Court said this was to impose too stringent a standard. Lord Phillips of Worth Matravers, Master of the Rolls, said the interest was that of the public in a modern democracy in free expression and the need to promote a vigorous press to keep the public informed. He continued:

> The corresponding duty on the journalist (and equally his editor) is to play his proper role in discharging that function. His task is to behave as a responsible journalist. He can

have no duty to publish unless he is acting responsibly any more than the public has an interest in reading whatever may be published irresponsibly. (*Loutchansky v Times Newspapers Ltd (the liability appeal)* [2001] EWCA Civ 1805, [2002] QB 783)

But suppose the paper is acting with malice? In the *Loutchansky* case the Court of Appeal said that unless the publisher was acting responsibly qualified privilege could not arise. If it did arise, the privilege was a complete defence, which could not be rebutted by a finding of malice.

The other important Court of Appeal decision was in the *Al Fagih* case, which recognised that the media have a right, in appropriate circumstances, to report what people are saying about matters of public interest, without necessarily having to check that it is true.

Accounts of some successful and unsuccessful defences by the media, including *Loutchansky* and *Al Fagih*, follow in the next passage. References to the *Loutchansky* and *Reynolds* cases in The Investigative Journalist, earlier in this chapter, have drawn attention to the importance of reporters keeping adequate notes of their conversations with sources. (There were no adequate notes in either case.)

The same passage also refers to the *Leeds Weekly News* case, where the existence of the reporter's notebook was crucial in the successful defence. Being able to produce a good note is particularly important when attempting to show the 'steps taken to verify the information' (point 4) when using the Reynolds defence.

The leading libel lawyer, Andrew Caldecott QC, explained why. He said: 'Since the media are necessarily reporting what others have told them, proof that they have fairly and accurately reported what they were told is the starting point of any privilege.'

The defence in practice

Although the House of Lords in the *Reynolds* case decided such a privilege existed, it also decided, by a majority, that the *Sunday Times* could not take advantage of it. In this case the former Irish prime minister, Albert Reynolds, had sued the paper for an article about the political crisis that culminated in his resignation in November 1994.

The article alleged he had deliberately misled the Irish Parliament and his coalition colleagues about circumstances surrounding the appointment of the President of the High Court.

Clearly the matter was of public concern (Lord Nicholls' point 2) but the paper had conspicuously failed to 'give the gist of the subject's response' (point 8). When the reporter was asked at the trial why his account contained no reference to Reynolds' explanation, he said: 'There was not a word of Mr Reynolds' defence because I had decided that his defence . . . there was no defence.' Reynolds had addressed the Dail (the Irish Parliament) on the matter, but the paper had not reported his statement.

When the court was attempting to establish the steps the reporter had taken to verify his story (point 4), and asked him why he had taken no notes during his inquiries, he replied, 'I was not in note-taking mode.'

Similarly, in the *Loutchansky* case, *The Times* failed, even after it had persuaded the Court of Appeal that the standard of duty required by the trial judge was too high.

The appeal judges sent the case back to the judge for reconsideration, and in 2002 Mr Justice Gray again rejected the paper's claim ([2002] EWHC 2490). He said the issue in relation to each of the articles was whether the paper had behaved responsibly in publishing them. That was dependent on whether, irrespective of the truth or falsity of the articles, it was in the public interest to publish the articles. Applying that test, and taking into account the 10 factors set out in Reynolds, the defence of qualified privilege had not been made out.

The articles, alleging that Loutchansky had committed serious criminal offences on an international scale, dealt with matters of public concern (point 2). However, to implicate him in misconduct of the utmost gravity was manifestly likely to be highly damaging to his reputation. For that reason a proportionate degree of responsibility was required of the journalist and the editor (point 1). But they failed to show this, in particular because the allegations made were vague, the sources were unreliable, sufficient steps had not been taken to verify the information, and no comment had been obtained from Loutchansky before publication.

The judge said 'such steps as were taken' by the reporter in his unsuccessful attempts to contact either Loutchansky or his company Nordex or their lawyers were far less diligent than was required by the standards of responsible journalism (point 7).

On the question whether the article met the Reynolds test of containing the gist of the claimant's side of the story (point 8), the judge said the article carried the bare statement that Loutchansky had 'repeatedly denied any wrongdoing or links to criminal activity'. This was insufficient, given the seriousness of the unproven allegations to be published.

The reporter was asked in court to produce the note he had made of the vital conversation he claimed to have had with his most important source. He said he thought he must have made the note on a scrap of paper which he had subsequently thrown away (point 4).

Readers may well reach the conclusion that the journalistic standards exhibited in the Reynolds and Loutchansky stories were such that it was unsurprising the courts found the new defence did not apply. But another case that came to court showed the Reynolds ruling could provide a defence to a newspaper even in circumstances where many editors would have hesitated to publish without making more effort to 'stand the story up'.

In 2000 a judge found for the *Leeds Weekly News*, a free newspaper, which was being sued for an article warning readers against the activities of doorstep salesmen selling karate club membership. It appeared on the front page under the headline 'Give 'em the chop' and a sub-head 'Doorstep salesmen flog dodgy karate lessons'. The judge assessed the story against Lord Nicholls' points.

He said the fundamental question was one of public interest. The court had to assess whether it was in the public interest for a newspaper to publish information as it did and whether the interest in protecting reputation from false defamatory attacks was outweighed by the interests of the free flow of information, even if that information was defamatory and false.

The firm's counsel had argued that, given the serious allegations contained in the article, which included allegations of dishonesty, the reporter had fallen far short of the standards of responsible journalism. She had made no adequate investigation before publication (point 4). Working on a hard-hitting story which accused the firm, GKR Karate (UK) Limited, of criminal offences, she had telephoned the firm and left a message with its paging service, but the firm did not reply and in the end the story carried no statement or comment from it (points 7 and 8).

The reporter phoned the trading standards officer in Leeds to ask whether there had been any complaints against the firm locally and was told no. She did not report this in her story, but she did report the officer saying there had been complaints about GKR clubs 'in other UK cities'.

But the judge said he found the reporter to be an honest, sensible and responsible person on whose evidence he could rely and who was naturally concerned by the dangers, particularly to children, resulting from this organisation. 'I reject the view that she was indifferent either to accuracy or truth. She based her article on what she believed, honestly believed, was reliable evidence.'

The judge said he was clearly of the view that counsel's criticisms neither individually nor cumulatively outweighed the interest in the free flow of information in this case.

Neutral reportage

In the *Al Fagih* case, in 2001, the Court of Appeal ruled that a newspaper was entitled to rely upon the Reynolds defence where it had reported, in an entirely objective manner, an allegation about someone made in the course of a political dispute by one of his opponents. The defence was not lost merely because the newspaper had not verified the allegation (*Al-Fagih v HH Saudi Research & Marketing (UK) Ltd* [2001] EWCA Civ 1634, [2002] EMLR 215).

The paper's counsel, Andrew Caldecott QC, referred to the newspaper's account as 'reportage', a word described later in the judgment by Lord Justice Simon Brown as 'convenient . . . to describe the neutral reporting of attributed allegations rather than their adoption by a newspaper'.

Saad Al-Fagih brought libel proceedings against an Arabic newspaper which was part-owned by the Saudi Arabian royal family and which was generally supportive of the Saudi Arabian government. The newspaper had published an article alleging that a political colleague of Al-Fagih's had told it that Al-Fagih had spread malicious rumours about him and had accused his mother of procuring women for sexual intercourse.

The newspaper, among other defences, claimed qualified privilege. It argued that, where two politicians had made serious allegations against each other, it was a matter of public importance that the dispute be reported, provided that this was done fairly and accurately and an opportunity was given to the parties to explain or contradict.

At first instance, the judge rejected the defence of qualified privilege. In doing so, she relied heavily on the fact that the journalist had made no attempt to verify the truth of the allegations (point 4). The judge also ruled that the potential harm to Al-Fagih in the reporting of the allegations outweighed the public interest in publication.

But before the Court of Appeal, the newspaper argued that the disinterested reporting of a political dispute should more readily attract qualified privilege than an article in which the newspaper made allegations of its own.

A majority of the Court of Appeal allowed the newspaper's appeal. While it noted that the media will normally need to verify a third party's allegations if a defence of qualified privilege is to succeed, circumstances can arise where the public is entitled to be informed of a political dispute that is being fairly reported.

This could be the case even though, at the time of publication, the publisher had not yet sought verification of the allegations in order to commit himself one way or the other. On the facts of this case, the failure to verify the story did not outweigh the public interest in publication.

In sharp contrast to the *Al-Fagih* case, in 2004 *The Daily Telegraph* failed in its claim that its coverage of documents said to have been discovered by a reporter in the ruins of the Foreign Ministry in Baghdad was 'neutral reportage'. (This case has been referred to earlier under 'Fair Comment'.) A judge held that the paper's allegations that the left-wing MP George Galloway had received funds diverted from Iraq's oil-for-food programme conveyed a defamatory meaning that was not protected by qualified privilege (*George Galloway MP v Telegraph Group Ltd* [2004] EWHC 2786 (QB).

Mr Galloway was awarded £150,000 damages and the paper had to pay costs estimated at £1.2 million

The articles and leader comments complained of were published in April 2003, just a month after the invasion of Iraq by coalition forces. Mr Galloway said the articles conveyed the impression that he had taken large sums of money from Saddam Hussein's regime for his own personal benefit, and had requested more, and that his campaign for medical assistance to Iraq and the lifting of sanctions had been used by him as a front for his own financial advantage.

The newspaper did not say the allegations were true, but disputed the defamatory meaning of the articles and claimed qualified privilege and (as discussed earlier) fair comment. The paper argued that the public had a right to know the contents of the documents, even if they were defamatory of Mr Galloway and irrespective of whether the allegations were true or not. The paper argued that the effect of the words complained of was that the Baghdad documents consisted of strong prima facie evidence that Mr Galloway had arranged for his political campaign against the Iraq war and/or other political activities to be financed by the Iraqi government.

But the judge said the Reynolds privilege protected the neutral reporting of attributed allegations rather than their adoption by a newspaper and the articles did not 'fairly and disinterestedly' report the context of the Baghdad documents. They went beyond assuming them to be true and drew their own inferences as to the personal receipt of funds diverted from Iraq's oil-for-food programme, something not alleged in the documents themselves.

The newspaper had made no attempt at verification of the allegations (Lord Nicholls' point 4) and had not told Mr Galloway, in interviewing him, that it was proposing to publish allegations of personal enrichment and thus given him a chance to reply (point 7). It could not be said that the newspaper was under a social or moral duty to make the allegations about Mr Galloway at that time.

Replies to attacks

There is also qualified privilege at common law for a defamatory statement made by a person in reply to an attack upon his character or conduct. There would be no privilege for any response wider than necessary to meet the specific allegations. A newspaper carrying a lawful response would share in the privilege.

Reports of judicial and parliamentary proceedings

Finally, there is qualified privilege at common law for fair and accurate reports of judicial proceedings in this country and reports of the proceedings of Parliament. If a journalist refers to court proceedings that are not contemporaneous his report does not attract absolute privilege but he may still be able to plead qualified privilege for any defamatory statements in his report.

Accord and satisfaction

This is a plea that the matter has been otherwise disposed of, for example by the publication of a correction and apology which has been accepted by the claimant in settlement of his complaint.

'Without prejudice'

A complaint to a newspaper may be made by a telephone call to the editor or another member of the staff; by a letter from the complainer direct, or from his solicitors.

A solicitor writing on behalf of a client demanding a correction and apology will always avoid suggesting that this action by a newspaper will be enough in itself to settle the dispute and will make it clear that the request is made 'without prejudice' to any other action that may become necessary.

The journalist, through ignorance, may fail to safeguard his interests in this way, particularly in the early stages of a complaint, before he has had the chance to take legal advice. He should not do anything that will prejudice the outcome of any legal action.

In any letter or conversation arising from the complaint the journalist should make it clear that what is said or written is 'without prejudice'. This identifies the exchange of views as merely exploratory. The words should be typed at the top of any letter, or introduced into the conversation. If they are omitted, what is said or written may be taken as an admission, can be used in evidence, and may defeat any effort by the lawyers to put up a defence.

Anything said without prejudice is legally off the record, and the contents of any statement or letter made or written without prejudice normally cannot be referred to in evidence if proceedings follow.

Care with corrections

It is no defence for a newspaper to publish a correction and apology not accepted by the claimant. Such a publication may be found by a court to constitute an admission that the matter was wrong and possibly that it was defamatory.

It may even be thought to make matters worse. In the *Stationery Trade News* case referred to in chapter 18 the magazine, after receiving a complaint from the envelope importers, carried an article on the front page of the following month's edition saying:

> Referring to our lead story last month, 'Counterfeits—retailers warned', envelope distributor Charles Freeman has asked us to point out that its Great West range, which is mentioned in one section of the story, is a 'high quality line' and not in the same category as the counterfeit notepads from China, also mentioned. The envelopes, which come from Ireland and Germany, are now origin marked to that effect and therefore there is no question of the consumer being misled.

The company said the correction made matters worse. The judge said the wording was curious and might be taken by the ordinary reader to mean the company had been counterfeiting and now was not, having origin-marked the envelopes.

On the other hand, if the jury finds for the claimant, the fact that the newspaper took prompt and adequate steps to correct the error, and to express regret, will provide a plea in mitigation of damages—that is, it will tend to reduce the size of damages awarded.

And an aggrieved person may be prepared to sign a waiver—that is, a statement saying he waives his right to legal redress in exchange for the publication of a correction and apology—and such a waiver will provide a complete defence.

The defence of accord and satisfaction does not depend upon the existence of any formal written agreement, but clearly the newspaper has a stronger case if it can produce a signed paper (known as a waiver) in the following terms:

> I confirm that the publication of an apology in the terms annexed in a position of reasonable prominence in the next available issue of the [name of paper] will be accepted in full and final satisfaction of any claim I may have in respect of the article headed [give headline] published in the issue of your newspaper for [date].

A practical danger for an editor who asks a complainer to sign a waiver is that the reader may not have realised previously that he has a claim for damages and, thus alerted, he may consult a lawyer. The waiver is therefore most useful when the complainer has already threatened to consult a lawyer.

Journalists should take care that in correcting one libel they do not perpetrate another.

For example, to say that allegations contained in a speech by X about Y were untrue could amount to calling X a liar—a damaging allegation and likely to be costly.

Newspaper editors are often asked to publish a correction of a statement made in judicial proceedings and reported in the paper. The mistake was not the newspaper's—the account was a correct report of the proceedings and is therefore privileged (see 'Privilege', above). The correction, however, carries no statutory privilege, and if it is defamatory the newspaper's only defence may be qualified privilege at common law (see 'Privilege at common law', above), which is likely to be difficult to mount.

An editor receiving such a request should suggest to the aggrieved person that by arrangement with the magistrates he or his solicitor should make a statement in open court. This statement can then be safely reported, under the cloak of privilege.

A final word of advice on corrections. Inexperienced reporters will sometimes try to avoid the consequences of their errors without referring them to their editor. They may be approached directly by the person making the complaint and try to shrug it off. Or they may incorporate a scarcely recognisable 'correction' (without apology) in a follow-up story.

Either course of action is highly dangerous. It may further aggravate the offence and annoy the person concerned, and he may well take more formal steps to secure satisfaction. In such circumstances the reporter should immediately tell his editor so that he may deal with the matter promptly and correctly.

Payment into court

Another way to 'satisfy' a claimant is by payment into court. This means that the newspaper lodges a sum of money with the court and the claimant can take out this money at any time to end the litigation. If he does not accept it, however, the action continues.

Neither the judge nor the jury Is told at the trial how much money has been paid in. If the award is less than, or the same as, the amount paid in, the claimant will usually be ordered to pay his own and the defendant's costs after the date the money was paid in. This legal device, intended to keep down the number of libel claims, is generally considered an important inhibition preventing people of modest means from suing newspapers.

Offer of amends

There are various ways in which the media can defame a person unintentionally. The classic example was the case of Artemus Jones. Here a journalist introduced a fictitious character into a descriptive account of a factual event in order to provide atmosphere.

Unfortunately the name he chose was that of a real person, a barrister. Stung by the comments of his friends, who either genuinely or for fun associated him with the report, the real Artemus Jones sued and recovered substantial damages.

Another example occurs where an account relating to one 'real' person is understood to refer to another. We considered the case of Harold Newstead in the section on identification.

Another is the case where a statement is on the surface innocuous but, because of circumstances unknown to the writer, is defamatory. In *Cassidy v Daily Mirror Newspapers Ltd* [1929] 2 KB 331, Cassidy, at the races, was photographed with a woman he described as his fiancée, and this was the way she was described in the caption to the photograph used by the newspaper. But Cassidy was already married, and his wife sued on the ground that people who knew her would assume she had been 'living in sin'.

A person can still be defamed in these various circumstances, but the Defamation Act 1996 provides for a defence known as 'offer to make amends'.

To avail himself of the defence, a defendant must make a written offer to make a suitable correction and apology, to publish the correction in a reasonable manner, and to pay the claimant suitable damages, although the precise terms on which this will be done may be left to be agreed at a later date.

The defence can only be used where the defendant did not know and had no reason to believe that the statement complained of referred to the claimant and was false and defamatory of him. The claimant has the onus of showing that the publication was not 'innocent'.

If the offer of amends is not accepted, the defendant will have a defence to the action provided the court holds that he did not know and had no reason to believe that the words complained of were false and defamatory of the claimant.

Other defences

Defences that may be available in certain circumstances are:

(1) *That the claimant has died.* The action for libel is a personal action. A dead person cannot be libelled (except in criminal libel: see chapter 21). Similarly, an action begun by a claimant cannot be continued by his heirs and executors if he dies before the case is decided. The action dies with him.

(2) *That the claimant agreed to the publication.* Short of obtaining a signed statement to that effect before publication, this might be extremely difficult to prove. It is no defence to say that you have shown the offending words to the claimant and he has had the chance to respond to the allegations.

(3) *That proceedings were not started within the limitation period.* This constitutes a complete defence, unless there is a new publication of offending material (as in a bygone days column: see preceding chapter). The period, formerly three years, was reduced to one year by the Defamation Act 1996. Reporters should keep their notebooks carefully in case they are required to produce them in court, particularly as the court has a discretion to extend the time for commencing proceedings.

(4) *That the matter has already been adjudged.* The court will not entertain a second action based on the same complaint against the same defendant, or against any other person jointly liable with him for that publication.

To sell copies of a publication containing the offending words after proceedings have begun, or the libel has been proved, would however constitute a separate publication, and could result in another action.

Note that this defence does not stop a claimant taking action against any number of defendants who are separately responsible for publishing the statement in different newspapers. See, for example, the case of Princess Bagaya mentioned in the previous chapter ('Publication').

Criminal libel, slander, and malicious falsehoods

In the preceding chapters we have been looking at libel as a civil wrong for which damages are recoverable (ie a tort). It is also a criminal offence.

Criminal libel occurs in two forms: (a) defamatory libel, (b) blasphemous, seditious, and obscene libel. There are important differences between the two types, and we must deal with them separately.

It may be that some elements of criminal libel would not survive a challenge under the European Convention on Human Rights. In a case in 1999 the European Court of Human Rights held that a conviction of a journalist for criminal libel constituted a violation of article 10 of the Convention (*Dalban v Romania*; see chapter 19).

Criminal defamatory libel

Many defamatory statements might be dealt with either in the civil courts or in the criminal courts; indeed, the same publication could be the subject of proceedings in both places, and the defamer could be sent to prison and made to pay damages.

In 1975 the satirical magazine *Private Eye* published an article which Sir James Goldsmith, the financier, claimed was defamatory of him. He said the article meant that he was the ringleader in a conspiracy to obstruct the police in their search for Lord Lucan, who was wanted in connection with the murder of the family's nanny. Sir James also claimed that the magazine was conducting a campaign of vilification against him.

He sued *Private Eye* and its editor, and he also began a private prosecution for criminal libel against them.

As we saw in chapter 18, the civil law gives a remedy for defamation because an attack on a man's reputation may injure him as much as a physical attack, and he ought to be compensated for such an attack.

The reason behind criminal libel is different. The publication of a libel is a crime because it is an act which might lead to a breach of the peace.

Sir James Goldsmith told the magistrate hearing committal proceedings against *Private Eye* that after the magazine article there were bomb scares at the offices of his solicitors. He added, 'When a campaign of vilification takes place the repercussions can sometimes lead to a breach of the peace.'

But it seems that it is not essential for the prosecution to prove that the libel was likely to provoke a breach of the peace. A prosecution may be brought where either the publication is likely to cause a breach of the peace, or the publication seriously affects the reputation of the person involved.

In practice, comparatively few cases of defamatory libel are heard in the criminal courts. Judges would be disinclined to jail a person if they felt that the payment of damages was sufficient to right the wrong that had been done.

Prosecutions are reserved for extreme cases where the libel is particularly monstrous or where it is persistently repeated, or where the defendant is impecunious and the complainant would otherwise be left with no redress.

The *Private Eye* case did not come to trial. Sir James withdrew the prosecution after the magazine withdrew its allegations about his involvement in the Lord Lucan affair, paid for an apology in a newspaper, and undertook not to pursue a vendetta against him.

But the law is still available to private prosecutors, and gives them advantages that would not be available under the civil law.

In 1977, a convicted sexual offender, Roger Gleaves, began a series of prosecutions against journalists. He had just left prison after serving a sentence for wounding and for committing homosexual offences at hostels he ran for homeless young people in London. At his trial, the judge had called him a 'cruel and wicked man with an evil influence on others'. Gleaves's activities had aroused considerable public concern and had been the subject of many articles.

He prosecuted among others the two authors of a paperback book *Johnny Go Home*, based on a TV programme by them which was screened in 1975, and three reporters of the *Sunday People*.

A magistrate committed all five to trial. She remanded the three newspaper reporters in custody to Brixton prison, because she said she felt they were likely to commit other offences, but they were released the following day by a judge in chambers.

Later the Director of Public Prosecutions took over the case against them and offered no evidence.

The television journalists were not so lucky. Their trial in 1980 lasted two and a half weeks. If they had been sued in a civil court, they could have brought evidence under the Civil Evidence Act 1968 that Gleaves had been convicted of the offences they had written about, and this would have been conclusive evidence that he had committed them. But this defence was not open to them in a criminal trial, and instead they had to prove Gleaves's offences again. They succeeded, and the jury acquitted them.

Legal aid is not available in a civil libel suit, but in this criminal libel case the entire cost of the action and the hearings leading to it, estimated at from £50,000 to more than £75,000, was paid from public funds because Gleaves had no money.

To sustain a prosecution for criminal libel the words must be written, or be in some permanent form, but there need be no publication to a third party: it is enough that they are addressed to the person injured by them. This is quite logical because it is the person defamed who is most likely to be angered to the point of hitting the person who insults him, and that would be a breach of the peace.

As we have seen, there can be no civil libel of the dead. But in criminal libel the position is different: words spoken of a dead person may be the subject of a prosecution, but only if it can be proved that they were used with the intention of provoking his living relatives to commit a breach of the peace, or that they had a tendency to do so.

In dealing with civil defamation, we saw that proving the truth of the offending words constituted a complete answer to an action.

This defence is available also in criminal proceedings for libel, but in addition the defendant has to satisfy the court that the words were published for the public benefit.

Failure to do so would result in a conviction.

The old saying 'The greater the truth the greater the libel' has no meaning in civil libel. In criminal libel it indicates that passions are more likely to be aroused and a breach of the peace more likely to occur if the allegation is true.

But even so the libeller has a defence if he has spoken out for the public benefit.

A further difference between criminal and civil libel is that it is a crime to libel a class of people, provided the object is to excite the hatred of the public against the class libelled. But a journalist guilty of such conduct is more likely to be prosecuted under the race relations legislation.

For publishing a defamatory libel a person may be sent to prison for up to a year, and/or fined. If it can be proved that he knew the libel to be untrue, the period of imprisonment may be doubled.

Blasphemy, sedition, and obscenity

The publication of blasphemous, seditious, or obscene matter is a criminal offence whether it is published in writing or by word of mouth.

It is no defence to prove that the words complained of are true, or that they form part of a fair and accurate report of what was said on a privileged occasion. Only with obscene libel is it any defence to prove that publication of the words was for the public benefit.

Changes of fashion and outlook affect decisions about whether words are or are not criminal. Statements that in Victorian times might have been held to be blasphemous are freely made today. Sex, once almost taboo, is a subject for open discussion in speech and in the printed word today.

Blasphemy

Blasphemy consists in the use of language having a tendency to vilify the Christian religion or the Bible. As with criminal libel, the law is seeking to prevent words likely to cause a breach of the peace. It is therefore concerned with the form and expression of language used, and not the substance of the statements or the intention of the author.

Even fundamental tenets of the faith may be questioned without fear of a prosecution unless—and this is the important proviso—scurrilous and irreverent language is used.

The test is whether what is written is likely to shock and outrage the feelings of believers.

In 1977 *Gay News*, a newspaper for homosexuals, and its editor were convicted of blasphemous libel for publishing a poem written as if by a homosexual Roman centurion recalling his feelings towards Christ after the Crucifixion.

The poem stated that Christ had had homosexual relations with a number of men, and went on to describe homosexual acts by the centurion with the dead body. The defence claimed the poem was an expression of the ecstasy of loving God, but they were not allowed to bring evidence on the literary merits of the poem or the author's intentions.

Gay News was fined £1,000. The editor was fined £500 and given a suspended prison sentence of nine months. On appeal, the fines were upheld, but the suspended sentence was set aside.

The law of blasphemy applies only to words concerning the Christian religion, as the Queen's Bench Divisional Court confirmed in 1990 when refusing to allow the prosecution of Salman Rushdie for comments in his book *The Satanic Verses* which had offended Muslims.

In 2004 the UK Government proposed a law extending the existing provisions on incitement to racial hatred to cover incitement to religious hatred (see chapter 25). The Government said that 'at the moment' it had no plans for repealing the law of blasphemy, but was keeping it under review.

Sedition

Any words that are likely to disturb the internal peace and government of the country constitute seditious libel.

The tests to apply to determine whether words constitute a seditious libel are these:

- Do they bring the sovereign or her family into hatred or contempt?
- Do they bring the government and constitution of the United Kingdom into hatred or contempt?
- Do they bring either House of Parliament, or the administration of justice, into hatred or contempt?
- Do they excite British subjects to attempt, *otherwise than by lawful means* (our italics), the alteration of any matter in Church or State by law established?
- Do they raise discontent or disaffection in British subjects?
- Do they promote feelings of ill-will and hostility between different classes?

From these tests, it seems that the law is very strict, but in fact the law will hesitate to interfere with an honest expression of opinion so long as it is couched in moderate terms. Thus criticisms of the monarchical and parliamentary systems, constructively advanced, would not be regarded as seditious.

Muslims tried to prosecute Salman Rushdie for sedition as well as blasphemy (see above) on the grounds that his words had created discontent among British subjects, had created hostility between classes, and had damaged relations between Britain and Islamic states.

But a magistrate rejected the attempt saying: 'The essential part of [the offence of seditious libel] is that any action should be directed against the state.'

The divisional court in 1990 agreed, saying the intention required to found a prosecution for seditious libel was an intention to incite to violence or to create public disturbance or disorder against the Queen or the institutions of government.

Not only had there to be proof of an incitement to violence, but it had to be violence or resistance or defiance for the purpose of disturbing constituted authority.

Obscenity

The test of obscene libel is whether the words or matter, if taken as a whole, would tend to deprave and corrupt those who are likely, having regard to all the circumstances, to read them.

The law used to be that, as with blasphemous libel, no evidence could be brought to show the literary merits of any work which was the subject of proceedings.

In 1928, for example, *The Well of Loneliness*, a literary work dealing with female homo-sexuality, was condemned as obscene. Evidence as to its literary merit was ruled inadmissible.

The Obscene Publications Act 1959 introduced a defence that the publication was 'for the public good . . . in the interests of science, literature, art, or learning, or of other objects of public concern'.

The publishers of D H Lawrence's *Lady Chatterley's Lover* were acquitted of obscenity as a result of this defence.

Before 1964, the law of obscene libel had caught only those who published obscene works. By the Obscene Publications Act of that year, it is an offence to have an obscene article for publication for gain.

Slander

The most obvious difference between libel and slander is that, as we have seen, libel is in some permanent form (eg written words, a drawing, or a photograph), while slander is spoken or in some other transient form.

The exceptions are (i) a defamatory statement broadcast on radio or television, or in a cable programme, which by the Broadcasting Act 1990 is treated as libel, (ii) a defamatory statement in a public performance of a play, by virtue of the Theatres Act 1968.

In slander, as with libel, there must be publication to a third person for a statement to become actionable.

There is one further difference between libel and slander. Whereas actual damage will be presumed in a libel action, it must be proved affirmatively by the claimant in a slander action, except in four cases.

A slander of this kind is said to be actionable per se (by itself). The four cases are:

(1) any imputation that an individual has committed a crime punishable by death or imprisonment;

(2) any imputation that an individual is suffering from certain contagious or objectionable diseases, such as venereal disease or leprosy: the test is whether the nature of the disease would cause the person to be shunned or avoided;

(3) any imputation of unchastity in a woman;

(4) any statement calculated to disparage an individual in his office, profession, calling, trade, or business.

In these four instances, actual pecuniary loss does not have to be proved.

The journalist is less likely to become involved personally in a slander action than in a libel action, but he must be aware of the danger of slander.

Let us suppose that X has said that Y, a member of a borough council, has used his office to secure building contracts. This is clearly actionable because it disparages him in his office of councillor. The reporter detailed to check the story will have to interview a number of people to arrive at the truth, and in these interviews he must be wary of laying himself open to a writ.

In 1987 a cargo airline sought an injunction to prevent a freelance journalist inquiring into the question of whether the airline had carried armaments, an allegation it denied (*Seagreen Air Transport v George*). The airline said that by simply asking the question the reporter was slandering the firm.

The matter was not tested in court because the judge refused an injunction on the preliminary point that it was not defamatory to allege, even wrongly, that a cargo airline carried arms; the words did not, of themselves, carry any improper implications.

Malicious falsehoods

Publication of a false statement, though it may cast no aspersions on the character of a person, or upon his fitness to hold a certain office or to follow a particular calling, may still be damaging to him.

For example, to say of a doctor that he has retired from practice would no doubt cause him pecuniary loss, if false. But it is clearly not defamatory.

Because it is not defamatory, a wronged person cannot bring an action for either libel or slander.

He may, however, be able to bring an action for malicious falsehood.

In such an action, the claimant must prove that the statement is untrue. Note the contrast with libel, where the court will assume that a defamatory statement is false.

The claimant in an action for malicious falsehood must also prove that the statement was published maliciously. If he fails to prove malice his action will fail.

As with the defence of qualified privilege in libel, malice means a statement made by a person who knows that it is false or who is reckless as to its truth, or who is actuated by some improper motive (*Spring v Guardian Assurance plc* [1993] 2 All ER 273, CA). Negligence is not malice.

It used to be the case that, to establish malicious falsehood, the claimant had to prove he had suffered actual damage.

By the Defamation Act 1952, the rule no longer applies to words in permanent form, such as printed words, provided they are calculated to cause financial damage.

Nor does it apply to words, whether spoken or written, that are likely to cause financial damage to the claimant in his office, profession, calling, trade, or business.

In 1990, when the television actor Gorden Kaye was in hospital seriously ill, his representative sued the *Sunday Sport* and its editor for malicious falsehood.

A journalist and a photographer had gained access to the hospital and taken photographs of Kaye, and in a proposed article the *Sunday Sport* planned to say Kaye had agreed to be interviewed and photographed.

The Court of Appeal said the words were false because Kaye was in no state to be interviewed or give any informed consent. Any publication would 'inevitably' be malicious because the reporter and photographer knew this.

As to damage, Kaye had a potentially valuable right to sell the story of his accident to other newspapers for 'large sums of money' and the value of that right would be seriously lessened if the *Sunday Sport* were allowed to publish.

The court made an order that until the matter came for trial the *Sunday Sport* should not publish anything that could convey to a reader that Kaye had voluntarily permitted the taking of photographs (see also references to the case in chapter 32, 'Privacy').

Another very important difference between libel and malicious falsehood used to be that, although a claimant could not get legal aid for a libel action, he might be able to do so for malicious falsehood.

In 1992 a former lady's maid to the Princess Royal wished to sue *Today* newspaper over claims that she stole intimate letters to the Princess from Commander Tim Laurence, later the princess's husband, but was too poor to do so. She was granted legal aid for an action in malicious falsehood and in a landmark decision the Court of Appeal ruled that her action was not an abuse of the process of the court. The following year she was paid out-of-court damages of about £25,000. But legal aid for malicious falsehood cases was ended by the Access to Justice Act 1999.

In the past another important difference between libel and malicious falsehood has been the 'limitation period'. A claimant had three years from the date of publication in which to sue for libel, but six years for malicious falsehood. The Defamation Act 1996 reduced the limitation period to one year for both actions.

Suppose an editor receives a solicitor's letter drawing attention to comments about a person or his goods which, the solicitor claims, are false and are likely to cause damage. The editor realises that his facts are wrong, but they were not defamatory and it was an honest mistake. The editor should act quickly to put the mistake right by means of an adequate correction to avoid any suggestion in subsequent legal action that he acted with malice.

The *Camden Journal* (later the *Camden New Journal*) carried a front-page story 'Baking days of Rumbold and Son come to an end', giving the impression the closure of the well-known bread shop was definite and imminent. The paper had jumped to the wrong conclusion after a planning application had been submitted to transform the shop into a restaurant and penthouse. A letter from the shop's solicitors said trade had suffered as a result of the story. The letter demanded a correction, and 'reserved their clients' rights' [to damages].

The paper's solicitor told the editor the report was not defamatory and was actionable as an injurious falsehood only on proof of malice. He said the reporter's assumption was a reasonable one, and he was clearly not malicious. 'You should publish the enclosed statement on the front page of this week's issue of *Camden Journal*. This will negative any possible suggestion of malice on your part and reassure the burghers of Hampstead that they will still be able to buy freshly baked bread.'

Two types of malicious falsehoods are known as slander of goods, false and malicious statements disparaging the claimant's goods, and slander of title, false and malicious denial of the claimant's title to property.

The word slander is misleading in both cases. The damaging statement can be in permanent form or in spoken words.

Rehabilitation of Offenders Act

The Rehabilitation of Offenders Act 1974 is intended to allow people with comparatively minor convictions to live down their past. Such convictions become spent after a specified length of time known as the rehabilitation period. This period varies according to the severity of sentence.

The Act limits in two ways the defences available to a journalist who has mentioned a person's spent convictions and is being sued for libel as a result:

(1) If the journalist pleads justification—that is, that the report of the plaintiff's previous convictions was true—the defence fails if the plaintiff can prove the journalist acted with malice.

(2) If the journalist reports a reference made in court to a spent conviction, and that conviction was held to be inadmissible in evidence, he cannot plead privilege.

The Act breached for the first time the established principle of the civil law that truth is a complete answer to an action for defamation.

Investigative reporters often need to mention the previous convictions of villains whose activities they intend to expose. Suppose, for example, a journalist discovers that a person who is starting a youth club in his area has a large number of previous convictions for indecency and that these convictions have become spent.

The journalist can defend the defamatory statement that the man has previous convictions by pleading either qualified privilege or justification. His story also carries the defamatory inference that a man guilty of these offences is unfit to run such a club, and he may be able to defend that allegation by pleading fair comment.

However, as we saw in chapter 20, if a claimant can show the journalist acted with malice, his defences of qualified privilege and fair comment fail. Under the 1974 Act, his defence of justification fails as well, if the claimant can prove malice.

It should be emphasised that if the journalist is not motivated by malice, he can still use justification, privilege, and fair comment to defend a reference to a spent conviction—except as to privilege in the situation mentioned under (2) above.

In 1977 the Labour Party presented a party political broadcast on television which took the form of a fierce attack on the right-wing party the National Front. The presenters wished to mention the spent convictions of John Tyndall, leader of the NF. Tyndall's most recent conviction was six months' imprisonment in 1966, 11 years previously, for having a loaded pistol without a licence. At the time he was a member of another right-wing party. The reference was deleted from the broadcast on the advice of the broadcasting authorities.

The lawyers were probably worried that, if the spent conviction had been mentioned and the case had come to court, Tyndall would have argued that the Labour Party's purpose was to speak out not in the public interest but for party political advantage, and that might amount to an improper motive—or malice as the law calls it.

Tyndall's convictions were published the following Sunday by the *News of the World* on its front page under the headline: 'We say you have the right to know the truth about such men as this.'

When a conviction has become spent it is as though, for all legal purposes, it has never occurred. If a person is giving evidence in any *civil* proceedings he should not be asked any questions about spent convictions and he is entitled to refuse to answer such questions unless the court tells him he must.

The Act does not apply to later *criminal* proceedings. If a rehabilitated person appears again before a criminal court after his conviction has become spent he can still be asked about it and the court can be told about it for the purpose of deciding sentence if he is found guilty.

Privilege applies to court reports of such references to spent convictions, unless ruled by the court to be inadmissible.

But the Lord Chief Justice has directed, in accordance with 'the general intention of Parliament', that spent convictions should never be referred to in criminal courts if such reference could be avoided and that no one should refer in open court to a spent conviction without the authority of the judge.

If a newspaper report contains any reference to spent convictions that were not referred to in open court, or that were referred to but held to be inadmissible, that part of the report will not be privileged.

The Act does not impose any criminal penalty on the journalist who mentions a spent conviction, but it is an offence for a public servant or someone involved in contracted out services to reveal details of spent convictions other than in the course of his official duties.

Obtaining information of spent convictions from official records by fraud, dishonesty, or bribery is also a criminal offence.

Rehabilitation periods

Excluded from the provisions of the Act are sentences exceeding two and a half years of imprisonment, of youth custody, of detention in a young offender institution, or of corrective training: they can never become spent. Nor can a term of preventive detention or an extended sentence for public protection after a violent or sexual offence.

The rehabilitation period varies between ten years (for a term of imprisonment exceeding six months) and six months (for an absolute discharge). But a further conviction during the rehabilitation period can have the effect of extending it.

There are *three* fixed rehabilitation periods that are reduced by half for offenders under 18.

- *Ten years* for prison sentence, detention in a young offender institution, youth custody, or corrective training for more than six months but not more than two and a half years; or for cashiering, or discharge with ignominy, or dismissal with disgrace from the armed services.
- *Seven years* for prison sentence or detention in a young offender institution or youth custody for six months or less; or dismissal from the armed services.
- *Five years* for fine, or some other sentence (such as a community order) for which the Act does not provide a different rehabilitation period, or for detention in the services.

There are *three* fixed rehabilitation periods relating to sentences that apply to young offenders.

- *Seven years* for borstal training or for armed services detention for more than six months.
- *Five years* for detention for more than six months but not more than two and a half years.
- *Three years* for detention or a custodial order for six months or less, or for a detention centre order.

For an absolute discharge the period is six months.

For a probation order or community order the period is five years for an offender over 18, and until the order expires (with a minimum of two and a half years) for those under 18.

There are also *five* variable rehabilitation periods.

- *The period runs until the order expires (with a minimum of one year)* for conditional discharge, or binding over; and for fit person orders, supervision orders, or care orders under the Children Act 1989.

- *The period runs on for one year after the order expires* for custody in a remand home, attendance centre orders, approved school or secure training orders.

- *The period runs on for two years after the order expires (with a minimum of five years from the date of the conviction)* for hospital orders under the Mental Health Acts.

- *The period lasts for the period of the disqualification* for disqualification and disabilities.

- *The period lasts for the duration of a supervision order, an approved school order, a community supervision order for a person in the armed forces, or a youth offender contract.*

Suspended sentences are treated as if they were put into effect.

Journalists requiring further information about rehabilitation periods for particular sentences should consult *Stone's Justices' Manual* (Butterworths, 2005).

Breach of confidence

This branch of the law is based upon the principle that a person who has obtained information in confidence should not take unfair advantage of it. The main means used to achieve this is the interim injunction—that is, a pre-trial order of the court directing a party to refrain from doing something, in this case from disclosing the confidential information.

The law was of little concern to journalists until the 1970s, and indeed editions of this book before then made no mention of it. But since then it has been developing rapidly and has become an important part of media law.

Governments use breach of confidence frequently to protect information they regard as secret. Individuals use it for the same purpose and also as a way to protect privacy, and this use of breach of confidence received a strong boost when the Human Rights Act was implemented in 2000, incorporating the European Convention on Human Rights into English law.

Breach of confidence is also used to protect commercial interests based upon personality rights, and this happened most notably in the case in which *OK!* magazine was awarded more than £1 million in damages in 2003 after *Hello!* magazine published 'snatched' pictures of the wedding of film stars Michael Douglas and Catherine Zeta-Jones.

Law books, quoting Mr Justice Megarry giving a judgment in 1968, say there are three elements of a breach of confidence:

(1) the information must have 'the necessary quality of confidence';

(2) the information must have been imparted in circumstances imposing an obligation of confidence; and

(3) there must be an unauthorised use of that information to the detriment of the party communicating it (*Coco v AN Clark (Engineers) Ltd* [1969] RPC 41 at 47).

But judges have taken a less strict view of requirement (b) over the years (see 'Obligation of confidence' below). At first, the obligation was recognised only where there was a clear business or domestic relationship. Later, judges inferred such a relationship where no obvious obligation existed. Then, in the *Douglas* case in 2000, a judge in the Court of Appeal said there was no need to construct 'an artificial relationship of confidentiality' when using breach of confidence to protect privacy because the law recognised privacy itself. This declaration, if followed by other judges, seemed likely to extend the ambit of breach of confidence considerably (*Douglas v Hello! Ltd* [2001] 2 All ER 289).

In 2001 a judge reviewed recent pronouncements before deciding she could use breach of confidence to impose an unprecedented ban preventing the disclosure of the new identities of two killers about to be released into the community. Eight years earlier, when they were ten, they had murdered the child James Bulger. The judge granted the injunction after pointing out that as the youths were now 18 no other means was available to her (*Venables and Thompson v News Group Newspapers Ltd* [2001] 1 All ER 908; see below, 'Breach of confidence and privacy').

Many basic questions about breach of confidence remain unclear. Development of this branch of the law is expected to accelerate in the years ahead.

See also chapter 30, 'Human Rights Act'; and chapter 32, 'Privacy'.

Protecting 'public secrets'

For many years judges have granted injunctions preventing breaches of confidence.

The law they developed had a useful role in protecting commercial and trade secrets; in a characteristic leading case the confidential information related to a blister treatment for horses. In the *Douglas* case, referred to above, in which in 2003 *OK!* magazine was awarded huge damages against *Hello!* magazine for publication of 'snatched' pictures, the judge found that the wedding was protected by the law of confidence as a 'valuable trade asset' (*Douglas v Hello!* [2003] EWHC 786 (Ch)).

In developing this branch of the law over the years the judges were using the discretionary powers available to them when dealing with equitable matters (see chapter 1: Sources of law). When they explained the legal concepts behind their decisions, individual judges put forward different ideas and sometimes reached apparently inconsistent conclusions. This is still a confusing characteristic of breach of confidence cases. The answers to many fundamental questions remain unclear.

A landmark in the development of the law of confidentiality was the declaration of the Lord Chief Justice in 1975 that the kind of secrets to be protected could include 'public secrets', which sounds like a contradiction in terms but means simply information emanating from state or public business. Journalists consider their role includes the investigation of such secrets and, in appropriate cases, publication in the public interest.

As *The Times* newspaper declared during a confrontation with government in 1852: 'The first duty of the press is to obtain the earliest and most correct intelligence of the events of the time, and instantly, by disclosing them, to make them the common property of the nation.'

In the 1980s, the law of confidentiality was used for the first time by local authorities against local newspapers.

In the late 1980s, the law of confidentiality was used by the British Government in attempts to silence former members of the security services (in particular Peter Wright, author of *Spycatcher*) and journalists trying to report their disclosures. Previously, such disclosures in this country would have resulted in prosecution under the Official Secrets Act 1911, but juries had generally shown themselves unwilling to convict and the legislation had become unworkable (see chapter 29).

Applications for interim injunctions on the ground of breach of confidence come before judges sitting without juries and if granted are enforceable under the law of contempt — again by judges sitting without juries; and the judges have generally shown themselves more amenable than juries to government claims of national security.

In spite of the greater effectiveness of the Official Secrets Act 1989, UK governments have continued to use breach of confidence in an attempt to buttress their powers to impose secrecy on former members of the security services (see chapter 29). In the late 1990s and early 2000s the Government used both injunctions and prosecutions under the Act against two former intelligence officers, David Shayler and Richard Tomlinson, who made disclosures to the media.

Journalists complain that governments also use breach of confidence as a means of enforcing news management in cases when no genuine issue of confidentiality is involved. In 1999 the Home Secretary, Jack Straw, obtained an injunction against the *Sunday Telegraph*, which was in the process of printing information from a leaked report of a public inquiry into the police handling of investigations into the murder of black teenager Stephen Lawrence.

The report was due to be made public some days later. The judge granted the injunction by phone at night. The presses were stopped, but substantial numbers of the paper had already been distributed. The injunction, which forbade the paper from publishing any information from the report, also had the effect of restraining all other English media (see Injunction against one is against all, below).

The injunction was later varied to allow publication of and comment on those parts of the report already published. The ban on further disclosure of the report's findings, before its official publication to the public, remained.

Journalists hoped that a provision of the Human Rights Act 1998 would in future make it more difficult for a government to obtain such injunctions (see chapter 30, 'Human Rights Act'; and below, 'Injunctions'). Section 12 of the Act applies if a court is considering whether to grant an injunction which affects the exercise of the right to freedom of expression.

Injunction against one is against all

In 1987, in a decision of great importance for the press, the Court of Appeal held that when an injunction is in force preventing a newspaper from publishing confidential information, other newspapers in England which know of the injunction can be guilty of contempt of court if they publish that information, even if they are not named in the injunction.

The court said papers committed a serious offence against justice itself by taking action which destroyed the confidentiality that the court was seeking to protect and so rendered the due process of law ineffectual. In 1989 two papers were fined £50,000 each for publishing extracts from *Spycatcher* because at the time of publication they knew that interim injunctions were in force against the *Observer* and the *Guardian* preventing them from publishing this material.

The fines were later discharged, but the convictions were upheld and the ruling on the law was confirmed by the House of Lords in 1991.

The implications of the 1987 decision quickly became clear when officials of the Department of Trade and Industry telephoned all national newspapers to warn them that an injunction existed against the *Observer* preventing it from publishing details of a leaked Department of Trade and Industry report on the takeover of House of Fraser; the other papers were unable to publish details from the report in case they committed contempt.

This legal device for silencing the press is all the more effective because the injunction is sometimes phrased in such a way that journalists are forbidden even to mention the existence of the proceedings. This happened in legal actions brought by the newspaper magnate Robert Maxwell. Robertson & Nicol's *Media Law* says: 'The danger of injunctions covering up iniquitous behaviour is demonstrated by the fact that six months before Robert Maxwell's corporate failing came to light upon his death, he was able to obtain injunctions preventing the press from publishing any suggestion that his companies had indulged in "dubious accounting devices" or had "sought to mislead . . . as to the value of the assets of the company". The media were even banned from reporting the fact that this order had been made.'

An injunction obtained in an English court does not prevent publication in another country. In particular, it does not prevent publication in Scotland—though Scottish judges may be asked to impose their own injunction, known as an interdict.

Breach of confidence and privacy

Until 2000, English law recognised no right to privacy (see chapter 32, 'Privacy'). But on many occasions people who believed their privacy was about to be infringed attempted to use the law of breach of confidence to prevent intrusions.

Their main difficulty lay in 'the essentially different nature of the two kinds of right', as the Law Commission's report on breach of confidence said in 1981 (Cmnd 8388). An obligation of confidence, by definition, arises firstly from the circumstances in which the information is given. By contrast, said the commission, a right of privacy in respect of information would arise from the nature of the information itself; it would be based on the principle that certain kinds of information are categorised as private and for that reason alone ought not to be disclosed. In many cases where privacy is infringed this is not the result of a breach of confidence.

As stated earlier, the judges used to take a strict view on the circumstances in which an obligation of confidence could be implied; it was only where there was a recognised relationship between the parties, such as that of doctor and patient, employer and employee, or husband and wife.

In 1978 a telephone subscriber was complaining that his line was tapped by the Post Office at the request of the police. The judge said:

> No doubt a person who uses a telephone to give confidential information to another may do so in such a way as to impose an obligation of confidence on that other: but I do not see how it could be said that any such obligation is imposed on those who overhear the conversation, whether by means of tapping or otherwise. (Sir Robert Megarry, the Vice Chancellor, in *Malone v Metropolitan Police Comr* [1979] Ch 344)

But the judges were beginning to abandon their strict view on the cirumstances in which an obligation of confidence could occur. In the *Spycatcher* case in the House of Lords in 1988 Lord Goff of Chieveley said:

> . . . a duty of confidence arises when confidential information comes to the knowledge of a person (the confidant) in circumstances where he has notice, or is held to have agreed, that the information is confidential, with the effect that it would be just in all the circumstances that he should be precluded from disclosing the information to others . . .

Lord Goff said he had expressed the duty in wide terms to include the situation where an obviously confidential document was wafted by an electric fan out of a window into a crowded street, or when an obviously confidential document such as a diary was dropped in a public place and then picked up by a passer-by.

In 1995 another judge said:

> If someone with a telephoto lens were to take from a distance and with no authority a picture of another engaged in some private act, his subsequent disclosure of the photograph would, in my judgment, as surely amount to a breach of confidence as if he had found or stolen a letter or diary in which the act was recounted and proceeded to publish it. In such a case, the law would protect what might reasonably be called a right of privacy, although the name accorded to the cause of action would be breach of confidence. (Laws J in *Hellewell v Chief Constable of Derbyshire* [1995] 4 All ER 473)

Then, when the European Convention on Human Rights was in effect incorporated into English law in 2000, guaranteeing a right to privacy, the judges started to abandon altogether the legal contrivance of implying a relationship where none existed.

In the *Douglas* case in 2000 Lord Justice Sedley said in the Court of Appeal:

> The law no longer needs to construct an artificial relationship of confidentiality between intruder and victim: it can recognise privacy itself as a legal principle drawn from the fundamental value of personal autonomy.

In that case the court was considering whether to lift an injunction which prevented *Hello!* magazine from publishing pictures of the wedding of the two filmstars who had sold exclusive rights to their wedding photographs to *OK!* magazine. At that time, there was no evidence who had taken the pictures. In fact they were taken by an intruder.

The two film stars had argued that publication of the photographs had infringed their privacy, but when the case came to trial in 2003, in spite of the declaration of Lord Justice Sedley three years earlier, the judge declined to hold that there was an existing law of privacy under which they were entitled to win. He said there were conflicting views in the authorities as to whether such a law existed, and therefore the matter should best be left to

Parliament. In the following year, however, the House of Lords, in the case involving the model Naomi Campbell, held unanimously that English law provided a cause of action for the unjustified publication of private information. See chapter 32, 'Privacy'.

In 2001, as reported earlier, a judge used breach of confidence to impose an injunction banning all the media from identifying the two killers of the child James Bulger, who were expected to be given new identities on their release from custody. The ban was to last throughout the lives of the two. Their counsel had argued for the injunction because, among other things, their lives would be at risk if they were identified, and because their rights under the European Convention to life, to privacy, and to protection from torture outweighed the freedom of expression of those who might wish to identify them.

The judge, Dame Elizabeth Butler-Sloss, said there was no other means of imposing a ban. She said:

> Under the umbrella of confidentiality there will be information which may require a special quality of protection. In the present case the reason for advancing that special quality is that, if the information was published, the publication would be likely to lead to grave and possibly fatal consequences. In my judgment, the court does have the jurisdiction, in exceptional cases, to extend the protection of confidentiality of information, even to impose restrictions on the press, where not to do so would be likely to lead to serious physical injury, or to the death, of the person seeking that confidentiality, and there is no other way to protect the applicants other than by seeking relief from the court.

The two cases, *Douglas* and *Venables*, appeared to provide a new general-purpose measure allowing courts to prevent publication of information in a wide range of cases where human rights enshrined in the European Convention were involved. But later comments by judges seemed to raise doubts on these matters (see 'Obligation of confidence' in 'Privacy', chapter 30).

The journalist's dilemma

The law of confidentiality regularly presents journalists with an awkward dilemma, a difficulty reduced but not removed by a measure in the Human Rights Act 1998 (see next section: 'How the media are affected', 'Injunctions'). Suppose a reporter learns about some newsworthy misconduct from a source who has received his information confidentially. The journalist is impelled, both by his instinct for fair play and by his respect for the law of libel, to approach the person against whom the misconduct is alleged to get his side of the story.

balanced & fair reporting.

If he does, however, he faces the risk that the culprit will immediately obtain an injunction preventing the use of the information and thus killing the story.

In 1977 the *Daily Mail* obtained a copy of a letter from the National Enterprise Board to British Leyland, the nationalised car manufacturer, that appeared to show BL was paying bribes and conspiring to defraud foreign governments to win overseas orders. It published the story under the headline 'World-wide bribery web by Leyland'.

No doubt the journalists assumed that if they checked the story with BL the firm would immediately get an injunction preventing them from publishing. In fact the letter turned out to be a forgery and the paper had to pay substantial libel damages.

By contrast, in several of the cases mentioned below—eg the *Bill Goodwin* case—the journalist attempted to check the story with the source and was then prevented by injunction from using it until it was no longer news.

You should certainly check the story if it is defamatory, but in doing so you would be wise to phrase your questions in such a way that you do not reveal that you have confidential material in your possession, thus laying yourself open to an injunction. It is better to use the information at your disposal to try to get the facts from a different, non-confidential, route. You can then return to the original source of the information to check.

Bear in mind that the court can order you to 'deliver up' confidential material, and this can result in the identification of your source. In the Bill Goodwin case the reporter refused to hand over his notes and was heavily fined (see below).

In a case brought under the Official Secrets Act the *Guardian* was forced to hand over confidential material that revealed the identity of its source, who was jailed. If you wish to avoid the risk of having your source identified, you should destroy the documents after writing the story.

Lord Denning said: 'It is contempt deliberately to mutilate a document which is likely to be called for in a pending action.' It is thought this danger should not arise if the 'mutilation' or destruction of the document takes place before a court order is made.

How the media are affected

Injunctions

The law of confidentiality affects the media because a person who passes information to a journalist may have received it confidentially. If the person to whom the confidence belongs (the confider) discovers, before the paper is published or the programme is broadcast, that the information is to be disclosed, he can try to get a temporary injunction prohibiting publication of the confidential material.

The Human Rights Act contains a section (section 12) which is intended to provide some protection against injunctions in matters involving freedom of expression (see chapter 30, 'Protection against injunctions').

The confider's lawyer applies to a High Court judge. He has to persuade the judge, under section 12, that the confider is 'likely' to establish at the trial that publication should not be allowed.

The limitations of the defence under section 12 were shown in the case referred to in chapter 1 where the *Liverpool Echo* wanted to publish a story about financial irregularities at the firm Cream Holdings, an event organiser, based on confidential information it had obtained from the firm's former financial controller.

The paper had published one story, then asked the directors of Cream to answer some questions about their activities. Cream immediately applied for, and was granted by a judge, an injunction to prevent further details being published.

The paper appealed to the Court of Appeal which, by a 2–1 majority, rejected the paper's case because it considered the firm was likely to win at trial in the sense that it had established a 'real prospect of success'. The paper then took the case to the House of Lords, and the Lords found in its favour. For the Lords' ruling, see chapter 30, 'Protection against injunctions'.

Before the Act was implemented, the application might be without notice, which meant that only one party was represented, and the newspaper might learn about the proceedings only when it was told that an injunction had been granted. That can still happen.

Section 12 says that if the journalist is not present when the application is made, the court must not grant an injunction unless it is satisfied the person seeking the injunction has taken all practicable steps to notify the journalist or that there are compelling reasons why the journalist should not be notified.

But these matters are generally conducted at speed, and it may not be possible to tell the journalist. In the *Douglas* case, referred to above, *OK!* and the two stars won a temporary injunction from a judge, granted at night over the telephone, banning distribution of the 750,000 print run. The court was told *OK!* had tried to contact the editor of *Hello!* but 'a security guard who answered the phone at their premises had been unable to help'.

In the past injunctions have sometimes been granted at a stage when a newspaper has been printed and ready to go on sale, or a programme has been ready for broadcasting, and such an injunction has caused great inconvenience and expense, but defiance of the order would have been a serious contempt of court.

On many occasions, temporary injunctions which appeared to be harsh and wide-ranging in their terms have been lifted when the newspaper's case was heard. This did not mean that the judges made a mistake, legally speaking, the first time. The purpose of a temporary injunction is to 'hold the ring' (in the words of Lord Donaldson, a former Master of the Rolls), until the matter can be fully argued later.

In the *Douglas* case the judges lifted the temporary injunction. They argued that if *Hello!* published the story, then lost its case at the trial, it would have to pay an 'enormous' bill by way of damages or an account of profits which would be adequate recompense for OK! In fact, when the case came for trial in 2003, the judge awarded *OK!* £1,003,156 damages, as well as £14,600 for the film stars.

Local papers

The following two examples show the effect of injunctions on local newspapers.

In 1982, the *Watford Observer* planned to publish a story based on a document which showed that the publisher Robert Maxwell's printing operation, Sun Printers, was losing money, and he wanted to reduce the workforce.

The day before press day, a reporter telephoned the company asking for comments. At midday on press day, Maxwell telephoned the paper's editor and asked for an assurance that the material would not be published, on the grounds that it was confidential and that negotiations with the trade unions were at a delicate stage. When the editor declined, Sun Printers' lawyers applied to the High Court for an injunction and telephoned the paper at 4.30pm to say an injunction had been granted. By this time all editorial and typesetting work on the paper would normally have been completed.

Fortunately, the paper, alerted by the call from Maxwell, had prepared alternative material for use in its pages. The injunction was later lifted (see this chapter).

In 1984, Medina Borough Council, on the Isle of Wight, got an injunction preventing the *Southern Evening Echo*, of Southampton, from publishing details of a consultant's report on plans for development in Newport, the island's capital.

As the papers were unloaded from the hydrofoil taking them from the mainland, an officer of the Newport county court stood on the quayside with the injunction. The papers could not be distributed, and another edition had to be sent to the island.

The *Spycatcher* affair

This affair arose out of attempts by the British Government to prevent publication of information acquired by Peter Wright, a former senior officer of MI5, Britain's internal security service. The Government acted against Wright and a number of newspapers in many courts in several countries. Only a brief summary is given below. Those wishing to study the cases in detail should refer to The *Spycatcher* Cases (European Law Centre) by Michael Fysh QC.

In 1985 the British Attorney-General began proceedings against Wright in New South Wales, Australia. Wright was living in Tasmania.

Wright's book recounted his experiences in MI5; among other allegations, it said that MI5 officers had plotted to destabilise the government led by the Labour Prime Minister Harold Wilson in the mid-1970s, and that officers of the security services had plotted to assassinate President Nasser of Egypt.

The Attorney-General sought an injunction or an account of profits (see below, 'Account of profits'), arguing that former members of the security services had an absolute and lifelong duty not to reveal any details of their employment.

In June 1986 the *Observer* and *Guardian* newspapers both carried stories reporting the forthcoming hearing in Australia. The stories contained brief accounts of some of the allegations. An English court granted the Attorney-General interim injunctions against both newspapers preventing them from disclosing any information obtained by Wright in his capacity as a member of the British security service.

The following year, as mentioned earlier in this chapter, other newspapers published information from *Spycatcher*, believing they were not prevented by the injunctions, but the courts held they were guilty of contempt of court.

In 1988, after many legal actions involving the Government and a number of newspapers, both in the United Kingdom and abroad, and after *Spycatcher* had been published in the United States, the House of Lords held, among other things, that the original articles in the *Observer* and *Guardian* in 1986 had not been published in breach of confidence; that the Government was not entitled to a permanent injunction preventing the two papers from further comment on the book and use of extracts from it; and that the Government was not entitled to a general injunction restraining the media from future publication of information derived from Wright or other members or former members of the security service. By the time the two papers were free to publish the material legally, the story was history rather than news.

Later the European Court of Human Rights (ECtHR) held that the UK Government had been right to obtain the initial injunctions against the *Observer* and the *Guardian* in 1986, but that the injunctions should not have been maintained once the book had been published. (For the comments of the ECtHR on the use of injunctions in this case, see chapter 1, 'The rule against prior restraint'.)

Security service cases

While the *Spycatcher* cases were dragging on the Government became committed to taking legal action whenever members and former members of the security services breached what the Government saw as their lifelong duty of confidence, and many actions followed. (The *Shayler* and *Tomlinson* cases continued the trend into the new millennium.)

A characteristic of the injunctions imposed by courts was their very wide scope. The Government was granted an injunction preventing BBC Radio 4 from broadcasting a series of programmes 'My country: right or wrong'. The injunction was at first in terms that prevented the BBC from broadcasting all information of whatever kind about the security services from former members, or even naming former members of the security services.

But the courts have been willing to make variations if newspapers apply with good supporting evidence that the material is publicly available or there is public interest in publication.

The Bill Goodwin case

In 1989 an engineering company, Tetra Ltd, obtained injunctions against the magazine *The Engineer* and Bill Goodwin, a trainee reporter. The company, which was in financial difficulties, had prepared a business plan for the purpose of negotiating a substantial bank loan.

A copy of the draft plan 'disappeared' from the company's offices and the next day an unidentified source telephoned Goodwin and gave him information about the company, including the amount of the projected loan and the company's forecast results.

Goodwin phoned the company and its bankers to check the information. The company obtained a without notice injunction restraining the magazine from publishing information derived from the draft plan and later obtained an order requiring Goodwin and the Engineer to hand over notes that would disclose the source of the information. Goodwin refused to comply with the order and was fined £5,000. In 1996 the European Court of Human Rights held that the court order and the fine violated his right to freedom of expression under article 10 of the European Convention on Human Rights (see also chapter 24, 'The journalist's sources').

Cost of injunctions

As a condition for the granting of an interim injunction the person seeking the inju
has to give a cross-undertaking in damages—that is, an undertaking that he will pay any
damages to the defendant if, at the trial, it is held that the interim injunction should not
have been granted.

The defendant may also get costs. In a case in 1994, Camelot, organisers of the
National Lottery, was granted an injunction preventing the media from identifying the
winners of the first major jackpot. When newspapers succeeded in having the injunction
lifted, Camelot had to pay them £5,000 costs.

Even so, the cost to a newspaper that decides to challenge an injunction may be considerable. The *Liverpool Echo* risked costs perhaps as high as £600,000 when it took its
challenge over the Cream Holdings story to the House of Lords; fortunately it won, but still
faced a large bill. The *News of the World* claimed in 1987 that it had spent £200,000 in
an unsuccessful attempt to defeat an injunction granted to a health authority preventing
the paper using information from personal medical records supplied by one or more of the
authority's employees. The records showed that two practising doctors employed by the
authority had the HIV virus.

Fines

Disobeying an injunction can result in an action for contempt of court. The *News of the
World* was fined £10,000 for publishing a story headlined 'Scandal of Docs with AIDS'
after the granting of the injunction mentioned above.

Order to reveal source

A court can order a journalist to reveal the name of his informant, as happened in the *Bill
Goodwin* case (see next chapter, 'The journalist's sources').

Delivery up

A court can order that confidential matter be 'delivered up' or destroyed.

Account of profits

A person misusing confidential information may be asked to account for the profits to the person who confided the information.

Damages

If confidential matter is published, the person whose confidences have been breached may be able to claim damages. As mentioned earlier, *OK!* magazine was awarded more than £1 million damages against *Hello!*, which had published 'snatched' pictures. The judge based this figure on losses of sales he estimated *OK!* to have suffered as a result of *Hello!*'s 'spoiler'. In addition the two film stars were awarded £14,600 for distress and incidental costs.

Supermodel Naomi Campbell was awarded £2,500 damages for distress and injury to her feelings in 2002 against Mirror Group Newspapers when she sued for breach of confidence and infringement of the Data Protection Act 1998. The *Daily Mirror* had published a story about her receiving therapy from Narcotics Anonymous for drug addiction. She was awarded an additional £1,000 for 'aggravated damages' as a result of an additional article published by the paper The finding was overthrown by the Court of Appeal, but in 2004 the House of Lords restored the trial judge's award (*Campbell v Mirror Group Newspapers* [2004] UKHL 22). See details of the case in chapter 32, 'Privacy'.

Elements of a breach

As stated in the introduction to this chapter, there are three elements of a breach of confidence—the quality of confidence, the obligation of confidence, and detriment.

The quality of confidence

Quality of confidence

The law of breach of confidence safeguards ideas and information. In general, information is not confidential if it is in the public domain—that is, if it is public knowledge.

In the *Watford Observer* case, mentioned above (Local papers), the injunction was discharged by the Court of Appeal because, among other reasons, the document upon which the story was based could not properly be regarded as confidential. It had started life as a highly confidential document, with a limited distribution. It was distributed personally, and the recipients were told it was confidential. Later, however, the report was circulated on a wider and wider basis throughout the company to management and trade union officials, so that all concerned could discuss it. It had thus lost the quality of confidentiality.

In the *Spycatcher* case, the Government finally lost largely because, in the words of one of the many judges who considered the issue, the cat had been let out of the bag. Mr Justice Scott (later Lord Scott) said that the book and its contents had been disseminated on a worldwide scale. In Britain, anyone who wanted a copy could obtain one.

But information in the public domain cannot always be used with impunity. In 1981, the Court of Appeal confirmed an injunction restraining Thames Television Ltd from showing a programme, '*The Primodos Affair*', about a pregnancy-testing drug because the TV producer got the idea for the programme while doing private consultancy work for the company concerned, Schering Chemicals Ltd, even though Thames said the programme would contain no material not freely available from other sources.

The information, though in the public domain, had been gleaned originally by diligent work, and the conduct leading to the injunction was, in the court's view, reprehensible.

Obligation of confidence

An obligation of confidence can arise in a variety of ways (and see also the views expressed above, Breach of confidence and privacy).

Contractual relationship

The most frequent is a contractual obligation. People working for others may have signed a contract to say that they will not reveal their employer's secrets, but even if they have not there is an implied term in every contract of employment that the employee will not act in a way detrimental to his employer's interests.

Membership of security services

Members have no contract of employment with the crown, but in the *Spycatcher* cases the courts accepted the view that they had a duty of confidence that resulted from the nature of their employment and the requirements of national security and which lasted for life, subject to the defences of public domain and public interest.

Disclosure

Under the process of 'disclosure' (previously known as 'discovery') in legal proceedings, parties have to disclose relevant documents to the other side. This information is protected until the information has been read to or by the court or referred to at a public hearing.

Domestic relationship

In 1967 the Duchess of Argyll prevented the *People* newspaper, and her former husband, from publishing marital secrets. By the 1980s the courts were willing to extend the protection to prevent the publication of kiss-and-tell stories originating from less formal relationships. In 1988 a woman was given leave to sue the *Mail on Sunday* for damages for a story about her love affair with another woman.

But information about transient affairs (for example, with a prostitute) is unlikely to be protected (see details of the *Theakston* and *Flitcroft* cases in chapter 32, 'Privacy').

Third parties—such as a journalist

The information may have been obtained indirectly from the confider. A third party, such as a journalist, who comes into possession of confidential information and realises it is confidential may come under a legal duty to respect the confidence.

For example, in the *Primodos* case, mentioned above, the chemical company supplied the TV producer with the information about the drug for the purpose of public relations work he was doing for the company. Thames TV, the third party, was prevented by injunction from using the information for a television film.

Unethical behaviour

It was once considered doubtful whether an obligation of confidence could arise because of the reprehensible means by which the information was acquired. It now seems to be established that there is an obligation of confidence on those who obtain confidential information by unethical means such as trespass, theft, listening devices, or long-range cameras.

Detriment

The detriment suffered by the confider does not have to be a financial loss. In the *Spycatcher* case in the Lords, Lord Keith of Kinkel said it would be a sufficient detriment to an individual that information he gave in confidence was to be disclosed to people he would prefer not to know of it.

That applied even if the information to be disclosed was to the person's credit.

But a government was in a different position from an individual. It had to show that publication would be harmful to the public interest.

In the *Spycatcher* case, he said, the book's contents had been disseminated worldwide, and general publication in this country would not bring about any significant damage to the public interest beyond what had already been done.

In 1994 a judge refused to order journalist Neil Hyde to reveal the source of a story derived from a confidential report on the escape from Broadmoor Hospital of two convicted killers. The judge, Sir Peter Pain, said a health authority was 'an emanation of the state' and therefore could not obtain an order requiring a journalist to reveal his source unless it could show that it was in the public interest that such an order should be granted.

The party communicating

By 'the party communicating it' is meant the person communicating the information originally, that is, the person to whom the confidence is owed. This person may be several stages removed from the one who eventually passes on the information to, say, a journalist.

Disclosure in the public interest

The Human Rights Act 1998, in section 12, says that when a court is considering imposing an injunction in a matter affecting freedom of expression, and where journalistic material is involved, it must have particular regard to the extent to which it is, or would be, in the public interest to be published.

Even before the Act was implemented, journalists could plead that the disclosure of confidential information would be in the public interest. The *Watford Observer* did in the case referred to above (Local papers). The judge, Lord Denning, said that when considering applications for an injunction on grounds of confidentiality, courts had to hold the balance between two competing interests. On the one hand there was the public interest in preserving confidence. On the other was the public interest in making known to people matters of public concern.

In this case, he said, the balance came down in favour of publishing the matters in the report. They were of great interest to all the many people in the Watford area who were concerned with printing. They were fit to be discussed, not only with the immediate workers in the Sun Printers' works, but also those outside connected with the printing industry or interested in it. Other judges have also taken the view that they had to balance the two interests.

Section 12(3) of the Human Rights Act says there shall be no prior restraint in a media case 'unless the court is satisfied that the applicant (that is, the person asking for the injunction) is likely to establish that the publication should not be allowed' when the case comes to trial. That means that the person seeking the injunction has the burden of persuading the court, and that the court must assess the likely outcome of a full trial by weighing up the competing factors.

In the *Douglas* case in 2000, after the Act came into force, Lord Justice Sedley said that the right to free expression referred to in article 10(1) of the European Convention could not have priority over the limitations to the right contained in article 10(2), which included 'preventing the disclosure of information received in confidence' (see wording of the article in chapter 30). He said: 'Everything will ultimately depend on the proper balance between privacy and publicity in the situation facing the court.'

In 2001, the Human Rights Act helped the media to publish material in the face of opposition, in this case from the Government. The *Sunday Times* wanted to publish information that originated from a former intelligence officer Richard Tomlinson. The paper argued that the material had been published elsewhere and was therefore not confidential, but the Attorney-General insisted the paper should prove the information was in the public domain. The Court of Appeal agreed with the newspaper, holding that its application was in harmony with article 10 of the European Convention and section 12 of the Human Rights Act (*A-G v Times Newspapers Ltd* [2001] EWCA Civ 97, [2001] 1 WLR 885).

In the case in 2002 in which Naomi Campbell sued Mirror Group Newspapers for a story about her receiving therapy from Narcotics Anonymous for her drug addiction, the paper argued that this was published in the public interest because the model had previously gone out of her way to tell the media that, in contrast to other models, she did not take drugs, and this was untrue. The House of Lords, in 2004, agreed that in the circumstances it was in the public interest to report the fact of Ms Campbell's drug addiction and that she was receiving treatment for that addiction, but there was no justification for reporting the fact that she was receiving treatment at Narcotics Anonymous, or giving details of the treatment and her reaction to it, or surreptitiously obtaining photographs of her emerging from a treatment session.

Section 12 of the Human Rights Act also says that a court considering a matter affecting freedom of information must have particular regard to 'any relevant privacy code'. In the *Douglas* case the relevant privacy code, which was considered by the court, was that of the Press Complaints Commission (see chapter 31, 'The Codes'). In this code, privacy is among the topics where the code makes clear that there may be exceptions to the rules set out if the information can be demonstrated to be in the public interest.

This phrase is said to include:

(1) detecting or exposing crime or a serious misdemeanour;

(2) protecting public health and safety; and

(3) preventing the public from being misled by some statement or action of an individual or organisation.

The editor must be able clearly to demonstrate how the public interest is served by publishing private/confidential information.

People in the public eye

Public interest may give a defence for matters concerning people in the public eye. In 1977 Tom Jones and other well-known singers tried unsuccessfully to get an injunction to prevent publication in the *Daily Mirror* of articles in which their former press agent gave details of their private lives.

The court held that the pop singers, who had sought and welcomed publicity of every kind, were not entitled to an injunction pending the trial of a court action. Lord Denning said that if there were another side to their image it was in the public interest that this should be made known.

The same principle was applied by a court in 1993 when the *Daily Mirror* published material from *The Downing Street Years*, memoirs of Lady Thatcher, the former Prime Minister. The *Sunday Times*, which had bought exclusive rights to the book, was planning to run lengthy extracts but the *Daily Mirror* obtained a leaked copy and published first, leading on the story three days running. *The Sunday Times* tried to obtain an injunction.

The Conservative Party conference was in progress when the Mirror published its first splash 'What she said about him' (referring to John Major, her successor). 'Intellectually he drifted with the tide.' On the following day the paper's headline was 'What she says about them' (leading members of the Party). 'Thatcher sticks the knife in Major's men.'

The judge rejected the application for an injunction. He said that because the Conservative Party was making a public show of unity in Blackpool, the publication of the Mirror's claims could be in the public interest. The Court of Appeal agreed.

In 2000, a judge refused an injunction sought by Lord Levy against Times Newspapers. The story was about his tax affairs, and was clearly obtained in breach of confidence. The judge said that Lord Levy was a prominent supporter of the Labour Party, which had a manifesto commitment to closing tax loopholes, and his own tax affairs would shed light on the integrity of that position, which was in the public interest.

In the case brought by Naomi Campbell against the *Daily Mirror* Lord Phillips, Master of the Rolls, said the Court of Appeal did not believe that because an individual had achieved fame, that meant that his private life could be laid bare by the media:

> We do not see why it should necessarily be in the public interest that an individual who has been adopted as a role model, without seeking this distinction, should be demonstrated to have feet of clay.

But he said the Human Rights Act, which gave a right to respect for family and private life, must be balanced against freedom of expression in the media. He continued:

> Where a public figure chooses to make untrue pronouncements about his, or her, private life, the press will normally be entitled to put the record straight.

Disclosure to whom?

Even if the information obtained ought to be disclosed in the public interest, it does not necessarily follow that it should be disclosed in the media. The answer to this question depends upon the circumstances.

In the *Operation Snowball* case, which involved allegations of miscarriages of justice and police corruption, the judge lifted an injunction imposed on the *Daily Express*. He said it had been suggested that disclosure should be made not to the public at large, but to certain holders of high office, such as the Commissioner of Police. However, the allegation concerned the administration of justice. Such corruption was properly a matter of public interest as opposed to a matter which should be taken up and dealt with by the authorities.

The *Daily Mirror* was not so fortunate when it wanted to publish information, obtained from tapes made illegally, that revealed alleged breaches of Jockey Club regulations and possibly the commission of criminal offences. The newspaper's lawyers argued that the paper would use the tapes to expose iniquity. But the judges rejected the argument, saying the best thing would be for the paper to tell the police or the Jockey Club. Publication would serve the newspaper's interests rather than any public interest.

24

The journalist's sources

It is a matter of professional principle that a reporter does not reveal his source of confidential information.

The journalist's job is to discover and record news. Wherever he looks he will find people with vested interests trying to prevent him from doing so.

For this reason, to get his story he must often rely on information passed to him by people who would be injured if it became known that they had done so.

The journalist will sometimes be asked, 'Where did you get that story?'

'Where did you get that story?'

If a judge asks

Sometimes the person asking will be a judge. At common law judges have the power to order disclosure of the identity of wrongdoers whenever the person against whom disclosure is sought has got 'mixed up' in wrongful conduct that infringes a claimant's legal rights (*Norwich Pharmacal Co v Customs and Excise Comrs* [1974] AC 133).

Like any other citizen, the journalist is under an obligation to answer questions properly put to him in a court of law. Failure to answer may constitute contempt of court. That can lead to a fine or even prison, but it may be that the journalist will feel impelled to preserve the anonymity of his source even at the risk of his personal liberty.

In 1989, Bill Goodwin, a trainee reporter on *The Engineer* magazine, was ordered by a judge to reveal the source of information he had been given in a telephone call that an engineering company was in financial difficulties and seeking a large loan. He refused to do so and, after fears that he would be imprisoned, was fined £5,000 for contempt of court (see 'Sources and the Human Rights Act', below; also chapter 23, 'The Bill Goodwin case').

In 1992 Channel 4 and the independent production company Box Productions were fined £75,000 for contempt of court after refusing to comply with an order requiring them to disclose the identity of a source used in a television programme '*The Committee*', part of the *Dispatches* series (see 'Anti-terrorism legislation', below).

In 2001 a group of news organisations was ordered to hand over documents wanted by Belgian brewers Interbrew, in an attempt to find the person responsible for circulation of false information that resulted in a fall in share prices (*Interbrew SA v Financial Times Ltd, Independent Newspapers, Guardian Newspapers Ltd, Times Newspapers Ltd and Reuters Group plc* [2002] EWCA Civ 274, [2002] 2 Lloyd's Rep 229).

The organisations refused to do so, and the sequel included a threat by the firm to seek a sequestration order seizing the assets of *The Guardian*. Later the brewer dropped its actions, leaving the matter in the hands of the financial regulatory authority, the Financial Services Authority, which has strong powers to compel people to produce documents (see 'Statutes giving disclosure powers', below).

In 2002 a freelance journalist, Robin Ackroyd, declined to reveal his source for a *Daily Mirror* report on Moors murderer Ian Brady. It was accepted that the source was someone within Ashworth Hospital, where Brady was detained, who obtained the information about the killer from a database. Attempts by the hospital to get Ackroyd to reveal his source led to a series of court hearings, and as this edition of *McNae* went to press in 2005 a trial was still awaited (see 'Sources and the Human Rights Act', in this chapter).

If an official asks

Sometimes the person asking the journalist for his source will be a tribunal chairman or an official. Increasingly in recent years Parliament has given authorities the power to demand information on specific issues and provide penalties under these Acts.

In 1963 two journalists appearing before a tribunal of inquiry were jailed for refusing to identify sources of information in stories in the *Vassall* case. Vassall had been convicted of spying. A number of newspapers suggested he was a known homosexual, a fact considered to make it inadvisable that he should be employed on secret work because it rendered him susceptible to blackmail. The tribunal had been set up under the Tribunals of Inquiry (Evidence) Act 1921, which gave tribunals wide powers to send for and examine witnesses.

Three journalists who refused to name the sources of stories about the Bloody Sunday killings in Northern Ireland were threatened with contempt of court actions by Lord Saville, chairman of the inquiry set up under the same Act to report on the incident. The journalists were Tony Harnden, of *The Daily Telegraph*, former Channel 4 news producer Lena Ferguson and Alex Thomson, the station's chief news reporter. Mr Harnden refused to name a soldier whose recollection formed the basis of a story published in 1999. The journalist had given him an undertaking not to say or do anything that might identify him. In 2000 Mr Harnden was 'placed in contempt' of the inquiry and told the matter had been referred to the High Court in Belfast, which would decide what action to take, but in 2004 the court was told contempt proceedings were being dropped. For five years Mr Harnden had lived with the threat that he could be imprisoned or face an unlimited fine. The inquiry agreed to pay the journalist's legal costs, believed to amount to £110,000. The two other journalists were declared to be in contempt of the tribunal in 2000. Both said they were prepared to go to jail rather than name the soldiers who had co-operated in a number of broadcasts. They also were told in 2004 that the proceedings would be dropped.

In 1988, Jeremy Warner, of the *Independent* newspaper, was fined £20,000 and ordered to pay costs estimated at £100,000 after refusing to disclose to government inspectors his sources for articles on takeover bids which involved insider dealing, a criminal offence (see Statutes giving disclosure powers, below).

If a police officer asks

Sometimes the person asking the journalist for his source will be a police officer. Like other citizens, the journalist has no legal duty to provide information to the police for their inquiries, except in the special circumstances mentioned below. This would seem an elementary item of civic knowledge, but in 1990 a *Westmorland Gazette* reporter who declined to tell a police inspector his source for a story about the leak of a council document was threatened with prosecution for obstructing the police in their duties.

If the police need to obtain 'journalistic material' to assist their investigations they normally have to apply to a judge first. They also generally need the consent of a judge before searching a journalist's premises for such material. These provisions are contained in the Police and Criminal Evidence Act 1984 (see section on the Act, below).

The opportunities for police officers lawfully to gain access to confidential information held by citizens, including journalists, were increased by the Police Act 1997 (see 'An Englishman's Home is his castle', below, and section on Police Act), the Regulation of Investigatory Powers (RIP) Act 2000 (see below), the Terrorism Act 2000 (see 'Anti-terrorism laws', below) and the Anti-terrorism, Crime and Security Act 2001 (see

'Anti-terrorism laws', below). It seemed that the Serious Organised Crime and Police Act, which received Royal Assent in 2005, would still further increase police powers.

Under the RIP Act, authorities do not need a judge's approval when seeking the disclosure of journalistic sources obtained through e-mail, through non-intrusive surveillance methods, or by way of communications data disclosure. (They do, however, need the approval of the Secretary of State.)

The Terrorism Act went a step further than other legislation by making it an offence, punishable by a prison sentence of up to five years, for a person to fail to tell a police officer if he believes or even suspects, as a result of information that comes to his attention in the course of a trade, profession, business, or employment, that certain terrorist offences concerned with the funding of suspected terrorists have been committed.

The Anti-terrorism, Crime and Security Act 2001 went further still by extending the offence of withholding information to all such information concerned with terrorist investigations.

Search powers

Increasingly authorities that have been given the power to demand information are also given the power to search the premises of the person they believe to have the information. This contravenes the traditional principle that 'an Englishman's home is his castle'.

A famous case in 1765 concerned a clerk called Entick whose house had been entered by 'the king's messengers' and his papers seized on the authority of a warrant from the Secretary of State (*Entick v Carrington* (1765) 19 State Tr 1029). The court said firmly the action was unlawful.

That case was referred to and given a ringing endorsement in the Queen's Bench divisional court in 2000 when the court refused an application by the police to order *The Guardian* and *The Observer* to hand over all files, documents, and records in their possession relating to a letter in *The Guardian's* letter column from the former M15 officer David Shayler and an article by reporter Martin Bright in *The Observer*.

Both publications repeated allegations that M16 officers had been involved in a failed attempt to assassinate the Libyan leader Colonel Gaddafi. The police in particular wanted an e-mail letter sent by Shayler so that they could discover his e-mail address (*R v Central Criminal Court, ex p Martin Bright* [2001] 2 All ER 244; the case is referred to below as the *Martin Bright* case).

Lord Justice Judge said that the Englishman's home principle was linked with freedom of speech. He continued:

> Premises are not to be entered by the forces of authority or the state to deter or diminish, inhibit or stifle the exercise of an individual's right to free speech or the press of its freedom to investigate and inform, and orders should not be made which might have that effect unless a circuit judge is personally satisfied that the statutory preconditions to the making of an order are established, and, as the final safeguard of basic freedoms, that in the particular circumstances it is indeed appropriate for an order to be made.
>
> Inconvenient or embarrassing revelations, whether for the security services, or for public authorities, should not be suppressed. Legal proceedings directed towards the seizure of the working papers of an individual journalist, or the premises of the newspaper or television programme publishing his or her reports, or the threat of such proceedings, tend to inhibit discussion. When a genuine investigation into possible corrupt or reprehensible activities by a public authority is being investigated by the media, compelling evidence will normally be needed to demonstrate that the public interest would be served by such proceedings. Otherwise, to the public disadvantage, legitimate enquiry and discussion, and 'the safety valve of effective investigative journalism' . . . would be discouraged, perhaps stifled.

Legislators have declined to conform with the common law principles in recent measures. Under the Police Act 1997, a chief police officer can authorise entry upon property, and the placing of surveillance devices ('bugging and burgling'), without any authorisation by a judge. In 'sensitive' cases authorisation is subject to prior approval by a government-appointed commissioner, unless the matter is urgent (see 'The Police Act', below).

Under the Security Service Act 1996 the security service, which now has police functions, also is enabled to enter on and interfere with property if it is investigating serious crime in the United Kingdom. Again, no authorisation by a judge is necessary, but in this case curiously a warrant from the Home Secretary is required.

Under the Terrorism Act 2000, a justice of the peace can issue a warrant enabling police investigating a terrorist offence to search premises, provided he is satisfied that the material sought does not consist of or include 'excluded' or 'special procedure' material (as defined under 'Police and Criminal Evidence Act 1984', below).

In urgent cases a police superintendent (or above) can issue the equivalent of a search warrant for excluded or special procedure material, normally available only from a circuit judge. The Secretary of State has to be notified as soon as is reasonably practicable.

See also the information on search powers given in chapters 25 and 33.

Sources and the Human Rights Act

In the *Martin Bright* case, Lord Justice Judge said that counsel had drawn the attention of the court to a number of decisions of the European Court of Human Rights (ECtHR), but he did not find it necessary to refer to any of these decisions to discover the principles that applied in this case because the principles contained in article 6, right to a fair trial, and 10, right to freedom of expression, 'are bred in the bone of the common law'.

This view would surprise those journalists who have been ordered to reveal their sources of information and/or suffered seizure of their papers by judges who often seemed more concerned with backing authority or property interests than with freedom of expression.

In the *Bill Goodwin* case (referred to above and, more fully, in chapter 23), Goodwin was fined for refusing to comply with a judge's order to reveal his sources in a story that most journalists would have regarded as unexceptionable. He appealed against the order unsuccessfully first to the Court of Appeal and then to the House of Lords and all three courts held that disclosure was 'necessary in the interests of justice'.

Then, backed by the National Union of Journalists, he took the case to the ECtHR, where it went first before the European Commission, which at that time had the job of considering matters before they reached the European Court itself. In 1994 the commission found for Goodwin, saying:

> Protection of the sources from which journalists derive information is an essential means
> of enabling the press to perform its important function of 'public watchdog' in a demo-
> cratic society.

If journalists could be compelled to reveal their sources, this would make it much more difficult for them to obtain information and, as a consequence, to inform the public about matters of public interest.

Any compulsion must be limited to exceptional circumstances where vital public or individual interests were at stake.

In 1996 the European Court reached the same conclusion in the case. It said protection of journalistic sources was one of the basic conditions for press freedom, as was reflected in the laws and the professional codes of conduct in a number of contracting states and was affirmed in several international instruments on journalistic freedoms. An order of source disclosure could not be compatible with article 10 of the Convention unless it was justified by an overriding requirement in the public interest.

In the case involving *The Daily Mirror* report on Moors murderer Ian Brady (referred to above), the hospital in 2000, not knowing at first that the story had come from Robin

Ackroyd, applied for and was granted an order against the paper, requiring it to reveal the source. The paper appealed unsuccessfully against the order.

Lord Phillips, Master of the Rolls, said in the Court of Appeal that the decisions of the ECtHR had demonstrated that the freedom of the press had in the past carried greater weight in Strasbourg than it had in the courts of this country. But the court went on to find against the media, after considering the ECtHR test.

Lord Phillips said an English court, when considering whether a production order was 'necessary', should apply the same test as the ECtHR did when considering article 10 of the Convention. But Ashworth Security Hospital could argue that identification of the source was in the interests of the protection of health, the protection of the rights of others, and preventing the disclosure of information received in confidence. The disclosure of confidential medical records to the press was misconduct that was not merely of concern to the individual establishment in which it occurred. It was an attack on an area of confidentiality that should be safeguarded in any democratic society. This was an exceptional case.

In 2002 the House of Lords agreed and rejected the *Mirror*'s appeal. The judges recognised that the disclosure of sources had a 'chilling effect' on the freedom of the press, but found that it was 'necessary and proportionate and justified' in this case (*Ashworth Security Hospital v MGN Ltd* [2002] UKHL 29, [2002] 4 All ER 193).

So the paper was ordered to reveal its source, but reporter Robin Ackroyd admitted it was he. As mentioned above, *he* refused to identify *his* source, after which he was ordered to do so on the basis that he had no defence after the *Ashworth* case. He appealed.

In May 2003 the Court of Appeal found for the reporter, saying the case against him was different from the earlier case against the paper, and he had an arguable defence that he ought to be allowed to put at trial (*Mersey Care NHS Trust v Robin Ackroyd* [2003] EWCA Civ 663). The court had now learnt, as the earlier court had not, that the source for the story (the person who had given the information to Ackroyd) had not been paid for it. If that person had a public interest defence to a claim by the hospital for breach of confidence or contract, a claim based on the *Norwich Pharmacal* case (see above) could not succeed against Ackroyd because there would be no wrongdoer.

Even if Ackroyd failed to establish that his source had a public interest defence, it did not automatically follow that the public interest in non-disclosure of medical records should override the public interest in maintaining the confidentiality of his source. Lord Justice May said: 'Protection of journalistic sources is one of the basic conditions for press freedom in a democratic society. An order for source disclosure cannot be compatible with article 10 of the European Convention unless it is justified by an overriding requirement in the public interest.' Although there was a clear public interest in preserving the confidentiality of medical records, that could not automatically be regarded as an overriding requirement without examining the facts of a particular case. Ackroyd's trial was awaited as this edition of *McNae* went to press.

A rare case in which a newspaper successfully contested a disclosure order, arguing its rights to freedom of expression under article 10 of the Convention, involved the Belfast-based newspaper the *News Letter*. In 2001 a Northern Ireland judge refused to order the paper to reveal its sources for a story that indicated it had possession of confidential police paper naming people responsible for a bombing.

The judge said he had to undertake a balancing act. He held that, important as the claimant's legitimate interests in establishing the identity of the people who had provided the information to the defendants with a view to suing them were, these did not outweigh the public interest in the protection of the newspaper's confidential sources in order to ensure free communication of information to and through the press.

Contempt of court

Courts claim to recognise that there is a public interest in journalists being able to protect their sources, but have ordered disclosure when they considered it necessary.

In 1980, a court ordered Granada Television to reveal the identity of a 'mole' who had passed on confidential documents belonging to the British Steel Corporation. The documents, which were used for a current affairs programme, revealed mismanagement at the corporation, which was then making huge losses. Fortunately for Granada, the mole himself came forward and revealed his identity.

The following year, the Contempt of Court Act gave statutory form to the courts' recognition of the public interest in allowing journalists to protect their sources.

Section 10 says:

> No court may require a person to disclose, nor is any person guilty of contempt of court for refusing to disclose, the source of information contained in a publication for which he is responsible, unless it is established to the satisfaction of the court that disclosure is necessary in the interests of justice or national security, or for the prevention of disorder or crime.

Three cases have illustrated that the protection given to the journalist by the section, as interpreted by the courts, is not as great as many had hoped (and probably not as great as Parliament had intended).

The first case showed the scope of the phrase 'national security'. In 1983 *The Guardian* newspaper was ordered to return to the Government a leaked photostat copy of a Ministry of Defence document revealing the strategy for handling the arrival in Britain of Cruise missiles.

The Guardian did not know the identity of its informant, but realised the identity might be revealed by examination of the document, and claimed that as a result of section 10 it did not have to hand it over.

But the House of Lords said the interests of national security required that the identity of the informant must be revealed; publication of the particular document posed no threat to national security, but there was a risk that the person who leaked that document might leak another, with much more serious consequences for national security.

The *Guardian* handed over the document and the informant, a Foreign Office clerk, Sarah Tisdall, was convicted under the Official Secrets Act and jailed for six months.

Journalists should note that had *The Guardian* destroyed the document after it was used to prepare the article but before its handing over was ordered, the paper would have escaped the painful necessity of having to reveal the identity of its source.

The case involving Jeremy Warner showed what the courts understood by the word 'necessary' and the phrase 'prevention of crime'.

Inspectors investigating insider dealing asked for a court order compelling Warner to reveal his sources. Action was taken under the Financial Services Act (see Statutes giving disclosure powers, below). The Act provides that if a person has no reasonable excuse he shall be punished as if he had committed contempt of court, and the court therefore considered whether he would have had a defence under section 10 of the Contempt of Court Act.

The House of Lords rejected the idea that disclosure was 'necessary' only if it was the only means of preventing further insider dealing, and that it was the 'key to the puzzle'. Lord Griffiths said 'necessary' had a meaning which lay somewhere between 'indispensable' on the one hand and 'useful' or 'expedient' on the other.

And Lord Griffiths rejected Warner's argument that 'prevention of crime' was limited to the situation in which identification of the source would allow steps to be taken to prevent the commission of 'a particular identifiable future crime'.

He said it was not the job of inspectors to take immediate action to frustrate a particular crime. Their task was to probe into and lay bare the whole dishonest web of suspected insider dealing so that measures could be taken to deter and contain it. Warner's evidence was 'really needed' by the inspectors for the purpose of their inquiry, the aim of which was the prevention of crime.

In the case involving William Goodwin and *The Engineer*, the House of Lords in 1990 considered the phrase 'interests of justice'. Earlier, in the 1984 case against *The Guardian*, the distinguished judge Lord Diplock said this phrase meant 'the administration of justice in the course of legal proceedings in a court of law' (*Secretary of State for Defence v Guardian Newspapers* [1985] AC 339).

But there was no suggestion of immediate legal proceedings in The *Engineer* case, and Lord Bridge said the phrase could simply refer to the wish of a private company to discipline a disloyal employee 'notwithstanding that no legal proceedings might be necessary to achieve this end' (*X Ltd v Morgan-Grampian (Publishers) Ltd* [1991] 1 AC 1).

The issue was central to the *Ashworth Hospital* case and the *Interbrew* case in 2002. When the *Daily Mirror* appealed to the House of Lords against the order that it should disclose the hospital source of its story about the Moors murderer, Ian Brady, its counsel argued that the court should accept Lord Diplock's explanation of the phrase 'interests of justice'. But the court rejected the argument in favour of Lord Bridge's interpretation (*Ashworth Security Hospital v MGN Ltd* [2002] UKHL 29, [2002] 4 All ER 193).

The cases were regarded as a setback by the media, some commentators drawing the conclusion that the judges' interpretation of the words of the section made its protection for journalists' sources illusory.

Earlier, commentators had detected a more benevolent attitude to the media after the pronouncement of the European Commission in the *Goodwin* case in 1994.

In that year, a court declined to require Neil Hyde, head of the news agency INS News Group, to reveal the source of a leaked confidential report because this was not 'necessary'.

The top-security Broadmoor Hospital wanted Hyde to reveal the source of a report on the escape of two convicted killers while on trips out of the hospital.

But the judge said the hospital authorities had failed to make any attempt themselves to find out who leaked the documents and had instead relied on the court application.

In 1996 two chief constables failed to have a journalist, Daniella Garavelli, jailed over her refusal to reveal the sources of a story to a police disciplinary tribunal. The reporter refused to say who supplied her with information for a front-page exclusive in the *Journal*, Newcastle, over allegations that Northumbria police crime figures had been massaged.

A High Court judge said Garavelli 'put before the public, fully and fairly, a question which had been raised of considerable public importance'. The police had failed to show that the 'interests of justice' outweighed her right not to disclose her source.

In 2000 the Court of Appeal overturned a judge's order that the *Express* newspaper should disclose who handed one of its reporters a confidential legal document containing advice on Sir Elton John's financial affairs. It turned out the document had been stolen from the dustbins of a set of barristers' chambers, and the court held Sir Elton (like the Broadmoor hospital authorities in the case referred to above) had not carried out sufficient investigations of his own before launching the proceedings (*John v Express Newspapers plc* [2000] 1 WLR 1931).

Statutes giving disclosure powers

As stated above, increasingly statutes give authorities the power to demand information on *specific* issues and provide penalties under these acts. The Vassall tribunal, which led to the jailing of two journalists, and the Bloody Sunday tribunal, which declared a journalist to be in contempt, were set up under the Tribunals of Inquiry (Evidence) Act 1921, which gives tribunals wide powers to send for and examine witnesses.

Another example is the Criminal Justice Act 1987, which empowers the director of the Serious Fraud Office to summon before him any person he believes has information relevant to an investigation and the person must answer questions or give information about any relevant matter. If he fails to do so he faces a maximum prison sentence of six months or a fine.

The director is also empowered to demand from any person documents relating to his investigation. The obligation to hand over information contains no public interest defence similar to that contained in the Police and Criminal Evidence Act (below).

In 1996 Westcountry Television journalists were forced to hand over video footage and documents to the SFO, which was investigating the collapse of a local computer firm.

The Serious Organised Crime and Police Act extends to the Serious Organised Crime Agency, the police, and Customs and Excise powers to compel the production of documents and to demand information on specific issues. These powers already affect financial journalists when the Serious Fraud Office demands information and when the Department of Trade and Industry is investigating criminal misconduct in the City.

However, there will continue to be protection for journalistic documents and records held in confidence, because the Act provides that no one can be compelled to disclose 'excluded material' (see 'Excluded material' below).

The Financial Services Act 1986, which was used to prosecute Jeremy Warner (see above), was enacted after newspaper disclosures of criminal misconduct in the City. It made it an offence for a person without reasonable excuse to refuse to comply with a request to attend before inspectors of the Department of Trade and Industry, or to assist them or to answer any question put by them about any matter relevant to their inquiries.

The Financial Services and Markets Act 2000 places the Financial Services Authority on a statutory basis, and gives its inspectors similar powers. Failure to comply with requests for information and documents could lead to contempt proceedings.

The Criminal Justice Act 1993 created offences of failing to disclose suspicion or knowledge concerning money laundering and insider dealing. There is a defence of 'reasonable excuse'. The Home Office Minister assured the Guild of Editors (later the Society of Editors) the legislation on insider dealing would not criminalise the conduct of a financial journalist preparing editorial analysis and news items.

Police and Criminal Evidence Act (PACE) 1984

The Police and Criminal Evidence Act 1984 requires the police to make a formal application before a judge to obtain journalistic material they want to help with their investigations. In several of the cases brought under the Act the application has concerned photographs or film taken in public places where disturbances were taking place.

Most editors take the view that they should hand over such material only after careful consideration and generally only after a court order. Their argument is that if it becomes routine for the police to obtain unpublished photographs or untransmitted film journalists will be seen as an arm of the police.

They will thus lose credibility as impartial observers and, in practical terms, will be subjected to violence. Journalistic no-go areas will be created during disturbances. In this way, they will be prevented from fulfilling their role as the 'eyes and ears of the general public' (see Lord Donaldson's comments, chapter 1).

A judge may reject the application if, among other things, he does not consider it in the public interest to grant it. In court, media lawyers have argued that it is not in the public interest that the media should be prevented from doing their job. But in nearly every case that has come to court judges have considered that argument outweighed by the police's need for evidence to convict.

For example, a judge rejected the media's argument in November 1994 when the police were successful in obtaining film and photographs by the major press and broadcasting organisations after a demonstration against the bill that became the Criminal Justice and Public Order Act 1994 even though counsel pointed out that at the demonstration 'class war' leaflets were distributed that showed the media were being branded 'agents of the police'.

The provision was intended to provide a new protection for journalistic material, but in practice has led to accelerating demands for the handing over of such material.

Special procedure material

Special protection is given to 'journalistic material' in the sections of the Act that lay down the procedure whereby the police may gain access to documents or search premises for evidence of serious arrestable offences.

Journalistic material is defined as 'material acquired or created for the purposes of journalism'.

The police have to apply to a High Court judge, a recorder or a circuit judge if they want to obtain journalistic material under the 'special procedure'. If they succeed the judge will make a 'production order'.

The application will normally be 'on notice' (formerly 'inter partes'), which means that the holder of the evidence is present to argue against disclosure if he wishes.

Before the judge makes an order he has to be satisfied that there are reasonable grounds for believing that a serious arrestable offence has been committed; that the evidence would be admissible at a trial for that offence and of substantial value to that investigation; that other methods of obtaining it have been tried without success, or not tried because it appears they are bound to fail; and that its disclosure would be in the public interest, having regard to

(1) the benefit likely to accrue to the investigation if the material is obtained; and

(2) the circumstances under which the person in possession of the material holds it
    that the material should be produced or that access to it should be given.

The Act therefore appeared to give useful protection to journalists. However, judges have interpreted the Act in such a way that (as with section 10 of the Contempt of Court Act) the protection is not as valuable as had been hoped.

In 1986, after a police operation in Bristol led to disturbances, the *Bristol Evening Post*, the *Western Daily Press*, and a freelance picture agency were asked by the police to hand over unpublished pictures and refused to do so.

The police applied to the court and the judge ordered that the pictures be produced.

The judge did not require the police to specify the offence which had been committed, nor the value and relevance of the material, nor the *particular material* which was sought; they asked for all the pictures taken between two specific times, and 264 pictures and negatives had to be handed over.

In 1990, 25 newspapers and television companies were ordered to hand over unpublished photographs and untransmitted film of a Trafalgar Square riot against the poll tax. Two weeks later the police applied successfully for similar orders against four other news organisations. The case illustrated again the way in which the courts would apply the test that material must be admissible at trial and of substantial value to the investigation.

At the second hearing the news organisations' counsel said the applications were premature because the police had not yet examined all the material handed over by the other 25 organisations. But the judge said that until the police had seen the material they could not say if it was relevant or not.

A more liberal view of PACE was taken in the *Martin Bright* case in 2000, when the police were using the Act in an attempt to obtain an e-mail sent by David Shayler to the reporter Martin Bright. Lord Justice Judge said that a judge is not restricted in his interpretation of public interest by the 'somewhat limited conditions' referred to above. Other matters such as the importance of open discussion in the media of questions of importance could be considered when a judge decides whether to exercise his discretion over making an order.

Excluded material

Excluded material is exempt altogether from compulsory disclosure. It includes journalistic material which a person holds in confidence and which consists of documents or records.

The protection is not limited to professional journalists, but extends to any material acquired or created for the purposes of journalism.

Evidence which was already liable to search and seizure under the previous law is not protected. For example, if a journalist acquired a stolen document, even on a confidential basis, it would not be excluded material because such documents are already liable to seizure under a warrant issued under the Theft Act 1968.

If the journalist is ordered to produce either special procedure material or excluded material on the ground that a warrant for its seizure would have been available under another statute, and if he fails to do so, the police can apply for a search warrant (see below).

Search warrants

Instead of asking for an order that a newspaper shall produce material, the police can apply to a circuit judge for a search warrant under PACE to obtain either non-confidential or confidential material. The newspaper does not have to be told of the application, and does not have the right to be heard by the judge.

Before the judge grants a warrant, he must be satisfied that the criteria for ordering the production of the material (see above) are satisfied, and that one of the following four circumstances applies:

(1) it is not practicable to communicate with anyone entitled to grant entry to the premises;

(2) it is not practicable to communicate with anyone entitled to grant access to the material;

(3) The material contains information which is subject to an obligation of secrecy or a restriction on disclosure imposed by statute (for example, material subject to the Official Secrets Act) and is likely to be disclosed in breach of that obligation if a warrant is not issued; or

(4) that to serve notice of an order to produce may seriously prejudice the investigation.

In the *Zircon* case in 1987, police used a warrant under these provisions to raid the offices of the *New Statesman* and the journalist Duncan Campbell (see chapter 29). Although material was 'excluded', it was not protected because a warrant could previously have been issued under the Official Secrets Act (see below).

Once inside a newspaper office, lawfully executing their search warrant, the police have powers under the Police and Criminal Evidence Act to remove additional journalistic material without getting a new production order or warrant.

The Serious Organised Crime and Police Act 2005 seems likely to widen police access to journalistic material by PACE when that material is said to be needed to assist their investigations. The Act largely abolishes the category of 'serious arrestable offence' and replaces it by 'indictable offence' in the criteria for PACE production order applications. Subject to the PACE procedure for search warrants for journalistic material (above), the Act allows police to obtain a warrant to search all property occupied or controlled by the person in the warrant and not merely specific premises. This would appear to allow access to journalists' houses and other premises owned by a media organisation.

But the Act adds additional criteria before a judge issues an all-premises warrant. He must be satisfied that:

(1) there are reasonable grounds for believing that it is necessary to search premises occupied or controlled by the person in question which are not specified in the application, as well as those which are, in order to find the material in question; and

(2) it is not reasonably practicable to specify all the premises which he occupies or controls which might need to be searched.

Police Act 1997

The Police Act 1997 gives the police the power to authorise themselves to break into premises and place bugs provided they believe this action will help them to investigate serious crime. Under section 89 of the Act, entry to or interference with property or with 'wireless telegraphy' is lawful when a chief constable or, in urgent cases, an assistant chief constable, 'thinks it necessary . . . on the ground that it is likely to be of substantial value in the prevention or detection of serious crime'.

The authorising officer must be satisfied that what the action seeks to achieve cannot reasonably be achieved by other means.

Police and customs officers had been carrying out similar operations for years against major criminals without any statutory permission, on the authority of chief constables, under guidelines laid down by the Home Secretary in 1984. But they had no legal right to do so and technically could have been sued for trespass if 'caught in the act'.

Under the Act, the Government appoints a small number of commissioners, existing or former High Court judges, and the police have to get the prior approval of a commissioner for the bugging of homes, offices, and hotel bedrooms, and in respect of doctors, lawyers, and 'confidential journalistic material'. Prior approval is not necessary in urgent cases, but the chief officer has to apply for approval as soon as reasonably practicable and specify why he could not do so before.

A commissioner approves the operation if he is satisfied that there are reasonable grounds for believing that the action is likely to be of substantial value in the prevention or detection of serious crime and that what the action seeks to achieve cannot reasonably be achieved by other means.

A commissioner can order that an operation be abandoned if he regards it as 'blatantly unreasonable'. Authorisation lasts for three months.

Serious crime is defined very broadly. It covers offences which involve 'the use of violence, results in substantial financial gain, or is conduct by a large number of persons in pursuit of a common purpose'. Those opposing the measure as it went through Parliament said the 'common purpose' clause could embrace groups such as environmentalists protesting at road developments, and the Act contains no exemption to protect journalists pursuing their inquiries.

Official secrets

The Official Secrets Act 1920, as amended by the Official Secrets Act 1939, operates where a chief officer of police is satisfied that there is reasonable ground for suspecting that an offence under section 1 of the Act, which is concerned with espionage, has been committed and for believing that any person is able to furnish information about the offence.

The officer may apply to the Home Secretary for permission to authorise a senior police officer to require the person to divulge that information. Anyone who fails to comply with any such requirement or knowingly gives false information is guilty of an offence.

Where a chief officer of police has reasonable grounds to believe that the case is one of great emergency and that in the interests of the state immediate action is necessary, he may demand the information without the consent of the Home Secretary.

Section 9 of the Official Secrets Act 1911 gives the police wide powers to carry out searches. A magistrate may grant a warrant authorising the police to enter at any time any premises named in the warrant, if necessary by force, and to search the premises and every person found there; and to seize any material which is evidence of an offence under the Act. If a police superintendent considers the case one of great emergency, he can give a written order which has the same effect as a warrant.

This was the section used to carry out the raids on the offices of BBC Scotland in the *Zircon* case. (The search provisions of the 1984 Act do not apply to Scotland.)

Regulation of Investigatory Powers Act 2000

Journalists were concerned about several aspects of this Act. In particular, they feared that the ability of the police to gain access to their e-mails would prevent them from assuring contacts that their confidentiality would be protected. If the Act had been in force when the police were attempting to access the e-mail sent from David Shayler to *The Guardian*, there would have been no need for the authorities to have asked a judge for an order; they could simply have got a warrant from the Home Secretary.

Interception

The Home Secretary can issue a warrant authorising interception (that is, disclosure of the contents of communications) after an application from specified officials of the police, security services, and Customs and Excise. He must not do so unless he believes:

(1) that the warrant is necessary

    (a)   in the interests of national security;

    (b)   for the purpose of preventing or detecting serious crime;

    (c)   for the purpose of safeguarding the economic well-being of the United Kingdom; or

    (d)   for the purpose . . . of giving effect to the provisions of any international mutual assistance agreement.

(2) that the conduct authorised by the warrant is proportionate to what is sought to be achieved by the conduct.

He must consider whether the necessary information could reasonably be obtained by other means.

Disclosure of 'communications data'

The phrase 'communications data' does not include the content of the communications, but does include much information that may be of interest to the police and other investigatory bodies, such as telephone numbers dialled, the date and time of calls, the identity of people to whom e-mails are sent, and much more. 'Dynamic' metering (obtaining such information while the call is in progress), can help identify the location of a person making calls on a mobile telephone.

The Act allows not only the police but the Customs and Excise, the Inland Revenue, any of the intelligence services, and any other 'public authority' specified by the Secretary of State to demand such information on the basis of internal authorisation. The designated person can grant authorisations for others within the authority to engage in such conduct.

The grounds for obtaining communications data are wider than for interception. Such data can be obtained in the interests of public safety; to protect public health; to assess or collect any tax, duty, levy, or other imposition, contribution, or charge payable to a government department; in an emergency, to prevent death or injury, or damage to any person's physical or mental health, or to mitigate any such injury or damage; or for any purpose specified by order of the Secretary of State.

In 2002 the Government announced plans to give access to communications data to many additional public bodies including the Environment Agency, the Information Commission, the Gaming Board, the Food Standards Agency, NHS trusts, the Financial Services Authority, the Royal Mail and more than 430 local authorities.

The plan caused an outcry. It was denounced as a 'snoopers' charter' by the media and was withdrawn; however the following year it was reintroduced, covering the same bodies, but with additional safeguards against misuse.

If the media are required to disclose communications data, the person giving the authorisation ought to have regard to the need to respect freedom of expression, but there is no express statutory provision within the Act to do so. The procedure will take place in secret, and investigating authorities do not always value freedom of expression.

Surveillance

Surveillance can be 'directed' or 'intrusive'. 'Intrusive surveillance' for the purposes of the Act, is covert and involves use of a surveillance device, or the presence of a person, in residential premises or a private vehicle. Confusingly, any other surveillance is described as 'directed' however intrusive it in fact is.

Schedule 1 to the Act gives a lengthy list of public authorities whose designated representative can give authorisation for directed (but not intrusive) surveillance. The list includes any police force, the intelligence services, the armed forces, the customs and tax authorities, government departments, the National Assembly for Wales, any local authority, and a number of other bodies including the post office.

Authorisation for intrusive surveillance, which must be given by a designated person (for example, a chief constable), must be approved by a surveillance commissioner, a person who holds or who has held high judicial office.

In both cases, the grounds are broadly similar to those for interception. The Home Secretary may also give authorisation in intelligence and defence matters.

Investigation of electronic data protected by encryption

A person (including a journalist) may be required to disclose the encryption code of his e-mails, and if he tips anybody off that his e-mails are compromised he could face a prison sentence. Written permission must be given in England and Wales by a circuit judge, in Scotland by a sheriff, or in Northern Ireland by a county court judge.

Anti-terrorism legislation

The Terrorism Act 2000 uses a wide definition of terrorism: 'the use or threat of action where the threat is designed to influence the government or to intimidate the public or a section of the public and the use or threat is made for the purpose of advancing a political, religious, or ideological cause'.

Failure to disclose information

The Anti-Terrorism, Crime and Security Act 2001 amended the 2000 Act by introducing a new offence, with severe penalties, of withholding information on suspected terrorist offences. 'Withholding' information includes failing to volunteer it. The offence is committed under section 38B(2) of the 2000 Act if a person, without reasonable excuse, fails to disclose information that he knows or believes might be of material assistance in preventing the commission by another person of an act of terrorism, or in securing the apprehension, prosecution or conviction of another person in the United Kingdom for an offence involving the commission, preparation or instigation of an act of terrorism.

The penalties for the offence are, on indictment, imprisonment for up to five years, or a fine or both; or on summary conviction, imprisonment for up to six months or a fine or both.

A reporter may be at risk of prosecution for the offence if he discovers information about terrorism by, for example, interviewing a terrorist leader or by witnessing a paramilitary display.

The amendment does not affect the offence, contained in the 2000 Act under section 19, committed by a person who withholds information when he believes or suspects that another person has committed an offence under certain sections of the Act that concern the funding of terrorists. He is required to contact a police officer as soon as is reasonably practicable and disclose the information on which his belief or suspicion is based.

Under section 19 only, the information must have come to the person's attention in the course of his trade, profession, business, or employment. It is a defence for a person charged with the offence to prove that he had a reasonable excuse for not making the disclosure or that he disclosed matters in accordance with a procedure established by his employer for the making of such disclosures. The penalty on indictment is the same as under section 38(B).

Recording information

Under section 58 a person commits an offence if he collects or makes a record of information of a kind likely to be useful to a person committing or preparing an act of terrorism, or he possesses a document or record containing information of that kind. The journalist has a defence if he can prove he has a reasonable excuse for his action or possession.

Investigation powers

Schedule 5 of the 2000 Act provides the police with a battery of powers to assist in investigations. These are the successors of powers in the Prevention of Terrorism (Temporary Provisions) Act 1989, under which Channel 4 and Box Productions were fined £75,000 for contempt of court after refusing to disclose the identity of a source (see 'If a judge asks', above).

Under paragraph 1 of the Schedule a constable can obtain a warrant from a magistrate to enter premises, to search them and any person found there, and to seize and retain any relevant material.

Under paragraph 2, a senior police officer can make an application which does not relate to residential premises. It is intended to allow for mass searches, such as searches of lock-up premises in a given area where it is suspected that bomb-makers are active.

Paragraph 3 relates to areas cordoned off by police in bomb scares. A police officer of at least the rank of superintendent can himself authorise a search of specified premises that are wholly or partly within a cordoned area.

Paragraph 5 deals with the production of, or access to, 'special procedure material' and 'excluded material' (both as defined in PACE). As stated above, under PACE, excluded material is exempt altogether from disclosure, but under paragraph 5 of Schedule 5 of the 2000 Act, a constable may apply to a circuit judge (or, in Northern Ireland, a crown court judge) for an order in respect of such material for the purposes of a terrorist investigation.

PACE does not apply in Northern Ireland and in 1999 a judge made an order under the 1989 Act referred to above that Ed Moloney, northern editor of the Dublin-based *Sunday Tribune*, should hand over to police notes of an interview with a loyalist later charged with murder. But the order was quashed by the Lord Chief Justice of Northern Ireland, Sir Robert Carswell. He said:

> Police have to show something more than a possibility that the material will be of some use. They must establish that there are reasonable grounds for believing that the material is likely to be of substantial value to the investigation.

It is unclear how this power would be affected by section 12(4) of the Human Rights Act 1998, which requires particular regard for the importance of freedom of expression before any order is granted.

If this power is considered inadequate, a constable can apply to a judge for the issue of a warrant permitting entry, search and seizure of such material for the purposes of a terrorist investigation.

Under paragraph 13, a constable may apply to a judge for an order requiring any person to provide an explanation of any material seized, produced or made available. This was the power used in the Channel 4 and Box Productions case.

Paragraph 15 deals with cases of urgency. A police officer of at least the rank of superintendent may himself give written authority equivalent to a warrant if he has reasonable grounds for believing that the case is one of great emergency and that immediate action is necessary.

And in emergencies, under paragraph 16 a senior officer may himself sign a written notice requiring a person to provide an explanation of any material seized.

The next three powers apply only to Northern Ireland. Under paragraph 19, the Secretary of State for Northern Ireland may, by a written order, give to any constable in the province an authority equivalent to a search warrant relating to specified premises.

Paragraph 20 allows the Secretary of State to make an order requiring any person in the province to produce or give access to special procedure material and excluded material.

And paragraph 21 enables the Secretary of State to issue a written order to require any person in Northern Ireland who is specified in the order to provide an explanation of any material seized as a result of the use of the two previous powers.

Making damaging disclosures

The Act also creates, under section 39, two offences of making disclosures that may damage the effectiveness of ongoing terrorist investigations. These measures could apply to journalists who come by the information.

Subpoenas and witness summonses

Occasionally reporters may be asked to supply evidence of what they themselves have seen, rather than to say where their information came from.

For example, in 1992 a *Wales on Sunday* photographer was asked to give evidence against eight defendants allegedly involved in riots. Cuttings from the paper had been produced in court, and the photographer's byline appeared on the pictures.

In this situation, most journalists will wish to retain their reputation for neutrality and will agree to give evidence only after receiving a subpoena (in civil cases) or witness summons (in criminal cases).

Then if the journalist does not attend the hearing and give evidence, he will be in contempt of court.

Sometimes journalists accompany police officers on raids. Where such a raid leads to an arrest, the defendant's lawyers can demand that the prosecution produces all the material gathered in the investigation. For this reason the journalists are required to sign an indemnification agreement in which they acknowledge that any recording or film may be liable to be used as evidence.

Whistleblowers

The Public Interest Disclosure Act 1998 (the whistleblowers' charter) now provides a defence to disciplinary charges for breach of confidence (see chapter 27, 'Central government').

Race relations

The law that may affect a journalist when he is reporting matters involving race is contained in the Public Order Act 1986.

It is an offence for any person to display, publish, or distribute written material that is threatening, abusive, or insulting if he intends thereby to stir up racial hatred or if, having regard to all the circumstances, racial hatred is likely to be stirred up thereby.

Notice that the offence can be committed without any *intent* to stir up racial hatred. As a result, a newspaper and its staff reporting an inflammatory speech or election manifesto (such as that of an extremist politician), or other expression of anti-immigrant propaganda is as liable to prosecution as the person who originally made the statement.

An editor must decide in the light of all the circumstances if hatred and not just ill-will is likely to be stirred up, and whether the words of an election candidate or other speaker should be paraphrased instead of being reported directly.

How does a paraphrase help? The words have to be 'threatening, abusive, or insulting'. The tone of the language must be objectionable for an offence to be committed. The expression of views in a moderate or reasoned, non-threatening manner is not caught by the act.

'Racial hatred' is defined as being 'hatred against a group of persons in Great Britain defined by reference to colour, race, nationality (including citizenship), or ethnic or national origins'. Religion as such is not covered, and an attempt by the Government to introduce an offence of incitement to religious hatred failed in 2005 (see below).

The phrase 'having regard to all the circumstances' was inserted into the 1986 Act at the insistence of the Guild of Editors, because its inclusion in earlier legislation had been seen as a protection for bona fide news reports of, for example, a racist rally, because it required the court to consider the publication in its context.

The Attorney-General has to give his consent to any prosecution, and in 1987 the

Attorney-General said that in making a decision to allow the prosecution of a newspaper he would probably take into account the nature of the publication, its circulation, and the market at which it was aimed, as well as any special sensitivity prevailing at the time of publication which might influence the effect on those who read the material.

Handling readers' letters calls for particular care. During the passage of the bill leading to the 1986 Act, the Home Office wrote to the Guild saying it was wrong to suppose newspapers could publish inflammatory letters provided they juxtaposed them with other letters or editorial comment putting a contrary view. A single letter written in inflammatory language which was likely to stir up racial hatred would contravene the Act and could not be saved by countervailing comments elsewhere. But in deciding *whether* racial hatred was likely to be stirred up, the courts would not look at the letter in isolation, but would consider all the surrounding circumstances, which would include the context of the publication in which it was printed.

It is also an offence under the Act for a person to have in his possession written material which is threatening, abusive, or insulting, with a view to its being displayed, published, distributed, broadcast, or included in a cable programme service, if he intends racial hatred to be stirred up thereby or if, having regard to all the circumstances, racial hatred is likely to be stirred up thereby.

Editors who receive unsolicited racialist material do not commit an offence, even if such material is kept for background information, provided they do not intend to publish the material itself.

The police can get a warrant from a justice of the peace to enter and search premises where they suspect a person has possession of racialist material. The protections contained in the Police and Criminal Evidence Act do not apply.

Penalties for any of the offences mentioned are up to six months' imprisonment or a fine, or both, on summary conviction and up to two years' imprisonment or a fine, or both, on conviction on indictment.

The Act does not apply to fair and accurate reports of proceedings in Parliament or to fair, accurate, and contemporaneous reports of public proceedings in courts or tribunals.

Religious hatred

In 2005 the Government attempted to amend the 1986 Act to cover incitement to religious hatred. The amendments were contained in the Serious Organised Crime and Police (SOCP) Bill.

Part III of the 1986 Act, 'Racial Hatred', was due to be re-named 'Hatred against persons on racial or religious grounds'. The term 'religious hatred' was to be defined as 'hatred against a group of persons defined by reference to religious belief or lack of religious belief'.

The proposal met strong opposition both in Parliament and out by those who believed it would inhibit freedom of expression. The comedian Rowan Atkinson told a protest meeting:

> To criticise a person for their race is manifestly irrational and ridiculous, but to criticise their religion, that is a right. This is a freedom. The freedom to criticise ideas, any ideas—even if they are sincerely held beliefs—is one of the fundamental freedoms of society and a law which attempts to say you can criticise and ridicule ideas as long as they are not religious ideas is a very peculiar law indeed.

The Government dropped the proposal because it ran out of time before Parliament was dissolved for the general election. It realised that otherwise opposition from the Lords would lead to the failure of the entire SOCP Bill.

Election law

Special codes of practice on the reporting of elections that apply to broadcasters and not to print journalists are referred to in chapter 34. But print journalists should be aware of some dangers they share with the broadcasters while elections are pending, whether municipal, parliamentary, or European.

Anyone who, after an election has been called, makes or publishes a false statement of fact in relation to the personal character or conduct of a candidate for the purpose of affecting his return is guilty of an illegal practice and is liable on summary conviction to a fine and disqualification as an elector for five years.

In 1998 a journalist who published false allegations on the Internet about a candidate in the run-up to the 1997 general election was fined £250. He claimed the candidate, who was later elected to Parliament, was homosexual. Where a company (eg the owners of a newspaper) is guilty of the offence, the directors are liable to the fine and disqualification.

Note that the falsity must be contained in a statement of fact, not an expression of opinion.

Note also that the false statement must relate to the personal as opposed to the political character or conduct of the candidate. A statement that a candidate supports a political splinter group, for example, would not come within the section.

It is a defence to this charge if the person accused can show that he had reasonable grounds for believing that the statements made by him were true. This law is contained in the Representation of the People Act 1983.

The publisher of such a false statement might also be liable in defamation.

It is also an offence under the 1983 Act to publish, in order to promote or procure the election of a candidate, a false statement that another candidate has withdrawn from an election.

Section 66A of the Representation of the People Act 2000 and regulation 30 of the European Parliamentary Elections Regulations 2004 prohibit the publication of exit polls before the poll has closed. Specifically, they prohibit the publication of any statement relating to the way in which voters have voted where that statement is (or is seemingly) based on information given by voters after voting, as well as any forecast as to the result of the election which is (or is seemingly) based on such information. On election day for the European Parliament in June 2004, *The Times* published an opinion poll that asked people how they had voted in areas using all-postal ballots. The Electoral Commission, the independent elections watchdog, said this amounted to an exit poll and should not have been published. The editor of *The Times*, Robert Thompson, said extension of postal voting would have implications for the freedom of the press to sound out and report public opinion.

Only the candidate himself or his agent may incur any expenses for, among other things, publishing an advertisement. It is an offence for anyone else unless he is authorised in writing by the election agent to do so. This precludes well-wishers from seeking to insert advertisements in a newspaper on behalf of a candidate without his express authority. But the Act states that this rule does not restrict publication of editorial matter relating to the election.

The law of libel is, however, a serious restriction at election times.

Journalists should remember that there is no statutory privilege for the publication of election material, although a good deal of cover is given by the privilege for fair and accurate reports of public meetings and press conferences.

Remember also that there is no privilege for remarks, even when made at a public meeting, which are not 'of public concern and the publication of which is not for the public benefit' (see chapter 20, 'Qualified privilege'). The defence of fair comment may not be available for personal attacks which impute base motives (see chapter 20, 'Fair comment').

Be careful of associating members of such parties as the Labour and Conservative parties with extremist parties of the left or right wing. In particular, be careful of the terms 'fascist', 'communist', and 'racist'.

When reporting speeches by extremist candidates, remember that such reports are subject to the provisions of the Public Order Act 1986 relating to inciting racial hatred (see chapter 25).

Do photographers have a right to be present at election counts? Admission is at the discretion of the returning officer and there is no national policy.

According to advice to the Newspaper Society and to the Guild (now Society) of Editors, the position is different if television cameras are present. In that case the Newspaper Society has established precedents whereby the press has an equal right to have cameramen present and pass film out of the count.

Freedom of information

For democracy to work, citizens must have access to information so that they can reach valid decisions. Journalists have a crucial role to play in enabling the public to take such informed decisions, by seeking out and communicating information that those in power might sometimes prefer the public did not have; but journalists have no greater legal rights to obtain that information than members of the public have.

The Freedom of Information Act (FOI Act) 2000 for the first time gives people a general right of access to information about the work of government and other public authorities in the United Kingdom. The Act came fully into force on 1 January 2005 and, in the short time between then and the date *McNae* went to press, some of its strengths and shortcomings became apparent.

A Labour government came to power in 1997 with a 23-year-old manifesto commitment to give people a legal right to know. It published a radical white paper 'Your right to know' in December that year, which was warmly welcomed by the media and campaigners. But the Act that emerged three years later was an emasculated version of the white paper and appeared to owe more to ministerial caution than to a strong desire for open government. Many journalists concluded the Act provided so many exemptions, allowing authorities lawfully to refuse information, that its value was limited.

When the Act was passed there was a general expectation that the right to make requests for information under the Act would begin to come into force, in stages, in 2002. But in November 2001, the Government announced that this would not happen until 1 January 2005. Until that time, the Government explained, groups of public authorities would be required, in stages, to adopt publication schemes. There was much scepticism about the reason the Government cited for the delay—that four years were needed for public authorities to get their records into sufficiently good order to allow them to find the information people were asking for.

There is a strong tradition of secrecy in British governments arising historically from the wish of authoritarian regimes to govern with as little interference as possible. But a white paper on open government published by a Conservative government in 1993 said: 'Open government is part of an effective democracy. Citizens must have adequate access to the information and analysis on which government business is based.'

The white paper was followed in 1994 by a Code of Practice on Access to Government Information. This code was superseded by the FOI Act.

By contrast with central government, since 1960 local government has been increasingly under statutory obligations to be open to the public and the press. This position was threatened by the bill that became the Local Government Act 2000. It gave councils the power to introduce cabinet systems of government and initially did not ensure that the meetings of such bodies should be in public.

The bill was later amended so that cabinet-style executives must meet in public when discussing 'key decisions'. But the Government's definition of key decisions appeared to give ample opportunity to local authorities to take important decisions in secret if they wished (see 'Local Government Act 2000', below).

Many activities in British life are controlled by quangos (quasi-autonomous non-governmental organisations), which spend huge amounts of public money. According to Dan Lewis, author of *The Essential Guide to British Quangos 2005*, there were 529 of them in the United Kingdom, 111 of which had been created since Labour came to power in 1997. However, owing to differing definitions, this may well be an underestimate.

Their position in 2005 was much as described by Patrick Birkinshaw in his book *Freedom of Information* in 1988: 'In the world of quasi-government, there is no elected representation, no public voting and no political accountability, and very rarely are there duties to inform the public in even the most exiguous of terms of what is being carried out on the public's behalf.' The last element of this description has altered since the duty for most quangos to adopt a publication scheme under the FOI Act came into force in November 2002, but real scrutiny had to await the right of access coming into force in January 2005.

The House of Commons select committee on public administration urged in a report in 2001 that the Government should seek to dispel popular suspicions of these bodies by creating 'a very open regime', allowing public access so far as possible. 'In principle, we believe that public bodies should be at least as open as is required of local authorities under the Local Government Act 2000.'

Central government

With certain rare exceptions, before the FOI Act, the press and public had no rights to know about the workings of central government. Without that information it was difficult to judge the real effects of government policies on, for example, unemployment, the council tax, the crime rate, the health service, and education.

If policies are not working a government is in a good position to conceal the facts if it wishes to. Whether the FOI Act has remedied that situation will become clear as more applications are made using it.

In addition, citizens had no rights to know about most of the activities for which central government is responsible. For example, they had no rights to know about the hygiene of their food or any side effects of the medicines they may be prescribed.

In substantial areas of life, relating to 'official secrets', the handful of people who know the facts face criminal prosecution if they tell the journalist about them and the journalist faces criminal prosecution if he publishes them (see chapter 29, 'Official Secrets').

In 1984 Sarah Tisdall, a Foreign Office clerk, was jailed for six months for giving the *Guardian* details of government plans to deploy Cruise missiles. The *Guardian* published information from a memo dealing with the public relations aspect of the deployment.

Clive Ponting, a senior Ministry of Defence official, was prosecuted for revealing to a member of Parliament in 1984 that ministers had misled Parliament over the sinking of the Argentinian cruiser *The Belgrano* during the Falklands war, and was acquitted only because of the obstinacy of the jury trying him, who disregarded the ruling of the judge.

Governments can also use the civil law of breach of confidence to prevent the media from publishing information (see chapter 23, 'Breach of confidence').

Civil servants too are under an obligation of confidentiality, and the unauthorised disclosure of information is a disciplinary offence that can lead to dismissal.

But the Public Interest Disclosure Act 1998 (the whistleblowers' charter) now provides a defence to disciplinary charges for breach of confidence. It applies to a wide range of misconduct and offers full protection to almost any worker who is dismissed or victimised for making a protected disclosure of information. In terms of disclosures by civil servants to journalists, the Act is most likely to come into play where the misconduct is serious and there is evidence of a cover-up. Civil servants can lose this new protection only if they have been convicted of a secrecy offence or if the government shows effectively, to a criminal standard of proof, that they would have been convicted.

The Freedom of Information Act 2000

The FOI Act 2000 gives a general right of access to all types of recorded information held by public authorities, sets out exemptions from that right and places a number of obligations on public authorities.

As stated, the right to make requests under the FOI Act came into force on 1 January 2005. The requirement on groups of public authorities to adopt publication schemes came into effect in stages from November 2002 to June 2004. The programme began with central government in November 2002, took in local government in February 2003 and extended to the police, armed forces and health bodies later in the same year, and to schools and universities in early 2004.

The Lord Chancellor produced annual reports on the progress being made with implementation of the FOI Act and these can be found on the DCA website at http://www.dca.gov.uk/foi/foiact.htm together with more information about the Act.

The FOI Act is enforced by the Information Commissioner, a renaming of the previous post of Data Protection Commissioner to reflect the fact that the Commissioner supervises both the Data Protection and Freedom of Information Acts.

Organisations covered

The FOI Act has a wide scope and applies to public authorities and those providing services for them. The list, contained in Schedule 1 to the Act, includes:

- government departments
- local authorities
- National Health Service bodies (such as hospitals, as well as doctors, dentists, pharmacists and opticians)
- schools, colleges and universities
- the police
- the Houses of Parliament
- the Northern Ireland Assembly, and
- the National Assembly for Wales.

The Schedule also contains a long list of other public bodies, ranging from various official advisory and expert committees, to regulators and organisations such as the Post Office,

National Gallery and the Parole Board. In total the FOI Act covers about 100,000 public authorities. The Act also provides for other authorities to be named later and for private organisations to be named as public authorities for relevant parts of their work—a company undertaking the processing of benefits claims for a local authority, for example. But the security and intelligence bodies, MI5, MI6, and GCHQ are excluded from the Act.

The Act in brief

Any person (including a journalist) who makes a request in writing to a public authority for information must be told whether the authority holds that information and must be supplied with the information he is seeking, unless an exemption applies. However, in the majority of cases where an exemption applies, the public authority will then have to consider whether the information must be released in the public interest.

Before making an FOI application the journalist may want to look at the organisation's publication scheme—usually available on its website—which may contain the information needed. If that is unsuccessful, an informal request may be the quickest way of eliciting the information. If this does not work then an application under the FIA is the next step. Such requests must be in writing, although e-mail is sufficient. It might perhaps be wise to check if an e-mail, or letter, has arrived at its intended destination, as it has been known for authorities to deny having received a request.

The Act does not allow public bodies to distinguish between media requests and requests from 'ordinary' members of the public. Some journalists experienced in using rights of access laws believe press officers receive copies of FOI requests and the response to them, thus getting early notice of subjects a journalist is inquiring about; but press officers are not allowed to be involved in the process of responding to a request, or manipulating the information provided as a result of a request.

It is important to understand that the right to be told whether information is held by an authority is distinct from the right to be supplied with the information; sometimes it may be lawful to withhold the information from the requester, but this does not mean that the authority should refuse to confirm that it holds the information sought. An example of this might be where details of a contract which has not yet been signed might be withheld by the authority on grounds of commercial confidentiality, but confirmation that the information is held could nevertheless be supplied.

Every public authority is required to adopt and maintain a publication scheme setting out how it intends to publish various classes of information it holds. However, the Act is almost silent as to what information should be contained in a publication scheme, leaving it instead to the public authority and Information Commissioner to decide what authorities should make available.

Critics complained that the Information Commissioner had not been demanding enough information to be included in the schemes. This had meant that many schemes contained little more than was previously available to the public, although some central government departments had been rather more open, publishing, for example, the minutes of the meetings of their management board meetings.

Authorities are also able to add new classes of information to their publication schemes without having to seek reapproval of the whole document from the Information Commissioner.

The Campaign for Freedom of Information (CFOI) told *McNae*'s editors: 'Journalists who obtain previously unpublished information from public authorities via other access regimes should encourage the authority to add the information to its publication scheme, so that over time these documents become a better tool for greater routine disclosure of previously secret information.'

A code of practice issued under section 45 of the FOI Act in November 2002 provides guidance to public authorities about responding to requests for information, operating publication schemes and associated matters. The Information Commissioner supervises compliance with this code by authorities. The Department of Constitutional Affairs website carries a model action plan, published in December 2003, for organisations that need to comply with the FOI Act.

Authorities must, where possible, provide the requested information in the manner asked for by the applicant. This may be in the form of a copy or summary, or the applicant may ask to inspect the record; he may also request that the information be supplied to him in an electronic format if that is what he would prefer. There is no need to mention the Act when making a request, although since it is possible that some public servants will be unaware of the Act and its requirements, it might be helpful—both for the journalist and the public authority—to do so. Requests can be made to the officer responsible for the subject that the journalist is inquiring about, should the reporter know his name and contact details. Otherwise requests should be made through the authority's officers charged with implementing the FOI Act. Journalists can make such applications through the organisation's press office.

In general, public authorities have to respond to requests within 20 working days. Proposals for charging a fee were dropped in 2004, although costs of photocopying and postage may be required. If such photocopying charges are to be made, the person making a request should be told in advance. The authority's 20-day deadline countdown to providing the information will stop until the fee is paid. In cases where an exemption applies, but an authority is then required to release the information because it is in the public interest to do so, it must disclose 'within a time that was reasonable in the circumstances'. The CFOI points out this might lead to substantial delay.

The Information Commissioner, Richard Thomas, warned in an interview with *The Times* on the eve of the full implementation of the FOI Act, that he would be 'naming and shaming' those organisations that failed to comply with the 20-day deadline, and that, given the fact there had been a four-year lead-in to implementation, excuses of lack of time or poor record management systems would not be acceptable.

Authorities have a duty to provide advice and assistance to applicants.

Although the proposed fees for information were dropped, limits were placed on the cost of providing such information. Authorities are entitled to refuse to provide information if collating it would be too expensive. The limits are £600 for a government department— which equates to three and a half days work at a fixed rate of £25 per hour. For other authorities the limit is £450—two and a half days at the same rate. If an applicant agrees to pay these costs then the information can be provided, but for many people this would be prohibitive.

Bearing the above in mind, journalists making requests for information may do well to heed the advice of the CFOI and make their requests as specific as possible. Asking for data that spans several years could take much longer to collate than data covering just a few months. Requests that are specific might stand a better chance of avoiding refusal because of excessive cost.

However, journalists may want records over several years in order to make comparisons between them, in which case a way round this might be to make a number of separate requests for individual years.

Where an authority has grounds not to release the information requested, it must give reasons for its decision and must tell the applicant of his right to complain. Appeal against refusal goes to the Information Commissioner.

It is an offence to destroy or alter requested records. In the month before full implementation of the FOI Act claims emerged in national newspapers that ministries had been shredding files for months to avoid disclosure, although the Information Commissioner said he had found no hard evidence that such shredding had taken place.

In the first month of its full implementation more than 4,000 requests for information were made, and some notable successes and failures were recorded. The Government refused to disclose legal advice it had been given in advance of the invasion of Iraq, a refusal that resulted in a number of complaints to the Information Commissioner.

Successful applications were made to release documents on the British Army's torture of Mau Mau rebels in Kenya in the 1950s and on so-called 'deep interrogation' of suspects in Northern Ireland using techniques such as 'hooding', deprivation of food and sleep, and exposure to noise.

One paper used the FOI Act to obtain the list of people who had been entertained at Chequers, the Prime Minister's country residence.

In February 2005 documents relating to 'Black Wednesday', the day in 1992 when the United Kingdom dropped out of the Exchange Rate Mechanism while interest rates rose five per cent in four hours, were released by the Treasury in response to newspaper requests. The documents showed the Conservative Government of the time in a bad light. Days after the release of the documents, the Conservative leader, Michael Howard, wrote to the Home Office permanent secretary asking that papers relating to his time as Home Secretary be released immediately. It was reported that he had done this to prevent political opponents making capital from an FOI application. At the same time the Lord Chancellor suggested former ministers should have early warning that an application had been made in relation to them under the FOI Act, so they could voice opposition to such disclosure

The public interest test

Public authorities are not required to disclose any information that is covered by one or more of the exemptions. However, in the majority of cases where a disclosure is not required, the public authority will then have to consider whether the information must be released in the public interest.

The information may be withheld only if the public interest in withholding it is greater than the public interest in releasing it.

However, the Act does not define what the public interest actually is and it is left to the authorities to make a judgment based on individual circumstances.

In *The Freedom of Information Act: An Introduction* (an Information Commission publication) the Commissioner lists the following public interest factors that would encourage disclosure and these may be useful to journalists wishing to challenge a refusal to disclose:

- Furthering the understanding and participation in the public debate of issues of the day. This factor would come into play if disclosure would allow a more informed debate of issues under consideration by the Government or a local authority.

- Promoting accountability and transparency by public authorities for decisions taken by them. Placing an obligation on authorities and officials to provide reasoned explanations for decisions will improve the quality of decisions and administration.

- Promoting accountability and transparency in the spending of public money. The public interest is likely to be served, for instance, in the context of private sector delivery of public services, if the disclosure of information ensures greater competition and better value for money that is public.

- Allowing individuals and companies to understand decisions made by public authorities affecting their lives and, in some cases, assisting individuals in challenging those decisions.

- Bringing to light information affecting public health and safety. The prompt disclosure of information by scientific and other experts may contribute not only to the prevention of accidents or outbreaks of disease but may also increase public confidence in official scientific advice.

The CFOI has stressed the importance of applicants pursuing their requests all the way to the Information Commissioner and not accept an initial rebuff from a public authority. In the case of the Government's refusal in January 2005 to release the legal advice given by the Attorney-General on the legality of the war in Iraq, newspapers immediately appealed against that decision to the Commissioner

The CFOI points out that, valuable though the public interest test in the Act is, there are two drawbacks.

First, the test in practice will require the applicant to demonstrate the public interest in openness. He should not assume that the Information Commissioner will automatically recognise the public interest case for disclosure. The applicant will have to set out the arguments.

Second, notices issued by the Commissioner requiring government departments to disclose on public interest grounds can be vetoed by cabinet ministers. Ministers' certificates over-ruling the Commissioner can be challenged only by judicial review. This power of veto is available to cabinet ministers only in relation to requests made to their own department. However, a minister acting alone can veto the release of information. This contrasts with the position in New Zealand, where any veto preventing the release of information requires the collective agreement of the Cabinet; and many jurisdictions with freedom of information legislation, including the US, Canada, and South Africa, operate effectively without any power of executive veto at all. Local authorities, the police and the many other thousands of public authorities covered by the Act are not able to veto the Commissioner's orders that they disclose exempt information in the public interest.

The exemptions

There are 23 exemptions in the FOI Act. They can be divided into:

(1) those that apply to a whole category of information (the 'class' exemptions), for example:

- information relating to investigations and proceedings conducted by public authorities;
- court records; and
- trade secrets.

Information covered by these class-based exemptions can be claimed as exempt without the authority having to show that any harm would result from disclosure; and

(2) those that are subject to a prejudice test, for example, where disclosure would prejudice, or would be likely to prejudice:

- the interests of the United Kingdom abroad; or
- the prevention or detection of crime.

Information becomes exempt only if disclosing it would prejudice or would be likely to prejudice the activity or interest described in the exemption.

The public interest test applies to most of the exemptions. Those to which the test does not apply are called the 'absolute exemptions' and these are set out in section 2 of the FOI Act. One example is information supplied by, or relating to, bodies dealing with security matters.

Three class exemptions are of particular concern to journalists.

1 Policy formulation

Section 35 of the FOI Act permits a government department to claim exemption for all information relating to policy formulation, including the facts on which decisions were taken, scientific advice on potential health hazards, research findings and technical assumptions. Only statistics about decisions that have been taken are excluded from this exemption. Most of the information whose suppression featured in the BSE ('mad cow') crisis would have been caught by this elastic provision. The public interest over-ride applies, subject to a ministerial veto, both in this and in the following two cases.

2 The effective conduct of public affairs

Section 36 applies to all public authorities and is what Lord Falconer, the minister who piloted the FOI Act through the Lords, described as a 'catch-all' exemption. It protects any information whose disclosure 'would in the reasonable opinion of a qualified person be likely to prejudice the effective conduct of public affairs'. The qualified person will be a minister or senior official.

The FOI Act places no limit on the matters that can be caught by this exemption. By giving legal weight to the authority's opinion about what will cause prejudice, the decision is protected from review by the Commissioner, unless the person complaining can convince the Commissioner that judicial review standards of unreasonableness underpin the claim for exemption from the duty to disclose the information.

3 Investigations and proceedings

Section 30(1) exempts information held in connection with criminal investigations and proceedings, including information held by safety and other prosecuting authorities in connection with investigations or inspections which could lead to a decision to prosecute.

The exemption applies even if it is decided not to prosecute. Information can be withheld even if there is no possibility of prejudice to legal proceedings. It will apply to all leading safety authorities, including the Railway Inspectorate, Nuclear Installations Inspectorate, Civil Aviation Authority, trading standards officers, Maritime and Coastguard Agency, Environmental Health Officers, Drinking Water Inspectorate and even DEFRA, the Department for the Environment, Food and Rural Affairs, which retains some prosecution functions in relation to BSE.

The CFOI points out that the danger of this exemption is that it protects evidence of hazards that safety authorities observe, but fail to act on. Complacent authorities are shielded from scrutiny.

Enforcement of the Act

A person who has made a request for information may apply to the Information Commissioner for a decision as to whether the request has been dealt with according to the FOI Act. In response the Information Commissioner may serve a notice on the public authority and applicant setting out any steps that are required to be taken by the authority in order to comply.

In certain circumstances the Information Commissioner may issue a notice requiring disclosure of information in the public interest. However, this may be subject to a ministerial veto for central government departments. In such a case the department will have 20 days from receipt of the notice to obtain a signed certificate from a cabinet minister overriding the Information Commissioner's notice.

All notices may be appealed to an independent Information Tribunal, both by the applicant and the public authority. The CFOI has pointed out that unscrupulous authorities may appeal to the tribunal simply in order to delay the disclosure of the information sought, rather than because they think they have a valid case. It says that journalists should be ready to challenge such appeals. The Information Commissioner may also issue a 'practice recommendation' in respect of non-conformity with either code of practice under the FOI Act.

The veto

The veto can be used in limited circumstances. It is available only to cabinet ministers, the Northern Ireland First Minister and the Welsh First Minister, and those public authorities to which the Government decides to extend the power. A veto cannot be used against the Commissioner's order to disclose information because it does not fall within the scope of an exemption or because it would not prejudice one of the interests. It can be used only where the Commissioner orders disclosure on public interest grounds. Nor can it be used by a cabinet minister to block disclosure of information by another public authority (eg a local council) unless the Government decides to extend the veto power to these bodies.

However, the CFOI comments that the FOI Act makes the exercise of the veto relatively easy. It is issued by a cabinet minister after consulting his cabinet colleagues. The obligation to consult does not appear in the Act itself and will presumably be required under the Ministerial Code. There is no suggestion that the cabinet will meet to discuss or endorse any veto. The proposal is merely that cabinet colleagues be consulted before it is exercised so that the doctrine of collective responsibility is maintained.

The text of this complex Act is available on www.legislation.hmso.gov.uk/acts/acts-2000.htm. More information is available from the website of the Information Commissioner and is available on the office's website at www.informationcommissioner.gov.uk. Journalists requiring further explanation of freedom of information (and data protection) are invited to consult the office on 01625 545700.

Environmental information

If environmental information is requested, it is not dealt with by use of the FOI Act, but rather by the Environmental Information Regulations. These implement a European Union Directive and have been described by the CFOI as giving more powerful rights of acess than the FIA.

Information about the environment covers air, water, land, natural sites, and living organisms—which include GM crops. It covers discharges as well as noise and radiation.

The EIR covers more bodies than the FOI Act and has fewer exemptions. For example, information about emissions cannot be withheld for reasons of commercial confidentiality.

All bodies subject to the FOI Act are also subject to the EIR and the same 20-day deadline applies to requests made for information.

The regulations require that authorities make environmental information available to the public through electronic means—the internet. They must also, as with the FOI Act, assist those making a request.

Requests for information can still be turned down on grounds of national security. However, all refusals are subject to a public interest test and requests can be turned down only if the public interest in non-disclosure far outweighs the public interest in disclosure.

A 'reasonable' fee can be charged for requests.

The EIR is enforced by the Information Commissioner, as with the FOI Act.

Local government

Changes brought about by the Local Government Act 2000 had major implications for the access of journalists to decision-making meetings. Previously, decisions were made at meetings that the public (including the media) had the right to attend.

The right applied, under the Local Government (Access to Information) Act 1985 and the Public Bodies (Admission to Meetings) Act 1960, to full council meetings and the meetings of committees and sub-committees except where the information was confidential or exempt. The public still have the right to attend such meetings, except when confidential or exempt matters are under discussion.

The LGA 2000, however, introduced 'cabinet-style' government. Executive decisions are now taken at meetings that may he held in private except where 'key decisions' are to be made. Local authorities have had to reorganise using one of three models, leader and cabinet, directly elected mayor and cabinet, or directly elected mayor and council manager.

Executive decisions are taken at meetings (described below as 'cabinet meetings') that are permitted to be held in private except where 'key decisions' are to be made.

The Government's definition of key decisions appears to give ample opportunity to local authorities to make important decisions in secret if they wish. Even if key decisions are being made, press and public may be excluded if exempt or confidential information or the advice of a political adviser would be disclosed.

Local Government Act 2000

The act in brief

Cabinets must meet in public when they are discussing or voting on key decisions, unless the item is confidential or exempt or would disclose the advice of a political adviser.

Agendas and reports to any public meeting must be made available at least five days beforehand.

A written record of all key decisions and other executive decisions must be made available 'as soon as is practicable' after the meeting. This also applies to decisions taken by individual members.

These documents must include a record of the decision, any alternatives considered and rejected, and a record of any conflict of interest.

Every council must publish a 'forward plan', containing details of the key decisions it is likely to make over a four-month period. The plan, which must be updated monthly, must include documents related to those decisions and information on who will take the decision and on those the council will consult.

Meetings of backbench 'scrutiny committees' are open to the press and public, with advance agendas and papers available beforehand.

The regulations covering access to information under the LGA 2000 are contained in a statutory instrument, the Local Authorities (Executive Arrangements) (Access to

Information) (England) Regulations 2000, SI 2000 No 3272. This SI was amended in 2002 by the Local Authorities (Executive Arrangements) (Access to Information) (England) Amendment Regulations 2002, SI 2002 No 716.

These complex rules are summarised below, but journalists needing to challenge councils may need to refer to the text, which is available on www.legislation.hmso.gov.uk. The regulations, which came into effect in January 2001, need to be read together with chapter 7 of the revised guidance on the regulations, issued in March 2002, available on the website of the Office of the Deputy Prime Minister www.local-regions.odpm.gov.uk/ncc/guidance/index.htm.

The regulations apply to unitary authorities, London borough councils, county councils, and district councils in England that are operating executive arrangements under the Act. They cover public access to meetings of local authority executives and their committees and of joint committees of local authorities where these are solely comprised of executive members and are discharging an executive function. The regulations also cover access to documents when executive decisions are made by individual members or officers.

When cabinets must meet in public

A cabinet meeting must be held in public when a key decision is to be made. A key decision means one that is likely:

(1) to result in the local authority incurring expenditure or making savings that are significant having regard to the local authority's budget for the relevant service or function; or

(2) to be significant in terms of its effects on communities living or working in an area comprising two or more wards or electoral divisions.

The meeting must also be in public when there will be discussion of matters relating to a key decision to be made subsequently and an officer, other than a political adviser or assistant or council manager, will be present.

Who decides when expenditure or savings are 'significant', requiring the meeting to be in public? The guidance notes say 'It will be for the potential decision-maker to decide.' To help him, the full council must agree limits above which items are significant, and the agreed limits must be published.

Journalists were worried that this measure would enable those authorities with less commitment to openness and accountability to choose high financial thresholds for key decisions. The revised guidelines said in February 2001 that the Secretary of State intended to issue further guidance to ensure consistency between councils of the same type and size but, in the event, the Government decided not to do this, so that nothing prevents authorities taking a restrictive view of the regulations.

Journalists were also worried about the second test, referring to a decision affecting 'two or more wards'. The revised guidelines, which appear to indicate second thoughts on this, say:

> Nevertheless, local authorities should, unless it is impracticable to do so, specify that they will treat as if they were key any decisions which are likely to have a significant impact on communities in one ward or electoral division. For example, a council should regard as key a decision to close a school . . . notwithstanding the thresholds of financial significance and that there may be an impact in only one ward.

A special procedure applies where an executive decision has been made but it was not treated as being a key decision, and an overview and scrutiny committee of backbenchers says the decision should have been treated as a key decision.

Papers that must be made available

Records of decisions

'As soon as reasonably practicable' after a cabinet meeting, either in private or public, at which an executive decision has been made, a written statement must be produced. The statement must include:

(1) a record of the decision;

(2) a record of the reasons for the decision;

(3) details of any alternative options considered and rejected;

(4) a record of any conflict of interest and, in that case, a note of any dispensation granted by the authority's standards committee.

An executive decision made by an individual or a key decision made by an officer must be recorded similarly.

The record must be made available for inspection by the public, again 'as soon as is reasonably practicable', at the council offices. With it must be any report considered at the meeting or, as the case may be, by the individual member or officer making the decision.

Where a newspaper asks for a copy of any of the documents available for public inspection, those documents must be supplied on payment of postage, copying, 'or other necessary charge for transmission'.

A copy of a list of background papers to the report must be included in the report and at least one copy of each of the documents included in that list must be available for inspection by the public.

Journalists failing to get information through official sources may need to know that members of local authorities are given additional rights to access to information under the LGA 2000. In certain circumstances members of overview and scrutiny committees can have access to exempt or confidential information in relation to decisions they are scrutinising, but note that they might be liable in breach of confidence for any information they give you (see chapter 23).

Reports to be considered

Where an executive member or officer receives a report that he intends to take into consideration when he makes a key decision, he must not make that decision until the report has been available for public inspection for at least five clear days. (This improvement on the previous requirement to make papers available only three clear days before the meeting was implemented in October 2002 and resulted from lobbying by journalists and the CFOI during the passage of the Act.)

The officer must make the report available 'as soon as is reasonably practicable' after he receives it. With the report must be included a list of background papers. Sufficient copies of the background papers must be available, or facilities must exist for the production of sufficient copies, 'to meet every reasonable request from members of the public'.

Agendas and reports

A copy of the agenda and every report for a public meeting must be available for inspection by the public when they are made available to the members of the cabinet. As a matter of procedure, the regulations say that an item of business shall be considered at a public meeting *only*:

(1) where a copy of the agenda or part of the agenda, including the item, has been available for inspection by the public for at least five clear days before the meeting; or

(2) where the meeting is convened at short notice, a copy of the agenda including the item has been available for inspection by the public from the time that the meeting was convened.

If 'the proper officer' thinks fit, he may exclude any report that relates only to the transaction of an item of business during which, in his opinion, the meeting is likely not to be open to the public.

In that case, the report, or part of the report, must be marked 'not for publication' and carry a statement saying it contains confidential information or exempt information (for an explanation of these terms, see below, 'Powers to exclude press'), or because the report or part of it contains the advice of a political adviser or assistant.

When a meeting is convened at short notice a copy of the agenda and associated reports must be available for inspection at the time the meeting is convened.

When an item that would be available for inspection by the public is added to the agenda, a copy of the revised agenda, and of any report relating to the item for consideration at the meeting, must be available for inspection by the public when the item is added.

During the meeting, the authority must make agendas and reports available for members of the public.

On request from a newspaper, a local authority must supply it with:

(1) a copy of the agenda for a public meeting and a copy of each of the reports for consideration at the meeting;

(2) such further statements or particulars, if any, as are necessary to indicate the nature of the items contained in the agenda; and

(3) if 'the proper officer' thinks fit in the case of any item, a copy of any other document supplied to members of the executive in connection with the item.

The newspaper must pay for postage charges 'or any other necessary charge for transmission'.

Forward plans

Each authority must publish every month a 'forward plan' giving details of key decisions to be taken in the following four months. These plans must be available for inspection 'at all reasonable hours' and free of charge. Each plan must contain a list of the documents to be considered. The guidance requires authorities with websites to publish their forward plans on these websites.

A plan must give the address from which copies of the documents are available and explain the procedure for obtaining documents submitted later as they become available.

It must also give the dates in each month in the following 12 months on which each forward plan will be published.

A notice drawing attention to the plan must be published in 'at least one' newspaper circulating in the area of the local authority and annually on a date between 14 and 21 days before the first forward plan of that year comes into effect.

A forward plan must include the following information: the matter to be decided, the identity of the decision-maker or makers, the identity of the principal groups or organisations to be consulted on the decision, the means of consultation, the way people may make representations, and a list of the documents to be considered.

Where the regulations permit the public to be excluded or documents not to be disclosed, the forward plan 'shall contain particulars of the matter but may not contain any confidential or exempt information or particulars of the advice of a political adviser of assistant'.

A special procedure applies if the inclusion of a matter in the forward plan is 'impracticable' and the matter would be a key decision. The decision may be made only if the 'overview and scrutiny committee' of backbenchers and the public has been told. This procedure does not apply in cases of special urgency, where agreement must be obtained from one of a number of specified office holders. A quarterly report must be submitted to the authority giving details of each executive decision taken under the 'special urgency' procedure.

Powers to exclude press

Even when key decisions are being discussed, a cabinet can exclude the press and public in three situations:

(1) it is likely that if members of the public were present, confidential information would be disclosed;

(2) the cabinet has passed a resolution excluding the public because otherwise it is likely exempt information would be disclosed;

(3) the cabinet has passed a resolution excluding the public because otherwise it is likely the advice of a political adviser or assistant would be disclosed.

'Confidential information' has a special meaning. It means information provided to the local authority by a government department upon terms (however expressed) which forbid the disclosure of the information to the public or information the disclosure of which to the public is prohibited by or under any enactment or by the order of a court.

A resolution to exclude on the grounds of exempt information must identify the proceedings, or part of the proceedings, to which it applies and state the category of exempt information involved.

Exempt information may be summarised as:

(1) information relating to a particular employee, job applicant, or office holder of the

council, or an employee, applicant, or official of the magistrates courts or the probationary committee;

(2) information relating to a particular council tenant or a particular applicant for council services or grants;

(3) information relating to the care, adoption, or fostering of a particular child;

(4) information relating to a particular person's financial or business affairs;

(5) information relating to the supply of goods or services to or the acquisition of property by the council, if to disclose the information would place a particular person in a more favourable bargaining position or otherwise prejudice negotiations;

(6) labour relations matters between the council and its employees, if and so long as to disclose the information would prejudice negotiations or discussions;

(7) instruction to and advice from counsel;

(8) information relating to the investigation and prosecution of offenders, if to disclose the information would enable the wrongdoer to evade notice being served on him.

The public can be excluded only for the part of the meeting during which the matter is being discussed.

The authority is not required to disclose to the public a document likely to disclose confidential information, exempt information or the advice of a political adviser or assistant.

Obstruction is an offence

A person who has custody of a document that is required to be available for inspection by members of the public commits an offence if he intentionally obstructs any person exercising a right conferred under the regulations to inspect the document or make a copy of it, or if he refuses to supply a copy of it.

Local Government (Access to Information) Act 1985

The Local Government (Access to Information) Act 1985 says that all meetings of principal authorities, their committees, and sub-committees must be open to the public unless dealing with confidential or exempt information.

The position regarding working parties and advisory or study groups, which may in effect act as sub-committees without the name, is unclear. It is possible that a court would take into account whether the meeting was that of a genuine working party or merely a device for decisions to be taken without the use of the name sub-committee.

Another view is that a local authority can delegate the exercise of power, or the fulfilment of a duty, only to a committee or sub-committee, and a working party acting in this way is thus a sub-committee.

In a case in 1988 involving a member of Eden District Council in Cumbria, Lord Justice Croom-Johnson said officers of the council were present at a working party as members (and not as advisers) and this was inconsistent with its being a sub-committee. It was not therefore covered by the LG(AI)A 1985.

Principal authorities, their committees and sub-committees must exclude the public when confidential information is likely to be disclosed (for an explanation of confidential information see above, 'Power to exclude press').

A local authority may, by passing a resolution, exclude the public when it is likely that exempt information will be disclosed (for an explanation of exempt information, see above, 'Power to exclude press'). The resolution must state to what part of the meeting the exclusion applies and must describe the category in the schedule of the exempt information.

Occasionally attempts are made to exclude the press when the matter to be discussed does not fall under any of the categories.

While the meeting is open to the public, 'duly accredited representatives' of newspapers or news agencies reporting the meeting must, under section 5(6)(c) of the LG(AI)A 1985, be afforded reasonable facilities for taking their report and for telephoning it, at their own expense, unless the premises are not on the telephone.

A newspaper or news agency must on request (and on payment of postage or other transmission charge) be supplied with (a) agendas, (b) further particulars necessary to indicate the nature of the items on the agenda, and (c) if the 'proper officer' thinks fit, copies of any other documents supplied to council members. The 'proper officer' may exclude from what he sends out any report, or part of a report, relating to items not likely to be taken in public.

Late items, reports and supplementary information can be admitted at the meeting only if the chairman regards the matter as urgent and specifies the reason for the urgency. Oral reports will be admissible only if reference to them is on the agenda or is covered by the urgency procedure.

Copies of agendas and of any report for a meeting of a council must be open to public inspection at least five clear working days before the meeting (except for items not likely to be taken in public). Where a meeting is called at shorter notice they must be open to inspection from the time the meeting is convened.

Copies of minutes and reports and summaries of business taken in private must be open to public inspection for six years (except for confidential or exempt information).

A list of background papers must be included in each officer's report considered at a meeting, and a copy of each background paper must be open to public inspection for four years. Background papers are those unpublished papers on which a report for a meeting is based and which, in the officer's opinion, have been relied upon to a material extent in preparing the report.

Publication of a fair and accurate copy or extract made in this way is subject to qualified privilege.

Any person who intentionally obstructs the right of any person to inspect agendas, minutes, and reports is liable to a fine on summary conviction.

The LG(AI)A 1985 applies also to combined police or fire authorities, to meetings of joint consultative committees of health and local authorities, and to some joint boards.

The LG(AI)A 1985 does not apply to parish and community councils. The Public Bodies (Admission to Meetings) Act 1960 still applies to these councils.

Public Bodies (Admission to Meetings) Act 1960

The Public Bodies (Admission to Meetings) Act 1960 says that these bodies must admit the public to their meetings and to meetings of their committees consisting of all the members of the body.

The PB(AM)A 1960 says, however, that such a body or committee can exclude the public for the whole or part of a meeting, 'whenever publicity would be prejudicial to the public interest because of the confidential nature of the business to be transacted or for other special reasons stated in the resolution and arising from the nature of that business or of the proceedings'.

It says that public notice of the time and place of the meeting must be given by posting it at the offices at least three days before the meeting, or if the meeting is convened at shorter notice, then at the time it is convened.

On request and on payment of postage, if demanded, the body must supply to any newspaper, news or broadcasting agency, a copy of the agenda as supplied to members of the body, but excluding if thought fit any item to be discussed when the meeting is not likely to be open to the public, 'together with such further statements or particulars, if any, as are necessary to indicate the nature of the items included', and copies of reports and other documents, if thought fit. The PB(AM)A 1960 gives no indication when the copies have to be supplied.

The PB(AM)A 1960 says that, so far as is practicable, reporters shall be afforded reasonable facilities for taking their report and, unless the meeting is held in premises not belonging to the body or not having a telephone, for telephoning a report at the reporter's expense.

Rights to admission and to reporting facilities, agendas, and telephones under the terms of the PB(AM)A 1960 also apply to:

(1) parish meetings of rural parishes where there are fewer than 200 electors;

(2) a number of bodies set up under the Water Act 1989. These are: regional and local flood defence committees, regional rivers advisory committees, salmon and freshwater fisheries advisory committees, and customer service committees.

Council meetings held in private

If after a local authority meeting held in private under any of the three Acts referred to above an official statement was issued to the press, a copy of or extract from such a statement would be privileged under the Schedule to the Defamation Act 1996 (see chapter 20).

Information about such meetings, held when the press is excluded, and obtained from an unofficial source would not be so privileged under the Acts should it be defamatory.

Minutes of the proceedings of a parish or community council must, under the Local Government Act 1972, as amended by the LG(AI)A 1985, be open to inspection by a local government elector for the area who may make a copy or extract. Publication of a fair and accurate copy or extract from such minutes is protected by qualified privilege.

Access to council accounts

Many journalists miss the chances to dig out local authority stories provided by the provisions of the Audit Commission Act 1998 and the Accounts and Audit Regulations 2003 (SI 2003 No 533). 'Local authorities' includes police and fire and civil defence authorities.

Under section 15 of the ACA 1998, 'any persons interested' may inspect a local authority's accounts and 'all books, deeds, contracts, bills, vouchers and receipts related thereto', and make copies. The previous version of the regulations said that each authority must make these accounts and documents available for public inspection for 15 full working days before a date appointed by the auditor, but this period has been extended to

20 working days in the 2003 update to the regulations. (A Government consultation paper in the autumn of 2002 proposed making them available throughout the year, but this appears to have been dropped in the face of local authority opposition.) An advertisement about this right must be published in at least one newspaper 14 days before the date the accounts and documents become available, but the best way to find out is to ask the authority directly.

Lawyers differ as to whether 'any persons interested' include reporters as such, but if the reporter is also a local elector there is no problem.

In 2004 ITV West won a court battle with Bristol City Council over its request to examine accounts relating to the authority and a former employee. ITV West was a non-domestic ratepayer in Bristol and, as such, qualified as 'an interested person.' However, the broadcaster's claim that its role in disseminating information made it an interested person was rejected by the court.

From this it would appear that to be an interested person a media organisation needs to be paying non-domestic rates to the authority concerned. Alternatively one of its reporters, or a freelance, who pays council tax to the authority could ask to examine the records as an interested person.

The *Express and Star*, Wolverhampton, has used the ACA 1998 to great effect in many stories. It revealed, for example, the details of a Birmingham City car pool equipped with expensive chauffeur-driven cars which were readily available to those in the know. The pool cost about £350,000 a year.

Jonathan Leake, a journalist formerly with the *Express and Star*, points out that the sheer volume of the 'treasure trove' made available by the ACA 1998 is a problem. He recommends alternative approaches.

First is going in knowing what you are looking for. If you suspect some dubious deals have been struck, ask for all the original documents relating to them, and go through the ledger to check. Get the original invoices and tenders, and don't be palmed off with ledger entries or computer print-outs.

Or go to a particular department equipped for a general trawl. Demand access to the files containing original invoices and receipts and go through them one by one.

Your reception from the council officers may not be welcoming, so you may need to insist on your rights. In 1994 the Kent Messenger Group had to employ a solicitor before forcing Kent County Council to provide a copy of a document containing details of an agreement between the council and a developer expected to create 10,000 jobs.

In that case the document was described as confidential, but the duty of disclosure under the ACA 1998 overrides such claims.

A council officer refusing a proper demand for a copy or obstructing a person entitled to inspect one of these documents is in fact committing a criminal offence. The London Borough of Haringey was prosecuted and fined in 1996 for refusing to disclose documents relating to the audit which had been requested by a resident.

An exception to the general rule is that there is no right to examine documents relating to personal expenses incurred by officers of the council.

The Local Government (Allowances) Regulations 1986 enable electors at any time of the year to demand to see a breakdown of allowances and expenses paid to councillors.

Before 1995 a local authority had to make available to the public information showing the amounts paid to councillors in the previous financial year. Since 1995, the local authority has been required to send this information to the local media.

Under the Local Government Finance (Publicity for Auditors' Reports) Act 1991 a council must make available any report produced by the auditors immediately on a matter of particular concern.

The above rights of access may be of use when making an application under the FOI Act, which meets with an initial rebuff. A threat to use these rights of access might well result in the information being provided.

Health authorities and NHS Trusts

NHS organisations are all subject to the requirements of the FOI Act.

Admission to meetings of local health authorities and NHS Trusts, and rights to their agendas, are subject to the Public Bodies (Admission to Meetings) Act 1960.

Department of Health guidance to these bodies in 1998 (Health Service Circular 1998/207) said that the government was 'committed to ending what it sees as excessive secrecy in decision making in public bodies' and that although authorities and trusts could exclude press and public in the public interest under the terms of the PB(AM)A 1960, they were expected to conduct their business in public in as open a manner as possible.

Authorities and trusts should seek to keep the public informed about their work, aims, and objectives. The circular envisaged that 'closed sessions should be limited to those areas of board business where real harm to individuals may result. This might include discussion about particular members of staff for disciplinary or other reasons, or relate to independent reviews on complaints. It should not be used however as a means of sparing board members from public criticism or proper public scrutiny'.

The minister of state in the Department of Health went further and said that 'in future, there will be no more secrecy concerning NHS trust board meetings and no more commercial-in-confidence information held concerning trust boards.' (*Hansard* 9 December 1997, column 785).

The 1998 circular makes clear that complaints from the press or public about access to meetings or papers should be dealt with in line with the NHS code of practice: that is, first complain to the senior officer accountable to the chief executive for compliance with the code, then to the Health Service Ombudsman.

Under the PB(AM)A 1960, the same rights of admission are given to any committee of a health authority consisting of all members of the authority.

Community health councils in England ceased to operate in September 2003, abolished by the NHS Reform and Health Care Professions Act, although they continued to exist in Wales. The English CHCs were replaced by patient forums (PPI forums—that is, patients and public involvement forums), There are 572 of them, one for each primary care trust and NHS trust and NHS foundation trust in England.

According to the Commission for Patient and Public Involvement in Health, established in January 2003, the forums would:

- be the main vehicle for the public to influence strategic priorities and day-to-day management of health services in their local area;
- be an independent critical friend on wider health matters in their community such as environmental health; and
- review services from the patient perspective and monitor responses from local health services to complaints from patients.

Each forum would comprise 15 to 20 locally recruited volunteers.

The government has the power to make regulations on access to information from these forums which apply the LG(AI)A 1985 with modifications.

More information about the commission and its work with the forums can be found at www.cppih.org

The Health and Social Care Act 2001 provided new powers to overview and scrutiny committees of those local authorities with social services responsibilities (county councils, London borough councils, unitary authorities), and these are subject to similar access to information provisions as other committees covered by Local Government (Access to Information) Act 1985.

An extended set of exemptions applies however, which can be found in Schedule 1 to the Health and Social Care Act 2001. These go further than the exemptions in the LG(AI)A

1985 by exempting also information on (1) a person providing or applying to provide NHS services (2) an employee of such person or (3) information relating to a person's health. Minutes, agendas, and reports are open to public inspection for only three years and background papers for only two years.

Health authorities are required to publish details each year about maximum waiting times for beds in each speciality, the number of complaints received and how long it has taken to deal with them, and how successful the authority has been in relation to national and local standards under the Government's patients' charter.

Police authorities

The Police and Magistrates' Courts Act 1994 gave added power to central government over policing and the workings of magistrates courts. The Act changes the membership of police authorities and empowers the Home Secretary by order to determine objectives for them.

The authorities have to draw up local policing plans that acknowledge the objectives set by the Home Secretary. Publication of the plans is arranged by the authorities in such manner as appears to them to be appropriate. The plan must state the authority's priorities for the year, the financial resources available and its objectives.

The authority must also issue an annual report as soon as possible after the end of the financial year and arrange its publication. The report must include an assessment of the extent to which the local policing plan has been carried out. Police authorities are subject to the requirements of the FOI Act.

Magistrates courts committees

The public must be admitted to a meeting of the magistrates courts committee at least once a year. The minutes of every meeting must be open to public inspection at the committee's office, except that confidential information can be excluded: in that case, the committee must state its reason. For a fee, copies must be made available.

The Lord Chancellor can require a committee to submit reports and plans and make these available to the public for a reasonable fee. Magistrates courts committees are subject to the requirements of the FOI Act.

Schools

Regulations made under the Education Acts 1996 and 1997 require both state and independent schools to provide information on examination results, truancy rates, rates of pupils staying on after 16, and employment or training undertaken by school leavers.

The regulations do not require schools to provide the names of examination candidates, with their results, but some schools do so and papers publish them. The previous Information Commissioner has told the editors of *McNae* she would expect schools to tell parents if it is their practice to issue the names and to withhold any if a parent objected (see also chapter 35, 'Children'). If a parent did object after a name was published, the Commissioner would take the matter up with the school, rather than the paper (see chapter 33, 'Data Protection Act 1998, Enforcement').

Governing bodies of every county, controlled, and maintained school must, under the Education (No 2) Act 1986, keep written statements of their conclusions on policy matters. Regulations require the head teacher to make the statement available at all reasonable times to persons wishing to inspect it.

Governing bodies of grant-maintained schools are required to make an annual report available for inspection at all reasonable times. Schools and other public sector education institutions were required to have adopted a publication scheme under the FOI Act by the end of February 2004.

Quangos

Many of the day-to-day services to the public that used to be administered by bodies on which representatives of the public served have been hived off to semi-independent agencies on the ground that they would become more efficient when exposed to the disciplines of the market. The managing bodies are staffed by appointees rather than representatives.

The term quango (quasi-autonomous non-governmental organisation) is conveniently used to describe non-elected public bodies that operate outside the civil service and that are funded by the taxpayer.

They include grant-maintained schools, further education colleges, urban development corporations, learning and skills councils, and a wide variety of other bodies.

Government prefers to use the term non-departmental public bodies (NDPBs), which includes only public bodies in the formal sense. It does not cover bodies that in legal terms are private enterprises, even if they are spending public money. Government divides these bodies into executive NDPBs and advisory NDPBs. Another term used by government is 'appointed executive bodies'.

As a result of this difference in definition, estimates of the number of quangos in existence vary from 2,000 to 5,000 and estimates of the amount of money spent annually also vary widely. A report published in 1994 claimed they exercised more power and influence than the entire structure of local government (Stuart Weir and Wendy Hall (eds) *Ego trip: Extra-governmental Organisations in the UK*).

When a new Labour government came to power in 1997 it committed itself to reducing the number of NDPBs, but figures given in a report by the all-party parliamentary select committee on public administration in 2001 showed that the total figure for executive NDPBs serving government departments—the most important and powerful category of quangos—had fallen by only two, from 189 to 187, since 1997.

The committee said it was disappointed at the low priority attached to public access to executive NDPBs, commenting, 'There are more black holes than examples of open governance'.

There was what the committee referred to as an 'unprecedented eruption' of advisory quangos in the first 18 months of the new government when ministers established 295 'task forces' to give policy advice on a wide range of issues.

Before the rapid increase in quangos in the 1980s and 1990s, it was generally accepted that the bodies that then had corresponding duties were accountable to the public and should provide information about their activities to the public. Many of them— for example, the old water authorities but not the new water companies—were required to admit the press to their meetings. They were generally required to provide documentation. In most cases, fair and accurate reports of their meetings and statements were covered by qualified privilege.

The argument on accountability no longer applies in the same way. Demands for information can be countered by the argument that the body cannot operate in market conditions when the details of its operations are known to its competitors. Public access to information would therefore work against normal commercial confidentiality.

The minister in charge of the water companies justified the clamp-down on public access by saying these companies were no longer operating like public corporations but more like private bodies under the Companies Act, with executive and business responsibilities.

In general, there is no right of access to the meetings of quangos but there is now a right to information to most of them under the FOI Act.

Websites for further information

Freedom of Information Act 2000

The Act: www.legislation.hmso.gov.uk/acts/acts2000/20000036.htm

Department of Constitutional Affairs information about the Act and bringing it into force: http://www.dca.gov.uk/foi/index.htm

The Information Commissioner: www.informationcommissioner.gov.uk

The Campaign for Freedom of Information: www.cfoi.org.uk

Local government

Office of the Deputy Prime Minister guidance on Local Government Act 2000: www.local-regions.odpm.gov.uk/ncc/index.htm

Office of the Deputy Prime Minister consultation on exemptions from the rights of access to meetings and papers: www.local-regions.odpm.gov.uk/consult/review/index.htm

Environmental information

Department for the Environment Food & Rural Affairs page on rights of access to environmental information: www.defra.gov.uk/environment/pubaccess/index.htm

28 Copyright

A journalist needs to know the basic rules of the law of copyright if he is to determine how much of other people's words, artistry, or photographs he can use in his paper.

What is protected

Copyright is a branch of intellectual property law—that is to say, it protects the products of people's skill, creativity, labour, or time.

Under the Copyright, Designs and Patents Act 1988, copyright protects any literary, dramatic, artistic, or musical work, sound recording, film, broadcast, or typographical arrangement. Artistic works include photographs and graphics (see below). Typographical arrangements cover the way the page is set out. Copyright does not have to be registered.

A judge once said: 'Anything worth copying is worth protecting.' Reproduction of a substantial part of a copyright work may constitute infringement. Whether the part of a copyright work which is copied is a substantial part may depend as much on the quality (the importance) of what is reproduced as much as on the quantity (*Sweeney v MacMillan Publishers Ltd* [2001] All ER (D) 332 (Nov)).

However, for a work to be protected by copyright it must satisfy the test of originality. Some work or effort must have gone into it. Brief slogans and catchphrases have been ruled to be too trivial to be protected by copyright.

There is no copyright in facts, news, ideas, or information. Copyright exists in the form in which information is expressed and the selection and arrangement of the material—all of which involves skill and labour.

Sir Nicolas Browne-Wilkinson, Vice Chancellor (later Lord Browne-Wilkinson), said in the Chancery Division in February 1990 that it was very improbable that the courts would hold there was copyright in a news story, *as opposed to the actual words used*.

He said the law as to copyright in a verbatim report of the spoken words of another was settled in a case in 1910 which established that the mere reporting of the words of another gave rise to copyright, so long as skill, labour, and judgment had been employed in the composition of the report. That case, he said, was still good law.

While there is no copyright in a news story, persistent lifting of facts from another paper, even if there is rewriting each time, may still be an infringement because of the skill, labour, and judgment that went into research on the stories. In an 1892 case, a judge made the distinction between lifting from another paper now and again at long intervals, and not likely to be repeated, and deliberate, persistent abstraction from the first paper.

The defence of fair dealing for reporting current events will however sometimes allow some quoting from another paper (see later this chapter).

Literary work is protected by copyright as soon as it is recorded in writing or otherwise and it includes newspapers and the writing that goes into them.

Copyright in material supplied to newspapers by outside contributors, whether paid or not, will normally be owned by the contributor. For example, a person sending a reader's letter for publication will by implication have licensed the newspaper to use his or her copyright work freely on one occasion, while still retaining the copyright. On the other hand an editor who uses a freelance writer's article sent in without first negotiating the fee may be in difficulty.

An official of a sporting or trade association may find it part of his duty to make material available to the paper free of charge but the copyright is still the association's and it can withdraw the facility, or start to make a charge, or prevent another journal from copying it.

This applies to much material available to newspapers—TV and radio programmes, sporting fixtures, lists of events, and tide tables. The company whose employee compiled the material owns the copyright.

The Football League many years ago established in a test case against Littlewoods Pools that the league owned the copyright in the fixture lists and could control copying. The league is thus able to charge pools promoters for the use of the fixtures while allowing newspapers to use them free.

Publication without permission of a photograph of the whole or a substantial part of a television image is an infringement under section 17 of the Copyright Act.

Under the Broadcasting Act 1990, those who provide a broadcast service (and own the copyright in the programme listings) must make information about the programmes available to any newspaper or magazine publisher wishing to use it, through a licensing scheme. In case of dispute as to the charge to be made by the broadcasting organisation for the use of the information, the matter is decided by the Copyright Tribunal.

Copyright in maps and drawings

To publish without permission the whole or part of an artistic work such as a map or drawing, where the copyright is owned by another, will constitute infringement, as for example where an artist on a newspaper or magazine adapts a map as a basis for his own sketch to illustrate a story or feature. In 2001, Centrica, the company which owns the Automobile Association, agreed to pay £20 million in an out-of-court settlement to Ordnance Survey for the use of OS maps as its source material to create its own maps. Ordnance Survey had introduced small subtle errors into its maps to catch out plagiarists using them as a basis for their own maps.

Copyright in speeches

Under the 1988 Act, there is copyright in spoken words, even if they are not delivered from a script, as soon as they are recorded, with or without the speaker's permission. This raises many questions on the reporting of meetings, etc, some of which will not be answered until there is a test case.

The speaker, as the author of a literary work, owns the copyright in his words, unless he is speaking in the course of his employment.

Under section 58 of the Act, it is not infringement to use the record of the words for reporting current events, subject to four conditions:

(1) The record is a direct record and not taken from a previous record or broadcast.

(2) The speaker did not prohibit the making of the record and it did not infringe any existing copyright.

(3) The use being made of the record, or material taken from it, was not of a kind prohibited by the speaker or copyright owner before the record was made.

(4) The use being made of the record is with the authority of the person who is lawfully in possession of it.

Could a speaker have second thoughts about his remarks and prohibit the reporting of them afterwards? It seems not. He must have prohibited the note being taken or the tape being made, before the speech, or have said he did not want the record to be used in a certain way, for example in a newspaper.

What is the position in copyright law if reporters attend a meeting which they would normally wish to report but they are barred from taking notes?

One of the difficulties in this situation would be knowing how much of the speech could be reproduced before it would constitute a substantial part in law. In recent years, courts have been ruling that a substantial part may not necessarily be of great length. Substantial part can, in any case, refer to the quality or importance of the material reproduced as well as to the quantity or length.

There is, as we have already seen, no copyright in facts conveyed in the speaker's words and it is possible that the courts would take the view that if the actual words were not used and the arrangement of the facts was altered, there had been no reproduction of a substantial part. It is also possible that limited use of a speaker's words might be covered by fair dealing (see later, this chapter).

Another problem in section 58 is in defining current events and how far back they stretch.

It seems however that surreptitious recording of a speaker's words is not a breach of copyright in itself. Once the words have been recorded however, there is copyright in them and it will be owned by the speaker. In many cases, there will be a separate copyright in the record because of the skill involved in making it. In certain circumstances there might be an action available for breach of confidence (see chapter 23).

Copyright in the speaker's words is not infringed in reporting parliamentary or judicial proceedings.

Apart from any copyright in the spoken word, there is a copyright in the manuscript from which a speaker reads.

In this way, Buckingham Palace made legal history in 1993 when it used copyright law to take legal action for breach of an embargo. The *Sun*, together with other newspapers, had been sent copies of the Queen's 1992 Christmas Day message, embargoed until after it had been broadcast. The *Sun* published the message on 23 December under the headline 'Our difficult days, by the Queen'. After Buckingham Palace started proceedings for a breach of the Queen's copyright, the *Sun* agreed to pay a large sum to a charity nominated by her. The owner of copyright material has the right to enforce his or her own terms for the use of it and can take action if those terms are breached. In this case Buckingham Palace had by implication licensed reproduction of the Queen's speech, but only after the broadcast.

Who owns the copyright

The first owner of a copyright work created after 31 July 1989 (when the 1988 Act came into force) is the author but in the case of work done in the course of employment the employer is the owner, subject to any agreement to the contrary. Thus in the absence of any contrary agreement the employer can sell the work of an employee to whom he wishes.

There is no automatic right on the part of a newspaper or magazine or periodical to the copyright of work done by non-members of the staff, even if the work has been ordered.

The copyright can be assigned to the newspaper, or magazine, or periodical but an assignment is not effective unless in writing signed by the copyright owner. He can license the publisher to use his work but if it is an exclusive licence this also must be in writing.

Where a photograph is commissioned from a freelance or commercial photographer today, the copyright is owned by the photographer (or his employer) unless there is an agreement to the contrary. If the photograph was taken before the 1988 Act came into force, however, the copyright will be owned by the person or company who commissioned it, even though the photographer or his employer will own the negatives or film.

A person who commissions a photograph for private and domestic purposes is protected by one of the 1988 Act's moral rights—the right not to have copies of the photograph issued to the public even if he does not own the copyright.

This has implications for the reporter who borrows a photograph, say of a wedding, when the bride or bridegroom comes into the news months or years afterwards. The relative who lends the photograph to the reporter is unlikely to own the copyright and may not have commissioned the taking of it in the first place.

If the paper were to publish the photograph (provided it was taken after 31 July 1989) two rights may be said to have been infringed—that of the photographer (who owned the copyright unless there was an agreement to the contrary) and that of the bridegroom who commissioned it and has the right not to have it made available to the public.

The photographer may be glad to accept a fee for publication of his copyright picture but the response of the bridegroom may raise problems under the 1988 Act.

In 2004 the wife of Charles Bronson, a man sometimes referred to as Britain's most dangerous prisoner, failed in a High Court bid to obtain a ruling that she could use pictures of their wedding in an autobiography. The pictures had been taken by a prison officer using prison equipment, giving rise to Crown Copyright in the pictures, although the photos themselves were in Mrs Bronson's possession. The judge in the case ruled that Prison

Service was entitled to ban their use to prevent those trading on a 'Bronson cult' from further profiting from his notoriety.

For ownership of copyright in broadcast material, see chapter 34, 'Copyright in broadcasting'.

Fair dealing

Fair dealing with a copyright work (apart from a photograph) for the purpose of reporting current events will not constitute infringement provided it is accompanied by sufficient acknowledgement of the work and its author and provided the work has been made available to the public. The courts continue to use, as a test of whether the dealing is fair, the criteria of whether the use competes commercially with that of the copyright owner and whether the amount and importance of the extracts are such as to negative fair dealing.

In 1991, Mr Justice Scott dismissed a copyright action brought by the BBC against British Satellite Broadcasting over the use on the satellite company's sports programme of highlights from BBC coverage of the World Cup finals. The BBC had bought exclusive rights. He held that the use of short clips varying from 14 to 37 seconds, with a BBC credit line, up to four times in 24 hours was protected by the defence of fair dealing for reporting current events. The managing director of BBC Television had said anarchy would result if the case went against the BBC but the judge said that was the frequent cry of those who saw a monopoly they had enjoyed being threatened, and was often shown by later events to have been exaggerated.

Fair dealing with a copyright work (including a photograph) for the purposes of criticism or review of that work or of another will also not be treated as infringement, subject again to sufficient acknowledgment and to the work having been made available to the public. This allows for reporting which quotes from books, plays, films, and broadcasts, when writing a criticism, story, or feature.

The importance of a work having been made available to the public is emphasised by changes to copyright law brought about as a result of the implementation of the European Information Society Directive 2001/29/EC by way of the Copyright and Related Rights Regulations 2003 (SI 2003 No 2498). This directive said that only works that had been lawfully made available to the public could be used for criticism or review by way of fair dealing.

This goes contrary to previous cases such as that of *Hubbard v Vosper* [1972] 2 QB 84, a case involving the Church of Scientology and someone within the church who had obtained previously unpublished material. Lord Denning in the Court of Appeal held that though the material was previously unpublished, its use was fair dealing for the purposes of criticism of Church of Scientology.

The potential implications of this change for journalists are clear from the use by former Royal butler, Paul Burrell, of extracts from letters in a book published in 2003 giving intimate details of the Royal Family. His book was published shortly before the implementation of the above directive and so he and his publisher were able to rely on fair dealing for protection. This defence will no longer apply to confidential material, such as private letters, and has been seen as a shift in favour of the copyright holder.

The Court of Appeal held in 1998 that the subjective intention of the user of an extract from a copyright work was relevant to whether the use satisfied the test of fair dealing for criticism or review. The court held that Carlton UK Television and Twenty-Twenty Television had not infringed the copyright of Pro Sieben Media in using a 30-second extract from Pro Sieben Media's broadcast interviews with Mandy Allwood, who was found to be carrying eight live embryos, and with her boyfriend, even though Pro Sieben Media had bought exclusive rights. Lord Justice Robert Walker said the degree to which the use competed with that of the copyright owner was a very important consideration but it was not the only one.

The broadcast which was the subject of the complaint was, as a whole, made for the purpose of criticism of chequebook journalism, contained only a short extract from the Pro Sieben Media programme, did not unfairly compete with Pro Sieben Media, and used that company's logo, which constituted sufficient acknowledgment. Lord Justice Walker said Ms Allwood's pregnancy and its eventual outcome were events of real interest to the public and the use of the extract would have been fair dealing both for the purpose of reporting current events and for criticism or review (*Pro Sieben Media AG* (*formerly Pro Sieben Television AG v Carlton UK Television* [1999] 1 WLR 605).

If the copyright work is obtained by unfair means this may be outside the scope of fair dealing, as would use of quotations from the work merely to avoid having to pay.

Copying which prevented the copyright owner from gaining financial benefit from the sale of rights to his work would also be ruled to be not fair dealing.

If more of the work is quoted than is necessary to make the point in reporting current events or in criticism or review, this may not be fair dealing. It is difficult to put a figure to the proportion of a copyright work that can be used. Authors and publishers tend to think in terms of low percentages.

It is not an infringement of copyright to extract or copy an abstract of a scientific or technical article which is published with the article, for example a blurb or standfirst used with a feature.

There is no copyright infringement in reporting Parliament, the courts, or public inquiries, but this does not permit copying of a published report. There is normally no copyright infringement in copying material which must be open to public inspection by Act of Parliament.

The use by the *Sun* of stills from a security video showing the length of a visit by Princess Diana and Dodi Al Fayed to the Villa Windsor, a house in Paris, was held by the Court of Appeal in 2000 to be an infringement of copyright which could not be defended as either as a publication in the public interest or as fair dealing for reporting current events.

The Court of Appeal allowed an appeal against Mr Justice Jacob's rejection of a claim for damages by Hyde Park Residence Ltd, which provided security services to Dodi's father, Mohamed Al Fayed and family. The *Sun* had maintained that the use of the video was necessary to expose Mohamed Al Fayed as having lied about the marriage plans of the princess and his son and their intention to live at the Villa Windsor. Mr Justice Jacob had said use of the stills to support a matter involving the mother of a future sovereign was of public interest and was fair dealing for reporting current events.

Lord Justice Aldous giving judgment in the Court of Appeal said fair dealing could not provide a defence for the *Sun*. 'I do not think a fair-minded and honest person would pay for the dishonestly-taken stills and publish them knowing that they had not been published or circulated when their only relevance was the fact that the Princess and Mr Dodi Al Fayed stayed only 28 minutes at the Villa Windsor—a fact that was known and did not establish that the Princess and Mr Dodi Fayed were not to be married.' The information could have been made available by the *Sun* without infringement of copyright (*Hyde Park Residence Ltd v David Yelland* [2000] EMLR 363).

(The *Sun* would have been prevented from putting forward the fair dealing defence at all had the pictures been ordinary photographs but the 1988 Act does not regard a still from a film, broadcast or cable programme as a photograph.)

Public interest defence

The 1988 Act states that nothing in the Act affects 'any rule of law preventing or restricting the enforcement of copyright on the grounds of public interest or otherwise'. But the extent of a public defence in copyright, and even its existence, remains unclear.

In the *Hyde Park Residence* case, the Court of Appeal also rejected the *Sun*'s submission that the action could be defended on the grounds that publication took place in the public interest. It held that the 1988 Copyright Act did not give a court general power to enable an infringer to use another's copyright in the public interest. Lord Justice Aldous said the basis of a public interest defence in a copyright action was not the same as the basis of such a defence in a breach of confidence action. The jurisdiction to refuse to enforce copyright came from the court's inherent jurisdiction and was limited to cases where enforcement of copyright would offend against the policy of the law.

A court would be entitled to refuse to enforce copyright if the work was:

(1) immoral, scandalous or contrary to family life,

(2) injurious to public life, public health or safety or the administration of justice, or

(3) incited or encouraged others to act in a way injurious to those matters.

Lord Justice Aldous said *Lion Laboratories Ltd v Evans* [1985] QB 526 was such a case.

(In that case, the *Daily Express* was successful in asking the Court of Appeal to lift injunctions granted to restrain breach of confidence and infringement of copyright. The Court of Appeal held that publication of material which cast doubt on the accuracy of the Lion Intoximeter, a device providing evidence for drink driving convictions, was such a matter of grave concern as to justify publication in a national newspaper. The material did not reveal misconduct on the part of Lion Laboratories but that did not mean publication had to be restrained. The Court of Appeal stressed the need to differentiate between what is interesting to the public (which is not covered by the defence) and what is in the public interest to be made known, where the defence might be available.)

(See also chapter 23, 'Breach of confidence'.)

In 1994 the Department of Trade turned down a suggestion that the Act should be amended to allow a clear statutory defence to copyright infringement for newspapers which publish private photographs issued to them by the police, usually in order to trace persons wanted for serious crime or as witnesses. The Department took the view that a public interest defence would be upheld by the courts.

Copyright in newspapers

There is, as stated, copyright in the typographical arrangement of newspaper pages. However, the House of Lords held in 2001 that a facsimile copy of the cutting of an article from a page which gave no indication of how the rest of the page was laid out was not a substantial part of the published edition and thus was not an infringement of the copyright of the typographical arrangement (*Newspaper Licensing Agency v Marks & Spencer plc* [2001] UKHL 38, [2001] 3 All ER 977).

In 2004 IPC failed in a breach of copyright action against Highbury Leisure Publishing where they claimed Highbury's *Home* publication was copied from IPC's market leading magazine *Ideal Home*.

IPC's claim related to the design or 'template' of the magazine and it was claimed *Home* copied several key features of *Ideal Home*. Mr Justice Laddie backed Highbury and said any alleged similarities were slight, scattered and superficial. He went on to point out that the law of copyright had never protected general themes, styles or ideas and that Monet, for example, had acquired no right to prevent others from painting water lilies.

Length of copyright

The Government extended the length of copyright in 1995 from 50 years to 70 years from the end of the year of the author's death, to conform with a European Union directive. Copyright in a broadcast is retained at 50 years.

In 1996, under the Copyright and Related Rights Regulations, a person publishing for the first time a previously unpublished photograph which has gone out of copyright establishes a publication right for 25 years from the end of the year of that first publication.

European Convention on Human Rights

The right of freedom of expression under article 10 of the European Convention on Human Rights was held by Sir Andrew Morritt, Vice-Chancellor, in the Chancery Division in 2001, to provide no defence for infringement of copyright over and above those defences already provided by the Copyright Act 1988. The *Sunday Telegraph* had published an article by its political editor which incorporated substantial sections of a confidential note kept by Paddy Ashdown, then leader of the Liberal Democrats, of a meeting with the Prime Minister. The vice-chancellor said it was not open to an infringer of copyright to defend it on the basis that article 10 entitled him to deal with a copyright work in a manner not hitherto permitted by the 1988 Act. There was no defence with any reasonable prospect of success to the claim for breach of copyright. The decision was upheld in the Court of Appeal (*Ashdown v Telegraph Group Ltd* (2001) Times, 1 August).

Moral rights

The 1988 Act, to meet the needs of the Berne Convention on copyright, gave moral rights to authors of copyright work.

These gave the author the right to be identified, not to have his work subject to derogatory treatment, and not to have a work falsely attributed to him.

The rights to be identified and not to have the work subject to derogatory treatment do not apply to any copyright work created for publication in a newspaper, magazine, or periodical or to any work made available for such publication with the consent of the author.

The right not to have a work falsely attributed to a person does not have these exceptions. If a person gives an interview and the newspaper publishes an article purporting to have been written by the person himself and that person has not consented, he may have an action for false attribution.

See also chapter 34, 'Copyright in broadcasting'.

Remedies for breach of copyright

Civil action The owner of the copyright can obtain an injunction in the High Court or county court to restrain a person from infringing his copyright. He can also seek damages and an order for the possession of infringing copies of the work and of material used in the infringement.

Where the court decides there has been a deliberate or reckless infringement of copyright, this can be reflected in the level of damages awarded. In 2002 the *Sun* was ordered to pay £10,450 for its use of a confidential photograph from the medical notes of a convicted killer who had been allowed on day release from Rampton Hospital. The Nottinghamshire Healthcare NHS Trust was awarded £450, plus £10,000 to reflect the flagrancy of the breach: *Nottinghamshire Healthcare NHS Trust v News Group Newspapers* [2002] EWHC 409.

Criminal law Under the 1988 Act a person guilty of infringement can be prosecuted.

Innocent infringement

If the infringer did not know and had no reason to believe the work was subject to copyright, for example if he genuinely believed the copyright had run out, the copyright owner is entitled to an account of profits but not to damages.

Acquiescence

If the owner of a copyright work has encouraged or allowed another to make use of that work without complaint, this may destroy a claim for infringement of copyright.

Mr Justice Carnwath held in the Chancery Division in 1996 that the owner of copyright who was:

> aware of a breach of that copyright, but did not complain or take any action to stop it, had acquiesced and was therefore not entitled to claim. In a case before him involving the use of adult films, the company owning the copyright became aware in early 1993 that use, beyond what was permitted in a licence it had granted, was being made of its films. The judge said that the defence of acquiescence was made out at least from the middle of 1993 (*Film Investors Overseas Services SA v Home Video Channel Ltd*, Chancery Division, Times Law Report, 2 December 1996).

29

Official secrets

The Official Secrets Acts of 1911 and 1989 are concerned with national security and breaches of official trust.

Journalists were jailed for offences under the 1911 Act in 1916 and 1932, but as this book went to press no journalist had been successfully prosecuted, let alone jailed, for many years. However, journalists need to be aware of the acts principally because they are part of an armoury of weapons available to governments wishing to prevent or punish the publication of information derived from government sources which may or may not be related to national security.

Though you may not be sent to prison for your story, your source may be. Your home may be raided and you may be arrested and threatened with prosecution, an experience you are likely to find intimidating. You may be prevented from publishing your story as a result of an injunction aimed to prevent you committing an offence under the Act. Your source may be subjected to a variety of civil penalties, including actions for breaches of confidence, contract, or copyright.

The acts are therefore considered to have a chilling effect on journalists investigating and publishing matters which may be in the public interest, and their sources.

It is tempting to government departments to use the legislation to prevent the publication of information merely because it is embarrassing. But, as Lord Hutchinson QC, defence counsel in the *ABC* official secrets trial in 1978 said, it is the task of a vigorous press 'to examine, probe, question, and find out if there are mistakes and abuses and to embarrass governments, of whatever complexion, and not just accept handouts from people in high places and churn out what they are told to say' (for summary of the *ABC* trial, see website article 'Official Secrets Act').

The legislation also has a wider effect. In a surprising contribution to an official committee on government communications in 2003 Rear Admiral Nick Wilkinson, secretary of the Defence, Press and Broadcasting Advisory Committee (the 'D-Notice committee'), said the 1989 Act had a 'pernicious influence' on the dialogue between officials and the public, including the media, and was in need of a 'post-Cold War review'. He said the review was necessary not so much because of the content of the Act or the frequency of its use in litigation but because of its influence on government communications in the widest sense. He said it induced in officials an attitude of 'how little can I get away with saying?' rather the 'What must I really not say at present?' He said: 'This attitude is only partly a reflection of the civil service's tradition of serving the government of the day: it is largely a reflection of the instinct of self preservation inherent in all bureaucracies.'

Here are some examples of the way the legislation has been used against journalists. In 1998 Tony Geraghty, former *Sunday Times* defence correspondent, was charged with an offence under the 1989 Act after publication of his book *The Irish War*, which disclosed the extensive use of computerised surveillance by intelligence agencies in Northern Ireland.

The Government was aware of the contents before the book was published, but did not attempt to stop it. Then, three months after publication, Ministry of Defence police raided Geraghty's home and arrested him. It was not until a year later that the charge against him was dropped.

In 2000 Julie-Ann Davies, a broadcast researcher, was arrested and questioned for possible breach of the Act on the basis that she had been in communication with David Shayler, a former MI5 officer who had provided the *Mail on Sunday* with security-related information. She was not prosecuted.

In 2003 armed police raided the home of Liam Clarke, the Northern Ireland editor of the *Sunday Times*, and arrested him and his wife Kathryn Johnston after they published an updated version of their book *From Guns to Government*. The book contained transcripts of tape recordings, taken from a joint police/MI5 surveillance operation, which detailed bugged telephone conversations that were acutely embarrassing to the UK Government. Sacks of documents and several computers were removed. The police also raided the Belfast office of the *Sunday Times*, battering the door down, though Mr Clarke had offered them the key.

Later that year the police admitted the raid had been unlawful because, although a search warrant had been issued, it had been authorised by a JP, not a county court judge, as the law required. In the High Court in Belfast Mr Justice Kerr quashed the warrant and ordered the police to pay the paper's costs in its application for judicial review. In 2004 the police ombudsman called for disciplinary action to be taken against the police officers.

Sources were less fortunate. Richard Tomlinson, a former MI6 officer, was sentenced to one year's imprisonment in 1997 for having sent an Australian publisher a synopsis of a planned memoir-cum-exposé of his work.

In 1998 Stephen Hayden, a Royal Navy chief petty officer, admitted breaking the Official Secrets Act by selling to the *Sun* newspaper details of an anthrax threat to Britain by Iraqi leader Saddam Hussein. He pleaded guilty and was jailed for a year. The *Sun* published the story but was not prosecuted.

Geraghty's source, Nigel Wylde, a former army colonel, was arrested and charged at the same time as Geraghty. The charge against him was dropped, but not until November 2000, 15 months after his arrest.

Shayler, the former M15 officer, was sentenced to six months' imprisonment in 2002. The stories he provided to the *Mail on Sunday* in 1997 included the disclosure that the Government kept secret files on certain Labour politicians. The newspaper published the story, but was not prosecuted.

Later Shayler accused MI5 of failing to react on prior knowledge of a terrorist attack on the Israeli embassy, and alleged that MI6 officers had plotted to assassinate the Libyan leader, Colonel Gaddafi. He was arrested in France and held without charge for four months while the UK Government attempted without success to extradite him.

He returned to the United Kingdom voluntarily in 2000, was arrested and charged with three offences under the 1989 Act.

The cases referred to above raise the question why the source was so often prosecuted, but the journalist was not. As explained on our website, the section of the Act, section 5, under which it is assumed a journalist will normally be prosecuted, provides defences that are not available to the source. In most cases the journalist will have a defence that the disclosure of the information was not 'damaging'.

But the usual criminal law concepts also apply to official secrets offences, and a journalist might be found guilty of inciting or of aiding and abetting the source to commit an offence under the stringent terms of section 1, the section under which Shayler was prosecuted.

Alarmed by the position, seven national newspapers made representations to the Court of Appeal when it was hearing Shayler's appeal, and the Lord Chief Justice, Lord Woolf, after pointing out that section 5 of the Act provided protection to the press that was not available to Shayler, said that only in exceptional circumstances would the Attorney-General authorise a prosecution of the press for incitement to commit an offence under section 1.

McNae's editors asked John Wadham, director of the civil rights organisation Liberty, and Shayler's lawyer, why journalists were not prosecuted. He said: 'It is partly because governments don't like to be seen to be trying to put journalists in prison and partly because juries are less sympathetic to civil servants, who are employed to keep their mouths shut, who are aware of the rules but break them, and who breach the trust with employers and colleagues, compared with journalists, who are paid to find things out and publish them.'

Penalties for the offence of disclosure under the 1989 Act are a maximum of two years' imprisonment or a fine or both. If the case is tried summarily (by the magistrates) the maximum is six months or a fine or both.

There is no generally recognised definition of national security. A general guidance note added to the introduction of the DA Notices says they cover anything that 'involves grave danger to the state and/or individuals'.

For a fuller version of this chapter, which gives a detailed explanation of the two Acts, see our website. The 1989 Act is extremely complicated. In effect it creates more than a dozen offences. But don't panic if you don't know whether disclosure of particular information would be an offence and your local lawyer cannot tell you. The table accompanying the chapter in our website will give you the answer if you work through it carefully.

The website article also explains the operation of the D-Notice system.

Human Rights Act 1998

The Human Rights Act 1998 came into force on 2 October 2000, and immediately began to have an impact on media law. The Act guarantees basic human rights, such as the rights to life and liberty. For journalists in their day-to-day work, the most important rights to note are those to freedom of expression, to privacy, and to a fair trial. All the rights guaranteed are set out in the European Convention on Human Rights (ECHR), which the Act, in effect, incorporates into British law.

The right to freedom of expression is set out in section 1 of article 10 of the Convention. It could equally well be called the right to freedom of information because it includes not only the right to hold opinions but also 'to receive and impart information and ideas' without interference by public authority.

Section 2 of article 10 says this right is subject to a number of limitations, which lawyers refer to as 'derogations' from the rights. These limitations apply only when they are 'necessary in a democratic society', and the European Court of Human Rights (ECtHR), which adjudicates upon cases involving the Convention, has ruled this means only when they answer a 'pressing social need'.

The ECtHR has also ruled that interference with freedom of expression, even when lawful, must be 'proportionate to the legitimate aim pursued'. The article reflects the great importance that is attached to freedom of expression by the ECtHR. (The full wording of the article is given below.)

An English judge has said:

> It cannot be too strongly emphasised that outside the established exceptions, or any new ones which Parliament may enact in accordance with its obligations under the Convention, there is no question of balancing freedom of speech against other interests. It is a trump card which always wins (Lord Justice Hoffmann, later Lord Hoffmann in a case in 1994).

From the journalist's point of view it is encouraging to be told that freedom of speech is 'a trump card', but it is important to understand that this is subject to 'the established exceptions', such as the right to privacy, which need to be 'balanced' against the article 10 right (see chapter 32, 'Privacy').

The Act says that:

(1) a court determining a question in connection with a Convention right must take account of decisions of the ECtHR;

(2) new legislation must be compatible with the Convention rights and old and new legislation must be construed so far as possible to conform with Convention rights;

(3) courts have no power to strike down legislation that is incompatible with Convention rights, but may declare it to be incompatible, leaving it to the discretion of the minister, if he considers that there are compelling reasons, to introduce amending legislation;

(4) it is unlawful for public authorities to act in any way that is incompatible with Convention rights.

Where English law is based on common law, the courts are free to disregard previous common law authorities if they are inconsistent with the Convention. But they have discretion in this matter. Under the Act domestic courts can decide the extent to which Convention case law is relevant to any particular issue, and how that case law should be applied. Once the domestic court has reached a decision on the point, that decision becomes a 'precedent' and in this way it is possible for judges to develop a body of human rights law, influenced by the Convention, but built upon the existing foundations of English law.

For this reason, the full implications of incorporation will remain unclear until fully tested in the courts.

Section 19 of the Human Rights Act requires the minister responsible for the introduction of legislation to certify its compatibility with Convention rights. This section took effect in 1998 and bills since then have carried the required certificate, but it is arguable whether this has led to improvement (see chapter 1, 'Freedom of speech').

The European Convention

The European Convention includes rights to a fair trial, respect for private and family life, and freedom of expression.

Article 6, Right to a fair trial (the article is quoted in part)

1. In the determination of his civil rights and obligations or of any criminal charge against him, everyone is entitled to a fair and public hearing within a reasonable time by an independent and impartial tribunal established by law. Judgment shall be pronounced publicly but the press and public may be excluded from all or part of the trial in the interest of morals, public order or national security in a democratic society, where the interests of juveniles or the protection of the private life of the parties so require, or to the extent strictly necessary in the opinion of the court in special circumstances where publicity would prejudice the interests of justice.

Article 8, Right to respect for private and family life

1. Everyone has the right to respect for his private and family life, his home and his correspondence.

2. There shall be no interference by a public authority with the exercise of this right except such as is in accordance with the law and is necessary in a democratic society in the interests of national security, public safety or the economic well-being of the country, for the prevention of disorder or crime, for the protection of health or morals, or for the protection of the rights and freedoms of others.

Article 10, Freedom of expression

1. Everyone has the right to freedom of expression. This right shall include freedom to hold opinions and to receive and impart information and ideas without interference by public authority and regardless of frontiers. This article shall not prevent states from requiring the licensing of broadcasting, television or cinema enterprises.

2. The exercise of these freedoms, since it carries with it duties and responsibilities, may be subject to such formalities, conditions, restrictions or penalties as are prescribed by law and are necessary in a democratic society, in the interests of national security, territorial integrity or public safety, for the prevention of disorder or crime, for the protection of health or morals, for the protection of the reputation or rights of others, for preventing the disclosure of information received in confidence, or for maintaining the authority and impartiality of the judiciary.

Impact on media law

Even before the incorporation of the Convention into UK law, the country was 'a party to' the Convention, and the Convention articles were referred to in English courts.

In July 2000, before incorporation, the BBC won a High Court challenge to a gagging order granted to the family of a missing teenager amid fears that the cult he was believed to be with was using the boy as a platform for its own ends. The BBC based its case on article 10(1). The teenager's family argued that this right was overridden by the derogations in article 10(2), but the court held that the right was overridden only when it was 'necessary' to do so. It was not a question of balancing freedom of expression against one or more of the interests identified in 10(2).

The Convention principles assumed even greater importance when the Act came into effect.

On 13 October, 11 days after incorporation, the *Sunday People* succeeded in overturning orders granted to the Defence Secretary which prevented it from publishing details of the security forces' alleged role in sectarian murders in Northern Ireland. The judge said the paper's counsel had drawn his attention to article 10.

He emphasised that the scales in respect of the state and the defendants did not start level. The defendant's rights started higher than the state's and the state should succeed only if it proved that it was strictly necessary and proportionate to the legitimate aim which grounded the public interest for the court to limit the right to freedom of expression.

The paper's counsel had also drawn attention to section 12(4) of the Act (see below, 'Protection against injunctions'), which requires the court, when granting injunctions, to have particular regard to the importance of freedom of expression and, when the proceedings relate to journalistic material, to the extent to which it is or would be in the public interest for the material to be published.

On the same day (13 October) the *Mail on Sunday* successfully overturned what it described as a draconian court order that prevented the paper reporting that a council had removed a black girl from her loving white foster parents in accordance with the council's fostering policy.

The judge repeated that no balancing exercise was involved in her decision to lift the ban. She said:

> I find it is not a balancing exercise in which the scales are evenly positioned at the commencement of the exercise. On the contrary, the scales are weighted at the beginning so that article 10 prevails unless one of the defined derogations applies when given a narrow interpretation.

'Trump card' does not always win

But the 'trump card' does not always win, as the Court of Appeal said in December 2000. The judges had to apply the Convention in a case concerning *Hello!* magazine, which had acquired photographs of the wedding of film stars Michael Douglas and Catherine Zeta-Jones (*Douglas v Hello! Ltd* [2001] QB 967). The pictures had been taken surreptitiously. The newly-weds had sold the exclusive rights to photographs of the occasion to *OK!* magazine, and they and *OK!* initially obtained an injunction preventing *Hello!* from publishing.

The Court of Appeal overturned the injunction and the edition of *Hello!* was allowed to be published, but the comments made in the court ensured the case would be a landmark in the development of privacy law in the United Kingdom.

Counsel for the filmstars argued that *Hello!'s* proposed actions breached their right to privacy. Previously English law had not recognised a common law right to privacy, but now the court accepted that such a right existed and would be protected by the law (see discussion of the case in chapter 23, 'Breach of confidence' and chapter 32, 'Privacy').

But what of the argument that freedom of speech was a 'trump card' that always won? Would not that deny the stars their injunction? In the Court of Appeal Lord Justice Sedley referred to the 'trump card' quotation from Lord Justice Hoffmann (above) but pointed out that the judge also referred to the limitations on that freedom. 'In other words,' said Lord Justice Sedley, 'if freedom of expression is to be impeded ... it must be on cogent grounds recognised by law.' These grounds included, in article 10(2), the protection of the rights of others, and these rights in turn included the article 8 right to privacy.

In such a case, he said, the judge had to weigh the two rights, determining the outcome principally by considerations of *proportionality*, that is, the principle that interference with freedom of expression, even if lawful, must be 'proportionate to the legitimate aim pursued'.

(When the case proceeded to trial in April 2003, the judge decided that *Hello!'s* publication was an infringement of the rights of the Douglases and *Hello!*, but not on the basis of infringement of privacy.)

In another case in 2001, concerning the two killers of James Bulger, the court held that the media's right to freedom of expression was outweighed by those contained in article 2, the right to life, article 3, the prohibition of torture, and (again) article 8, privacy. The president of the Family Division imposed a breach of confidence injunction preventing the media from identifying the two young men when they are released with new identities after she concluded that their lives would be at risk if they were to be identified (the case is discussed more fully in chapter 23, 'Breach of confidence').

A problem for court reporters

The area in which journalists were most likely to come into contact with the Convention rights was court reporting. Defence lawyers were quick to use the Act to argue for restricted reports involving their clients on the ground that otherwise their right to a fair trial under article 6 would be infringed.

A farmer accused of cruelty to animals had his case switched to a court 90 miles away because it was argued he was well known to the bench and could not have a fair trial before the court. In another case it was argued that a man accused of murdering his girlfriend should not have his address published in the press because the fear of reprisals against his family meant he could not prepare for his trial.

Walter Greenwood, joint editor of *McNae*, drew attention to this development at a law seminar for editors run by the National Council for the Training of Journalists in 2000. He said that defence lawyers citing article 6, and also article 8 (privacy), rarely mentioned article 10 and the duty of the court to balance the competing interests. The reporter might have to put the other side, he said, and he urged that reporters should be instructed in the implications of the act.

The *Liverpool Daily Post & Echo* defeated an attempt to use the Act to prevent publication of the addresses of three former social workers accused of physically and sexually assaulting young boys at a residential care home. The defendants' lawyers asked for an order under section 11 of the Contempt of Court Act 1981, citing article 8 of the Convention. They claimed that in the prevailing climate of hostility and violence towards sex offenders, they would be at risk of serious attack on their homes and families if their addresses were published.

But the Recorder of Liverpool, Judge David Clarke QC, rejected the request. He said there was no 'pressing need' for the addresses to be withheld. The two articles of the Convention, 8 and 10, were in conflict in the case, but the position of the defendants was no different from that of anyone facing any criminal charge. He added: 'Unless and until some statutory prohibition is enacted, I do not consider that there is any warrant for prohibiting publication of their addresses' (*R v Carroll* (2000) Media Lawyer 31).

In a case in 2004 counsel argued that article 8 required the court to ban the identification of a defendant in a criminal trial to prevent harmful publicity for the defendant's child, who was not involved in the criminal proceedings (*Re S (A Child) (Identification: Restrictions on Publication)* [2004] 3 WLR 1129). The Law Lords rejected the plea. Lord Steyn said courts had no power to create new exceptions to the general principle of open justice and the right of the press to report criminal trials except in the most compelling circumstances. See *Juveniles and the European Convention on Human Rights* in chapter 6, 'Children in the news'.

Protection against injunctions

When the Human Rights Bill was before Parliament, the media were worried that it would give the opportunity to wealthy and powerful villains to get last-minute injunctions against the publication of exposés on the ground that such publication would be an infringement of their privacy, and would therefore contravene article 8.

In response, the Government amended the Act to introduce a provision (section 12) that applies if a court is considering whether to grant 'relief' (principally an injunction) which affects the exercise of the right to freedom of expression.

If the journalist is not present when the application is made, the court must not grant an injunction unless it is satisfied the person seeking the injunction has taken all practicable steps to notify the journalist or that there are compelling reasons why the journalist should not be notified.

The court must not grant an injunction preventing publication before trial unless it is satisfied that the person seeking the injunction is likely to establish at the trial that publication should not be allowed.

The value of this defence depends crucially on the meaning the courts give to the word 'likely'. In a case in 2004 a newspaper argued unsuccessfully that it meant 'more likely than not'—that is, an interim injunction could be granted only if it was more likely than not that, at the trial which was to follow, publication would not be allowed.

On appeal, the House of Lords ruled in favour of the newspaper, lifting the injunction that had been imposed on it, but said this could not be the meaning in every case. Lord Nicholls said courts should be exceedingly slow to make interim injunctions where the applicant had not satisfied the court he would probably ('more likely than not') succeed at trial, but there would be cases where it was necessary for the court to depart from this general approach.

Such cases included those where the potential adverse consequences of disclosure were particularly grave or where a 'holding injunction' was required to enable the court to consider an application for an interim injunction or a pending appeal (*Cream Holding Ltd v Banerjee* [2004] UKHL 44).

Under subsection (4) the court must have 'particular regard' to the importance of the Convention right to freedom of expression.

The court must be especially cautious where the proceedings concern material which the journalist claims, or which appears to the court, to be journalistic, literary, or artistic material—or to conduct connected with such material, which would cover investigative work before the story is written. In this case the court must have particular regard to:

(1) the extent to which—

      (a) the material has, or is about to, become available to the public; or

      (b) it is, or would be, in the public interest for the material to be published;

(2) any relevant privacy code.

(See chapter 31, 'The codes'.)

The section does not apply to criminal proceedings, so cannot assist a journalist when challenging a reporting restriction imposed by a court.

UK cases before and after incorporation

Britain ratified the Convention in 1951 but before the HRA came into effect British citizens wishing to give effect to the provisions of the Convention had to petition the ECtHR at Strasbourg. They could not do so in English courts.

Important British cases involving freedom of speech that came before the ECtHR during this period included those of Bill Goodwin and Count Tolstoy.

In 1990 Bill Goodwin, a reporter on *The Engineer* magazine, was fined £5,000 by a British court after defying a ruling by the House of Lords that he must identify the source of a news story (see chapter 23, 'The Bill Goodwin case'). Backed by the National Union of Journalists, he took his case to the ECtHR which in 1996 ruled that the order breached his rights to freedom of expression under the Convention.

The court, answering the question 'Was the interference "necessary in a democratic society"?' said protection of journalistic sources was one of the basic conditions for press freedom. An order of source disclosure could not be compatible with article 10 unless it was justified by an overriding requirement in the public interest and the order in this case did not meet that criterion.

In 1995 the Court found in favour of the author Count Tolstoy, against whom and a co-defendant an English jury had awarded £1.5 million, the largest libel award ever, for allegations against the Conservative politician Lord Aldington, contained in a pamphlet. The pamphlet said Lord Aldington, when a brigadier in Austria at the end of the 1939–45 war, handed over 70,000 Cossacks and anti-Tito Yugoslavs to Communist forces knowing they faced imprisonment or death. Count Tolstoy was also ordered to pay nearly £1 million in costs.

The Court held that the award violated Count Tolstoy's rights to freedom of expression. It said that in 1987, when the words were published, the UK Court of Appeal did not have the power it acquired later (see chapter 18) to vary excessive jury awards, and the ECtHR said its decision had regard to the size of the award in conjunction with the state of national law at the time.

If the ECtHR found against the British courts, the United Kingdom was expected, in accordance with its treaty obligations, to change its law to conform with the Convention. The Government introduced a new defence for those accused of contempt of court after the ECtHR held that the House of Lords' decision preventing the *Sunday Times* from publishing an article about the drug thalidomide was an interference with the paper's freedom of expression (see chapter 17, 'Discussion of public affairs').

This was the case in which the ECtHR said a restriction was 'necessary in a democratic society' only if it answered a 'pressing social need'.

The Government also provided the media with a right to appeal against gagging and exclusion orders (now section 159 of the Criminal Justice Act 1988) after Old Bailey reporter Tim Crook challenged a secrecy order in the divisional court and established that the media had no effective remedy under English law. He claimed this was a breach of article 13 of the Convention, which requires that anyone whose rights are violated (in this case, his rights to freedom of expression) should have an effective remedy.

The House of Lords said in 1991 that UK courts had to enforce domestic law even when it conflicted with the Convention but added that when domestic law was ambiguous courts could apply the Convention, working on the assumption Parliament had intended the law to conform with the Convention.

There was an application of this principle in 1992 when the Court of Appeal considered the question whether a local authority could sue for libel. Derbyshire County Council wished to sue the *Sunday Times* for criticising its pension fund dealings. English law was unclear on whether a local authority could sue for libel.

The court, applying article 10, said a local authority had adequate remedies for protecting its reputation without having the right to sue in defamation and thereby be able to stifle legitimate public criticism of its activities. For this and other reasons the court found for the newspaper (see chapter 18, 'Who can sue').

(In 1994 the Law Lords upheld the decision without needing to rely upon the Convention, ruling that the common law matched article 10.)

The effect of all this was the creation of what Lord Steyn, in the House of Lords in 1999, described as 'the new legal landscape'. He was speaking in the case in which the Reynolds defence was formulated (see chapter 20). This is really a public interest defence, something against which the English judicial system had previously set its face, and is perhaps the most important consequence, for journalists, of that new landscape.

Lord Steyn said important issues regarding the reconciliation of the colliding right of free speech and the right to reputation needed to be considered afresh. He cited a number of cases determined by the ECtHR.

Exceptions to freedom of expression must be justified as being necessary in a democracy. In other words, freedom of expression was the rule and regulation of speech was the exception requiring justification. The existence and width of any exception could be justified only if it was underpinned by a pressing social need.

Another European Court of Human Rights case (the 'McLibel case') in which the right to freedom of expression featured involved two environmental campaigners who claimed they should have been given legal aid by the UK Government to help them fight a libel action brought against them by the multi-national fast food company McDonalds. The pair, who had handed out leaflets attacking the company's working practices and policies, had lost the case in 1997 and were ordered to pay damages to the firm. In 2005 the European Court found for the pair, saying their human rights had been breached. The court said the lack of legal aid effectively denied them the right to a fair trial as guaranteed by article 6 and also breached their right to freedom of expression under article 10.

Since incorporation, the effect of the HRA has been most obvious in cases involving conflict between article 10 rights (freedom of expression) and article 8 rights (privacy), most notably in the *Douglas* and *Venables* cases (see chapter 32).

Clibbery v Allan (2001) was a case which led to an important relaxation of the secrecy surrounding family court proceedings in cases not involving children. The court considered the conflict between the article 10 rights of a woman who wished to publicise proceedings concerning property which had taken place in private, and the article 8 rights of a man who wished the proceedings to remain private.

It was held that a blanket ban on disclosure was not 'necessary in a democratic society' and it would not be proportionate to the legitimate aim of protecting article 8 rights. An injunction that had prevented the woman from disclosing material put before the court was discharged, and an appeal against that discharge was rejected by the Court of Appeal (see chapter 17, 'Reports of hearings in private').

But all areas of media law have felt the impact of the Act. The HRA also made possible the triumph of the civil rights group Liberty, *The Guardian* newspaper and others who argued that the secrecy that shrouded the proceedings of the Investigatory Powers Tribunal was a violation of the Act. The tribunal deals with complaints involving unlawful telephone tapping or invasive surveillance by MI5, MI6, the police or other security agencies. It had until the start of 2003 dealt with all cases in private, without even having oral hearings. But in January that year, as a result of the media challenge, it met in public for the first time, and decided that preliminary hearings about two complaints could also be made public.

31

The codes

Codes of conduct attempt to encourage or enforce ethical standards in the media. For all journalists, the importance of these codes increased as the Human Rights Act and the Data Protection Act, both passed in 1998, came into force, and increased further as the courts extended the reach of the common law to provide protection for privacy.

Previously there was a significant difference in the status of the codes applying in the print and broadcast media. Codes for the print media were essentially voluntary, in the sense that there were no legal penalties for failing to observe them. By contrast, contravention of the broadcast codes could sometimes have serious legal implications leading, for example, to fines or even revocation of the licence to broadcast (see chapter 34, 'The broadcast journalist').

The reason for the difference was that the state has always retained the means to control the operations of the broadcast media, and the codes were part of this apparatus. But the state exercised no direct control over the operations of the print media.

There were increasingly strident calls during the 1980s and 1990s for regulation of the print media, and for the Press Complaints Commission (PCC), which adjudicates upon the editorial code, to have powers to fine or issue injunctions forbidding publication, but both Conservative and Labour Governments preferred voluntary self-regulation through the PCC.

However, the two Acts referred to above attempt to encourage observance of the editorial code, and other codes, by ensuring that the full benefit of defences provided in the Acts are available only to journalists whose conduct has conformed to the codes.

The Human Rights Act says in section 12 that a judge, when considering granting 'relief' (principally an injunction) against the publication of a story, must have particular regard to 'any relevant privacy code'. The Data Protection Act provides in section 32 a defence against challenges on data protection grounds to the use of personal data for journalistic purposes but one factor a court will take into account is an editor's compliance with 'any relevant code of practice'.

As stated, the conduct of the print media is required to conform to the editorial code adjudicated upon by the PCC (the code is given in full below). By contrast, until implementation of the Communications Act 2003, the conduct of most broadcasters was regulated by various codes, including six operated by three authorities, the Broadcasting Standards Commission (BSC), the Independent Television Commission (ITC) and the Radio Authority (RA).

The 2003 Act created the Office of Communications (Ofcom), which now has responsibility for regulating all the UK communications industries, apart from the print media, and its remit includes television, radio, telecommunications and wireless communications services. It was established on 29 December 2003 and assumed the functions of the ITC, the BSC and the Radio Authority. Ofcom has power to impose penalties on broadcasters that contravene the provisions of their licence.

The BBC has its own routine. Its governors' programme complaints committee hears appeals from members of the public dissatisfied with a finding from the BBC programme complaints unit. Producers must observe the BBC producer guidelines. Even after the establishment of Ofcom, the BBC governors continue to have responsibility for the conduct of the corporation except that the BBC also is subject to the external requirements of Ofcom.

Ofcom was required by the 2003 Act to draw up a code setting standards for programmes, sponsorship, fairness and privacy for all broadcasters. It published a draft code in July 2004, for consultation, and was due to publish the final version in 2005. Until publication of the new code, it continued to apply the provisions of the earlier codes, referred to as the 'legacy codes'. For that reason, in the 'Privacy' chapter (chapter 32) of this edition of *McNae* the editors continue to explain the rules on privacy as applied under the earlier codes. The new Ofcom code, when published, will be discussed in the *McNae* website, which will also give a link to the full code.

The Human Rights Act states that it is unlawful for public authorities to act in any way that is incompatible with Convention rights, so members of the public who consider they have been wronged by a decision of such authorities can seek judicial review of the decision in the courts.

However, following well-established principles, the courts are reluctant to overturn decisions of the authorities except in extreme cases.

Editorial Code of Practice (PCC)

A revised version of the code, drawn up by the Editors' Code of Practice Committee, was ratified by the PCC on 28 April 2004 and took effect from 1 June 2004.

Key changes were that the code:

- re-emphasises that editors and publishers have the ultimate duty of care to implement the code;

- stresses that its rules apply to all editorial contributors, including non-journalists;

- makes clear that it covers online versions of publications as well as printed copies;

- insists that publications which are criticised in adverse adjudications should include a reference to the PCC in the headline;

- extends the protection of private correspondence to include digital communications—prohibiting the interception of private or mobile telephone calls, messages or emails, unless in the public interest;

- introduces a new rule to prevent payment to criminals for material which seeks to exploit, glorify or glamorise crime;

- tightens the rules so that a newspaper which paid a criminal in the belief that it would elicit material in the public interest could not publish if no public interest emerged.

The asterisks in the code related to the public interest defence and are referred to in the final paragraph.

Introduction

All members of the press have a duty to maintain the highest professional standards. This Code sets the benchmark for those ethical standards, protecting both the rights of the individual and the public's right to know. It is the cornerstone of the system of self-regulation to which the industry has made a binding commitment.

It is essential that an agreed code be honoured not only to the letter but in the full spirit. It should not be interpreted so narrowly as to compromise its commitment to respect the rights of the individual, nor so broadly that it constitutes an unnecessary interference with freedom of expression or prevents publication in the public interest.

It is the responsibility of editors and publishers to implement the code and they should take care to ensure it is observed rigorously by all editorial staff and external contributors, including non-journalists, in printed and online versions of publications.

Editors should co-operate swiftly with the PCC in the resolution of complaints. Any publication judged to have breached the code must print the adjudication in full and with due prominence, including headline reference to the PCC.

1. Accuracy

i)   The press must take care not to publish inaccurate, misleading or distorted information, including pictures.

ii) A significant inaccuracy, misleading statement or distortion once recognised must be corrected, promptly and with due prominence, and—where appropriate—an apology published.

iii) The press, whilst free to be partisan, must distinguish clearly between comment, conjecture and fact.

iv) A publication must report fairly and accurately the outcome of an action for defamation to which it has been a party, unless an agreed settlement states otherwise, or an agreed statement is published.

2. Opportunity to reply

A fair opportunity for reply to inaccuracies must be given when reasonably called for.

3. * Privacy

i)   Everyone is entitled to respect for his or her private and family life, home, health and correspondence, including digital communications. Editors will be expected to justify intrusions into any individual's private life without consent.

ii) It is unacceptable to photograph individuals in private places without their consent.

Note—Private places are public or private property where there is a reasonable expectation of privacy.

4. * Harassment

i)   Journalists must not engage in intimidation, harassment or persistent pursuit.

ii) They must not persist in questioning, telephoning, pursuing or photographing individuals once asked to desist; nor remain on their property when asked to leave and must not follow them.

iii) Editors must ensure these principles are observed by those working for them and take care not to use non-compliant material from other sources.

5. Intrusion into grief or shock

In cases involving personal grief or shock, enquiries and approaches must be made sympathy and discretion and publication handled sensitively. This should not restrict the right to report legal proceedings, such as inquests.

6. * Children

i) Young people should be free to complete their time at school without unnecessary intrusion.

ii) A child under 16 must not be interviewed or photographed on issues involving their own or another child's welfare unless a custodial parent or similarly responsible adult consents.

iii) Pupils must not be approached or photographed at school without the permission of the school authorities.

iv) Minors must not be paid for material involving children's welfare, nor parents or guardians for material about their children or wards, unless it is clearly in the child's interest.

v) Editors must not use the fame, notoriety or position of a parent or guardian as sole justification for publishing details of a child's private life.

7. * Children in sex cases

1. The press must not, even if legally free to do so, identify children under 16 who are victims or witnesses in cases involving sex offences.

2. In any press report of a case involving a sexual offence against a child—

i) The child must not be identified.

ii) The adult may be identified.

iii) The word 'incest' must not be used where a child victim might be identified.

iv) Care must be taken that nothing in the report implies the relationship between the accused and the child.

8. * Hospitals

i) Journalists must identify them-selves and obtain permission from a responsible executive before entering non-public areas of hospitals or similar institutions to pursue enquiries.

ii) The restrictions on intruding into privacy are particularly relevant to enquiries about individuals in hospitals or similar institutions.

[handwritten: NB Not illegal to record ~~state~~ up an conversation on the phone only 3rd person]

9. * Reporting of crime

(i) Relatives or friends of persons convicted or accused of crime should not generally be identified without their consent, unless they are genuinely relevant to the story.

(ii) Particular regard should be paid to the potentially vulnerable position of children who witness, or are victims of, crime. This should not restrict the right to report legal proceedings.

10. * Clandestine devices and subterfuge

[handwritten: → refers to. bugs → recording someone else]

i) The press must not seek to obtain or publish material acquired by using hidden cameras or clandestine listening devices; or by intercepting private or mobile telephone calls, messages or emails; or by the unauthorised removal of documents or photographs.

ii) Engaging in misrepresentation or subterfuge, can generally be justified only in the public interest and then only when the material cannot be obtained by other means.

11. Victims of sexual assault

The press must not identify victims of sexual assault or publish material likely to contribute to such identification unless there is adequate justification and they are legally free to do so.

12. Discrimination

i) The press must avoid prejudicial or pejorative reference to an individual's race, colour, religion, sex, sexual orientation or to any physical or mental illness or disability.

ii) Details of an individual's race, colour, religion, sexual orientation, physical or mental illness or disability must be avoided unless genuinely relevant to the story.

13. Financial journalism

i) Even where the law does not prohibit it, journalists must not use for their own profit financial information they receive in advance of its general publication, nor should they pass such information to others.

ii) They must not write about shares or securities in whose performance they know that they or their close families have a significant financial interest without disclosing the interest to the editor or financial editor.

iii) They must not buy or sell, either directly or through nominees or agents, shares or securities about which they have written recently or about which they intend to write in the near future.

14. Confidential sources

Journalists have a moral obligation to protect confidential sources of information.

15. Witness payments in criminal trials

i) No payment or offer of payment to a witness—or any person who may reasonably be expected to be called as a witness—should be made in any case once proceedings are active as defined by the Contempt of Court Act 1981.

This prohibition lasts until the suspect has been freed unconditionally by police without charge or bail or the proceedings are otherwise discontinued; or has entered a guilty plea to the court; or, in the event of a not guilty plea, the court has announced its verdict.

*ii) Where proceedings are not yet active but are likely and foreseeable, editors must not make or offer payment to any person who may reasonably be expected to be called as a witness, unless the information concerned ought demonstrably to be published in the public interest and there is an over-riding need to make or promise payment for this to be done; and all reasonable steps have been taken to ensure no financial dealings influence the evidence those witnesses give. In no circumstances should such payment be conditional on the outcome of a trial.

*iii) Any payment or offer of payment made to a person later cited to give evidence in proceedings must be disclosed to the prosecution and defence. The witness must be advised of this requirement.

16. * Payment to criminals

i)   Payment or offers of payment for stories, pictures or information, which seek to exploit a particular crime or to glorify or glamorise crime in general, must not be made directly or via agents to convicted or confessed criminals or to their associates—who may include family, friends and colleagues.

ii) Editors invoking the public interest to justify payment or offers would need to demonstrate that there was good reason to believe the public interest would be served. If, despite payment, no public interest emerged, then the material should not be published.

*The public interest

There may be exceptions to the clauses marked *where they can be demonstrated to be in the public interest.

1. The public interest includes, but is not confined to:

i)   Detecting or exposing crime or serious impropriety.

ii) Protecting public health and safety.

iii) Preventing the public from being misled by an action or statement of an individual or organisation.

2. There is a public interest in freedom of expression itself.

3. Whenever the public interest is invoked, the PCC will require editors to demonstrate fully how the public interest was served.

4. The PCC will consider the extent to which material is already in the public domain, or will become so.

5. In cases involving children under 16, editors must demonstrate an exceptional public interest to over-ride the normally paramount interest of the child.

The Editorial Code of Practice is reproduced by permission of the Press Standards Board of Finance Ltd.

32

Privacy

Privacy has been described as the right of the individual to be protected against intrusion into his personal life or affairs, or those of his family, by direct physical means or by publication of information (Calcutt Committee on Privacy and Related Matters, 1990).

Until 2 October 2000 the law of England did not specifically recognise the right to privacy, but on that date the Human Rights Act 1998 came into force, in effect incorporating into English law the European Convention on Human Rights, which guarantees under article 8 the right to privacy.

Lord Justice Sedley in the Court of Appeal declared: 'It can be said with confidence that the law recognises and will appropriately protect a right of personal privacy'.

The judge was speaking in a case in December 2000 in which the court was asked to lift a temporary injunction preventing a magazine from publishing 'snatched' photographs of a wedding. Two film stars, Michael Douglas and Catherine Zeta-Jones, had granted exclusive rights to pictures of their wedding to the magazine *OK!*, but the magazine *Hello!* had its own pictures, which it planned to publish. (*Douglas v Hello! Ltd* [2001] 2 All ER 289; see below and also the fuller report in chapter 23, 'Breach of confidence and privacy'.)

But though the right to privacy existed, it was unclear how the courts would protect it. The remedy most favoured was breach of confidence, an area of the law where many uncertainties existed and still exist.

Journalists were concerned at the potential effect of the right to privacy on their freedom to publish true information of public interest. Section 12 of the Human Rights Act requires courts, when considering granting an injunction, to have 'particular regard' to the importance of freedom of expression, guaranteed by article 10 of the Convention.

But in the *Douglas* case Lord Justice Sedley rejected the view that the section gave greater weight to freedom of expression than to privacy rights. He said: 'Everything will ultimately depend on the proper balance between privacy and publicity in the situation facing the court.'

Uncertainty about privacy persisted. In the *Douglas* case the Court of Appeal lifted the injunction that prevented *Hello!* from publishing its snatched pictures of the wedding but did not have to decide whether such publication was unlawful; and in April 2003 the judge who had that task declined to hold that there was an existing law of privacy under which the stars and *OK!* could recover damages from *Hello!* He said there were conflicting views in the authorities as to whether such a law existed.

He did decide that they had won the case, but not on the grounds of privacy. He held the wedding was protected under the law of commercial confidence as a valuable trade asset. The publication of unauthorised photographs by a rival magazine was a breach of that confidence (*Douglas v Hello!* [2003] EWHC 786 (Ch)).

However in 2004, in a case involving the supermodel Naomi Campbell, the House of Lords authoritatively established 'unjustified disclosure of private information' as a new cause of action. The distinguished judge Sir Charles Gray referred to 'the new (or at least relabelled) tort' and said the judgment had, in effect, created a law of privacy for the first time.

The Lords agreed that Ms Campbell was entitled to damages after the *Daily Mirror* reported that she had a drug addiction, for which she was receiving treatment by Narcotics Anonymous, gave details of the treatment and her reaction to it, and surreptitiously obtained photographs, which they published, of her emerging from a treatment session (*Campbell v Mirror Group Newspapers* [2004] UKHL 22).

Another important development was the Princess Caroline case, in which the European Court of Human Rights held in 2004 that respect for the private life of the princess was breached by photographs of scenes from her daily life, shopping or on holiday with her family, in public places.

English courts had not prevented publication of such photographs, and the significance of the decision for the United Kingdom was that the Human Rights Act 1998 says that a court determining a question in connection with a right guaranteed under the European Convention must 'take account' of decisions of the European court.

Though there has been no specific common law protection for privacy, a number of laws have given limited protection. These include—in addition to breach of confidence—data protection, trespass, harassment, defamation, criminal libel, copyright, laws regulating press reports of court proceedings, the Wireless Telegraphy Act 1949, and the Regulation of Investigatory Powers ('RIP') Act 2000. These topics are covered in this chapter (see below and also the chapters on 'Breach of confidence', chapter 23, and the 'Data Protection Act', next chapter).

If none of these remedies is available, a person who considers his privacy has been infringed can appeal to the European Court of Human Rights. In 2003 the court ordered the United Kingdom to pay £7,900 (11,800 euros) compensation, plus costs and expenses, to Geoff Peck, after a local authority gave footage of his suicide attempt, recorded on closed-circuit television, to the BBC for its television programme *Crime Beat*.

The court found there had been a 'serious interference' with his rights under article 8. The court also found that the United Kingdom had breached article 13, the right to an effective remedy. It said the Broadcasting Standards Commission and Independent Television Commission, which were then the relevant regulatory bodies, could not offer an effective remedy because they had no power to award damages.

In 1996 Peck had applied to the High Court and later the Court of Appeal for a judicial review of the council's disclosure of the footage, but both requests were rejected.

The media's various codes of practice on privacy achieved greater importance as a result of implementation of the Human Rights Act (see chapter 31, 'The codes'). The way in which the codes deal with aspects of privacy is covered later in this chapter, 'What the codes say on privacy'.

Article 8 of the Convention

The right to privacy is guaranteed by article 8 of the Convention on Human Rights, which says:

1. Everyone has the right to respect for his private and family life, his home and his correspondence.
2. There shall be no interference by a public authority with the exercise of this right except such as is in accordance with the law and is necessary in a democratic society

in the interests of national security, public safety or the economic well-being of the country,

for the prevention of disorder or crime,

for the protection of health or morals, or

for the protection of the rights and freedoms of others.

The wording of article 8 suggests it gives protection for privacy only against a 'public authority', but in fact it gives protection also against the media because under the Act a court in the United Kingdom is a public authority and must take account of the judgments of the European Court of Human Rights (which adjudicates upon Convention matters) whenever it is hearing a case that involves one of the rights guaranteed by the Convention.

'Any relevant privacy code'

The Human Rights Act says in section 12 that where a court is considering imposing an injunction in a matter involving freedom of expression and journalistic, literary, or artistic material, it must have particular regard, among other things, to the extent to which the media defendant has complied with 'any relevant privacy code' (see chapter 30, 'Protection from injunctions').

In the *Douglas* case the judges considered clause 3 of the Press Complaints Commission code, relating to privacy. At that time the code said:

(i) Everyone is entitled to respect for his or her private and family life, home, health and correspondence. A publication will be expected to justify intrusions into any individual's private life without consent.

(ii) The use of long lens photography to take pictures of people in private places without their consent is unacceptable.

Note—Private places are public or private property where there is a reasonable expectation of privacy.

In 2004 the code was amended slightly, and (ii) now reads: 'It is unacceptable to photograph individuals in private places without their consent', which covers the Douglas and Zeta-Jones wedding.

In the code, privacy is one of the topics where there may be exceptions to the rules set out in the code on grounds of public interest, a phrase which includes, in the 2004 wording (the list is not exhaustive):

(1) detecting or exposing crime or serious impropriety;

(2) protecting public health and safety; and

(3) preventing the public from being misled by an action or statement of an individual or organisation.

Lord Justice Brooke (in the *Douglas* case) said it was not necessary to go beyond section

12 of the 1998 Act and clause 3 of the code to find the ground rules by which the court should weigh the competing considerations of freedom of expression on the one hand and privacy on the other.

So far as privacy was concerned, the case of Mr Douglas and Ms Zeta-Jones was not a particularly strong one. They did not choose to have a private wedding, attended by a few members of their family and a few friends, in the normal sense of the words 'private wedding'. They invited 250 guests.

Although by their agreement with *OK!* they undertook to use their best efforts to ensure that their guests 'shall not publish and/or broadcast . . . or write any article about, or give any extended comment, report or interview to any media concerning the wedding', there was no evidence before the court which showed that they took any steps to enforce that undertaking, so far as their guests were concerned.

The judge commented: 'I do not consider that their privacy-based case, as distinct from their confidentiality-based case, adds very much.' (The judges concluded that the stars and *OK!* were, in the words of section 12 of the Human Rights Act, 'likely to establish at the trial that publication should not be allowed', but they lifted the injunction, saying damages or an account of profits would be appropriate if the claimants were successful—which they were.)

Laws providing protection

Breach of confidence

Before the development of the 'new tort', the only remedies that British citizens had against intrusions into their private lives were those referred to in the introduction to this chapter. If none gave an appropriate remedy, a claimant had no legal protection.

As explained in chapter 23, the law of breach of confidence is based on the principle that a person who has acquired information in confidence should not take unfair advantage of it. Originally the obligation was understood to arise only where the parties had a recognised relationship (such as doctor and patient or employer and employee) but more recently the judges had modified the law so that they were ready to infer such a relationship where no obvious relationship existed.

In the *Douglas* case Lord Justice Sedley said:

> What a concept of privacy does . . . is accord recognition to the fact that the law has to protect not only those people whose trust has been abused but those who simply find

themselves subjected to an unwanted intrusion into their personal lives. The law no longer needs to construct an artificial relationship of confidentiality between intruder and victim: it can recognise privacy itself as a legal principle drawn from the fundamental value of personal autonomy.

The judges' comments in this case gave a considerable boost to the new right of privacy, which received another boost three weeks later when a judge, Dame Elizabeth Butler-Sloss, imposed an unprecedented injunction forbidding the media from revealing the new identities and whereabouts of the two killers of the three-year-old child James Bulger on the ground that such a disclosure would infringe their rights to privacy (article 8 of the European Convention), article 2 (right to life), and article 3 (prohibition of torture). She said she had no doubt, after the comments of the judges in the *Douglas* case, that disclosure would amount to a breach of confidence (*Venables and Thompson v News Group Newspapers Ltd* [2001] 1 All ER 908).

Quality of confidence

The elements of this legal remedy have traditionally been that: (a) the information must have the necessary quality of confidence; (b) the information must have been imparted in circumstances imposing an obligation of confidence; and (c) there must be an unauthorised use of that information to the detriment of the party communicating it.

The question whether the information has the 'necessary quality of confidence' is an issue that the judges frequently have to consider in privacy cases, particularly in 'kiss-and-tell' stories—that is, stories in which one of the parties gives the media details of the relationship.

Not all sexual conduct is entitled to be viewed as confidential or, indeed, deserving of legal protection at all. In 2002 the Court of Appeal lifted an injunction banning publication of details of the extra-marital affairs of a professional footballer, Blackburn Rovers' captain Garry Flitcroft (*A v B (A Company)* [2002] EWCA Civ 337).

The judge who granted the injunction had explained that the law afforded the protection of confidentiality to facts concerning sexual relations within marriage, and he ruled that in the context of modern sexual relations the position should be no different with relationships outside marriage. He granted an injunction preventing the *Sunday People* from identifying Flitcroft and publishing interviews with his former lovers—one a lap dancer he met in a club and the other a nursery teacher who claimed he used his wealth, fame and position to seduce her.

But the Court of Appeal, lifting the injunction, said there was a significant difference between the confidentiality that attached to what was intended to be a permanent relationship and that which attached to the category of relationships that Flitcroft was involved with in this case (*A v B (A Company)* [2002] EWCA Civ 337, [2003] QB 195).

Earlier that year a judge refused to grant an injunction to Top of the Pops presenter Jamie Theakston banning the *Sunday People* from publishing an article about his activities in a brothel. The judge said a 'fleeting' sexual relationship in a brothel was not confidential (*Jamie Theakston v MGN Ltd* [2002] EWHC 137 (QB)).

Incidents that take place behind closed doors do not necessarily have the 'quality of confidence'. In *Theakston* the judge did not regard a brothel as a private place at all. Nor are clubs and hotels, which featured in the *Flitcroft* case, likely to be viewed as very private.

It is clear, however, that information concerning health will be treated as of the utmost confidentiality. In 2002 the *Mail on Sunday* was barred by the Court of Appeal from revealing the identity of a local health authority where a health care worker, referred to as H, had quit his job after being diagnosed as HIV positive. Earlier the paper had won permission in the High Court to name the authority, but not the healthcare worker.

Lord Phillips, Master of the Rolls, said there was a public interest in preserving the confidentiality of health care workers who might otherwise be discouraged from reporting they were HIV positive. He said the *Mail on Sunday* believed H's patients were entitled to know they had been treated by someone who was HIV positive. But he said that if the authority was identified, it would inevitably lead to the disclosure of H's identity, because only his patients would be offered HIV tests and counselling. The paper was allowed to state that the healthcare worker was a dentist.

In the case in 2002 in which the supermodel Naomi Campbell sued Mirror Group Newspapers for a story about her therapy for drug addiction, there was no dispute that this information had the 'quality of confidence'. When her case reached the Lords in 2004, the court declared that in any claim based on the publication of private information, the initial question is whether the information is sufficiently private in nature to engage the article 8 right. This is determined by asking whether the person suing had a reasonable expectation of privacy. For example, a person could have a reasonable expectation of privacy in relation to the information conveyed by a photograph taken in a public place if the photograph captured a private activity. Thus the picture published by the *Daily Mirror* of Ms Campbell emerging from a therapy session was 'confidential' even though it was taken in a public street.

Obligation of confidence

In spite of Lord Justice Sedley's comment in the *Douglas* case, reported above, that the law no longer needs to construct an artificial relationship of confidentiality between intruder and victim, judges hearing cases involving privacy continued to consider whether an 'obligation of confidence' existed.

Where the relationship is a contractual one the courts will hold the confidante to a very high standard of confidence. Naomi Campbell, whose case against the *Daily Mirror* has been referred to, also won a summary judgment against her former personal assistant, who had given information to the *News of the World* for their story 'Fiery model attacks aide over secret love scenes with heart throb Joseph Fiennes'. (The judgment was overturned on appeal, partly on public interest grounds.)

Similarly, it is easy to find or infer a relationship of confidence with one's medical advisers, or fellow participants in therapy (as in Naomi Campbell's case against the *Mirror*). But it is unlikely that a relationship with a prostitute, as in the *Theakston* case, or other transient sexual partner (the *Flitcroft* case) will be viewed as confidential in nature.

Suppose the information is obtained by covert means, for example by bugging or long-lens photography? In that case, leading media lawyer Patrick Moloney QC stated in a lecture in 2002, the confidential relationship 'stretches to vanishing point . . . the unethical conduct imposes a duty, but in no real sense any relationship.'

In the *Douglas* case the wedding pictures were taken by an uninvited freelance photographer. In the *Campbell* case, photographs of the model leaving a Narcotics Anonymous therapy session were also taken surreptitiously.

Public interest

As stated in chapter 23 (see 'Disclosure in the public interest'), even before the 1998 Act was implemented journalists could plead that the disclosure of confidential information would be in the public interest. Judges are ready to accept the media case that the celebrity of the claimant can generate a public interest in his private conduct that would otherwise be protected.

The 'role model' status for young people of a disc jockey or a footballer was a real factor against the continuation of injunctions in the *Theakston* and *Flitcroft* cases. In the *Theakston* case the judge drew a distinction between the public interest in the fact of the relationship, which could be published, and in salacious details which would still be restrained.

In the case involving Naomi Campbell, publication of some of the information was held to be in the public interest, and some not. There were five distinct 'elements' of private information:

(1) the fact of Ms Campbell's drug addiction;

(2) the fact that she was receiving treatment for that addiction;

(3) the fact that she was receiving treatment at Narcotics Anonymous (NA);

(4) details of the NA treatment and her reaction to it; and

(5) surreptitiously obtained photographs of her emerging from an NA treatment session.

Because the model had publicly denied using drugs previously, the first and second facts could be published in the public interest. But the rest could not, because of the intrusiveness of the disclosure and the likelihood that disclosure would interfere with or disrupt her treatment. Three of the judges—the majority—held that article 10 considerations could not justify publication of the information.

Two of the judges considered that the third, fourth and fifth categories added little of significance to the disclosure of the first and second and that journalists should be given greater latitude—but as these two were in the minority their views did not prevail. The difference of opinion between the judges illustrates the difficult decisions that have to be taken by journalists when running such stories.

Data Protection Acts

The Naomi Campbell case alerted the media to the full implications for the law of privacy of the Data Protection Act (DPA)1998. She sued the *Daily Mirror* for both breach of confidence and infringement of the DPA (see next chapter).

A journalist collecting personal information intending to put it into a database or extracting information from a database could lay himself open to a claim for compensation if the person concerned suffers damage as a result of the unauthorised disclosure of that information.

Antony White QC, the lawyer who represented the model, pointed out the advantages, for a claimant, of suing under the DPA rather than for breach of confidence.

There is no general public domain defence under the Act.

If publication has taken place there is no blanket public interest protection for the media.

The requirements of the first data protection principle are stringent and in most privacy cases are unlikely to be satisfied.

There is an entitlement to compensation for distress even if no identifiable damage has been caused.

Under the Criminal Justice and Public Order Act 1994, the journalist is guilty of a criminal offence if he knowingly procures a disclosure of the data or if he sells or offers to sell the data (see next chapter).

Trespass

Trespass is a direct injury to land, to goods, or to the person. At first sight it would appear to impose significant restrictions on journalists' conduct, but the impression is largely illusory.

Trespass to land

This is a wrongful interference with the possession of 'land', which includes a building such as a house. Wrongful interference includes going there without consent.

It is a tort—a civil wrong—and the occupier of the land can sue for damages or get an injunction to stop it. No one else can.

In a case where a reporter and journalist from the *Sunday Sport* intruded into a hospital room where the TV actor Gorden Kaye was lying semi-conscious, and 'interviewed' and photographed him, Kaye could not sue for trespass because, as a hospital patient, he was not legally the occupier of the land; the hospital authority was.

The person who sues must show unauthorised physical entry upon the land. In 1977 Lord Bernstein, chairman of Granada Television, failed to get damages from a firm of aerial photographers who, he said, had trespassed in the airspace above his property and invaded his right to privacy by taking photographs of his house. The court found that, as the aeroplane had flown hundreds of feet above Lord Bernstein's property, no trespass was committed. This does not mean that any intrusion by low-flying aeroplanes would be justifiable.

As a result of this need for the occupier of the land to show unauthorised entry, a journalist cannot be sued for trespass for using binoculars to watch another person on his own land, or photographing that person on his own land, provided the journalist did not enter the land—although he might be sued if he were on a highway that technically formed a part of that person's property.

Note that a journalist's entry is unauthorised if he has obtained permission to enter by fraud—for example, by pretending to be a doctor. And even if his entry is legal, he may be trespassing if he takes advantage of his admission to do things, such as carrying out a search of the property, not covered by his permission to enter.

Suppose he accompanies police, at their invitation, on a raid. The Ofcom code requires him to make himself known 'as soon as practically possible' to the person responsible for the premises. If he does not do so, he may be trespassing.

Even if damages are awarded, they are not likely to be substantial. After all, how much actual damage to land is done, for example, by fixing a microphone to a bed?

But if the trespass has taken some particularly outrageous form the court may award heavy damages, known as exemplary or punitive damages. It may be that a journalist who forced his way into a house to get a story would be liable to pay substantial damages, even though he had done little or no damage to the house.

In addition to seeking damages, the occupier of the land can use reasonable force to eject the trespasser. The police may lawfully assist, though they have no duty to do so and when doing so are not protected by the special powers and privileges of constables.

So there is a civil action for trespass but there is no general criminal offence. After an intruder was found in the Queen's bedroom in Buckingham Palace in 1982, consideration was given to the creation of an offence of trespassing on residential property in a manner likely to cause the occupier alarm and distress, but no such law has been passed.

It is convenient to mention here provisions relating to trespass in the Criminal Justice and Public Order Act 1994, though these provisions are related to public order rather than privacy.

The Act created an offence of aggravated trespass, but this involves trespassing on land in the open air and doing anything intended to intimidate, obstruct, or disrupt some lawful activity. The law is aimed primarily at hunt saboteurs and those protesting about road developments. It carries a penalty of up to three months' imprisonment.

What is the position of the journalist covering this type of activity? A senior police officer can direct anyone to leave if he reasonably believes the person is committing, has committed, or intends to commit an offence. Failure to leave can be punished by imprisonment or a fine or both. The journalist may have a defence that he had a reasonable excuse.

The Act gives the police powers to deal with raves and with trespassory assemblies. They can direct those organising or attending to leave and they can stop and redirect any one on the way to such an event. Failure to comply with such a direction can lead to a fine.

Trespass to goods

If a journalist visiting a contact picks up and reads a letter on the contact's desk, while the latter has been called out of the room, the journalist commits a trespass to the goods and is liable. Only the person in possession of the letter can bring an action for trespass—even if someone else is injured by the information disclosed. (The injured person may have a claim for breach of confidence.)

The journalist cannot be sued for trespass for reading the letter while it is lying on the desk. If, however, he takes the letter away and intends permanently to deprive the owner of it, he risks the more serious tort of conversion or even the criminal offence of theft.

Trespass to the person This involves actual physical interference with a person, or threats of it. Such action, however, would probably lead to a criminal prosecution for assault rather than a civil action.

Harassment

In 1996 Diana, Princess of Wales, obtained an injunction against a freelance photographer whom she accused of persistent harassment. She was relying on the precedent of a case in the Court of Appeal in the previous year, when a man was consistently pestering a woman and the court stated that it would restrain conduct which might not be unlawful if it was necessary to protect 'legitimate interests'.

Until recently it was doubted that the English law recognised a tort (civil wrong) of harassment, but in the 1995 case referred to Sir Thomas Bingham, Master of the Rolls (later Lord Bingham), said: '. . . in the light of later authority . . . the view [cannot] be upheld that there is no tort of harassment.'

Under the Protection from Harassment Act 1997 harassers can be arrested and imprisoned. The Act declares that a person must not pursue 'a course of conduct' that amounts to harassment of another and which he knows or ought to know amounts to harassment. The Act does not define harassment, but says it includes 'alarming the person or causing the person distress'.

The Act introduced two new criminal offences and a civil measure. A high level offence, not expected to affect the work of journalists, is intended to catch the most serious cases of harassment, where, on more than one occasion, the conduct is so threatening that victims fear for their safety. This carries a maximum penalty of five years in prison, or an unlimited fine, or both.

A lower level offence catches harassment which may not cause the victim to fear that violence will be used. The action has to have occurred at least twice. This carries a maximum penalty of six months in prison, or a £5,000 fine, or both.

For these offences to have been committed, there does not have to be an intention on the part of the harasser to cause the victim to fear violence or feel harassed. The prosecution has to prove only that the conduct occurred in circumstances where a reasonable person would have realised that this would be the effect.

Both offences are immediately arrestable, without a warrant, and the police are able to search the harasser's property.

The courts also have the power to make a restraining order immediately after convicting a person of either of the two offences. A breach of this order is a criminal offence with a maximum penalty of five years in prison, or an unlimited fine, or both.

There is also a civil remedy. Victims are able to take action if they are subjected to the conduct described in the low level offence, and in 2001 the Court of Appeal upheld the ruling of a county court judge that subjects of media reports that cause 'alarm or distress' can sue for damages under the Act.

A civilian clerk for the City of London police, Esther Thomas, wanted to sue the *Sun* for articles that reported a complaint by her against the behaviour of four police officers and the following week a selection of readers' letters attacking her. These were followed by another article seeking readers' contributions to a fine imposed on one of the officers.

The publication of one article would not amount to a 'course of conduct', but Ms Thomas's lawyers argued that the publication of two or more did.

The Court of Appeal gave her the go-ahead to sue the paper. Lord Phillips, Master of the Rolls, said it could be argued that publication of the Sun articles would lead some readers to send hostile mail to the clerk, causing her distress. After the appeal judges' ruling, Ms Thomas was reported to be seeking up to £50,000 damages.

Someone who believes himself to be harassed can also attempt to stop the conduct by obtaining an injunction. For example, a journalist might be banned from telephoning the 'victim'. A breach of the injunction would be a criminal offence, carrying the power of arrest, with a maximum penalty of five years in prison, or an unlimited fine, or both.

The Home Secretary said the law would not prevent people going about their lawful activity, and the legitimate work of the police, the security service, journalists, and others would be protected. He was referring to provisions which say that the course of conduct will not amount to an offence if 'in the particular circumstances' it is reasonable or if it is pursued 'for the purpose of preventing or detecting crime'.

But journalists fear that the legislation may be exploited by those who want to gag the press or stop an investigation by a particular journalist. The media can effectively be restrained by police powers of arrest and by applications for injunctions by those who believe they might be subject to media harassment, even if no prosecution is brought, and even if the journalist can successfully defend his conduct as reasonable in particular circumstances.

There have been complaints that journalists in pursuit of a story have harassed people reluctant to be interviewed by massing on the pavement outside their homes. An Act of 1875 makes it a criminal offence, among other things, to besiege people's homes or workplaces with a view to forcing them to do something against their will. But there is no record of this Act being used against journalists.

The police normally move the press aside to allow people to pass, using powers under the Highways Act 1980 to prevent 'wilful' obstruction of the free passage along a highway. These powers include arrest.

Photographers are sometimes arrested and charged under the Public Order Act 1986, which makes it an offence to use 'threatening, abusive, or insulting words or behaviour' or disorderly behaviour '. . . within the hearing or sight of a person likely to be caused harassment, alarm or distress'

Problems generally occur when photographers are covering demonstrations or marches and the police believe their presence is likely to cause a breach of the peace because they may be attacked by demonstrators.

The Criminal Justice and Public Order Act 1994 created a new offence of intentional harassment; that is, using threatening, abusive, or insulting behaviour, intending to cause a person harassment, alarm, or distress. There is a defence that the accused's conduct was reasonable.

Defamation

Reporters and photographers embarking on conduct that might be considered intrusive must be careful to ensure that the resulting story or picture does not convey a meaning defamatory of the person concerned (see chapters 18–20).

The divorced Duchess of Bedford received substantial damages from the *Daily Mail*, which reported falsely that she had been to a marriage bureau. The defamatory 'implication' was that she was lacking in friends and social resources.

A Colonel Allan, of the Royal Military Academy, accepted an apology and his legal costs in settlement of an action against the *Observer* magazine and Express Newspapers for an advertisement for paint headlined 'Put a guard around your home'. A photograph showed Colonel Allan in full regimental dress and seated on a horse. The imputation was that he had behaved in an ungentlemanly way by allowing his picture to be used for advertising.

But in the absence of any defamatory meaning, the law of libel cannot help to protect privacy.

Criminal libel

A journalist might be prosecuted for criminal libel if his revelations were so damning about an individual that, nominally, a breach of the peace might occur (see chapter 21).

But this remedy is available only if the story is defamatory and the journalist cannot show it is true and in the public interest.

Malicious falsehood

In a case concerning the television actor Gorden Kaye (above), the *Sunday Sport* planned to say in an article that Kaye had agreed to be interviewed and photographed.

The Court of Appeal decided the article would amount to a malicious falsehood (see chapter 21) and made an order that until the matter came for trial the *Sport* should not publish anything that could convey to a reader that Kaye had voluntarily permitted the taking of photographs.

But the remedy is of very limited value in respect of privacy. In this case the court was appalled by the conduct of *Sunday Sport*'s journalists and appeared to go to extraordinary lengths in an attempt to help Kaye.

Copyright

If the journalist is using copyright letters, other documents, or photographs snatched from a family album he must be alert to the possibility of an action for infringement of copyright (see chapter 29).

Passing off

Passing off means selling one's goods or services so that they appear to be those of another business. In 2002 a well-known racing driver established that the unauthorised use of his picture in an advertisement for a radio station amounted to passing-off, implying that he had given the station a celebrity endorsement (*Irvine v Talksport* [2002] EWHC 367 (Ch), [2002] EMLR 679).

Court reporting restrictions

This book has explained the restrictions under which journalists work when reporting court proceedings, and the protection given to juveniles and the victims of sexual assaults, among others (see in particular chapters 5, 6, 8, and 9).

Contravention of these restrictions normally leads to prosecution before a criminal court.

However, the person who believes he or she has been injured by such a contravention may be able to sue. In 1994 a rape victim won £10,000 damages from a local freesheet that gave sufficient details about her to enable her to be identified. In so doing, the paper was liable for the tort of breach of statutory duty.

Wireless Telegraphy Act 1949

The Act prohibits the use without authority of wireless apparatus with intent to obtain information about the contents of any message, and prohibits the disclosure of any such information. The Act has been used against journalists listening in systematically to police radio messages. It is probably ineffective against journalists casually scanning the airwaves.

Regulation of Investigatory Powers ('RIP') Act 2000

The Act prohibits intentional and unlawful interception of communications by post or phone or other telecommunication systems. It supersedes the Interception of Communications Act 1985 but, unlike the 1985 Act, it applies to private systems as well as public systems. The gaps in the previous law were illustrated when a journalist tapped the phone of the actress Antonia de Sancha to record telephone conversations between her and David Mellor, a government minister. The journalist used a telephone extension leading from de Sancha's flat to the garden. The 1985 Act did not apply because no tap was put on the line between the private property and the operator and in any case the tap was 'authorised' because de Sancha's landlord had given the journalist permission. The RIP Act says that the sender or recipient of an intercepted message can sue, even if the person having the right to control the use of a private system gives permission, if such interception is 'without lawful authority'.

Journalists frequently record telephone calls. Under the 2000 Act, interception occurs in the course of transmission, so recording telephone conversations by a device at either end of the communication is not interception and is lawful.

What the codes say on privacy

The final part of this chapter lists the main topics covered by the privacy codes. As explained in chapter 31 ('The Codes'), from 2003 the Office of Communications (Ofcom) has had responsibility for regulating all the UK communications industries, apart from the print media, and as this edition of *McNae* was going to press was preparing its own programme code. Meanwhile, it was continuing to enforce the codes set up earlier by the 'legacy bodies', the ITC, the BSC and the Radio Authority. For that reason, the requirements of these bodies on privacy issues are given below, in addition to those of the Editors' Code of Practice Committee (the PCC code) and the BBC, which has its own routine.

This passage summarises the sometimes lengthy guidance given. It is not comprehensive, and each statement may not accurately represent the guidance given by *every* code. The full wording of the PCC code can be found in chapter 31.

In the following account, advice specifically for broadcasters that is not otherwise attributed is from the Broadcasting Standards Commission (BSC) code. The Broadcasting Act 1996 gave the BSC the duty to draw up a code giving guidance to broadcasters on, among other things, the avoidance of unwarranted infringement of privacy in television or radio programmes and each broadcasting or regulatory body had the duty to reflect that code.

The public interest

All the codes agree that everyone is entitled to his or her privacy. The PCC code says that intrusions into privacy can be justified only in the public interest, and gives a non-exhaustive list of what constitutes the public interest. To this list the BSC code adds 'disclosing significant incompetence in public office'.

In cases involving children, editors must demonstrate an exceptional public interest to override the normally paramount interests of the child. The revised ITC code, issued in 2001, echoes European Court of Human Rights language in stating:

> Any act that relies on a defence of public interest must be proportional to the actual interest served. This will be a balancing exercise which will depend on the individual circumstances of each case. Where, for example, there is a significant intrusion into an individual's private affairs, particularly where that individual is innocent of any offence and/or where there is a significant risk of distress, an important public interest is likely to be required.

Public figures

The codes agree that people in the public eye, either through the position they hold or the publicity they attract, are in a special position, but not all matters that interest the public are in the public interest. Even when personal matters relating to people in the public eye become the proper subject of inquiry, their immediate family or friends do not forfeit their rights to privacy and even the public figure may not forfeit all his rights.

BBC producers are told that news programmes should not report the private 'legal behaviour' (which presumably means lawful behaviour) of public figures unless broader public issues are raised either by the behaviour itself or by the consequences of its becoming widely known. The mere fact that private behaviour is 'in the public domain' (that is, that someone else has reported it), is not in itself sufficient to justify the BBC reporting it too.

The BSC says the location of a person's home or family should not normally be revealed unless strictly relevant to the behaviour under investigation.

Ordinary people in the news

The BSC code says that for much of the time the private lives of most people are of no legitimate public interest. It is important that when, for a short time, people are caught up, however involuntarily, in events which have a place in the news, their situation is not abused or exploited either at the time or in later programmes which revisit those events.

Obtaining material

The BSC code says privacy can be infringed during the obtaining of material for a programme, even if none of it is broadcast, as well as in the way in which material is used within the programme.

Filming events in public places

When broadcasters are covering events in public places, they should ensure that the words spoken or images shown are sufficiently in the public domain to justify their broadcast without the express consent of the individuals concerned. This applies particularly to material from closed-circuit television cameras of which the individual is unlikely to have been aware.

Surreptitious listening and recording devices

The PCC code says journalists must not obtain or publish material obtained by using clandestine listening devices, but this item is marked with an asterisk to indicate there may be exceptions to the rule where the procedure can be demonstrated to be in the public interest.

The BSC code says the use of secret recording should be considered only where it is necessary to the credibility and authenticity of the story. Recording secretly in public places should take place only when the words or images recorded will serve an overriding public interest.

An unattended recording device (a bug) should not be left on private property without the full and informed consent of the occupiers or their agent unless seeking permission might frustrate the investigation by the programme-makers of matters of an overriding public interest. The BBC says this should be done only 'for the purpose of gaining evidence of serious crime'.

The BBC says also that hidden cameras or microphones may be used on private property, in the absence of permission from the owner, occupier or agent, only where prima facie evidence exists of crime or of significant anti-social behaviour by those to be recorded.

The BSC code says that when secret recording is undertaken as part of an entertainment programme, the subjects of a recorded deception should be asked to give their consent before the material is broadcast. If they become aware of the recording and ask for it to stop, their wishes should be respected. In a live broadcast, especial care should be taken to avoid offence to the individuals concerned.

The ITC says that the use of hidden microphones and cameras for the filming or recording of individuals who are unaware of it is acceptable only when it is clear that the material so acquired is essential to establish the credibility and authority of a story where this cannot or is unlikely to be achieved using 'open' filming or recording techniques, and where the story itself is equally clearly of important public interest.

The BBC says that sometimes it is necessary for the safety of staff or for the style or content of the programme that journalists record surreptitiously in public places. Consent must be obtained in advance from a senior BBC executive.

Long lens photography

The PCC code used to say that use of long lens photography to take pictures of people in private places without their consent was unacceptable, except where justifiable in the public interest. The revised code in 2004 widened this requirement to say 'It is unacceptable to photograph individuals in private places without their consent'—that is, with or without the use of long lens photography.

The code defines 'private places' as public or private property where there is a reasonable expectation of privacy.

Conduct in institutions

Particular care must be taken when gathering news or filming in hospitals and similar institutions. The PCC says that journalists or photographers making inquiries at such places should identify themselves to a responsible executive and obtain permission before entering non-public areas.

The BSC says that when permission has been given to film or record in an institution, broadcasters are under no obligation to seek the consent of individual employees or others whose appearance is incidental or where they are essentially anonymous members of the general public. However, in clearly sensitive situations in places such as hospitals or prisons or police stations (the ITC gives the example of psychiatric or intensive care patients), individual consent should normally be obtained unless the individual's identity has been concealed.

Protecting the innocent

The BBC says that when broadcasters record surreptitiously for the purpose of exposing anti-social or criminal activity, whether in public or on private property, they must take care to protect the reputations of innocent people who may be caught inadvertently in the recording. Broadcasters should obscure their identities or make their innocence clear if there is any likelihood of confusion.

The PCC says the press must avoid identifying relatives or friends of persons convicted or accused of crime without their consent.

'Fishing expeditions'

BBC journalists and programme makers are told they must not go on 'fishing expeditions'—that is, they must not record secretly on private property in search of crime or anti-social behaviour by identifiable individuals if there is no prima facie evidence against them. This also applies when secret recording takes place on public property but is directed towards subjects who are on private property.

There may, however, be a legitimate case for the use of surreptitious recording in a narrow range of cases (including consumer research items and social research items) where there is no prima facie evidence of wrongdoing by the people concerned. (But note the Court of Appeal decision after the BBC filmed in a Dixons store; 'Some queries on privacy', above.)

Open recording when the subject is on private property

The PCC says journalists and photographers must not photograph individuals in private places (as defined above, 'Long lens photography') without their consent (subject to the public interest proviso).

The BBC says it is permissible to use cameras or recording devices openly on both public and private property when the subject is on private property, but such filming or recording must be appropriate to the importance or nature of the story. The broadcaster should not intrude unnecessarily on private behaviour.

The BBC says if the subject asks the journalist to stop he should do so, unless he is seeking to illustrate anti-social behaviour or expose people he has evidence to show are guilty of it.

Closed-circuit TV (CCTV)

Broadcasters using material recorded by closed-circuit TV (CCTV) cameras should take care (as with individuals in institutions) to ensure identifiable individuals are treated fairly.

Set-up situations

The ITC says unwarranted invasions of privacy must be avoided in 'set-up situations' where members of the public or celebrities are featured without their knowledge or without prior warning.

Where material is recorded, the consent of the subjects should be obtained before transmission. If the programme is live, particular care should be taken to avoid offence to the individuals concerned. Requests to leave private property or stop filming should be complied with promptly.

A different kind of set-up situation is one where the subject consents to being recorded for a different purpose from that secretly intended by the programme makers.

The use of such material without the subject's permission can be justified only if it is necessary in order to make an important point of public interest. The programme maker must get consent from the most senior executive.

A slightly lower test applies to celebrities and those in the public eye.

Interviews without prior arrangement

The ITC says interviews sought on private property without the subject's prior agreement should not be included in a programme unless they have a public interest purpose. The same consideration applies to restaurants, churches, and other places where the subject would reasonably expect personal privacy. Interviews in which criminal or other serious allegations are put to individuals should not be attempted without prior warning unless a previous request has been refused or received no response, or where there is good reason for not making a prior approach.

Particular care needs to be taken where the person approached is not the subject of the allegations—for example a relative, friend, or associate, to avoid the risk of unwarranted invasion of his privacy.

Recorded telephone calls

The PCC says that journalists must not obtain or publish material got by intercepting private telephone conversations, but this item, like the one on secret recording devices, is marked with an asterisk to indicate there may be exceptions to the rule where they can be demonstrated to be in the public interest.

The BSC code says a broadcaster wishing to broadcast a recording of a telephone call between him and an interviewee should normally identify himself to the other person from the outset, or get agreement from him.

Suppose a factual programme-maker takes someone by surprise by recording a call for broadcast purposes without any prior warning. Such approaches should take place only where there is reason to believe that there is an overriding public interest and the subject has refused to respond to reasonable requests for interview, or has a history of such refusal, or there is good reason to believe that the investigation will be frustrated if the subject is approached openly.

The BSC code says other recordings of telephone conversations for broadcast purposes made with the agreement of one of the parties but without the knowledge of the other party are to be assessed by the criteria which apply to secret recording on private property (see above).

The ITC's revised code, issued in 2001, says the requirements that apply to the secret recording of telephone conversations where these are intended for transmission are the same as those for 'surreptitious listening and recording devices' (see above). Permission must be sought from senior programme executives for the secret recording of phone calls and for the use of the recording in a programme.

Harassment

The PCC code says that, subject to the public interest proviso, journalists and photographers must neither obtain nor seek to obtain information or pictures through intimidation, harassment or persistent pursuit. They must not persist in telephoning, questioning, pursuing or photographing individuals after having been asked to desist; must not remain on their property after having been asked to leave and must not follow them.

The BSC says care must also be taken not to make it easy to locate or identify the refuser's address unless it is strictly relevant to the behaviour under investigation and there is an overriding public interest.

Doorstepping

The BSC says people who are currently in the news cannot reasonably object to being questioned and recorded by the media when in public places. If the approach is made by telephone, the broadcaster should make clear who is calling and for what purpose. Nevertheless, even those who are in the news have the right to make no comment or to refuse to appear in a broadcast.

Outside the daily news context, different considerations apply. Surprise can be a legitimate device to elicit the truth especially when dealing with matters where there is an overriding public interest in investigation and disclosure. Doorstepping in these circumstances may be legitimate where there has been repeated refusal to grant an interview (or a history of such refusals) or the risk exists that a person might disappear.

Intrusion into grief or shock

The PCC says that in cases involving personal grief or shock, inquiries should be carried out and approaches made with sympathy and discretion. Publication must be handled sensitively at such times—though this should not be interpreted as restricting the right to report judicial proceedings.

The BSC says that broadcasters should not add to the distress of people caught up in emergencies or suffering a personal tragedy. People in a state of distress must not be put under any pressure to provide interviews. The mere fact that grieving people have been named or suggested for interview by the police or other authorities does not justify the use of material which infringes their privacy or is distressing. Such use is justified only if an overriding public interest is served. Broadcasters should take care not to reveal the identity of a person who has died, or victims of accidents or violent crimes unless and until it is clear that the next of kin have been informed.

BSC says programme-makers should also be sensitive to the possibility of causing additional anxiety or distress when filming or recording people who are already extremely upset or under stress, for example at funerals or in hospitals. Normally, prior consent should be obtained from the family or their agents.

'Media scrums'

When a person suddenly features in a news event large numbers of media people may gather in the street outside—the 'media scrum'. In such cases, the BBC says, it is important that the combined effect of legitimate newsgathering by a number of organisations does not become intimidating or unreasonably intrusive. It may be possible for pooling arrangements to be reached, reducing the number of media present. BBC teams on the spot who are asked by the subject to leave should refer for guidance to editors who will reach a decision bearing in mind whether the subject is a private citizen or a public figure, whether he is victim, villain, or merely interested party, and whether he has expressed a clear intention or wish not to appear or give interviews.

Revisiting past events

The BSC says programmes intended to examine past events involving trauma to individuals, including crime, should try to minimise the potential distress to surviving victims or surviving relatives in retelling the story. So far as is reasonably practicable, surviving

victims or the immediate families of those whose experience is to feature in the programme should be informed of the programme's plans and its intended transmission, even
if the events or material to be broadcast have been in the public domain in the past.

Children

Print journalists should refer to the PCC's comprehensive guidance on avoiding intrusion
into the privacy of children and the reporting of children involved in sex cases
(chapter 31).

The BSC says children's vulnerability must be a prime concern for broadcasters. They
do not lose their rights to privacy because of the fame or notoriety of their parents or
because of events in their schools. Care should be taken that a child's gullibility or trust is
not abused. They should not be questioned about private family matters or asked for views
on matters likely to be beyond their capacity to answer properly. Consent from parents or
those in loco parentis should normally be obtained before interviewing children under 16
on matters of significance. Where consent has not been obtained or actually refused, any
decision to go ahead can be justified only if the item is of overriding public interest and the
child's appearance is absolutely necessary.

Similarly, children under 16 involved in police inquiries or court proceedings relating to
sexual offences should not be identified or identifiable in news or other programmes. The
ITC code's advice on how to avoid the identification of children who have been the victims
of sexual abuse within the family is given in chapter 6, 'Jigsaw identification'.

Filming on police operations

The ITC says that when permission is given to film police or similar official operations of
any kind involving members of the public in other than public places—for example, visits
to homes under warrant or raids on licensed premises—the journalist must make his
position known to the members of the public involved and identify the organisation for
whom he or she is working as soon as practically possible. If asked to leave, he should
'normally' comply.

Data Protection
Act 1998

Even before the passage of the Human Rights Act (chapter 30) the law in effect recognised rights of privacy for the vast amount of information held about people on computer and in some manual records.

These rights were provided for information on computer by the Data Protection Act 1984. The Data Protection Act 1998 strengthened those rights and extended them to information about people contained in 'structured manual files'. (In this chapter 'the Act' or 'the DPA' means the 1998 Act.)

The Act requires that the processing of personal data must be in accordance with the Act and the definition of data (see below) is so wide that it comprehensively describes the normal operations of any newspaper or media produced with the aid of integrated computerised systems.

A leading lawyer explained: 'Whenever a journalist obtains information which is to be put into a database the principles apply . . . Whenever a newspaper extracts information from its database and publishes it, that is disclosure' (Michael Tugendhat QC in 'The Data Protection Act 1998 and the Media', *OUP Yearbook of Copyright and Media Law* (2000)).

The Act aims to ensure that people handling personal data comply with eight data protection principles. In brief, data must be

- fairly and lawfully processed
- processed for limited purposes
- adequate, relevant, and not excessive
- accurate
- not kept longer than necessary
- processed in accordance with the data subject's rights

- secure

- not transferred to countries without adequate protection.

The Act affects journalists in two ways. Firstly, they may find it difficult to obtain information from authorities that are prevented from releasing such information, or believe themselves to be so prevented, or use the Act as an excuse for refusing to give information they do not wish to give. In 2004 David Blunkett, then Home Secretary, promised the Newspaper Society, representing the local and regional newspapers, that he would listen to the media's concerns over data protection, after editors in a survey stressed the frequency with which public services tried to block inquiries and obstruct reporting by claiming—rightly or wrongly—that they could not give the information sought because of data protection restrictions.

Elizabeth France, Data Protection Commissioner (later Information Commissioner), said in her annual report in 2000 that 16 years after the original Act there still remained data controllers (for a definition of this term, see below) who misrepresented the nature of data protection law. They 'grasp the Act and wave it as though it were some hybrid garlic which might ward off information hungry vampires'. She continued:

> Nowhere does the Act place blanket bars on the disclosure of information. The right to
> private life, which it seeks to provide the powers to protect, is not dependent wholly, or
> even mainly, on withholding information.

Four years later, Ms France's successor as Information Commissioner, Richard Thomas, told the Society of Editors the data protection law was being used improperly in 'many, many cases' where people found it difficult to respond to a legitimate request. He referred to a case where the organisers of a women's institute jam-making competition had not allowed the results to be published 'because of data protection'. Mr Thomas said: 'I am very intolerant of this sort of thing and am taking a very strong line on a commonsense approach to data protection.'

The second way the Act affects journalists is that, as people processing data themselves, they may have problems complying with the privacy rights of those about whom they hold information. In 2002 the supermodel Naomi Campbell was awarded £3,500 damages for breach of confidence and infringement of data protection rights over the Daily Mirror's publication of details about her therapy at Narcotics Anonymous (NA). (The finding was first overturned by the Court of Appeal, then, in 2004, upheld by the House of Lords (*Campbell v Mirror Group Newspapers Ltd* [2004] UKHL 22)).

The Act came into effect on 1 March 2000, but data already held in a manual filing system need not comply with many aspects of the new law until 2007.

The Act makes considerable use of its own jargon.

For journalists, the definition of 'data' in section 1(1) of the Act is particularly important.

Data means information that (among other things):

- is being processed by means of equipment operating automatically in response to instructions given for that purpose,
- is recorded with the intention that it should be processed by means of such equipment.

In the Naomi Campbell case, the 'data' were held to include photographs of the model leaving an NA meeting.

Personal data means information which relates to a living individual who can be identified from those data and which are either processed electronically or, if manual, are held in 'a relevant filing system'. In 2003, the Court of Appeal held that incidental references to a person involved in a matter or an event 'that has no personal connotations' is not 'personal information' under the Act (*Durant v Financial Services Authority* [2003] EWCA Civ 1746). Following that decision, the Information Commissioner issued revised guidelines on what 'personal data' means (available at www.informationcommissioner.gov.uk under 'Data Protection').

Processing means:

- 'obtaining, recording or holding the information or data or carrying out any operation or set of operations on the information or data, including:
  - organisation, adaptation or alteration of the information or data,
  - retrieval, consultation or use of the information or data,
  - disclosure of the information or data by transmission, dissemination or otherwise making available, or
  - alignment, combination, blocking, erasure or destruction of the information or data.'

A *relevant filing system* has a lengthy and complicated definition. The minister introducing the bill into Parliament said it would apply to highly structured systems such as card indexes, but would exclude collections of paper which only incidentally contained information about individuals. The Court of Appeal in the *Durant* case took the same view.

A *data controller* determines the purposes for which and the manner in which any personal data are processed. Data controllers include magistrates courts, the police, and local authorities, and also all newspapers that keep personal data about people on computer or in structured filing systems.

A *data subject* is a person about whom the information is held—in media terms, the person about whom the reporter is writing his story or any third parties who may be referred to or identified in the report.

Under the Act, data are processed for *special purposes* when they are processed for journalistic, literary, or artistic purposes.

The data protection principles

The principles, summarised above, are contained in Schedule 1 to the Act and are, in full:

(1) Personal data shall be processed fairly and lawfully and, in particular, shall not be processed unless certain conditions are met (see 'Fairly and lawfully', below).

(2) Personal data shall be obtained only for one or more specified and lawful purposes, and shall not be further processed in any manner incompatible with that purpose or those purposes.

(3) Personal data shall be adequate, relevant, and not excessive in relation to the purpose or purposes for which they are processed.

(4) Personal data shall be accurate and, where necessary, kept up to date.

(5) Personal data processed for any purpose or purposes shall not be kept for longer than is necessary for that purpose or those purposes.

(6) Personal data shall be processed in accordance with the rights of data subjects under this Act.

(7) Appropriate technical and organisational measures shall be taken against unauthorised or unlawful processing of personal data and against accidental loss or destruction of, or damage to, personal data.

(8) Personal data shall not be transferred to a country or territory outside the European Economic Area unless that country or territory ensures an adequate level of protection for the rights and freedoms of data subjects in relation to the processing of personal data.

'Fairly and lawfully'

As stated, personal data shall be processed fairly and lawfully. In particular, it must not be processed at all unless at least one of a number of conditions set out in the Act in Schedule 2 is met. For the purposes of a journalist attempting to obtain information to write a story the most relevant Schedule 2 conditions would seem to include (either because they apply to the journalist himself, or to the data controller from whom he hopes to obtain the information):

- Paragraph 1. The data subject has given his consent to the processing,
- Paragraph 3. The processing is necessary for compliance with any legal obligation to which the data controller is subject,
- Paragraph 5. The processing is necessary—

  (a) for the administration of justice,
  (b) for the exercise of any functions conferred on any person by or under any enactment,
  (c) for the exercise of any functions of the crown, a minister of the crown, or a government department, or
  (d) for the exercise of any other functions of a public nature exercised in the public interest by any person.

- Paragraph 6. The processing is necessary for the purposes of legitimate interests pursued by the data controller or by the third party or parties to whom the data are disclosed, except where the processing is unwarranted in any particular case by reason of prejudice to the rights and freedoms or legitimate interest of the data subject.

The Information Commissioner has stressed to the editors of *McNae* that the 'conditions' referred to in Schedule 2 and also Schedule 3 (below) are not 'exemptions'. The commissioner said:

> Once the condition for processing has been established then this merely means that the normal requirements of the fairness principle need to be met.
>
> It is conceivable that a data controller [eg a journalist] could have obtained the consent of a data subject to particular processing, where the data subject did not have a full appreciation of the likely consequences to him/her of any processing, and still process personal data in such a way that has unfair adverse consequences for that individual.

Sensitive personal data

The Act provides even stronger protection to 'sensitive personal data', which means information about:

(1) the racial or ethnic origin of the data subject

(2) his political opinions

(3) his religious beliefs or other beliefs of a similar nature

(4) whether he is a member of a trade union

(5) his physical or mental health or condition

(6) his sexual life

(7) the commission or alleged commission by him of any offence, or

(8) any proceedings for any offence committed or alleged to have been committed by him, the disposal of such proceedings or the sentence of any court in such proceedings.

The judge in the Naomi Campbell case held that the information about the nature of and details of the therapy that Miss Campbell was seeking was 'sensitive personal data' under (5).

Sensitive personal data can be processed only if *two* conditions are met, one of them from the Schedule 2 list above and the other from a list contained in Schedule 3: for example, the person gave 'explicit' consent; or he deliberately made the information public; or the use to which the information was to be put was necessary for the administration of justice.

As a result of media representations, the Government introduced a statutory instrument that extended the Schedule 3 list of conditions and included an additional 'special purposes' condition. The media had been concerned that the new law created new problems over access to information. The SI widened the grounds for any third party's lawful release of information to the media for publication by adding another 'gateway' for the lawful processing of sensitive personal data. Editors may wish to refer to this measure to resolve disputes with such organisations. It is the Data Protection (Processing of Sensitive Personal Data) Order 2000 and may be read on www.hmso.gov.uk/si/si2000/20000417.htm

The statutory instrument sets out 10 circumstances in which sensitive personal data may be processed. Several require that the processing is 'in the substantial public interest'.

For journalists the most important is contained in paragraph 3 which covers disclosures for journalistic, artistic, or literary purposes of personal data relating to:

(1) the commission by any person of any unlawful act (whether alleged or established),

(2) dishonesty, malpractice, or other seriously improper conduct by, or the unfitness or incompetence of, any person (whether alleged or established), or

(3) mismanagement in the administration of, or failures in services provided by, any body or association (whether alleged or established).

Other paragraphs include the following:

- Paragraph 1 covers certain processing for the prevention or detection of any unlawful act, where seeking the consent of the data subject to the processing would prejudice those purposes.

- Paragraph 2 is for cases where the processing is required to discharge functions which protect members of the public from certain conduct which may not constitute an unlawful act, such as incompetence or mismanagement.

- Paragraph 10 covers processing by the police in the exercise of their common law powers.

Why did this SI not provide a defence to the *Daily Mirror* against Naomi Campbell? Remember that the Schedule 2 and Schedule 3 conditions are not exemptions. Even if those conditions are met, processing must also be 'fair and lawful'. As the House of Lords reached the decision that the *Daily Mirror* coverage of Naomi Campbell's therapy for drug abuse breached her confidence, it could not be said to be 'lawful'.

The Information Commissioner points out also that the gratuitous disclosure of the identity of a victim of an unlawful act may be unfair/unlawful/unwarranted; and the disclosure of the alleged incompetence or dishonesty of someone may be unwarranted if the allegations are wild and wholly unsubstantiated.

Data protection and the Human Rights Act

Editors in conflict with public bodies proving reluctant to impart information should remind them that the Human Rights Act (HRA) 1998 requires public authorities to act in a way consistent with the European Convention on Human Rights (ECHR), which includes a guarantee of freedom of expression, including the right to receive and impart information.

'Media Guidelines' circulated by the Association of Chief Police Officers (ACPO) in

2000 remind chief constables that the HRA requires that each police officer and member of the civilian support staff, 'as a "public authority", must act in a way which is at all times consistent with the ECHR'.

The guidelines say that many of the Convention's provisions directly affect the release of information by police to the media. These provisions include article 3, which provides protection against inhuman and degrading treatment; article 6, which establishes the right to a fair trial; article 8, which concerns the right to respect for private and family life; and article 10, concerning the right to freedom of expression.

It is perhaps unfortunate that the right to freedom of expression is listed last. Editors should draw the attention of the police and other authorities to the emphasis that judges have paid to this right and to the need for the exemptions to it to be narrowly defined. In *Sunday Times v United Kingdom* (1979) 2 EHRR 245 the European Court of Human Rights said at paragraph 65: 'The court is faced not with a choice between two conflicting principles, but with a principle of freedom of expression that is subject to a number of exceptions which must be narrowly interpreted.'

The police guidelines say the principles of proportionality, legality, and necessity must all be considered in making decisions where questions of human rights are involved. (The right to freedom of expression may be restricted only where this is 'necessary in a democratic society', see chapter 30.)

Notification

The Information Commissioner keeps a public register of data controllers. The process by which their details are added to the register is called notification.

A data controller who wishes regularly to pass information to a third party, such as the press, must include this on its notification form. Part 1 of the form includes a section for 'Recipients', and the data controller simply has to enter R424, which is the standard description for the media.

A data controller handling a 'one-off' media inquiry can still do so lawfully under the provisions of section 32 of the Act, which gives a special exemption for personal data processed only for the 'special purposes'.

The fact of notification does not mean that a data user is free to release *any* information it wishes or the journalist wishes to receive. The data controller still needs to ensure that the disclosure complies with the data protection principles and the Commissioner has powers to enforce compliance (see below).

Data controllers are under a positive obligation to tell data subjects all the purposes to which they are going to put their data.

The requirement to register affects media managements principally, but freelances working from home and keeping their material on computer or in 'structured manual files' should register also because they are not holding that data simply for domestic purposes.

The comparable process under the 1984 Act was called registration. When the Act came into effect the Home Office advised all magistrates courts to register (see chapter 12), but for years newspapers were still having difficulties. In 1989 magistrates at Colchester and Southend said they were unable to release lists of defendants' names and ages and the charges because the information was now on computer.

The local newspapers had to call on the Home Secretary, the Lord Chancellor, and the local MPs before the courts agreed to comply with the Home Office advice.

The courts

Some journalists have had difficulty obtaining information from the courts. Magistrates courts use guidelines prepared by the Justices' Clerks' Society which state that a clerk could be found to have unfairly processed information in breach of the DPA if 'restricted' information were to be published. The guidelines were prepared with the assistance of the Data Protection Registrar (now Information Commissioner), who provided the following summary.

> The guidelines take into account the stage in the judicial process reached by a particular case—that is, whether it is pending, current, or completed.
>
> For current cases, disclosure of information that has been heard in open court may be appropriate. However, with regard to disclosure of information regarding completed cases, disclosure is at the discretion of the clerk because the court register is not a public document and is governed by the Magistrates' Courts Rules. However, the Department of Constitutional Affairs announced in 2004 that a register of fines in the magistrates courts, with name, date of birth and address would become available during 2005 ([see chapter 11, 'Magistrates court information').
>
> It is therefore for the clerk to determine disclosure policy. The guidance suggests that disclosure within a specific period might be appropriate but after that the clerk may wish to exercise more discretion.
>
> When exercising that discretion, it may be that if the court register is held on computer, he or she will need to consider the data protection implications of their actions.
>
> For that reason, on receipt of a request for disclosure, the clerk will need to consider:

- at what stage the proceedings are;
- whether the information requested has been given in open court; and
- whether there are any unfair implications for the individual.

The Data Protection Commissioner (later Information Commissioner) told the editors of *McNae* in 1999 that the guidelines represented her office's current thinking. She said they took into account the Home Office's guidance on disclosure of court results (see chapter 11).

The police

Journalists, even when engaged in routine reporting tasks, frequently have difficulty obtaining information from the police, who say they are prevented by the provisions of the Data Protection Act (in addition, in some cases, to the provisions of the Human Rights Act and their common-law duties to act within their powers and observe confidentiality). This view is frequently based upon a misunderstanding of the Act.

Two main problem areas are the identification of people involved in road accidents and the victims of crime.

Mrs Elizabeth France, the Data Protection Commissioner (Information Commissioner), said in her annual report in 2000 that there had been instances where data controllers, for a variety of reasons, had decided not to disclose personal information even though the Act would not restrict disclosure.

She said the media believed that guidance produced by ACPO on the issue provided sensible practical guidance on what might be disclosed to the media, but that the media believed the guidance was not being applied correctly or consistently by police forces around the country. She commented: 'This is a matter of concern to us. We do not wish to see what are often viewed as arbitrary restrictions on disclosure imposed where there is a quite proper basis in law for the disclosure to take place.'

ACPO guidelines

The revised ACPO guidelines referred to above were issued in December 2000. They say the wishes of the victim, witnesses or next of kin, where necessary, must be sought at the earliest possible stage before deciding how to publicise a crime, road collision, or any other incident, in accordance with the Data Protection Act.

The guidelines say that when victims or other people who have provided their personal details to police say that their details should not be released to the media, this should be honoured unless police feel on a case by case basis there is an exceptional reason why such details must be given. The maintenance of good relations with the media, while important, is not itself sufficient reason.

The Information Commissioner tells the editors of *McNae* that the 'exceptional reason' must be an 'exceptional policing reason' (see 'A policing purpose', below).

Except in certain circumstances (see below), victims, witnesses or next of kin are entitled not to have their personal details released without their permission. They are not, however, entitled to ask that police release no information of the incident what-soever, provided that the information the police do release does not lead to their identification.

Suppose victims, witnesses or next of kin have agreed to the release of their personal details but such a release may make them vulnerable to further crime (such as an elderly person living alone). The guidelines say a judgment may be made not to release those details. In such cases, the reasons for the decision should be explained to journalists to encourage them to follow suit should they find out the name from another source.

The Data Protection Act does not apply to dead people. Victims may therefore be named once positive identification has taken place and immediate relatives told. It may be help-ful to explain the reasons for any delay to the media to gain their support in withholding publication if they learn the identity from another source.

In certain circumstances, the guidelines say, the Data Protection Act allows for informa-tion to be released without the permission of the individual or individuals concerned. Police fully recognise that there may be some exceptional circumstances where wider policing interests might override the interests of individuals, but the decision to release information on such grounds can be made only in the light of each case.

The guidelines say that circumstances in which details might be released without the consent of the people concerned would include a major incident involving multiple vic-tims: in such an event it would be a legitimate 'policing purpose' to release casualties' identities before formal authority is obtained, to minimise public alarm and distress, and would thus satisfy the DPA.

The Information Commissioner, however, takes the view that the disclosure by the police of details where no permission has been provided must be justified by 'wider policing interests' rather than 'the wider public interest'. Thus, to justify releasing casualties' identities before formal authority is obtained, there would have to be a substantial impact on 'policing operations', for example switchboards being jammed preventing other calls getting through; or if there was some exceptional circumstance where it might be necessary to minimise widespread public alarm and distress.

The guidelines say there will be frequent occasions when media come to police seeking further details about information they have received from other sources. Even if authority has not been given, a judgment will have to be made on the course of action to take. As the person's identity is already in the public domain this will often provide an opportunity to give accurate information or to counter rumour and speculation.

Any active or imminent legal proceedings should be borne in mind when considering the release of names of those injured. For example, when victims have been injured while in a suspected stolen vehicle, their medical condition may have prevented an immediate arrest and proceedings are not, therefore, technically active.

Normally, if an early arrest is deemed likely, the identity of such a victim should be withheld until he or she is charged, even if consent has been given. When juveniles are charged their identities will not be released. If no criminal proceedings against individuals are instigated, their identities and other details could then be revealed as indicated above.

One criticism among many made by journalists is that the police, when asking victims if they object to identification, do so in a manner inviting the answer no. The guidelines, in a passage headlined 'Recommended question to victims and witnesses', say it is important when dealing with all victims, witnesses, or next of kin that police should ask a balanced question to establish consent, recorded in accordance with force procedure. In many cases they are likely to agree, as the experience in dealing with victims of crime is that they very often have no objection to their details being passed to the media.

It is recommended that the consent of victims and witnesses is sought in the first instance and, therefore, they should be asked the question 'We often find it helpful in our inquiries to pass on someone's details to the media. Do you object if we do that in your case?'

ACPO stresses that the notes are for the guidance of police forces only. It is a matter for chief constables to decide whether and how they should be implemented. ACPO recommends that police chiefs consult with local media and consider adapting the guidelines in the light of local circumstances.

If an editor is having difficulty getting information covered by the Act he should query whether the wishes of the victim have been sought, and a proper question put to him. If this has not happened, in accordance with the guidelines, then encourage the police to go back and ask for the victim's views.

If the victim has definitely declined the disclosure of his details, the editor could query whether there is any 'substantial policing interest' that would permit the over-riding of the victim's wishes. For example, do the victim's details need to be put into the public domain as an essential part of the investigation of the crime?

A 'policing purpose'

Data obtained and processed under the Act must be for a specified and lawful purpose. Under the 1984 Act this purpose was registered, in the case of the police, as being for a 'policing purpose'. The Data Protection Registrar (now Commissioner) defined this as:

> the prevention and detection of crime, apprehension and prosecution of offenders, protection of life and property, maintenance of law and order, and rendering assistance to the public in accordance with force policies and procedures.

The ACPO guidelines say that to this should be added 'reducing the fear of crime'.

The guidelines say this definition continues to be used for the guidance of forces when determining the balance between protecting a person's right to privacy and acting to achieve a 'policing purpose'.

Schools

In 2002 schools began to refuse media requests to photograph pupils, citing the Data Protection Act. Some newspapers were unable to publish their traditional photographs of first-year classes, sports teams and drama productions. During Christmas of that year, some schools banned filming or photographing of nativity plays. Fears that children would be targeted by paedophiles was behind the development, which intensified after media publicity about the murders of two schoolgirls (the Soham murders).

The then Education Secretary, Charles Clarke, later explained that some local authorities and schools had misinterpreted advice sent out by the Department for Education and Skills, given in response to inquiries from schools about using video and photographic images for their own publicity purposes, such as displaying images on websites.

Some schools wrongly used the advice to form the basis of policies relating to the publication of photographs in local newspapers, or applied it to the use of cameras and videos by parents when filming or photographing school events.

In 2003 the department sent out new advice, headed 'Photographic images and the press' and available on www.teachernet.gov.uk/wholeschool/familyandcommunity/child-protection/usefulinformation/pressphotos/

It said schools and local education authorities were free to develop and implement their own policies on arrangements with the press for local newspapers to take and publish photographs of pupils taking part in school activities and events. It said: 'We recognise that local newspapers play an important part in reporting the achievements and challenges facing local schools and their pupils, and therefore a cooperative arrangement should be beneficial.'

On the Data Protection Act, the department's advice note quotes Richard Thomas, the Information Commissioner:

- Where schools merely allow access to a local newspaper photographer, they are not caught by the DPA unless they provide the personal details of the pupils in the photographs.

- If the names of those in the photograph were collected directly from the participants (subject to the wishes of parents and guardians of pupils) the school would not be releasing personal data subject to the Act at all.

- Alternatively, if the school had canvassed the wishes of parents and guardians and they had agreed to the release then there would be no questions of the DPA preventing disclosure.

Bob Satchwell, director of the Society of Editors, picking up the commissioner's final point, recommended that papers should overcome DPA problems by suggesting to schools they should seek permission for photography at the beginning of term. 'They should tell parents that from time to time press photographers come into the school to publicise its achievements and those of the children. In other words get them to ask a positive question when seeking parents' permission.'

Rights of data 'subjects'

People have the right to find out whether an organisation, including a newspaper or broadcasting station, holds information about them and if so what it is. They must be told also the purposes for which such information is held and to whom it is or may be disclosed; and also the source of the information.

The 1984 Act had the effect of preserving the confidentiality of journalists' sources by stipulating that a data user did not have to comply with an access request if he could not do so without disclosing information relating to another individual who could be identified by that information unless the individual consented.

The 1998 Act says the access request must be complied with, even in the absence of the consent of the other individual, if it is reasonable in all the circumstances to comply without that consent. But lawyer Heather Rowe, a data protection expert, summing up the complex measure for *McNae*, said: 'To my mind the provisions all say, taken together, that you do not have to name a source unless there is something like a court order that makes you do so.'

A data subject has to make an access request, and the item must be supplied within 40 days of the request. He must pay a fee, and this must be paid before the item is supplied.

Under the 1984 Act the data subject could have the item corrected if it was wrong and claim compensation if he had suffered damage. Under the 1998 Act, where his rights have been contravened for special purposes (which include journalism), he does not have to prove any damage before claiming damages for distress.

Under the 1984 Act the right of compensation arose only from loss from inaccuracy of or unauthorised disclosure of personal data. The right of compensation now is for damage caused by any breach of the Act.

Damages for infringement of rights under the 1998 Act were awarded to the film stars Michael Douglas and Catherine Zeta-Jones, after *Hello!* magazine published snatched pictures of their wedding (see chapter 32, 'Privacy'). But they were awarded only £50 each, which led media lawyer Caroline Kean to comment that in the previous two years she had seen a proliferation of data protection claims from celebrities whose photographs had been published and that 'if £50 is the value of this kind of claim I would hope that they will become less attractive'.

A data subject has the right in some circumstances to require a data controller to cease processing data referring to him (see 'Protection from gagging orders', below).

Protection from gagging orders

An individual is entitled to require a data controller to cease processing any personal data referring to him on the ground that this would cause or be likely to cause substantial damage or substantial distress either to him or to another, and that the damage or distress would be unwarranted.

Thus, if there was no protection for the media, a villain being investigated by the press might make a subject access request to obtain a copy of information being held about him, and then use that information as evidence to support an application for an injunction ('gagging order') or other civil action.

But the Act does provide such a protection. Under section 32 an injunction to prevent the processing of data must be 'stayed' if the processing relates only to journalistic, literary or artistic purposes, the material concerned has not previously been published, and the other conditions referred to below are fulfilled.

The stay is until either the claim is withdrawn or the Commissioner determines whether or not the exemption applies.

Exemption for journalistic work

In the Naomi Campbell case, the paper argued that it had a defence under section 32 for its story about the treatment being received by the model, but the trial judge rejected this argument, saying the defence applied only to the processing of data before publication (that is, to prevent gagging orders), not after.

Fortunately for the media, the Court of Appeal rejected that ruling and held that the defence applied both before and after publication; 'fortunately' because the appeal judges said that section 32 provided the *only* defence available to the paper in this case.

Section 32 of the Act says that personal data which are processed only for 'special purposes' (journalistic, literary, or artistic purposes) are exempt from any provisions of the 1998 Act relating to:

(1) the data protection principles (except for requirements to keep data secure—the seventh data protection principle);

(2) subject access;

(3) the right to prevent processing likely to cause damage or distress;

(4) prevention of automated decision-taking; and

(5) rights to rectification, blocking, erasure and destruction.

The exemption applies only if the processing is undertaken with a view to the publication of special purposes material that has not been published; the Act says 'material which, at the time 24 hours immediately before the relevant time, had not previously been published by the data controller'.

In addition, the exemption applies only if the newspaper or broadcaster reasonably believes that:

(1) having regard in particular to the special importance of the public interest in freedom of expression, publication would be in the public interest; and

(2) in all the circumstances, compliance with the rules in the 1998 Act is incompatible with the journalistic purposes.

In considering whether the belief of the newspaper that publication would be in the public interest is reasonable, regard may be had to its compliance with 'any relevant code of practice'.

The *Daily Mirror* was able to persuade the Court of Appeal (but not the House of Lords) its story and pictures on Naomi Campbell was fair and lawful and complied with all these requirements. Under section 32(1)(a) of the Act, the processing of the data was undertaken with a view to the publication of journalistic material. Under section 32(1)(b), the data controller reasonably believed that publication would be in the public interest (to correct untruths told by Miss Campbell) and under section 32(1)(c) the data controller reasonably believed that, in all the circumstances, compliance with the provision was incompatible with the 'special purposes' [journalistic purposes] because the paper had approached Miss Campbell's agent, who had refused permission. The paper's case was helped also by the fact that it had complied with the PCC code, in accordance with section 32(3) of the Act.

The House of Lords, however, found for the model after a majority of the judges held that some elements of the *Daily Mirror's* coverage of her visit to a Narcotics Anonymous session breached her confidence and was therefore unlawful. Thus presumably (though the Lords did not spell this out) it failed to meet the 'fair and lawful' requirement of the First Data Principle, and so contravened the Data Protection Act.

Newspapers receiving a request for access to personal information contained in their electronic archives sometimes argue that section 32 allows them to withhold the information. The Information Commissioner argues that even if section 32 continues to provide a defence, after publication, against an accusation of infringing a person's rights under the Act, it cannot provide the media with a reason for withholding requested information after publication on the ground that this prejudices journalism.

Enforcement

If the Commissioner is satisfied that a data controller has contravened a data protection principle, he can serve an enforcement notice requiring compliance. Failure to comply with such a notice is an offence.

The Act includes wide powers of entry and inspection which may be exercised by the

Commissioner for the detection both of data protection offences and breaches of data protection principles. These powers can be exercised only under a warrant granted by a circuit judge (in Northern Ireland by a county court judge). A judge must not issue a warrant relating to personal data processed for the 'special purposes' (including journalism) unless the Commissioner has determined whether such data fall within the special purposes exemption.

Although the 1984 Act made it an offence for a data user (now data controller) to disclose data to someone he knew was not entitled to receive it, no specific criminal offence was committed by people *obtaining* such information.

Thus in 1992 the *Sun* newspaper was able to reveal, without infringing the Act, that the Chancellor of the Exchequer at that time, Norman Lamont, had exceeded his credit card limit 21 times, information held on computer which could have been obtained only by improper disclosure.

But the Criminal Justice and Public Order Act 1994 created three new offences that might affect the work of journalists. They were: procuring the disclosure of data covered by the 1984 Act, knowing or believing this to contravene the Act; selling the data; or offering to sell the data or information extracted from it.

Similar provisions are contained in the 1998 Act.

The broadcast journalist

Broadcast journalists encounter the same legal minefield in presenting news and features as their contemporaries in print. For example, Tyne-Tees Television was fined £10,000 in 1997 for the inclusion in a news broadcast of a few words which might have inadvertently led to the identification of an alleged victim of indecent assault although the company later successfully appealed (see chapter 8).

In addition to legal restrictions, some of which are peculiar to broadcasting, the Office of Communications (Ofcom) exercises a regulatory function. Under the Communications Act 2002, Ofcom assumed the functions of the Independent Television Commission, the Broadcasting Standards Commission and the Radio Authority. Among Ofcom's listed aims is to protect audiences against offensive or harmful material, unfairness or the unwarranted infringement of privacy on TV or radio (see 'Privacy', later this chapter).

The responsibilities of the BBC governors continue but the BBC is also subject to the external requirements of Ofcom.

A draft code giving guidance in these matters and replacing the codes of the previous bodies was prepared by Ofcom (see chapter 31, 'The codes'). Ofcom said the protection of children would be at the centre of its code. Ofcom can fine broadcasters if they breach the code. It can fine the BBC up to £250,000 and other channels up to five per cent of their revenue. Broadcasters can also be ordered not to repeat the offending programme.

Ofcom imposed its first fine, of £50,000, on the satellite channel Xplicit XXX in 2004 for showing hard core sex scenes before the 9pm watershed.

BBC output is also controlled on matters such as maintaining due impartiality and due accuracy through the licence agreement which is part of its charter. The Home Secretary has power to order that any item should not be broadcast either by the BBC or by the commercial companies.

Libel

The Broadcasting Act 1990 re-asserts that for the purposes of defamation, publication by broadcast is to be treated as libel rather than slander.

It is sometimes assumed that a broadcast defamatory statement is less likely to lead to an action because of the fleeting nature of the message. A person who claims that he has been defamed may, however, in the legal process of discovery, seek a court order requiring a recording of the broadcast to be made available to his lawyers. Television recordings must be kept for 90 days and radio recordings for 42 days.

Defamatory matter

A broadcast item may be construed as defamatory because of the combined effect of the spoken word and of film chosen to illustrate the topic, even when the film is shown for no more than a few seconds. This danger in 'wallpapering' arises where the voice-over is derogatory of a class of people and the film shows a recognisable face or someone's premises or car.

A Metropolitan Police detective was in 1983 awarded £20,000 against Granada Television for defamation arising in this way. During a documentary about police corruption, the voice-over said 'Some CID men take bribes' at the same time as film was shown depicting the claimant leaving West End Central Police station.

The problem for the broadcaster in finding suitable film for items criticising a class of people may be solved by the use of staff or actors, while making it clear in the broadcast that the film is a television reconstruction.

In another action, the choice of background music for a television programme led to an out-of-court settlement with payment of damages to a holiday company. The item about self-catering holidays included film which depicted the size of the rooms provided for the use of holidaymakers. As the film was shown, the theme from the *Colditz* series was used.

Identification

Broadcasts have often led to defamation actions because of the failure of the reporter or presenter adequately to identify a company or individual referred to, or portrayed in film, in a derogatory manner, with the result that innocent namesakes have claimed that reasonable people would understand the words to refer to them.

In 1973, the BBC was ordered to pay £15,000 damages to Mr Christopher Floris, the Queen's confectioner, and his company, the House of Floris. A television investigative programme on public health hazards included film of conditions in the premises of another company which was referred to simply as Floris. The plaintiffs claimed that viewers would think the item referred to the House of Floris.

Live broadcasts

Another hazard for radio and television is the broadcast of live discussions. In an unguarded moment, an invited guest or telephone caller may utter remarks which are clearly defamatory of an individual or company. Thus, not only may the person who utters the words be sued, but also the broadcast company which has published them. Many defamation actions have been brought in this way. In some cases the offending remarks have been made by leading politicians. Some commercial radio stations have an eight-second 'panic' button allowing the presenter to cut out offending words after they have been used but before they are transmitted.

Ideally, in items where there is potential for defamatory remarks being made, people should not be interviewed live nor calls taken directly on the air. If the words are spoken, the presenter should immediately dissociate himself and the station from the defamatory statement and should apologise without repeating the defamatory statement.

Section 1 of the Defamation Act 1996 provides a limited defence where the broadcaster of a live programme has no effective control over the maker of the defamatory statement. The Act requires that the broadcaster took all reasonable care and did not know and had no reason to believe that what he did caused or contributed to the publication of the statement. It says that in assessing whether this requirement is fulfilled, regard shall be paid to the nature or circumstances of the broadcast and the previous conduct of the broadcaster.

In establishing that it took all reasonable care the broadcaster may benefit if it can show that it had a system for reducing the risk of such defamatory statements being broadcast.

See also chapter 19, 'The section 1 defence'.

Qualified privilege

The Broadcasting Act 1990 provides for the qualified privilege, which, now under section 15 of the Defamation Act 1996, protects certain fair and accurate reports published without malice in a newspaper (see chapter 20), to be extended to similar broadcast reports, subject to the publication if requested of a reasonable letter or statement by way of explanation or contradiction.

The absolute privilege for fair, accurate, and contemporaneous reports of court proceedings and the qualified privilege for fair and accurate reports published without malice of certain other occasions, set out in the Defamation Act 1996 applies to all forms of publication including broadcasting. (See chapter 20, 'Privilege'.)

Gatley on Libel and Slander suggests that where a person complains of a defamatory statement broadcast as part of a report protected by qualified privilege, the broadcasting station should, if requested to broadcast a reasonable letter or statement under the requirements of the Defamation Act, do so as part of the same programme or service.

Contempt of court

Broadcasting runs all the same risks as newspapers and others and, additionally, judges have sometimes expressed concern that television broadcasts might bring some undesirable influence to bear on the proceedings, which might amount to contempt. However, in 1994 ITN was found not guilty of contempt in respect of an item in the early evening news which referred to the previous conviction of a man accused of terrorist offences. Lord Justice Leggatt said he was not persuaded that viewers would have retained the information for the nine months between the broadcast and the trial. He said a newspaper article would have been more likely to have been remembered than the broadcast since even a casual reader had the opportunity of reading a passage twice, an opportunity denied to the casual television viewer. (See chapter 17, 'Risk less than substantial'.)

In court reporting, judges desire the jury to reach its verdict on the basis of what is said in court and not on other interpretations of what might have happened at the scene of a crime, although there is no objection to straight reporting of the proceedings.

A judge at the Old Bailey in 1983 said it was folly for Independent Television's *News at Ten* to have broadcast a reconstruction, using actors in a street scene, of events related in evidence during the day's proceedings at a trial before a jury. 'Here was someone who was not there at the time and is not a witness trying to show all the world what he thinks may have happened', he said. He was concerned not so much with the words as the pictures that accompanied the words and added that he had reflected on whether he ought to have initiated proceedings for contempt.

Four years later the Lord Chief Justice granted an injunction to restrain Channel 4 from broadcasting a re-enactment of the Birmingham pub bombing appeal while the proceedings were still in progress, even though there was of course no jury involved in the appellate proceedings. He said the portraying of witnesses was of particular significance as it was pretending to be the real thing and was subtly inviting the viewer to make what he would think was his own comment on actual events. Such a representation would not directly affect the judgment of the court but it would or might affect the public view of the judgment of the court.

The Court of Appeal in 1991 criticised the filming of interviews with three people who were to be witnesses in a drugs trial. After an approach by a television company to customs and excise, they were interviewed as though they were giving their evidence at the trial. The item was broadcast after the end of the trial. Lord Justice Watkins said leading prosecution counsel had been wrong when he advised that customs and excise could properly co-operate in the filming. Lord Justice Watkins said the defence had not been told that three important witnesses had rehearsed their testimony before a television camera. If the defence had known, they would have cross-examined the witnesses as to any difference between their filmed evidence and the evidence they gave at the trial.

Like newspapers, television is at risk in using a photograph of an accused person where identification may be an issue at the trial because a witness's evidence could be affected.

The BBC was held to be in contempt and was admonished in the High Court in Glasgow in 1992 for screening film of a man accused of murder being led into court for his trial from a police van. The judge said the man was clearly identifiable from the film. 'The publication of a photograph, a film, or an artist's likeness of an accused during a trial poses a potential risk to justice,' he said.

In 1985, a Metropolitan magistrate referred to the Director of Public Prosecutions (although no action was subsequently taken) an Independent Television News report of committal proceedings involving six men and women on terrorist charges. The report included an artist's impression of the court scene, drawn away from the court. The suggestion was that the artist's drawing of two accuseds' faces was so accurate that it would prejudice their subsequent trial, where identification might be an issue.

In 1990, Central Television, the BBC, and Signal Radio successfully appealed against an order made by a judge at Stafford Crown Court under section 4 of the Contempt of Court Act 1981 that there should be no broadcast reports of a trial while the jury was spending a night at an hotel prior to returning its verdict. The crown court judge had said when making the order that he did not want the jury to be deprived of television or radio but the Lord Chief Justice said in the Court of Appeal that the judge was wrong to make the order. He very much doubted whether any restrictions were necessary on what the jury read or saw in newspapers or by way of television in the circumstances of the case.

Prosecutions for broadcasts which breach statutory court reporting restrictions are usually brought under the relevant statute and prosecutions treating a breach as contempt of court have been discouraged. In 2001 however BBC was fined £25,000 and one of its reporters £500 for contempt in a report which identified a man complaining of a sexual attack that took place while he was a child. The report was held to be contempt because it interfered with the administration of justice in that the man was distressed by it and initially refused to attend court (see chapter 8, 'Effect of contravening restrictions').

Copyright in broadcasting

The basic principle that the author (creator) is the owner of a copyright work is carried into broadcasting. For the purposes of ownership of a broadcast, the author is defined as the person transmitting the programme, if he has any responsibility for its content, *and* the person providing the programme, who, with the person transmitting, makes the arrangements necessary for the broadcast. The effect of this is that the copyright in a programme is owned jointly by the broadcasting authority transmitting it and the company providing it.

Separate copyrights, owned by different authors, may exist in the underlying literary, dramatic, or musical works incorporated in the broadcast, eg the script.

Copyright is not infringed by the incidental inclusion of a work in a television programme, eg a background shot of a painting in a documentary, or the loudspeaker music heard behind the commentator's voice during the interval at a football match.

Use in a broadcast of brief excerpts of a copyright work, eg film, can sometimes be defended as fair dealing for the purposes of reporting current events or of criticism or review. Use of the excerpts for criticism or review must be accompanied by sufficient acknowledgment.

(See chapter 29, 'Fair dealing'.)

The moral rights provided by the Copyright, Designs and Patents Act 1988 apply to some broadcasting. The right to be identified as author or director applies, except to employees and to those reporting current events. The right, where it exists, has to be asserted by the author, however. The moral right not to have the work subjected to derogatory treatment does apply to employees if they are or have been publicly identified in the work, except where it is made for reporting current events. Derogatory treatment is defined as treatment amounting to distortion or mutilation, or otherwise prejudicial to the honour or reputation of the author or director. The right not to have a work falsely attributed to a person applies to broadcasting as does the right of a person who has commissioned a photograph or film for private and domestic purposes not to have it made available to the public. (See also chapter 29, 'Copyright'.)

Privacy

Broadcast journalists who infringe privacy thereby contravene a code which can be enforced by sanction.

In 1992 the former Broadcasting Complaints Commission considered two complaints of infringement of privacy against Granada Television and found against the company. As a result, Granada was required to publish the finding. Granada appealed to the High Court.

Granada had included in a programme *How safe are our children*? a photograph of a child who had been raped and murdered two years previously. The company had not warned the parents before the broadcast. In the other programme, *The allergy business*, Granada had included a picture of a woman who had died three years previously aged 21. Again Granada had not warned the parents.

Granada argued that the photographs could not be an infringement of privacy because they were in the public domain and also that they did not relate to the people who complained but to their daughters.

But the court rejected Granada's argument, saying that the fact that a matter had once been in the public domain could not prevent its resurrection, possibly many years later, from being an infringement of privacy. And it would be an unacceptably narrow interpretation of the meaning of privacy and contrary to common sense to confine it to matters concerning the individual complainant, and not as extending to his family.

(See also chapter 31, 'The codes', and chapter 32, 'Privacy'.)

Covering election campaigns

Restrictions on programmes about a constituency or electoral area in which a candidate takes part, which existed for 17 years in section 93 of the Representation of the People Act 1983, have now been removed. These restrictions meant that a candidate who took part had to give consent to the programme being transmitted, effectively meaning that he was able to control any editing. Additionally, even if the candidate gave consent to transmission, all the other candidates had also to consent. No such programme could be broadcast at all between the election being called and nominations closing.

The Political Parties, Elections and Referendums Act 2000 substituted a new section 93 requiring each broadcasting authority, after consulting the Election Commission, to adopt a code of practice for the participation of candidates at a parliamentary or local government election in items about the constituency or electoral area during the election period. The effect of the change is that it is no longer necessary to secure the agreement of all candidates before any candidate can take part in an item about the constituency or electoral area and adopted candidates are no longer prevented from taking part in a broadcast between the election being called and the closing of nominations. The codes demand that broadcasters, while having a free hand to arrange items, should maintain strict impartiality and should offer candidates of each of the major parties a chance to take part.

The 2000 Act defines the period from which the codes must be applied as from the dissolution of Parliament in the case of a general election, from the issue of the writ in the case of a by-election, and the last date for publication of notice of the election in the case of a local government election. In all cases, the election period is defined as ending with the close of poll.

The new section 93 does not require the codes to apply to items in which only broadcasters rather than candidates take part. Nor does it cover items where a candidate is not participating in the broadcast but is, for example, canvassing and speaking only to an elector rather than to camera. Lord Denning, Master of the Rolls, said in the Court of Appeal in 1983 that control is exercisable only if the candidate has taken an active part in the programme. Candid camera shots of their canvassing did not require their consent because they were then the object of the film rather than participants in it (*Marshall v BBC* [1979] 3 All ER 80).

It also does not apply to broadcasts where a candidate takes part but which are not about his constituency, as where a leading politician is speaking in some other part of the country.

In 1994, the BBC was prevented by an interdict of the Court of Session in Edinburgh from broadcasting an interview with the Prime Minister, John Major, four days before the Scottish local elections on the grounds that it was a breach of the duty of impartiality set out in the annex to the BBC's licence agreement.

See also chapter 26, 'Election law'.

Obscenity and racial hatred

Under the Broadcasting Act 1990, the Obscene Publications Act 1959 was extended to television and sound broadcasting in the same way as it applies to books and films (see chapter 21). No prosecution can take place without the consent of the Director of Public Prosecutions but a magistrate may, if satisfied that there are reasonable grounds for believing that an offence has been committed, authorise the police to require that a visual or sound recording of a programme be handed over.

A similar procedure is possible if it is suspected that an offence has been committed under the racial hatred section of the Public Order Act 1986 (see chapter 25).

35

The photographer and the law

The newspaper photographer and TV camera operator share many of the legal risks faced by their reporter colleagues, and it is not the intention of this chapter to repeat the detailed guidance given elsewhere in this book on issues such as libel, contempt, data protection, copyright, privacy, and the PCC Code. All of these impinge upon the work of the photographer every bit as much as they do the reporter and it would be wise for photographers and picture editors to pay special attention to the chapters dealing with those topics.

Instead we will look at specific situations in relation to many of the issues mentioned above in an effort to illustrate the dangers they pose to a news photographer.

There were a number of important developments in the 2000s affecting the work of photographers, particularly in the areas of privacy, commercial confidentiality, and data protection. See in particular the cases referred to below and in chapters 32 (Privacy) and 33 (Data Protection Act) in which the model Naomi Campbell triumphed over the *Daily Mirror*, which had published a picture of her leaving a Narcotics Anonymous session; *OK!* magazine was awarded £1 million-plus in damages from *Hello!* magazine, which had published 'snatched' photographs of the wedding of two film stars; and Princess Caroline of Monaco won damages at the European Court of Human Rights for the publication of photographs of scenes from her daily life.

The courts

The Criminal Justice Act 1925, section 41, as stated in chapter 8, forbids the taking of photographs in court or its precincts. While what constitutes the court itself may be clear, the 1925 Act does not define what constitutes the precincts.

Different courts appear to hold different views on this matter and therefore it would be wise for photographers covering a specific court building to find out what the authorities consider to be its precincts to avoid incurring the displeasure of a judge when photographs are subsequently published.

It is common practice for papers to publish photographs of the various parties involved in a case, including witnesses, arriving or leaving court but remember common law contempt allows a judge to punish a photographer who takes such pictures in certain circumstances. However, if the photography amounted to 'molestation' which interfered with the administration of justice, then that would be punishable.

Photographing jurors could certainly be punishable as contempt, even where they leave the court to visit a crime scene.

Photographing an empty court would appear not to contravene the Act. Though this point has not been tested in law, in 2000 the clerk of Hertfordshire magistrates conceded he was wrong to have reprimanded *Hertfordshire on Sunday* when it carried a picture of an empty courtroom in connection with a rape case.

The march of technology has allowed for two new ways of picturing a courtroom.

Firstly mobile phones with the capability of taking digital photographs are now commonplace. In 2004 a teenager who used a mobile phone to shoot still and moving images in Bristol Crown Court was sentenced to six months in a young offenders' institution. The same year a man received a nine-month sentence for taking similar pictures in Birmingham Crown Court, and here the judge said he believed there was a 'sinister motive' to the taking of the images. In 2003 a man who took a picture of his brother in the dock at Liverpool Crown Court was jailed for a year, a sentence that was upheld on appeal.

The other advance that has allowed for the depiction of the interior of courtrooms is computer graphics. Broadcasters in particular, covering a hearing in a courtroom, can create a computer image of the room, using existing pictures of an interior and stock shots of key participants, such as defendants and barristers, to create an image of the scene. A case in which this technique was used was the trial of Ian Huntley and Maxine Carr for the Soham murders. It was also used by broadcasters covering the Hutton inquiry into the death of Dr David Kelly. Though not a court and not covered by the 1925 Act, it had been decided not to allow filming of proceedings.

According to the 1925 Act, any graphic artist who visited court to work on such an image could not create it while in the court but, as with a sketch artist, would have to work on the image from memory.

As this edition of *McNae* went to press a pilot scheme was being undertaken in the Court of Appeal to allow cameras into court (see chapter 7). The dangers of televising the courts and allowing the free access enjoyed by media in the United States was of concern to the Government when the pilot scheme was announced by the Lord Chancellor at the Edinburgh International Television Festival in 2004. He said: 'We will not have OJ Simpson-style trials in Britain. We must protect witnesses and jurors and victims. We don't want our courtrooms turned into US-style media circuses.'

Crime

While the mobile phone camera has given rise to difficulties in the courts, its widespread use has created new opportunities.

Before the advent of this new technology a picture editor could rely only on staff, agencies or freelance photographers for images, but the use of the digital camera has created a vast network of people capable of capturing pictures suitable for publication.

Pictures of disasters such as the tsunami that devastated countries around the Indian Ocean in 2004 and, closer to home, the immediate aftermath of a train crash in Berkshire in November of the same year, were sent to picture desks from the cameras or phones of members of the public.

This development also makes the photographing of the commission of crime far more likely. The question for a picture editor is whether the resulting photograph is usable legally. It would seem there is no good reason on grounds of potential contempt of court not to use such a picture (unless proceedings are 'active' under the Contempt of Court Act), although this may lead to the photographer being called as a witness and/or, as explained below, his film being requested by the police. Picture editors should also be aware that a picture apparently showing someone attacking another person, when in fact he was acting in self-defence, could be libellous.

During the 2000s newspapers have been paying greater attention to youth crime and many have obtained pictures of young people in the commission of crime—usually anti-social behaviour. Most papers carrying such pictures have pixellated the faces of the youths involved but whether they do so or not is essentially a matter of editorial judgment. Editors may wish to pixellate because of the tender years of those pictured, but as *McNae* went to press in 2005, there was no legal reason to do so because young offenders were entitled to anonymity only when they entered youth court.

The Youth Justice and Criminal Evidence Act 1999 contains a provision making it an offence to identify a juvenile offender once police have started a criminal investigation, but this provision had not been implemented in 2005. Clause 6 of the PCC Code gives protection to children, but this clause is subject to an exception in the public interest, an example of which is detecting or exposing crime.

It has been the practice of some photographers to steal a march on the opposition by using scanning devices to listen to emergency service radio messages. As is explained in chapter 8 ('Other statutory restrictions'), this is forbidden by the Wireless Telegraphy Act 1949.

Police evidence

The Police and Criminal Evidence Act 1984 (PACE) gives police powers to obtain material they believe would be of substantial value in investigating a 'serious arrestable offence' and the Serious Organised Crime and Police Act (2005) extended the PACE criterion to 'indictable offence'. Police can apply to a judge for an order giving access to 'journalistic material' and very often the material they are looking for is pictures.

Such orders have been sought following serious disturbances in Bristol in 1986; the poll tax riots in Trafalgar Square in 1990; and after public disorder at News International's print works at Wapping.

In opposing them the media argued that to allow police access to such material would compromise the partiality of photographers and TV camera crews if those involved in disturbance knew that their pictures and film could be the subject of such an order—it could in effect make them a target. The courts ruled that the public interest in catching the offenders outweighed the media interests (see chapter 24, 'Police and Criminal Evidence Act (PACE) 1984').

Risk of arrest

When covering events such as riots, photographers sometimes find themselves caught in the middle and subject to violence from rioters and to possible arrest, and on occasion, violence, by police.

Police officers covering major incidents can be under considerable pressure and it has been known for press photographers to be arrested at the scene of an accident, simply because one or other of the emergency services dealing with it does not like them being there.

Arrest in such situations is most likely to be under the powers granted by the Public Order Act 1986. This allows arrest if anyone uses behaviour likely to cause 'harassment, alarm or distress'. Though the photographer is not intending to cause such things, in some situations the mere fact that he is taking pictures, perhaps of someone or some group who do not want their picture taken, can give rise to this.

In 1995 a BBC cameraman filming scenes of a coach crash was arrested. Police said he had been arrested for his own safety, because he had refused to leave what was a volatile situation. Magistrates bound him over to keep the peace but this was overturned on appeal. However, at appeal the judge said the cameraman had acted with excessive enthusiasm and that he should remember others have feelings and rights too.

A photographer who took a picture of an army officer defusing an IRA bomb was arrested when the officer complained. He felt the pictures might put him or his family at risk of terrorist reprisals.

Other powers available to the police include those granted by section 121 of the Highways Act 1959. These allow police to arrest photographers who do not move on when asked to do so. If the photographer is on private land with the owner's permission the police cannot ask him to move on, although he can still be arrested for obstruction.

A photographer who persists in taking photographs and engages in argument with a police officer runs the risk of arrest under section 51 of the Police Act 1964. This Act says it is an offence to 'resist or wilfully obstruct a constable in the execution of his duty.'

In 1977 it was decided that 'wilfully' in this instance meant anything that made it more difficult for police officers to do their job. A photographer arguing with an officer may well be viewed by that officer as doing just that.

In 1995 an agency photographer in East Anglia covering an animal rights protest was arrested as he took pictures of police advancing on demonstrators who had sat down to block the road. Despite his protests and those of other media, he was held in a police van, and later, when he refused to accept a caution, he was charged with obstruction of the highway. Although acquitted by magistrates he was not awarded costs.

There are a number of laws forbidding trespass on the railways. This is a risk to photographers when venturing onto railway property to take pictures of rail crashes.

False imprisonment

If a photographer is subject to unlawful physical restraint, whether this is being locked up in the cells, or physically restrained in some other way by a police officer—or anyone else for that matter—it is possible to sue for false imprisonment. Movement must be completely restricted; barring a photographer from going in one particular direction, for example towards the scene of a crash, is not false imprisonment.

In 1995 a freelance photographer, David Hoffman, won £25,000 damages from the Metropolitan Police for assault, malicious prosecution, and unlawful imprisonment as a result of an arrest during a demonstration he was covering in 1989. Previous to this incident the same photographer had helped in the making of a Met video used for teaching officers about dealing with the media in public order situations.

Children

The law involving children is stated in chapter 6 and there are many situations where photographing a child can give rise to serious legal implications. An offence can be committed by publishing a picture of a child who is a ward of court or who is the subject of youth court anonymity, of a section 39 order, of adoption proceedings, or of Children Act proceedings.

Under the Children Act, it is an offence to identify the child as being the subject of proceedings only in respect of that Act. A photographer innocently taking a picture at a school—of a school play for example—and unknowingly including a child who is the subject of such proceedings, has not committed an offence, provided of course the accompanying text does not identify the child as being the subject of such proceedings.

Photographers encounter difficulty when visiting schools to be told by head teachers that they will not be allowed to photograph pupils or, where they are allowed to do so, they are not given pupils' names because of fears that the Data Protection Act may be infringed. For a discussion of this problem, see 'Schools', in chapter 33, 'Data Protection Act 1998'.

Libel

The ability to manipulate images with ease also gives rise to legal difficulties on occasion.

The libellous potential of pictures is demonstrated by the case of Ann Charleston and Ian Smith, the actors who played Madge and Harold Bishop in the Australian soap opera *Neighbours*. The *News of the World* carried a banner headline reading 'Strewth! What's Harold up to with our Madge?' accompanied by a picture appearing to show them engaging in pornographic activity. Only when reading the text did it become clear that the actors' faces had been superimposed on a pornographic picture without their consent. The paper was saved by the 'bane and antidote' rule in libel, with the court ruling a fair-minded reader of the complete text would not think less of the actors, who were clearly the victims of a hoax: *Charleston v News Group Newspapers* [1995] 2 AC 65.

However, the PCC can on occasion disapprove of such manipulation. *Luton on Sunday* was held to have breached the code of practice in 2003 when a story headlined 'Vice girls move into High Town' was accompanied by a picture of a street corner and a supposed 'vice girl' on the pavement. A complainant to the PCC said the picture was either posed, or else had been put together from two images. The paper admitted it was a composite image created from two pictures, but argued the use of an illustrative photograph was legitimate. The PCC, however, decided its code had been breached.

Use of file photographs to illustrate news stories or features is fraught with libellous possibilities. A photo of a social function, with people holding drinks, is perfectly acceptable. If it is later used as a stock shot to illustrate the perils of drinking, those pictured may sue, particularly if any of them are teetotal.

A paper in South Wales had to publish an apology after a library picture of football supporters was used to illustrate an article about hooliganism.

Trespass

The law of trespass forbids unlawful physical entry to land or buildings. The remedy is an action in the civil courts which can result in an injunction to prevent further trespass, or damages.

Trespass can also include 'trespass to the person', which might amount to compelling a person to be filmed by stopping him getting into his home or place of work. Trespass to goods means, for instance, picking up a document without permission and filming or photographing it.

With the exception of specific laws covering, among others, Ministry of Defence land, trespass is not normally a criminal offence and a police officer threatening an arrest for trespass is wrong in law. See also chapter 29, 'Official Secrets'.

However, the Criminal Justice and Public Order Act 1994 created the offence of aggravated trespass. This was intended to deal with travellers and those staging 'raves', but it is possible it might be used against photographers. The Act says that if two or more people are trespassing on land with the common purpose of intimidating persons so as to deter, obstruct, or disrupt lawful activity they may be ordered to leave, and if they return they have committed an offence. It is not hard to see how this might be applied to a 'pack' of photographers staking out a person's home.

There is no trespass where a picture is taken from public property, or property where the photographer has permission to be, of something or someone on adjoining private land (although see also chapter 31, 'The codes', and 32, 'Privacy'). Such a picture might amount to a breach of the PCC Code, particularly if it shows someone in a place where he has a reasonable expectation of privacy.

Privacy

Where once there was no law of privacy in the United Kingdom, it has now developed considerably as a result of a number of cases.

Michael Douglas and Catherine Zeta-Jones took action against *Hello!* magazine when it published snatched pictures of their wedding. They won in 2003, not on the grounds of privacy, but because of commercial confidentiality which made their marriage a valuable trade asset.

In 2004 the action by Naomi Campbell against the *Daily Mirror* went to the House of Lords. The *Mirror* had reported she had a drug addiction and that she was attending meetings of Narcotics Anonymous. They surreptitiously pictured her emerging from one such meeting.

The photograph of Ms Campbell was one of the key elements referred to by the House of Lords in its judgement and they made the point that a picture taken in a public place of a private activity could be 'confidential' and so its publication was a breach of Ms Campbell's rights. For a more detailed discussion of this case see chapter 32.

The European Court of Human Rights in 2004 held that Princess Caroline's right to privacy had been infringed by photographs of her daily life—shopping, or on holiday with her family, even though these had been taken in public places.

Harassment

It was not the intention of Parliament to target the press with the Protection Against Harassment Act 1997, which was a law designed to tackle stalkers. However, Esther Thomas, a former civilian clerk with City of London Police, took action against *The Sun* over stories about a complaint she made of racist behaviour against four police officers.

The Sun failed in its appeal to have the action struck out and, although this situation did not directly relate to photography, it would seem clear that, in spite of Parliament's intentions, the courts have found that the law can be used in such a manner.

The judge in Thomas's case said that harassment would require a 'course of conduct', so one story, or picture, would not be enough to amount to harassment. But behaviour which caused alarm or distress could find a photographer falling foul of this law. See also chapter 32.

See also chapter 17, 'Pictures' and chapter 34, 'Contempt of Court'.

Northern Ireland

The law in Northern Ireland, including the courts structure, is broadly the same as that in England and Wales—though Scotland has its own legal system with its basic differences protected by the Act of Union. This book does not attempt to explain media law in Scotland which is covered in *Scots Law for Journalists*.

In the few important cases involving the media that have come before the High Court in Northern Ireland, cases in England have been freely cited. The House of Lords is the final court of appeal for both criminal and civil cases in Northern Ireland.

The Lord Chief Justice of Northern Ireland is assisted by seven High Court judges and 15 crown court judges who try cases in the crown court. The crown court also hears appeals from magistrates courts. High Court judges sitting in the Northern Ireland High Court also hear civil cases, as do crown court judges sitting in the county court. Three lords justices of appeal, sometimes sitting with other High Court judges, hear appeals from the crown court, county court, or High Court in the Court of Appeal.

Most cases in magistrates courts are heard before resident magistrates, who are legally qualified and full time.

Defamation

The Defamation Act (Northern Ireland) 1955 is identical to the Defamation Act 1952, which covers the rest of the United Kingdom.

Under section 6 of the Defamation Act 1996, proceedings in Northern Ireland, as in England and Wales, must be started within 12 months of publication, although a court may extend this in special circumstances. Much of the rest of the 1996 Act has been implemented in Northern Ireland (see chapters 18, 19 and 20). Included in the parts now in operation are sections 1 (responsibility for publication, such as on the part of broadcasters of live programme), 2 and 4 (offer of amends), 8–11 (summary disposal of a claim), 14 and 15 (privilege). (See chapters 18 and 20.)

Sections 5 and 6 of the Defamation Act (Northern Ireland) 1955 (failure to prove every allegation of fact in the defences of justification and fair comment) are still in force.

The Rehabilitation of Offenders (Northern Ireland) Order 1978 contains similar provisions to those in the Rehabilitation of Offenders Act 1974 (see chapter 22).

Contempt of court

The Contempt of Court Act 1981 is effective in Northern Ireland and the many contempt decisions by the English High Court are equally applicable there.

The only reported contempt prosecution in Northern Ireland since the Act arose in 2003 when the *Sunday Life* in Belfast was fined £5,000 and its editor £1,000 over three articles about an alleged drug dealer. The final article, published in the month before the trial was due to start, referred to the accused as a drug dealer who had been on the run from police and from loyalist killers. The Attorney-General also claimed the article linked the accused to earlier articles mentioning that he had been on the run for more than six months, that cocaine had been found in a drugs squad raid on his home, that he had escaped over the fields and that he had continued to travel back to Belfast to maintain his criminal underworld contacts. Afterwards, the editor said they realised too late that the trial was imminent.

When special courts (the Diplock Courts) were introduced in Northern Ireland for the trial by judge alone of terrorists charged with scheduled offences, it was contended that the risk of contempt through creating a substantial risk of serious prejudice to these proceedings was much less in the absence of a jury. The danger remains however of witnesses being affected in that their evidence might be coloured by accounts given by others.

In 2002, a High Court judge in Belfast decided against an injunction preventing Ulster Television broadcasting a background feature after the conviction of two men on murder charges. The defence had said there would be an appeal and any retrial that was ordered might be affected. (See chapter 17, 'When proceedings cease to be active' and 'Appeal being lodged'.)

Reporting restrictions

Reporting restrictions in Northern Ireland broadly follow mainland lines although they often have different titles, based on Orders made by the Secretary of State.

Juveniles in court

A child under 10 cannot be charged with a criminal offence in Northern Ireland. Under the Criminal Justice (Northern Ireland) Act 2002 the threshold age for anonymity was raised to 'under 18' in April 2005, bringing it into line with the mainland and affecting reporting in adult courts where an order may be made for anonymity, as well as in youth courts.

Youth courts (set up in place of juvenile courts in 1999) deal with offences committed by those below the age of 18. The Criminal Justice (Children) (Northern Ireland) Order 1998. as amended, makes it an offence in reporting the proceedings to publish the name, address, or school, or any particulars likely to lead to the identification of anyone *under 18* involved in youth court proceedings, or an appeal from a youth court, as defendant or witness. It is also an offence to publish a picture of or including anyone under 18 involved. A youth court may lift or relax the restrictions on a convicted young offender in the public interest but must first afford parties to the proceedings an opportunity to make representations.

Under article 22 of the 1998 Order, an adult court may make an order that nothing should be published to identify those under 18 involved in the proceedings as a defendant, witness or party (see chapter 6 and chapter 12, both of which deal with the comparable section 39 orders on the mainland).

The 1998 Order empowers a court in any criminal proceedings to exclude everyone not concerned in the case, where it considers the evidence of a child is likely to involve matter of an indecent or immoral nature. There is no specific provision for the press to remain, unlike the position under the mainland section 37 of the Children and Young Persons Act 1933, which exempts the press from being excluded during the taking of evidence by a juvenile witness in a case involving indecency.

Under the Youth Justice and Criminal Evidence Act 1999 if it is fully implemented, the definition of what may lead to the identification of a child in the youth court, or in the adult court (if an anonymity order has been made there) will be widened to include the name, address, school, or other educational establishment, workplace, or any still or moving picture of the person.

In civil proceedings, under the Children Order (Northern Ireland) 1995 no publication must lead to the identification of any person under 18 as being involved in any (family) proceedings before a court where any power is being exercised under that order, which is comparable with the mainland Children Act 1989. The court also has power to sit in private when exercising a Opower under the order in relation to a person under 18 and may ban identification of a person under 18 in other types of civil case.

Sexual offences

The Sexual Offences Act 2003 and the Youth Justice and Criminal Evidence Act 1999 amend the mainland Sexual Offences (Amendment) Act 1992 as it applies in Northern Ireland.

The amended 1992 Act gives anonymity during their lifetime to complainants in rape cases and in any of the other offences to which the Sexual Offences Act 2003 applies (see chapter 8, 'Sexual offences and other statutory reporting restrictions').

It makes it an offence to publish any matter which identifies a complainant in any of these offences, in particular his or her name, address, school, other educational establishment or workplace or any still or moving picture of the complainant. No prosecution for a breach of these reporting restrictions can be started except by or with the consent of the Attorney-General.

An exception to the anonymity of complainants is made in any report of criminal proceedings other than proceedings for the offences listed or an appeal arising out of such proceedings (such as in proceedings arising from a false allegation of a sexual offence). Written consent by a complainant over 16 to being identified is a defence and a court has power to lift the restriction on the grounds that it imposes a substantial and unreasonable restriction on the reporting of the trial and it is in the public interest to lift it.

Sometimes, when a person is charged with incest the prosecution is brought under the Punishment of Incest Act 1908, which has been repealed on the mainland but is still, in part, in force in Northern Ireland. Section 5 of the Act says that all proceedings under the Act are to be held in private. (ie excluding press and public). This does not in itself appear to prevent publication of any report of the proceedings which may be obtained, either at common law or under section 12 of the Administration of Justice Act 1960 (see chapter 17, 'Reports of hearings in private'), unless a court, having power to do so, has specifically prohibited the publication. However the incest victim still has anonymity. The in-private rule of section 5 of the 1908 Act does not apply when a prosecution for a sexual offence is brought under any other Act.

Restrictions on identifying defendants

There is nothing in the 1994 order giving a court discretionary powers, in addition to the automatic restrictions, to impose further restrictions such as prohibiting identification of the defendant. All that article 19 does is to prohibit publication of particulars that would lead to the identification of the complainant and there is no provision in the article for a court to determine *which* particulars they might be. It appears to be up to newspapers to decide what particulars (eg relationships between the defendant and the complainant) they delete from the report to avoid identification of the complainant in any of the offences listed. If they publish particulars likely to lead to such identification they risk prosecution. (See also chapter 31, 'Children in sex cases').

A number of crown courts and magistrates courts have attempted to make orders banning the naming of a defendant, citing the 1994 order, on the grounds that publication of his name would either lead to the identification of the complainant or would be detrimental to the well-being of the defendant. Such purported orders would seem to be ultra vires (see also chapter 11, 'Addresses of defendants', where an unsuccessful application to restrict reporting was made under the Human Rights Act).

Newtownabbey magistrates court made an order in 1997 prohibiting the identification of a scoutmaster accused of indecently assaulting boys, to protect the physical and mental well-being of the defendant. His solicitor had asked for an embargo on the reporting of the case because publicity would be prejudicial to his client's welfare, following the murder of a Presbyterian minister who had been charged with offences of handling pornographic literature.

Later that year the *Sunday Life* newspaper in Belfast applied to the Northern Ireland Queen's Bench Divisional Court for judicial review.

The divisional court granted the application. It held that, in the absence of any other statutory power, there was no inherent power in a court to control the publication of any report of the proceedings in addition to the power contained in section 4 of the Contempt of Court Act (power to order postponment of reports of the proceedings or part of the proceedings to avoid the substantial of risk of prejudice to those or other proceedings). The order made by the magistrate was wrong.

Lord Justice McCollum giving judgment said the possibility of an attack on the defendant by ill-intentioned persons was merely speculative and could not be regarded as a consequence of publication which should influence the court. He said he would sum up the position for the benefit of other tribunals who might be faced with similar problems:

1. In our judgment the powers of the court to prohibit publication or postpone it which are contained in the Contempt of Court Act 1981 fully encompass existing common law powers and there are therefore no further powers inherent in the court outside the terms of that Act to prohibit or postpone publication of any part of the proceedings before it.

2. Under section 4(2) of the Act the court may order a postponement of publication for such period, defined either in relation to time or the occurrence of some event, such as the conclusion of a trial, as a court thinks necessary, and may only postpone where it appears to be necessary for avoiding a substantial risk of serious prejudice or impediment to the administration of justice in those proceedings or in any other proceedings pending or imminent.

3. Under section 11 of the Act the court may only give directions prohibiting the publication of the name or other matter in connection with the proceedings, where the court, during the course of the proceedings before it, has allowed the name or other matter to be withheld from the public in those proceedings, and the directions given by the court should be those that appear to be necessary for the purpose for which the name or other matter was so withheld.

In our view it is only in those specified circumstances, or where a statutory position makes specific exception, that there may be a departure from the general rule that a report of court proceedings should be freely available for publication. (*Re Belfast Telegraph Newspapers Application* [1997] NI 309.)

The court ordered the costs should be borne by the Crown Solicitor's Office, and Martin Lindsay, editor of the *Sunday Life* said afterwards that some £7,000 of taxpayers' money had therefore been spent in an attempt to defeat the newspaper's challenge to the ban on naming the scout leader. (See also chapter 12, 'Section 11 orders'.)

In 1999 when the prosecution and defence at Newtownabbey magistrates court in the case of a police officer accused of indecently assaulting a child made a joint application for the press to be excluded, Mr Phillip Mateer, a deputy resident magistrate, refused the application, referring to the *Sunday Life* case outlined earlier.

Photography at court

The Criminal Justice (Northern Ireland) Act 1945, operating in a similar way to the mainland Criminal Justice Act 1925 (see chapter 35), prohibits photography or sketching in a court or its precincts.

Disclosure of material to police

See chapter 24, 'Anti-terrorism legislation'.

Table of Cases

Table of Statutes

Table of Statutory Instruments

Table of European Conventions, Directives and Treaties

Glossary

Absolute discharge A decision of the court to impose no penalty and no conditions, even though the defendant has been convicted.

Actus reus A guilty action. *See also* mens rea.

Affidavit A statement given on oath to be used in court proceedings.

Age of criminality The age above which a child may be accused of a criminal offence and be brought before a court.

Arrestable offence An offence for which an arrest may be made without a warrant.

Assault In legal language, assault is a hostile act which causes another person to fear an attack. Battery is the actual application of force.

Asbo An anti-social behaviour order aimed at preventing further such behaviour by placing restrictions upon a person subject to it; imposed in magistrates court or in youth court.

Attachment, writ of An order to bring a person before the court to answer an accusation of contempt.

Bail The system by which a person awaiting trial, or appeal, may be freed pending the hearing.

Bailiff A representative of the court who enforces its orders.

Bill of Indictment An order made by a High Court judge, compelling a person to stand trial at crown court. A rare procedure, used to cut out the usual committal by the magistrates, or to overcome a decision by the magistrates that there is no case to answer.

Burglary Unlawful entry of a building and committing or intending to commit certain criminal offences, not just theft.

Case law The system by which reports of previous cases and the judges' interpretation of the common law can be used as a precedent where the legally material facts are similar.

Case stated Appeal by case stated is a procedure by which the magistrates court, or the crown court sitting as an appeal court may be asked to state the grounds on which it reached its decision. By this procedure either prosecution or defence can appeal a point of law to the Queen's Bench Divisional Court.

Chancery Division A division of the High Court that deals with companies, trusts, estates and intellectual property.

Child A person below 14.

Circuit judge A judge who has been appointed to sit at crown court or county court within a *circuit*—one of the regions of England and Wales into which court administration is divided. Unlike high court judges, circuit judges do not go on circuit, that is travel to various large centres dispensing justice.

Claimant *Previously known as* plaintiff. The person who takes an action to enforce a claim in the civil court. New civil justice rules in 1999 said the word claimant should be used instead.

Claim form *Previously known as* writ or default summons. A document that begins many forms of civil action.

Committal for trial Procedure by which a case involving an either-way offence, where the accused has indicated a plea of not guilty, is committed from the magistrates court to be tried at crown court before a jury. The procedure is also used where a juvenile is accused of any indictable offence and the case is committed to crown court.

Committed for sentence Tried at magistrates court and sent by them to crown court for sentence because magistrates' powers of punishment are insufficient. (There are no reporting restrictions on committals for sentence.)

Common law Law based on the custom of the realm and the decisions of the judges through the centuries rather than an Act of Parliament.

Community punishment An order that an offender must carry out unpaid work in the community under the supervision of a probation officer.

Concurrent sentences Two or more sentences of imprisonment imposed for different offences; the longest one is the sentence actually served.

Conditional discharge Decision of the court to impose no penalty even though a conviction has been recorded against the defendant, provided the defendant commits no further offences during a stipulated period.

Consecutive sentence To follow one after the other, rather than concurrently.

Coroner A solicitor, barrister, or doctor appointed by the Crown to conduct inquests in his or her area.

Corporation Only individuals and corporations can sue for libel. A corporate body is one that has rights and duties distinct from those of the people who form it. An incorporated company is a corporation formed for the purpose of carrying on a business.

Counsel Barrister (singular or plural), not solicitor.

Decree nisi A provisional decree of divorce, usually made absolute six weeks later, thus allowing the parties to remarry.

Derogatory assertions Assertions made in mitigation about a person's character that allege conduct that is immoral, improper or criminal. May be the subject of a reporting restriction.

Disclosure and inspection *Previously known as* discovery. The process whereby each side in a court action serves a list of relevant documents on the other. The other party then has the right to inspect those documents.

Discovery *See* Disclosure.

District judge An official of the county court who also adjudicates in the smaller cases, presides at public examinations in bankruptcy, and deals with cases under the informal arbitration procedure.

District judge (magistrates courts). The title given under the Access to Justice Act 1999 to full-time, legally-qualified magistrates, formerly known as stipendiary magistrates.

Drink driving Not drunk driving, in heads and intros.

Either-way offence Previously known as a hybrid offence. One triable either summarily at magistrates court or before a jury at crown court. On a triable-either-way offence, a defendant who has indicated a plea of not guilty has the right to opt for jury trial at crown court. But even if he chooses to be tried summarily at magistrates court, magistrates may overrule him by deciding on crown court trial.

Excluded material Such material is exempt from compulsory disclosure under the Police and Criminal Evidence Act 1984. It includes journalistic material that a person holds in confidence and that consists of documents or records.

Ex parte *See* Without notice.

Fair comment A defence to a libel action; the defendant does not have to show the words were fair. But he must show they were honest and published without malice.

Family proceedings Civil proceedings before magistrates, dealing with separation orders, maintenance of spouse or children, adoption orders.

Habeas corpus, writ of A writ issued by the Queen's Bench Divisional Court to secure the release of a person whom it declares to have been detained unlawfully by the police or other authorities.

Hybrid offence *See* Either-way offence.

In chambers Used to describe the hearing of an application heard in the judge's room. Such hearings are not confidential or secret, and the media should be granted permission to attend 'when and to what extent it is practicable' (*see* chapter 11).

Indictable offence One that may be tried on indictment before a judge and jury at crown court.

Indictabe-only offence One that can be tried only by a jury at crown court.

Indictment A written statement of the charges that are put to the accused when he stands trial at crown court.

Information A written statement alleging an offence, that is laid before a magistrate who is then asked to issue a summons or warrant for arrest.

In private *Previously known as* in camera. Proceedings of the court that are heard in the absence of the public and the press (eg Official Secrets Act cases).

Interdict In Scottish law, an injunction.

Jigsaw identification Where, for example, one paper gives details of a person's identity and another suppresses his name but gives details of his relationship to a child who is the subject of a section 39 order. The two reports read together form a jigsaw identifying the child.

Journalistic material Material acquired and created for the purposes of journalism. Special protection is given to journalistic material in the sections of the Police and Criminal Evidence Act 1984 that lay down the procedure whereby the police may search premises for evidence of serious arrestable offences.

Judicial review Review by the Queen's Bench Divisional Court of decisions taken by a lower court, tribunal, public body or public official.

Juvenile A young person below the age of 18. Above this age the accused will be tried at an adult court for any type of offence.

Justification The defence in libel actions that the words complained of were true. The word is misleading, because there is not requirement that the words were published justly or with good reason.

Lords Justices Not Lord Justices, or Lords Justice. Judges of the Court of Appeal. They are not members of the House of Lords.

Lords of Appeal They are usually known as the Law Lords. They sit in the House of Lords, not the Court of Appeal.

Malice In law not only spite or ill will but also dishonest or improper motive. Proof of malice can be used by a claimant in a libel action to deprive the defendant of the defences of fair comment or qualified privilege.

Mandatory order *Previously known as* mandamus. An order made by the Queen's Bench Divisional Court directing a lower court or public body to perform some duty for which it is responsible.

Mens rea Guilty mind, the intent required, along with the actus reus (see above) to be guilty of an offence. Not required in strict liability offences.

Narrative verdict The system of allowing a coroner or inquest jury, to make a short statement of the circumstances of a person's death, rather than the traditional one-word verdicts.

Plaintiff *See* claimant.

Plea and directions A preliminary hearing before a judge at crown court where the accused may indicate whether he will plead guilty, directions are given regarding such matters as which evidence will be admitted, and the defence has an opportunity to plead that there is insufficient evidence to go before a jury.

Pleadings *See* Statements of Case.

Prima facie At first sight.

Privilege A defence, absolute or qualified, against an action for libel which attaches to reports produced from certain events, documents or statements.

Quango The term stands for quasi-autonomous non-governmental organisation and is conveniently and loosely used to describe non-elected public bodies that operate outside the civil service and that are funded by the taxpayer.

Queen's Counsel The title given to a senior barrister recommended as counsel to the Queen by the Lord Chancellor. A system that was under review by the Department of Constitutional Affairs when *McNae* went to press.

Recorder An assistant judge at crown court who is usually appointed to sit part-time (eg for spells of a fortnight). Solicitors and barristers are both eligible for appointment as a recorder.

Remand An individual awaiting trial can be remanded on bail, or in custody.

Robbery Theft by force, or threat of force. The word is often used, wrongly, to describe simple theft.

Sending for trial The fast-track procedure by which an indictable-only offence (one that can be tried only by a jury) is transferred from the magistrates court to crown court, often leading to an early plea and directions hearing (see above).

Small claims court The county court procedure by which the district judge, generally sitting in private, deals by arbitration with claims for less than £5,000.

Special measures Measures taken under the Youth Justice and Criminal Evidence Act 1999 to protect a vulnerable witness, eg taking evidence over a video link.

Spent conviction A conviction that is no longer recognised after the specified time (varying according to sentence) laid down by the Rehabilitation of Offenders Act. After this time, a newspaper referring to the conviction may not have available some of the normal defences in the law of libel.

Statements of case *Previously know as* the pleadings. The set of documents that set forth the issues between the parties in a civil action. Anything not contained in the statements will not be adjudicated upon, unless the judge agrees to applications to amend or extend them.

Stipendiary magistrates *See* District judge (magistrates courts).

Strict liability A strict liability offence does not require the prosecution to show intent on the part of the accused. Statutory contempt of court is a strict liability offence.

Sub judice Literally under law. Often applied to the risk which may arise in reporting forthcoming legal proceedings. Frequently used by authority as a reason for not disclosing information. This is not the test for strict liability under the Contempt of Court Act (see chapter 17).

Subpoena A court order compelling a person to attend court to give evidence.

Summary proceedings Cases tried by magistrates. At the end of such a trial on an either way offence, however, magistrates can, if they consider their powers of sentence insufficient, send the defendant for sentence at crown court.

Summons An order issued by a magistrate to attend court at a stated time and date to answer a charge.

Supreme Court The name given to the Court of Appeal, the High Court and the crown court. It is not in fact *the* supreme court; the House of Lords is. In 2003 the Government published a position paper addressing the establishment of a free-standing Supreme Court, separating the court function from the House of Lords.

Surety A person to whom an accused released on bail may be entrusted under certain bail conditions. The person may provide a sum of money as surety and risk losing it if the accused fails to surrender to bail at the required date.

Taxation of costs The examination of costs lawfully chargeable to the unsuccessful party in a legal action to ensure they are not excessive.

Theft Dishonest appropriation of property with the intention to permanently deprive another of it.

Tort A civil wrong for which monetary damages may be awarded eg, defamation, negligence.

TWOC (taking a car without owner's consent) Court reporters must not confuse this with theft (see above) of a car; a more serious offence.

Ward of court A minor (a person under the age of 18) brought under the care of the court by the Family Division of the High Court.

Warrant for arrest An order issued by a magistrate to secure the arrest of a person suspected of a crime.

Without notice *Previously known as* ex parte, *of the one part*. An injunction without notice is one granted after hearing only one side of the case.

Writ *See* claim form.

Young person A person 14 years of age or above, but below 18.

Book List

Confidentiality
Confidentiality RG Toulson and CM Phipps (Sweet & Maxwell, 1996)

Courts
Anthony and Berryman's Magistrates' Court Guide TG Moore (Butterworths, 2003)

Stone's Justices Manual Paul Carr and Adrian Turner (Butterworths, 2003)

Children in the news
Review of Access to and Reporting of Family Proceedings (Consultation Paper, Lord Chancellor's Department, 1993)

Explanatory Notes, Youth Justice and Criminal Evidence Act 1999 (The Stationery Office)

Contempt of court
Arlidge, Eady & Smith on Contempt (Sweet & Maxwell, 2nd edn, 1999)

Contempt of Court CJ Miller (Oxford University Press, 3rd edn, 2000)

Copyright
Blackstone's Guide to the Copyright, Designs and Patents Act 1988 Gerald Dworkin and Richard D Taylor (Blackstone Press, 1988)

Defamation
Defamation. Law, procedure and practice David Price and Korieh Duodu (Sweet & Maxwell, 3rd edn, 2004)

Gatley on Libel and Slander Patrick Milmo QC and Prof WVH Rogers (Sweet & Maxwell, 10th edn, 2004)

Information from government
Blackstone's Guide to the Freedom of Information Act 2000 John Wadham and Jonathan Griffiths (Oxford University Press, 2nd edn 2005)

Your Right to Know Heather Brooke (Pluto Press, 2005)

Media law
Media Law Geoffrey Robertson and Andrew Nicol (Sweet & Maxwell, 4th edn, 2002)

Official secrets

Secrets, Spies and Whistleblowers (Liberty and Article 19, 2000)

Press Complaints Commission code

The Editors' Codebook (published by the industry's trade associations, 2005)

Privacy

The Law of Privacy and the Media edited by Michael Tugendhat QC and Iain Christie (Oxford University Press, 2002)

Privacy and the Media: the Developing Law Matrix Media and Information Group (Matrix Chambers, 2002)

Privacy and the Press Joshua Rozenberg (Oxford University Press, 2004)

Scots law

Scots Law for Journalists Alistair J Bonnington, Rosalind McInnes, Bruce McKain (W Green/ Sweet & Maxwell, 7th edn, 2000)

Terrorism

Blackstone's Guide to the Anti-terrorism Legislation Clive Walker (Oxford University Press, 2002)

The newsletter *Media Lawyer* records changes in this area of the law, and where necessary draws attention to the need to amend copies of *McNae*. Its editor and honorary consultant are editors of *McNae*.

Index